Responsible Management in Asia

# Responsible Management in Asia

## Perspectives on CSR

Edited by

Geoffrey Williams
*CEO, OWW Consulting*

First published 2011 by
PALGRAVE MACMILLAN

Palgrave Macmillan in the UK is an imprint of Macmillan Publishers Limited,
registered in England, company number 785998, of Houndmills, Basingstoke,
Hampshire RG21 6XS.

Palgrave Macmillan in the US is a division of St Martin's Press LLC,
175 Fifth Avenue, New York, NY 10010.

Palgrave Macmillan is the global academic imprint of the above companies
and has companies and representatives throughout the world.

Palgrave® and Macmillan® are registered trademarks in the United States,
the United Kingdom, Europe and other countries.

ISBN: 978–0–230–25241–7 hardback

This book is printed on paper suitable for recycling and made from fully
managed and sustained forest sources. Logging, pulping and manufacturing
processes are expected to conform to the environmental regulations of the
country of origin.

A catalogue record for this book is available from the British Library.

A catalog record for this book is available from the Library of Congress.

10   9   8   7   6   5   4   3   2   1
20  19  18  17  16  15  14  13  12  11

Printed and bound in Great Britain by
CPI Antony Rowe, Chippenham and Eastbourne

*This book is dedicated to my Sayang…who is all I need in the world*

# Contents

# Figures and Tables

## Figures

## Tables

# Acknowledgements

I have been able to prepare this volume because of the expertise, resources and support of my company OWW Consulting and the marvellous staff that I am fortunate to work with. We have been able to draw together the material, background and insights to bring the project to a conclusion. My business partner Luke Wood, Chief Technical Officer at OWW, was typically sceptical but generously allowed me the time off to complete the project while he held fort at the company.

I have also benefited from our partners at the Academy of Responsible Management (ARM), which is a new and exciting initiative in Corporate Social Responsibility (CSR) education in Asia and the Middle East. The ARM programmes, run in collaboration with the Malaysian Institute of Management and Universiti Sains Malaysia, have brought me into contact with many companies and practitioners in Asia who have offered their views and guidance on the development of CSR in the region.

These insights have also benefited from presentations and examples from participants at the first and second International CSR and SRI Conferences 2008 and 2009 in Kuala Lumpur, organized by OWW Consulting and the EU–Malaysia Chamber of Commerce and Industry (EUMCCI), and the first and second Global CSR Summits 2009 and 2010 in Singapore, organized by The Pinnacle Group International (TPGI) and supported by OWW Consulting. Events like these bring together leading practitioners and experts from Asia and around the world from all areas of CSR and SRI. They are vibrant forums for the exchange of ideas and sharing of experiences, which help us all to understand CSR as a living concept promoted by a dynamic and committed community of practice.

Of course, as for any edited volume, my main vote of thanks must be extended to the authors of the chapters, who have generously provided the material for each of the chapters and have shown dedication in editing and redrafting the material according to our suggestions. In this respect I must also thank Carlos Eduardo Oliveros at OWW and ARM, who helped in the administration of the requests made to the authors. I would also like to thank Amy Russell, who headed my team of editorial assistants, including Brian Brinker and Jack Hall, who together with Carlos and Amy put the changes into the document files more efficiently than I could have managed.

Finally, I would like to thank Virginia Thorp at Palgrave Macmillan for her commitment, dedication and support to this project. She and her assistant Paul Milner have both had the patience of saints in waiting for the final draft to be delivered.

# About the Authors

**Nelmara Arbex**

Nelmara Arbex joined the GRI Secretariat in July 2006 as Director for Learning and Services. She is responsible for developing the programmes and content for the inaugural learning services that support reporters and report users in their use of the GRI Guidelines. This also involves running the GRI Certified Training Program. In 2010 Dr. Arbex was appointed Deputy Chief Executive and her responsibilities now also cover future developments of the GRI Guidelines and development of strategic partnerships. Nelmara joined GRI with a wealth of experience in corporate responsibility and sustainable development. For three years she was manager for Corporate Responsibility at Natura Cosmetics, Brazil. There she developed and implemented a management system for corporate responsibility, led participatory processes of sustainable development planning with communities, implemented national social and environmental campaigns and was also responsible for the company's internal sustainability programme for managers. She also coordinated the preparation of the company's annual sustainability report. From 2001 to 2003, she was manager of Knowledge and International Relations at Ethos Institute – Business and Social Responsibility – Brazil. She was involved in developing CSR management tools, engaging partnerships with academia, managing relations with international partners and providing strategic guidance to companies about their social and environmental responsibilities and annual report processes. In addition to area coordination, Nelmara also collaborated on and co-authored several publications, including books, manuals and other research papers; she also coordinated learning activities such as a CSR course at FGV Business School and sessions at Ethos's annual conference. Prior to Ethos, she was an associate consultant at McKinsey in São Paulo, Brazil. Nelmara holds a PhD in theoretical physics from Marburg University, Germany (1997) and has been frequently involved in social and political activities in many civil organizations.

**Lisa Barnes**

Lisa Barnes has 15 years' experience in professional public accounting practice in Australia. She has taught, coordinated and developed a range of accounting and management courses and is currently a lecturer at Newcastle Business School in the University of Newcastle, Australia. She has taught internationally in Hong Kong and Kuala Lumpur and has presented her research findings in Sweden, New Zealand, Portugal and Turkey. She is a Certified Practising Accountant and a Fellow of the Australian Taxation Institute of Australia. She is currently an advisor to the NSW State Government Small Business Minister.

### Charles Bodwell

Charles Bodwell is the International Labour Organization (ILO) specialist, handling enterprise and private sector development in East Asia and the Pacific. Prior to this, he worked on developing a holistic approach to factory upgrading, later used in the ILO's Better Work and Factory Improvement Programmes. This integrated approach to enterprise improvement relies on improved social dialogue and workplace cooperation to achieve dramatic improvements in productivity, quality and labour practices. Previously, as a senior specialist based in ILO headquarters, his work focused on corporate citizenship and global supply chain issues. Before joining the ILO, he worked at the United Nations Industrial Development Organization (UNIDO), where he was Assistant to the Chief of Staff, as well as project manager for factory programmes in Africa. He has been a graduate researcher at Cambridge University while also serving as Visiting Professor at the Helsinki School of Economics and Visiting Scholar at Stanford University. He has worked for IBM, Agfa and Schlumberger. He has an MBA from McGill University and a Master's of International Management from ESADE as well as an engineering degree from Michigan State University. His research interests centre on the linkages at the factory level between productivity, quality and labour practices.

### Paul Boldy

Paul Boldy is an internationally experienced senior executive who has worked in a diverse range of industries including professional services management, business to business sales, FMCG, real estate investment, consultancy and training. He has worked across the globe, running regions in Europe, the Middle East, Africa, Australasia and North America. His roles include COO, Managing Director of Origination and Marketing, Global Head of Sales as well as Vice President of Sales, Marketing and Operations, all for large global companies. This level of experience has enabled him to look at CSR in Asia from both a cultural and a global perspective.

## Joëlle Brohier-Meuter

Joëlle is the Founder and Director of Anakout, a CSR (Corporate Social Responsibility) Consultancy Firm conducting research; and helping various organisations, from international institutions to companies and the non-for-profit sector, to raise awareness and build capacities on CSR, design and implement CSR programmes and projects across Asia. Her last jobs include organising an OECD-UNESCAP Asia CSR Conference, training on CSR at the French Chamber of Commerce in Singapore among others, providing reports and information on China-Europe CSR to the China-Europa Forum. She regularly speaks and moderates in CSR events. She has been studying and working in the field of CSR and Sustainable Development since 2002 in Hong Kong, London, Bangkok and now Singapore. She co-founded in 2006 www.RSE-et-PED.info, a non-profit initiative, consisting in an extensive French-language information website on CSR in developing and emerging countries, with a fortnightly newsletter. The website links to over 5,000 documents. Previously, Joëlle worked 11 years with Unilever, Bosch and Havas Advertising. She held Marketing, Research, Communication and Consultancy positions. In 1993, as a product manager with Unilever, she launched a range of eco-products. She received a Master In Management (MIM) from Rouen Business School, a DESS (Master) in Direct Marketing from Lille University, and a Postgraduate Diploma in Environmental Decision Making from the Open University UK. She speaks French, English, with some basic Mandarin Chinese and Thai.

## Rod Allan A. de Lara

Rod Allan A. de Lara is the Head of Postgraduate Studies and Research Center of KDU University College Sdn Bhd (Malaysia), and Programme Leader for the Executive Master's of Business Administration of KDU College School of Hospitality Tourism and Culinary Arts. Prior to joining academia, Dr de Lara was Senior Economic Specialist with the Congressional and Planning Department (CPBD) of the 13th Congress of the Philippines under the office of the speaker of the House of Representatives. The CPBD is the Policy Advisor and Think Tank agency of the Lower House of the Philippine Parliament. During his service in government, Dr de Lara regularly collaborated with local, national and international agencies and technical working groups such as the World Bank (WB), Asian Development Bank (ADB), the United Nations (UN) representatives in the Philippines and the National Economic

Development Authority (NEDA). He has authored a number of policy advisories and sector analyses that provided policy debates and inputs for legislation and legislative reforms of pertinent national economic policies. Dr de Lara has a doctorate in Business Administration from the Colegio de San Juan de Letran and is an alumnus of the prestigious Asian Institute of Management (Philippines).

### Josie M. Fernandez

Josie M. Fernandez is an Asian Public Intellectual Fellow under the Nippon Foundation Japan Programme for public intellectuals. She is founder Director of Philanthropy Asia – Centre for the Advancement for Philanthropy, and an independent researcher, writer and consultant. As an advocate of the rights of consumers, women, children, farmers and workers and an environmental and health activist, Josie has lobbied, written and spoken widely on these issues locally and internationally. Josie has served as a consultant to the Ministry of Domestic Trade and Consumer Affairs, Malaysia, and several UN agencies. Josie holds a Master's in Development Management from the Asian Institute of Management, Philippines and is also trained in education, mediation of environmental conflicts, advocacy, CSR, gender issues and library science. Among awards received are the Asian Public Intellectual Fellowship of Nippon Foundation, National Consumer Award, CIDA Scholarship and the Asia Foundation Fellowship for environmental mediation.

### Meena Galliara

Meena Galliara is Professor and Chair of Social Entrepreneurship at NMIMS University in Mumbai, India. She holds a Master's in Social Welfare Administration from Tata Institute of Social Sciences and her doctoral research is in the area of the Social Responsibility of the Corporate Sector towards Community Development. She is a recipient of the International Fellowship of the Government of the Netherlands. Prior to joining SVKM's NMIMS University, she was a full-time faculty member of the Department of Social Welfare Administration, Tata Institute of Social Sciences. In 1999–2000, she received a fellowship from the Business and Community Foundation, which is the Indian arm of the Prince of Wales Business Leaders Forum, London. As an outcome of this fellowship she has published a manual titled *'Sahaveeryam': Manual for Managing and Sustaining Sustainable Partnerships amongst Cross Sectors*. She is actively involved with the NGO sector in Maharashtra, India and has also conducted innovative field action projects in the area of management of rural entrepreneurship

About the Authors xvii

through self-help groups. Her major research work has been in the area of political empowerment of women at the grass roots and exploring cross-cultural issues affecting business and community development. In 2004–5, Dr Galliara was adjudged as the Best Faculty of NMIMS. In recognition of her efforts in teaching, research, training and consultancy to NGOs; the Bombay Management Association conferred the Best Faculty Award on her in July 2005. In 2007, she designed the Part-Time MBA Programme in Social Entrepreneurship, for which NMIMS won the prestigious 'Social Innovation Golden Peacock Award' in January 2008.

### Nicole M. Helwig

Nicole M. Helwig is Associate Intern at the Lariche Community, where she is focusing on social research and corporate-community engagement. Nicole is an experienced non-profit professional who has served as administrator and Board Director in Canada and Hungary respectively. She has a Bachelor of Arts degree – Distinction in Humanistic Studies from McGill University and is currently working on her Master's of Business Administration through the University of Strathclyde's international centre in Malaysia.

### Cheryl D. Hicks

Cheryl D. Hicks is an experienced business and sustainability professional, most recently working with leading multinational companies on collaborative action projects for sustainable development with The World Business Council for Sustainable Development (WBCSD) from 2004 to 2009. Cheryl worked with global companies on business and society issues and was the focal point for two workstreams: Sustainable Consumption & Consumers and Valuation & Capital Markets in the WBCSD's Business Role Focus Area. In 2008–9 Cheryl contributed to the WBCSD's Vision 2050 project, which outlines pathways to sustainability by 2050 and the future agenda for business. Cheryl has 14 years of business experience spanning many sectors, with nine years working at the intersection of business and sustainable development. She is co-founder and executive committee member of Sustainable Finance Geneva (Switzerland), advisory board member at BigRoom.ca (Canada), Transparence Source & Connect (Switzerland) and Steering Group member for the Green Awards 2010 (United Kingdom). Cheryl graduated from the University of Western Ontario in Canada with a BA with Honours in International Relations. She is Canadian, and throughout her career has worked and lived in Australia, Canada, Colombia,

France and South Korea. Cheryl is currently an independent advisor on sustainability, based in Geneva, Switzerland, working with leading businesses, governments and initiatives in the areas of sustainability-driven innovation, sustainable finance and sustainable consumption and lifestyles.

### Dewan Mahboob Hossain

Dewan Mahboob Hossain is Assistant Professor in the Department of Accounting & Information Systems, University of Dhaka, Dhaka, Bangladesh. He received his MCom in Accounting from the University of Western Sydney, NSW, Australia and holds an MCom in Accounting and a BCom (Honours) in Accounting from the University of Dhaka. His primary research interests include Corporate Social Responsibility Practices in Bangladesh, Corporate Social Reporting in the Developing Economies, Climate Change Issues, Social Entrepreneurship and Corporate Governance.

### Fiona Hovenden

Fiona Hovenden is an experienced researcher who uses the practice of ethnography as a main part of her work. For the past 18 years, through doctoral and postdoctoral research and in the business world, she has provided insight-based strategies for many organizations. These range from global consortia, Fortune 100 companies, government ministries, SMEs and philanthropic foundations. She has also worked with non-profits and start-ups – including a number of projects building innovation in the provision of education and social services in the US and Singapore. At Collective Invention, Fiona provides research direction, management and client support. This ranges from primary research, through analysis and integration of data, to rich persona and scenario-based recommendations and the design or redesign of social processes, policies and strategic direction. She has a BA in Philosophy from the University of London, an MS in Artificial Intelligence from Kingston University, UK, an MA in Counselling Psychology from JFK University, California and a PhD in Computing and Ethnography from Brunel University, UK.

### Brian Lariche

Brian Lariche is the Founder of the Lariche Community Sdn Bhd, a specialist in community liaison projects for corporations and international organizations, which was established in 2009. Brian has vast experience in the area of community development both in Malaysia and internationally. He worked as Project Advisor for the UNDP Malaysia in the area of HIV and also as a trainer–facilitator for the British Government on the Regional Young Global Community Leaders Program and also the Accelerated Learning Program for Regional Chevening Scholars. He is currently a Mentor for the SPROUT – Taking It Global online mentorship programme based in Canada, and continues to consult for international agencies. Brian started his career as a tutor of Malay language and Malaysian culture for local colleges and corporate bodies, but soon moved on to his interest of community development. He has published, written, translated and adapted numerous books and brochures on socio-medical issues. He sits on a variety of committees for both local and international organizations and conferences on social issues, including the Expert Panel for AIDS Accountability International, based in Sweden. Brian is currently finalizing his MBA and Master's in Public Administration (MPA) degrees.

### Ivanka Mamic

Ivanka Mamic is a technical specialist with the United Nations' International Labour Office (ILO), handling environment and corporate social responsibility issues with a particular focus on global supply chains. She is currently part of the ILO Regional Office in Bangkok, where, among other things, she is responsible for implementing projects in China, India, Bangladesh, Thailand and the Philippines relating to the promotion of decent work. Ivanka has extensive practical and research-based experience in the field of CSR in a number of sectors, including managing a factory training programme for multinational suppliers based in Vietnam. In 2007, she completed a series of research papers examining labour and social issues in global agri-food chains and, in 2004, published 'Implementing Codes of Conduct', an in-depth view into how businesses manage social performance across global supply chains in the sports footwear, apparel and retail sectors. Ivanka has a Master's of Philosophy degree from the University of Cambridge, UK, as well as a Bachelor of Law and a Bachelor of Economics from the University of Queensland, Australia. Her current research interests are focused on understanding how companies are marrying environmental and labour-related concerns in their supply chain operations.

### Falko Paetzold

Falko Paetzold works as a Senior Sustainability Analyst with Vontobel Asset Management in Zurich. He supports investment teams in integrating sustainability issues into investment processes, develops sustainable investment universes in cooperation with internal stakeholders and several external research partners, and supports Vontobel's position as a thought-leader in the sustainable investing field. A native German from Berlin, he draws from extended stays in North America and Asia, developing supply chain management strategies in China and Europe, working with the Canadian government on health care labour relations, sustainability topics with a leading strategy consultancy in Germany and a sustainability-related NGO in Singapore. Falko Paetzold studied for a Bachelor of Business Administration degree at OTA University in Berlin and Wilfrid Laurier University in Canada and an MBA at the University of St Gallen in Switzerland and Nanyang Technological University in Singapore.

### Kevin Teo

Kevin Teo is a Volans Founding Partner and Director. He runs Volans Asia and currently lives in Singapore. Kevin was previously Head of East and Southeast Asia at the Schwab Foundation of Social Entrepreneurship and Global Leadership Fellow at the World Economic Forum (2006–8). In 2003, Kevin co-founded the Southeast Asian Service Leadership Network (SEALNet), a California-based 501(c)3 organization that focuses on building a community of service leaders who are passionate about development in Southeast Asia. He currently sits on SEALNet's board and is an active mentor to the student chapters at Stanford University and the Massachusetts Institute of Technology. Every summer, you will find Kevin in some part of Southeast Asia working with a group of student leaders to dream up and execute plans that positively impact the region. Kevin graduated from Carnegie Mellon University with an MS in Information Networking and holds a BEng with Honours in Computing from Imperial College, London.

### Arno Thöny

Arno Thöny is the General Manager of Melia Kuala Lumpur. He has a wealth of experience drawn from 32 years of work in the hotel industry. Apart from Malaysia, Arno Thöny has significant international experience and has lived, worked and undertaken consultancy projects and assignments in a multitude of other Asian countries, including China, Hong Kong, Philippines, Singapore, Thailand and Australia, and his own home country of Switzerland for Hyatt, Hilton, Accor and Dusit Thani. Arno is a member of the Global Hotel Association and earned his undergraduate degree from the Hotel Management School at Belvoirpark, Zurich. He obtained his MBA from the University of South Australia, Adelaide. Arno is a Deputy-Chair of the EU Malaysia Chamber of Commerce and

Industry (EUMCCI) CSR Committee. Married with three children, Mr Thöny feels he is very much a global citizen and at home in multicultural societies.

## Wilfred Walsh

Wilfred Walsh is the Managing Director of Biosphere Capital Pte Ltd, a Singapore-based carbon finance advisory, specializing in CDM project development and renewable energy technologies, particularly concentrated solar thermal power. Dr Walsh has previously worked as an experimental physicist, operating astrophysical and atmospheric observatories in Australia and Antarctica.

## Geoffrey Williams

Geoffrey Williams is a founding director and Chief Executive Officer of OWW Consulting in Malaysia, Singapore and Indonesia. He is also a director of the Academy of Responsible Management Sdn Bhd and Opinion Tiger Sdn Bhd and a Deputy-Chair of the EU Malaysia Chamber of Commerce and Industry (EUMCCI) CSR Committee. Geoffrey's most recent work has focused on Corporate Social Responsibility in a global context and, in particular, on the factors that determine the success of CSR initiatives in different socio-political contexts. He has worked with leading international companies and organizations, including PETRONAS, UEM Group, PLUS Expressways Berhad, UMW Holdings Berhad, MRCB, Resorts World Berhad, du – the Emirates Integrated Telecommunications Company, Telekom Malaysia Berhad, Sime Darby Berhad, the Abu Dhabi Chamber of Commerce and Industry, the International Labour Organization, the European Commission and many others. Geoffrey has held academic positions at London Business School, Pembroke College, University of Oxford, and the Universities of London, Nottingham, Liverpool and elsewhere. He is Associate Member of the Centre for Business, Organisations and Society, School of Management, University of Bath, UK and was elected Fellow of the Royal Society of Arts (RSA) in 2004 and Fellow of the Malaysian Institute of Management (MIM) in 2010.

## Magdalene M. Kong

Magdalene M. Kong is currently the Director of Research at UNI Global Union – Asia & Pacific (UNI Apro). She holds a Master's of Sociology from the National University of Singapore (NUS), where she was a Teaching Assistant and an editorial member of the Asian Journal of Social Sciences from 2007 to 2008.

**Ruth Yeoh**

Ruth Yeoh is Director at Yeoh Tiong Lay & Sons Holdings Sdn Bhd and Director of Investments at YTL Corporation Bhd. She is also a Director at YTL-SV Carbon, YTL's in-house carbon credit and CDM consultancy. Ruth currently leads the environmental division at YTL, where she reports on her organization's environmental activities through writing its award-winning annual Sustainability Reports. Ruth also pioneered the highly successful 'Climate Change Week', YTL's flagship educational campaign designed to raise awareness on the important issue of climate change in her home in Malaysia and globally. She is a member of the Institute of Corporate Responsibility Malaysia (ICRM) and is an investment committee member of both the Asian Renewable Energy and Environment Fund (AREEF) and Renewable Energy and Environment Fund (REEF), investing in clean technology and renewable energy. Ruth was appointed as the youngest Board Member of Rare Conservation in 2008, with responsibilities in the Governance Committee of this US-based conservation organization. She has a degree in Architectural Studies (Hons) from the University of Nottingham, UK and an MSc in Management (Distinction) from Cass Business School in the City of London.

# Introduction
## Corporate Social Responsibility: Perspectives from Asia

*Geoffrey Williams*

The concept of Corporate Social Responsibility (CSR) in Asia differs in many ways from the current understanding and development of CSR in the West. CSR in Asia is distinctive and dynamic and reflects the diversity and vibrancy of a region that includes some of the most developed and some of the least developed economies in the world.

To the alarm of many Western observers, CSR in Asia does not always mirror, or even appear to acknowledge, Western standards, codes and compliance requirements.[1] This leads to a view that concepts of CSR are not understood or are even completely absent from the region. This, of course, is a misconception due in large part to a lack of information available about CSR activities among Asian companies. In fact, there is a strong emergence of a separate Asian dimension to CSR, with several key drivers which differ from those in the West. This in turn means that different processes are often used to deliver CSR outputs and the impact mechanisms are also different in important ways.

### Defining Asia: businesses in Asia and their CSR challenges

Talking about 'Asia' is, of course, itself misleading, since the region is one of the most diverse areas of the globe. The various countries of the region create a rich and dynamic mosaic of social, economic, environmental, political and cultural spaces in which businesses operate and perform their social responsibilities.[2]

There is also a wide array of company types, industries and business models in Asia, especially those that have emerged in recent times. These range from small-scale indigenous enterprises through back-end supply chain partners catering to the western markets, up to Asian multinationals and global corporate giants.

This diversity leads to some of the most pressing and difficult CSR challenges in the world, which often present themselves on a scale unknown in more developed markets in Europe and North America. The enormity of these challenges has produced creative responses from businesses in identifying and addressing the social and environmental impact of their activities.

## Setting the Asian CSR agenda

There are very few studies that document perspectives on CSR in Asia in a formal way.[3] Much of the available literature draws from the non-Asian perspective of CSR and focuses on global rather than local issues.[4] So far, most attempts to shed light on Asian CSR have been either microscopic, or studies through the Western lens, or generalization studies are used, where 'one rule fits all.'[5] Taken together, these studies often shed a bad light on CSR in Asia, because CSR efforts in the region often do not fit the frame of Western analysis.

To begin an understanding of Asian CSR, this volume draws on the experiences of people living and working in Asia as well as those in international organizations focusing on sustainability issues in Asian economic development. Each article refers in some way or other to the premise that Asia's emergence as a significant region for global businesses is widely expected to offer important economic opportunities and serious sustainability challenges in the current millennium. Given this premise, there is a need to understand Asian CSR in the context of several dynamic factors that affect Asian businesses and their role as agents of change in responsible and sustainable management.

## Charity and philanthropy as CSR in Asia

There is a widespread debate as to whether CSR in Asia is still at a fairly nascent stage where philanthropy and charity continue to be the dominant forms. In Chapter 1, Jose Fernandez addresses this issue directly by examining the importance and significance of Corporate Philanthropy and its successes and limitations in the context of Asian society and culture. Fernandez argues that there is a growing belief that governments in Asia cannot meet and sustain the social and economic development needs of their populations alone. Corporate Philanthropy is seen as a social intervention which can help fill this gap. Indeed, since companies exist within the context of society, there is an emerging consensus across Asia that companies have an obligation to accept their role and responsibility in social development.[6]

Corporate Philanthropy has a long history in Asian culture and has been seen as a way to promote and sustain social harmony. Philanthropy in Asia has historically gone beyond charity and has helped address numerous problems such as poverty, disease and providing jobs and education. Fernandez argues that, to continue to be effective, philanthropy must have an impact which succeeds at amassing, managing and allocating financial and human resources in ways that have the greatest positive impact in the sectors that corporate foundations choose to fund. As Asia has enjoyed increasing levels of development and its companies are enjoying more success, they are also facing increasing expectations of contributing to social needs in addition to generating profits. This matches changing attitudes as a whole, and more business leaders are starting to accept these social responsibilities, but designing effective philanthropic policies still poses challenges for many.

The chapter examines Strategic Philanthropy as a response to these challenges and its potential role as the next step in CSR. With corporations today helping with development and the achievement of the UN Millennium Development Goals, there is great potential for the development and growth of Corporate Philanthropy in Asia. This chapter outlines the various forms of philanthropy relevant to the Asian context and gives examples of how these could be adopted strategically to sit comfortably in a CSR context. Although there are challenges to be overcome, the author presents strong arguments in favour of a philanthropic approach to CSR, highlighting the social demand for such services. The implications for this within Asia are manifold.

## History, colonialism and CSR

Much of Asia has been under colonial rule of various forms for long periods in its history. This colonial past has left deep imprints on the social, cultural and political fabric of many Asian countries. It has played a significant role in economic growth, trade and business and the development of the corporate environment.

These themes are discussed in Chapter 2 by Meena Galliara, who provides an overview of CSR in India in the context of its historical and cultural development. Galliara argues that CSR is culturally and socially specific and its effectiveness depends on the ability of business to take these issues into account. The study highlights current and emerging trends in India and the interplay that CSR has with the societies in which it is carried out. The author highlights that business needs to play a more important role in society, and in particular within the marketplace, particularly in India, where the business sector is rapidly developing and inevitably encroaching into spaces it has previously never occupied, and so affects a larger number of citizens. The chapter identifies a need to develop market-oriented pressures, in order to assess companies according to more stringent criteria relating to CSR. It also highlights the need to ensure that CSR addresses gaps in income distribution, as well as ensuring sustainability of natural resources, and advocates CSR as a useful tool for development more widely.

The theme of how CSR develops within country-specific contexts is also discussed in Chapter 3 by Dewan Mahboob Hossain. In a study of Bangladesh, Hossain identifies the nature of CSR practices in the Bangladeshi business sector through various case studies. The organizations examined cover a wide range of industry sectors and include Banglalink, Dutch-Bangla Bank Limited, Citycell, Unilever, HSBC, Grameen Phone and British American Tobacco Bangladesh Limited. Information was also collected from sources such as newspapers, articles and websites as a way of gauging public awareness and discussion. Through his analysis Hossain brings to light two opposite pictures. On the one hand, the corporate sector of Bangladesh is performing CSR activities related to issues such as health, education, natural environment, empowerment for women and disabled people, cultural development and infrastructural development of the country. On the other hand, there is also evidence of persistent child labour, human rights violations, low wages, poor working environments and violations of governmental regulations.

## The role of governments and public policy in CSR in Asia

The role of governments in Asia is complex and varied due to their wide range of forms, from multiparty democracies through to one-party states and military dictatorships. The role governments have played in promoting or inhibiting the development of CSR is equally varied and has raised many challenges and issues for the extent and scope of corporate engagement in CSR across the region. In Chapter 4 Joëlle Broeher captures the essence of these experiences and highlights some of the key features of government policy as a driver of CSR in Asia. The chapter provides an overview of some existing frameworks for the analysis of public policy on CSR. These are used to examine various CSR policies across Southeast Asia and China and to compare and contrast various strategies. Broeher finds that the styles of promoting CSR range from a largely participatory model, as followed in Thailand, to top-down regulation, as followed in China, with everything in between.

The study outlines the specific features and achievements of CSR public policies in Asia using the frameworks presented and suggests some recommendations for the future. These include more direct measurement of CSR impact, broadening the range of tools used when conducting CSR activities and promoting public CSR policies that partner with a wider range of stakeholders. In conclusion, Asian governments need to include more participatory tools, create more oversight, coordinate regionally and engage internationally, among other things. The most effective policies will likely be those that encourage participation and generate commitment from the private sector and will include a mixture of voluntary and mandatory initiatives.

## Civil society and the third sector as a driver of CSR in Asia

Chapter 5 by Brian Lariche examines various non-government organizations (NGOs) as drivers that have played a role, both positive and negative, in the development of the CSR agenda within companies across Asia. Lariche argues that in many respects these are similar organizational drivers to those in the West, and include civil society organizations and international agencies as well as consumer groups, organized labour and the companies themselves, but there is a marked difference in the emphasis. In particular, non-government organizations adopt a non-lobbying role as well as lobbying and are likely to carry much more of the implementation load than their counterparts in the West.

In his study of these issues, Lariche discusses the role that home-grown NGOs and international non-governmental organizations (INGOs) and other forms of social organizations have played, and continue to play, in the CSR journey of Asia. The Asian story of NGOs and CSR includes the role of civil society in lobbying, such as the campaign against MNC operations in Myanmar or environmental concerns and indigenous people's rights in palm oil cultivation. It also includes non-lobbying interventions, such as the largely successful story of micro-credit, especially in Bangladesh, or the support of health infrastructure programmes and empowerment initiatives for marginalized groups region-wide. The chapter illustrates these issues by documenting many innovative and previously unpublished cases of several Asian NGOs engaged in eradicating poverty and hunger and addressing issues of health, population, education and human rights. Examples include Magic Bus and DASRA in India and Tenaganita in Malaysia and their programmes working towards development of healthier societies and stronger communities in Asia.

## Decent work and the role of organized labour in Asia

While CSR is an emerging trend, implementing CSR policies is a challenge in the disaggregated supply chains of the globalized economy. In Chapter 6 Ivanka Mamic and Charles Bodwell argue that successful CSR policies will start from a social vision of the company that requires the commitment of top managers in order to succeed. Implementing these codes of conduct involves several steps, such as evaluating structures and auditing CSR performance. Examining several case studies from the International Labour Organization (ILO) Factory Improvement Programme has revealed numerous success stories based on this premise. The chapter explores some of the results achieved through practical approaches from the ILO, the United Nations' specialized agency charged with the responsibility for promoting social justice and advancing decent work opportunities for all. These programmes have assisted companies in Asia in their quest for win–win solutions. The examples highlighted show that it is possible for companies to be more competitive while respecting the core labour rights of workers and operating in an environmentally sustainable way. In addition, this study argues that voluntary corporate initiatives are only successful in respecting workers' rights when implemented in the context of coherent labour laws and regulations that are backed up by credible systems of enforcement.

In Chapter 7 Magdalena Wong argues that many parts of Asia lack the powerful consumer lobbies, interested consumers and active unions that have helped fuel CSR initiatives in more developed nations. This may be one of the reasons for the relative lack of success of CSR in Asia, since the CSR agenda has been primarily driven by issues generated in the Global North that have little direct involvement with those in the Global South. Given this premise, Wong uses the case study of P.T. Hero Supermarket in Indonesia to examine a positive outcome and engagement in Asia-specific CSR programmes, particularly as they relate to decent work and labour practices. The negotiations between the Hero union and Hero management over labour issues demonstrate the success of a locally sustained initiative that did not rely on top-down Western support. Instead, both parties worked with each other to form a partnership and help achieve benefits for both the company and its workers.

## Consumers as drivers of CSR in Asia

In Chapter 8 Cheryl Hicks and Fiona Hovenden examine the relationship between consumers and corporations in the development of CSR in Asia. They argue that it is in the interest of businesses to protect their future by helping customers to adopt sustainable lifestyles and behaviour. To do this, Asian businesses have more to do to make sustainable products and services easy to buy and affordable. They would also benefit from taking a full life-cycle approach on high-performance products and leveraging the power of consumers by applying a deeper understanding of how people think and what motivates different people to act on CSR issues.

The chapter reviews recent insights into consumer trends, behaviour shifts and sustainable lifestyles. The study makes the case for the opportunities that are open to Asian companies from understanding the critical links between CSR, sustainability and triggers to behavioural change. The analysis draws on recent research on sustainable consumption and sustainable lifestyles from the World Business Council for Sustainable Development (WBCSD). It also uses approaches that link knowledge of sustainability and consumer behaviour to new opportunities in corporate and social innovation from the social innovation groups, Collective Invention and The Idea Factory.

A particular form of consumer behaviour important for many Asian countries is discussed in Chapter 9 by Rod Allan De Lara and Arno Thöny. The chapter examines the nature of tourism in Asia and takes a close look at how CSR should be undertaken in this industry. The chapter begins by looking at the development path of tourism in Asia, and goes back to its roots, which are historically embedded in war. It then goes on to examine the problems that arise in developing responsible tourism, including the significant cultural issues encountered within the sector. These challenges are unique in Asia for a number of reasons. The growth of Asian economies, along with growing interest in the region's rich history and culture, has resulted in well-meaning development of the continent's hospitality industry. In any industry, though, development and growth are attached to externalities, and the leisure and tourism industry is no exception to this rule. Due to the nature of the industry, the externalities affecting local communities in affected areas differ in form and scale from other industrial impacts.

For this reason, new challenges have been presented in the process of implementing responsible behaviour in the tourism industry. This in turn has given rise to concepts such as 'Sustainable Tourism', which has heightened concerns on issues such as preservation of ecosystems, bio-diversity and the quality of life of host populations. In addition, there has also been a steady rise in the codes of conduct and formal certifica-tion schemes for the sector.

## CSR innovation in corporations and enterprises in Asia

In Chapter 10, Cheryl Hicks and Kevin Teo argue that businesses have always had a responsibility to the societies in which they are licensed to operate, but now face more focused business and market incentives to develop CSR practices. Eco-efficiency and a more motivated work-force are just two possible outcomes of well-developed CSR practices. Further, there has been a growing awareness among consumers about the need to develop sustainable and ethical business practices, and cer-tain companies, such as Stonyfield Farms, have been able to use this awareness to tap new markets successfully. These innovations and mar-ket incentives have created a significant opportunity for growing Asian markets to redefine the notion of business success in the future econ-omy where sustainability and CSR drive innovation and entrepreneur-ship. Drawing on examples of businesses and organizations, such as the Schwab Foundation, Hicks and Teo show how collaborative initiatives can empower social entrepreneurs to use market forces to drive sustain-able innovation.

## Environmental sustainability in Asia

There has been a rise in Asian environmental consciousness within the corporate sector, civil society and community at large. From being a region with weak environmental enforcement, many Asian countries are developing strong and steady awareness on issues such as green-house gas (GHG), climate change and waste management. The complex and ever-emerging role of environment and CSR is one that offers both opportunities and challenges.[7]

In Chapter 11, Ruth Yeoh highlights the current energy issues fac-ing Asia and proposes sustainable alternatives. Three key areas are sug-gested as priorities on which to concentrate efforts in order to achieve sustainable development in the region. These are energy efficiency, energy diversification and climate change adaptation. Yeoh advocates the use of the Clean Development Mechanism (CDM) and presents arguments in favour of investment in these three key areas, highlighting areas of opportunity. In particular, a case is made for strengthening environmental reporting within firms and for stronger monitoring and evaluation in line with environmental achievements. Yeoh provides case study examples from Malaysia to illustrate successful investment in 'Green Business'. The chapter shows both the commercial value and the policy incentive for sustainability and renewable energy in Asia. Again concern is placed on the balance between the rights of future generations and the 'Triple Bottom Line' of economic prosperity, social equity and environmental protection. Yeoh highlights the link between society and business, with society able to put pressure on businesses to act in an ethical and sustainable way, since societies influence government regulation and provide licences for businesses to operate.

Chapter 12 provides a case study of Hong Kong Financial Institutions by Lisa Barnes and Paul Boldy. Dense urban development and high carbon emissions are causing Hong Kong's air quality to diminish. A large part of this is due to massive amounts of energy being used by buildings. Financial institutions operate and occupy many of these buildings, and this chapter highlights their power to reduce emissions, advocating that finance houses have a responsibility to act. The research focuses on the demand side, where pressure for 'Green Buildings' and environmentally friendly office space is beginning to form. Eight Hong Kong-based local and international financial institutions were interviewed to find out their perspectives on initiatives for Green Buildings. The findings presented in this chapter suggest that the financial sector is serious about environmental CSR and that it has become a normal part of doing business in the banking sector, although reporting and disclosure are weak.

In Chapter 13 Wilfred Walsh takes a pragmatic, somewhat personal, look at the problem of climate change and asks why the climate change debate became so tortuous, how opposing sides became so entrenched and how we might resolve this problem and avoid other ones like it. Walsh briefly explains the science of climate change, before showing its economic and environmental effects, providing impetus for businesses to act on this issue. To be pragmatic, relevant ethical considerations are construed as being purely emergent properties of macroeconomics. Walsh argues that ethical thinking has a role in providing guidance in matters such as the avoidance of potentially catastrophic events, such as climate change, which disrupt society and business.

## Sustainable and responsible investment as a driver of CSR in Asia

Sustainable and Responsible Investment (SRI) is a key market mechanism for achieving sustainability[8] and the recent rapid growth of SRI funds in Asia can have a significant impact on CSR developments. In Chapter 14 Geoffrey Williams offers a detailed discussion of the responsible investment scenario in Asia, with empirical data on the size, scope and growth of various forms of SRI. Using simple notions of company valuation, Williams shows how SRI adds value to shareholders. The chapter also examines how Asian governments and market regulators have used top-down, regulatory efforts to increase sustainability awareness amongst companies directly. This evolving attitude has resulted in increased pressure for companies to use more sustainable business models, and in turn has influenced the emergence of Sustainable Investment in Asia. This model differs from the Western model, which is largely market-driven and to an extent influenced by civil society pressure on material issues. While the amount of money invested in sustainable products in Asia is currently rather small, the introduction of SRI Indices, increasing regulation and changing attitudes amongst asset owners are making it an imperative for fund managers to consider sustainability issues in the companies in their portfolios. Importantly, Williams highlights cases where SRI outperforms conventional investments and so may be a superior long-term strategy for risk-averse investors and opportunity-seekers alike.

In Chapter 15 Falko Paezold argues that CSR in Asia should place priority on environmental, social and governance (ESG) issues in order to benefit from international investment. While Asia has become an economic success story, this has been based on an inherently unsustainable system of resource exploitation. Several factors, such as culture and the desire for quick economic growth, have also limited sustainability initiatives. The chapter examines the materiality of these issues to investors who want to focus on Asia and provides case study examples to illustrate their importance. Paezold argues that unless Asia addresses these problems its development may be hindered and investment opportunities lost. The chapter proposes that there is a great deal of opportunity in investing in Asia, and focusing on ESG issues in particular gives advantage over competitors. Using selected available investment products, investors can lend critical support to the drive towards sustainability, while reducing exposure to significant sustainability risk and profiting from the promising position of emerging Asia's sustainability leaders. He concludes with a strong case for sustainable investment in emerging Asia today.

## CSR reporting to international standards

CSR reporting is increasingly gaining acceptance in Asia, and is slowly moving from glossy CSR Reports published with a PR intent to adoption of structured and audited formats.[9] In Chapter 16, Nelmara Arbex discusses the experience of the Global Reporting Initiative (GRI) in working with corporations in Asia to improve the adoption of formal reporting using the GRI-G3 Guideline for Sustainability Reporting. She notes that Asia is one of the largest and most dynamic regions in the world, but it is also facing numerous sustainability problems that are becoming more urgent as economic development progresses. Sustainable development is in the interest of both business and society, as each depends on access to resources and the environment. In order to achieve greater sustainable development Arbex argues that more transparency and the promotion of GRI reports are needed. GRI reporting measures sustainable business practices and is becoming increasingly popular as more companies see reporting as being in their own interest. She highlights future efforts for GRI reporting which are being streamlined and expanded to include factors driven by economic globalization, such as issues with smaller companies, community investments and supply chain management.

## Conclusions and the future

The final chapter offers a discussion of the possible future of CSR in Asia, the different trends, the new areas of focus and the emerging possibilities for companies and their stakeholders. The chapter begins by reviewing the state of CSR in Asia as described by the authors. These look at the various initiatives for encouraging social responsibility, especially from the viewpoint of corporations and governments in Asian countries. With government promoting its participation and seeking to increase its CSR visibility in its association with corporations, there is a marked rise in the number of platforms, ranging from formal recognition processes and awards to joint initiatives in addressing social issues.

The chapter also explores the global impact of Asian CSR and offers an alternate perspective to the popularly accepted theory of dominance of Western CSR. There are plenty of arguments and evidence to support the view that Asian CSR is or has been influencing the global business scenario. This ranges from the assertive approach to the environmental and social balance of CSR, as demonstrated at the 2009 Copenhagen Summit, to laws and reforms on innovative principles of corporate community relationships. In many respects these new developments highlight the role of Asian companies in leading their own way in markets which are hugely complex and dynamic.

## Notes

1. See, for example, Gary Chan and George TL Shenoy, *Ethics and Social Responsibility: Asian and Western Perspectives* (Singapore: McGraw-Hill Education (Asia), 2009).
2. There are plenty of studies of this field, of which Juan J Palacios (editor), *Multinational Corporations and the emerging network Economy in Asia and the Pacific* (London, UK: Routledge, 2007), Rodolfo C Severino, *South East Asia: In search of an ASEAN Community* (Singapore: Institute of Southeast Asian Studies, 2006) and William E James, Seiji Naya and Gerlad M Meier, *Asian Development: Economic Success and Policy Lessons* (Madison, WI: University of Wisconsin Press, 1988) are just a few examples.
3. An example is Kyoko Fukukawa, *Corporate Social Responsibility in Asia* (London, UK: Routledge 2009).
4. See, for example, Andreas Georg Scherer and Guido Palazzo (editors), *Handbook of Research on Global Corporate Citizenship* (Cheltenham, Glos., UK: Edward Elgar, 2008) or Samuel O. Idowu and Walter Leal Filho (editors), *Global Practices of Corporate Social Responsibility* (Berlin and Heidelberg: Springer-Verlag GmbH & Co., 2009).
5. See, for example, Wayne Visser and Nick Tolhurst (editors), *The World Guide to CSR: A Country-by-Country Analysis of Corporate Sustainability and Responsibility* (Sheffield, UK: Greenleaf Publishing, 2010).
6. The general theme of CSR and Social Development in Asia is discussed in Manuel E Contreras (editor), *Corporate Social Responsibility in the Promotion of Social Development: Experiences from Asia and Latin America* (Washington, DC: Inter-American Development Bank, 2004).
7. See, for example, *Asian Environment Outlook 2005: Corporate Responsibility for Environmental Performance in Asia and the Pacific* (Manila, Philippines: Asian Development Bank, 2005).
8. See, for example, discussions of the importance of SRI in Rory Sullivan and Craig McKenzie (editors), *Responsible Investment* (Sheffield, UK: Greenleaf Publishing, 2006), Matthew J Kiernan, *Investing in a Sustainable World: Why GREEN is the New Color of Money on Wall Street* (New York, NY: AMACOM, 2009) or Cary Krosinsky and Nick Robins (editors), *Sustainable Investing: The Art of Long Term Performance* (London, UK: Earthscan Publications, 2008).
9. The issues of reporting and disclosure in developing markets in Asia are discussed, for example, in Ataur Rahman Belal, *Corporate Social Responsibility Reporting in Developing Countries: The case of Bangladesh* (Farnham, Surrey, UK: Ashgate Publishing, 2009).

# 1
# Pathways to Sustainability: Philanthropy, Charity, CSR

*Josie M. Fernandez*

Philanthropy is rooted in the ethical notions of giving and serving beyond immediate relief and has existed in all cultures and in most historical periods.

As a social intervention, philanthropy can help to eradicate poverty, provide access to basic needs such as health and education, promote global peace and security and conserve the environment. It can also be seen as a response to the growing belief that governments alone cannot meet and sustain the needs of their people.

Philanthropy therefore reflects the struggles and contexts of a nation or a culture at particular periods of its history. A study of philanthropy in the world's traditions shows that it becomes a location where cultural values and norms are often contested.[1] Today, the philanthropy spectrum includes charity and Corporate Social Responsibility (CSR).

The objectives of this chapter are to provide a clear understanding of the scope of strategic philanthropy, its needs, where there are overlaps, if any, and, more importantly, to examine where some synergies may be possible. Since this book is predominantly focused on CSR, this chapter will focus more on strategic philanthropy, with the view of allowing the reader to assess objectively the next step of CSR, which is strategic philanthropy. Philanthropy is what you do with your profits. CSR is how you make those profits.[2]

Philanthropy is a complex phenomenon influenced by values, organizational and community activities and a complex array of local, national and international institutions. Defining philanthropy is not easy, as there are different perceptions depending on the social location of the individual defining it. The influences on philanthropy are equally diverse and include factors such as religion, culture and economic development, with well-being and education taking critical roles.

The word 'philanthropy' is derived from the Greek 'phillen' (to love) and 'anthropos' (human), and can be taken to mean 'the expression of love to human beings'. Webster's Dictionary (2002) does not limit this expression of love to giving money or things, but includes activity or effort which increases the feeling of love for human beings and humanity.

The comprehensive mapping of philanthropic practices worldwide by various scholars has facilitated a global definition of the phenomena, as follows:

> Philanthropy is defined as voluntary giving, voluntary service and voluntary association for the benefit of people and the environment. We owe a debt to Robert L. Payton's definition of philanthropy as voluntary action for the public good.[3]

> Charity provides immediate relief while philanthropy is a long term commitment for building capacity of people, facilitating social change and promoting sustainable development.[4]
>
> Liffman, Michael (2009)

## Dimensions of Asian philanthropy

Some significant changes are taking place in the philanthropy terrain in Asia. Several studies on philanthropy in Asia in the first decade of the twenty-first century have observed the following new trends in the philanthropy spectrum:

- A new paradigm to mobilize indigenous resources through organized philanthropy is shaping the philanthropy field
- Community resources are being transformed into Social Investment rather than charity. Giving a loan or a job rather than a gift, so preserving the recipient's self-respect and encouraging self-help. Increasingly programmes of Strategic Social Investment have been developed in consultation with stakeholders and are informed by a wider vision of sustainable social improvement
- The development and growth of Social Justice Philanthropy is increasingly evident
- The pluriformity of philanthropy is being recognized given Asia's social, cultural and economic diversity
- The centrality of religion and culture in the expansion of philanthropy is profound

- The role of Corporate Social Responsibility in addressing economic disparities through establishing Philanthropy foundations is encouraged and sometimes necessary by legislation
- Issues of Sustainability and principles of Sustainable Development cut across philanthropic endeavours
- The cosmological values linked to philanthropy and cosmology-cum-economy societies are being recognized for example in Indonesia
- Models of community or horizontal forms of philanthropy exist throughout Asia

Fernandez, Josie (2009)[5]

Targets of philanthropic actions fall into three categories: individuals, groups or communities, and issues. Philanthropy is orientated towards charity, social development such as eradication of poverty, education and other social needs, welfarism or activism. The donors fall into several categories, including individuals, households, foundations (family-based, corporate and community-based), religious institutions, corporations, the high net worth (HNW) individuals, international aid agencies and governments.

Philanthropic practices are often driven by religion, cosmological practices, social justice and the need for Corporate Social Responsibility. Philanthropy is conditioned too by social, political and economic conditions of particular periods.

The main influences that promote philanthropy in addition to religion and culture are politics, economy, education, new information technologies, disasters and emergencies.

Based on studies in Pakistan, India, Thailand, Indonesia and the Philippines, Asian philanthropy can be said to be deeply rooted in the diverse cultural and religious traditions of Asians and is not as institutionalized or organized as in the United States and Europe. However, this is changing following the phenomenal giving for the 2004 Asian tsunami victims, according to the Asia Pacific Philanthropy Consortium based in the Phillipines.[6]

The patterns of giving among households in India, Indonesia, the Philippines and Thailand show that individuals and religious organizations are the main recipients of household giving. Direct support for individuals accounted for 40 per cent of total giving in Indonesia, India and the Philippines.[7]

The main areas of support were for social services (welfare) and education, and the primary motive for giving was compassion.[8] Support for organizations providing social services was high in Indonesia, Thailand and the Philippines, whereas donors in India gave the most for religious purposes and less to voluntary organizations. Door-to-door soliciting was high in Indonesia and the Philippines but low in India. Corporate philanthropy is growing in terms of cash donations, matching staff contribution and providing goods and services. This points to the growing role of philanthropy within Corporate Social Responsibility (CSR) in Asia.[9]

A 2010 report on Giving in Thailand states: 'Buddhist temples, situated in nearly all communities, still play an important role in Thai life, even in Bangkok. They instil from a young age the value of giving and volunteering for social good.'[10]

Local fund-raising activities in Bangladesh, India, Indonesia, Nepal, Pakistan, the Philippines and Thailand by Non-Profit Organizations tapped local (indigenous) resources successfully. Fund-raising was undertaken for a broad spectrum of social needs, including poverty alleviation, education, health and disasters.[11]

Corporate giving in Pakistan is extensive, according to Philanthropy in Pakistan (2000), a report of the Aga Khan Development Network. A survey of 120 companies showed that 93 per cent of companies engaged in philanthropic activities. Some companies made small one-time donations, while others undertook large projects with long-term commitments of cash, company personnel and material.[12]

A corporate citizenship report of 14 Asian countries showed that corporations were involved in charitable donations of cash/products for community programmes, advocacy against HIV/AIDS and environmental protection.[13]

A study of philanthropy in Malaysia shows that it is rooted in culture, ethnicity, religion and value systems. Religious influences on philanthropy are strong. A number of modern philanthropic institutions have also emerged and the type of giving is primarily welfare-focused. Corporations give from company profits and through public fund-raising events. There is also active use of the mass media for fund-raising.[14]

CSR is a relatively new phenomenon exclusive to corporations and for most corporations in Asia has been motivated by legislation requiring or encouraging companies to give back to society; for example, public listed companies in Asia are all encouraged to participate in CSR activities or be faced with adverse publicity. Thus, when CSR activities are externally driven and perhaps more drawn towards gaining publicity, one may argue that their effectiveness and impact may well be limited.

For example, in Indonesia, the last two decades have seen tremendous growth in Islamic philanthropy, given the huge potential for Islamic obligatory giving and voluntary contributions. Institutional philanthropy is on the rise. Indonesia has harnessed pluralism in philanthropy for strengthening diversity and addressing socio-economic needs.[15]

The traditional models of giving, which have essentially been charity-based, are now shifting to more organized forms of philanthropy. These organized philanthropic institutions are based on the principles of social justice, long-term social investments such as education and health, and community and environmental sustainability.

The potential for harnessing these informal avenues of philanthropy to increase their effectiveness and to make them sustainable is extensive.

## Some major trends
### Institutionalized philanthropy

Modern philanthropy is highly institutionalized; that is, resources are mobilized for grant-making, which goes through various stages such as identifying prospective beneficiaries and intermediaries. Wealthy individuals and families have often established grant-making foundations to enhance the efficacy of their contributions. These foundations are serviced by many supporting organizations such as research institutions and centres of excellence. The specialization of giving is also a feature of institutionalized philanthropy.

Philanthropy in Asia has not yet attained this level of institutionalization, but the growth of a civil society movement is changing the structure of philanthropy in Asia. The dependency on foreign aid, which will diminish as countries in Asia develop, has also triggered the need to develop institutionalized indigenous philanthropy.

A study in 2000 by the Public Interest Research and Advocacy Centre (PIRAC) showed a high level of giving among Indonesians. Almost all of those interviewed (96 per cent) stated they had given donations either in the form of cash, goods or time and energy. The factors that drive philanthropy in Indonesia include social justice, CSR, religion, culture and political changes.[16]

### Social Justice Philanthropy (SJP)

The notion that philanthropy, to retain its character, must remain non-controversial represents a fundamental misunderstanding of the institution which not only prevents its historical development but also destroys its essential values. The most traditional of charitable purposes ordinarily require the acquisition, development and dissemination of information and ideas and they are not rendered the less charitable because such information or ideas are disputable and disputed.

Albert M. Sacks (Quoted in chapter 4, Social Change Philanthropy in America, Rabinowitz Alan, 1990)

The concept of Social Justice Philanthropy was first developed in the United States by the National Committee for Responsive Philanthropy (NCRP). An operational definition of Social Justice Philanthropy is 'the practice of making contributions to non-profit organizations that work for structural change and increase the opportunity of those who are less well off politically, economically and socially'.

The goal of SJP is the creation of social justice, which involves, theoretically, 'addressing basic needs, redistribution of power, transformation of values in favour of diversity (race, gender, etc.), strong community capacity and public participation in decision making' Traditional philanthropy does not necessarily address basic needs, nor does it always contribute to the transformation of values, including prejudices about race and gender. Traditional philanthropy may redistribute power and improve capacity, but it is unclear who makes decisions, to whom power is redistributed and whose capacity is built. From the SJP perspective, philanthropic social services do not eradicate the root causes of social injustice.

Elements of charity, social investing and social justice shape religious philanthropy. This is evident in Christian missionary work. For example, schools, hospitals and orphanages were built and managed through donations from Catholics in many parts of Asia, including Indonesia. Democracy and human rights are the fundamentals of social justice, and the Catholic Church was an active participant in the struggle for independence from colonial rule in many Asian countries, especially Indonesia.[17]

## The pluriformity of philanthropy

One of the significant findings of a study on philanthropy in Indonesia is the pluriformity of philanthropy there. It is the pluriformity that has constructed an ethos that enables Indonesians to embrace philanthropic orientations based on various religions including Islam, Christianity, Hinduism, Buddhism and cosmological practices. In 2007, Indonesia celebrated 60 years of independence from Dutch colonial rule 'on the heels of national polemic on issues concerning liberalism, pluralism and secularism' (Jakarta Post, 2007). Foundations, organizations, corporations and Community Based Organizations (CBOs) carrying out philanthropic activities reflect the pluralistic nature of Indonesian society.[18]

### The evolution of corporate philanthropy

Corporate Philanthropy, which is part of CSR, was spurred in part by anti-corporate campaigns on social, environmental, workers' and human rights issues. The direct response from corporations was to repair their image in the eyes of the public, enhance the company's reputation and gain more leverage in society.

An in-depth analysis of 2008 Corporate Philanthropy data from 137 leading Fortune 500 companies in America reveals some interesting trends that challenge corporations. The report highlights the following:

* The Shifting Social Contract. Around 84 per cent of corporate executives believe that society expects businesses to take a more active role in environmental, social and political issues than it did 5 years ago. Corporate Philanthropy is one effective way to meet these new expectations, which goes beyond the scope of CSR as often conceived.
* Capturing the Corporate Philanthropy Opportunity. Companies are developing more sophisticated initiatives to address the three levels of their contract with society (laws and regulations, implicit non-legal expectations and frontier issues such as obesity or human rights) and employing broader resources for community impact, including volunteerism, product donations and capacity-building.
* The Complexity of Getting It Right. Fewer than 20 per cent of companies surveyed said their philanthropic efforts were very or extremely effective in meeting social or business goals. To help optimize these efforts, companies must define the focus of philanthropic efforts, gain public recognition for their programmes and allocate appropriate CEO time to philanthropy.
* Capturing the Corporate Philanthropy Opportunity. Examining the behaviour of leading corporate philanthropists uncovered three keys to philanthropic success: deep involvement from the CEO and board of directors, alignment between philanthropic and business strategy, and management of philanthropy as a business investment.
* The report underscores the fact that the scope of philanthropy includes CSR when Corporate Philanthropy extends beyond financial contributions and explicitly links company missions, organizational competencies and various stakeholders. Strategic Philanthropy

is therefore defined as the synergistic use of an organization's core competences and resources to address key stakeholders' interests and to achieve both organizational and social benefits.[19]

John Damonti, president of the Bristol-Myers Squibb Foundation, reflected: 'When you align your contributions with your business focus, you then can draw on the greater wealth of the corporation's people, information and resources.' Identifying optimal opportunities for philanthropic investments requires a healthy realism about both the funder's and the grantee's skill base, expertise and resources as well as a willingness to challenge conventional thinking and entrenched assumptions. Strategic philanthropy requires a careful and ongoing examination of each project's or organization's emphasis in order to narrow the array of possibilities, find ripe opportunities and assess where investments can have the greatest return.[20]

Ferrell (2008)[21]

Effective philanthropy has impact and succeeds at amassing, managing, then allocating financial and human resources in ways that have the greatest positive impact in the sectors that foundations choose to fund. To allocate resources effectively, philanthropic organizations must have vision and strategies for their grant-making that allow them to analyse issues and concerns they want to influence, identifying both challenges and potential resources. They must be able to find the Non-Profit Organizations most likely to produce the results they intend. They must be able to structure their grants in ways that will be most useful to their grantees. Philanthropic entities must evaluate what they do to ensure they achieve the intended impacts.[22]

According to Dr Madhav Mehra, President of the UK-based World Environment Foundation and the World Council for Corporate Governance, integrating business and social needs takes more than good intentions and strong leadership. It requires adjustments in organization, 'reporting relationships' and incentives. Few companies have engaged operations management in processes that identify and prioritize social issues based on their salience to business operations and their importance to the company's competitive context. Even fewer have unified their philanthropy with the management of their CSR efforts, much less sought to embed a social dimension into their core value proposition.

Doing these things requires an approach to both CSR and philanthropy far different from the one prevalent today. Companies must shift from a fragmented, defensive posture to an integrated, affirmative approach. The focus must move away from an emphasis on image to an emphasis on substance. The current preoccupation with measuring stakeholder satisfaction has its drawbacks. What needs to be measured is social impact. Operating managers must understand the importance of the influence of competitive context, while officials with responsibility for CSR initiatives must have a granular understanding of every activity in the value chain. Value chain and competitive-context investments in CSR need to be incorporated into the performance measures of managers with Profit & Loss responsibility. These transformations require more than a broadening of job definition; they require overcoming a number of long-standing prejudices. Many operating managers have developed an ingrained 'us versus them' mindset that responds defensively to the discussion of any social issue, just as many NGOs question the pursuit of social value for profit. These attitudes must change if companies want to leverage the social dimension of corporate strategy.

## Strategy

Strategy is always about making choices, and success in Corporate Social Responsibility is no different. It is about choosing which social issues to focus on. The short-term performance pressures faced by companies often rule out indiscriminate investments in social value creation. They suggest, instead, that creating shared value should be viewed like research and development, as a long-term investment in a company's future competitiveness. The billions of dollars already being spent on CSR and corporate philanthropy would generate far more benefit to both business and society if consistently invested using the principles outlined above. While responsive CSR depends on being a good corporate citizen and addressing the social harm business creates, strategic CSR is far more selective.

Companies are called on to address hundreds of social issues, but only a few represent opportunities to make a real difference to society or to confer a competitive advantage. Organizations that make the right choices and build focused, proactive and integrated social initiatives in concert with their core strategies will increasingly distance themselves from the pack.[23]

## Some challenges

It is globally accepted that the world economic power shift is taking place towards Asia. A PricewaterhouseCoopers (PwC) report, which projected relative size of economies in 2007 and 2050, clearly shows highest GDP growth rates especially in Asia, including China, India and Indonesia. The shift in growth rates in Asia will have several implications; such as:

1. Rapid high growth rates in Asia will create huge economic imbalances – a leading cause of social injustice
2. To alleviate the imbalances caused by rapidly developing economies, corporate philanthropy will need to play an important role
3. In Asia family businesses still have a significant role in driving economic growth. These wealthy family businesses will need to support emerging concerns such as social justice

But the scope and challenges of the current financial crisis and its impact on all countries and regions are unprecedented. Massive layoffs, shutdowns of plants and businesses, bankruptcies, unintended mergers and consolidation, and shrinking government resources take serious toll on human lives and the environment. Poverty and hunger will escalate, access to health care and other basic needs will be seriously eroded, and children will drop out of school, thus affecting generations in various known and unknown ways.

The climate change crisis is a far greater crisis than the current economic meltdown. Governments face a choice between serving the planet or the economy. There is a growing concern that, given the financial crisis, governments are losing interest in climate change. Recent reports are warning that we need two planets to sustain current consumption patterns and population growth. In every continent it is evident that global warming is man-made. The inadequacy of current responses to global warming is very worrying. Take the issue of carbon emissions. Some countries are saying theirs are 'survival emissions'. Some are guilty of 'luxury emissions'.

Hunger, floods and long periods of drought are daily news on TV screens around the world. Irreversible degradation and loss of resources seriously affect economic activities and livelihoods.

It is also becoming clear from the Copenhagen Dialogue G20 Summit of 2009 that we are struggling in the losing battle for sustainable development. Developed economies seem to be admitting that there are weaknesses in global economic growth.

Issues such as global climate change continue to highlight the structural imbalances that exist between the rich and poor nations. At the G20 summit in Pittsburgh in 2009, the most industrialized countries of the world came to the conclusion that they can no longer run the world on their own. By turning to the developed world, especially the emerging nations of the world, such as Brazil, China, India, South Africa and Mexico, the G8 and European Union were admitting that they were out of answers.

The role of philanthropy may be reduced as resources shrink. But it is now, more than ever, that people turn to philanthropy to keep themselves alive. It is in this financial meltdown that all forms of philanthropic resources are critically needed in addition to government stimulus packages to reduce the enormous and unprecedented effects of the economic and climate change crises.

It is in this context that we need to realize that philanthropic initiatives have a very long history and have survived many difficult periods in the history of human societies. Philanthropic interventions have been supported and given life by different groups at different stages of human history. Today, the corporate sector, through its CSR interventions, has taken the lead to strengthen philanthropy and contribute to social well-being.

It is true that economic and social objectives have long been seen as distinct and often competing. But this is a false dichotomy; it represents an increasingly obsolete perspective in a world of open, knowledge-based competition. Companies do not function in isolation from the society around them. In fact, their ability to compete depends heavily on the circumstances of the locations where they operate. Improving education, for example, is generally seen as a social issue, but the educational level of the local workforce substantially affects a company's potential competitiveness.

## In their own words

The following entrepreneurs have expressed their concerns on CSR:

> In 1895, in his work 'The Creation of Wealth', the founder of the Tata Group of Companies, Jamsetji Tata, said: 'We do not claim to be more unselfish, more generous or more philanthropic than other people. But we think we started on sound and straightforward business principles considering the interests of the shareholders our own and the health and welfare of the employees the sure foundation of our prosperity.'

> 'Corporate Social Responsibility, I don't think it's working. I think it's been taken over by the big management houses, marketing

houses ... it's a huge money-building operation now. I think maybe it's the word "corporate"...' – Anita Roddick

'A market system has not worked in terms of poor people.' – Warren Buffet

'We need to challenge the idea that you can live a morally decent life just by looking after your own family and not actually causing harm to others. We need to develop a sense that if we have an abundance, we are actually doing wrong if we don't share it.' – Peter Singer

Leon Davis, Chairman of Westpac Bank, Australia expressed his concerns as:

Communities can and will punish organizations that fail to meet modern expectations.

But the biggest and most enduring benefit of all lies in their heightened appeal to potential employees.

The best people – the people that companies want to attract and keep – are the people who like to feel proud about going to work every day.

They come to work to earn a living – but they also want to feel good about it.

Those corporations that fail to adapt will fail to succeed.

Corporations that embrace this new era will be rewarded by employees, customers and investors.

## Conclusion

Philanthropy and Social Responsibility go beyond charity and welfare. Philanthropy has made a significant impact in reducing hunger, poverty and disease, and providing jobs, access to education and healthcare. Today corporations are contributing to numerous causes such as education, achieving the UN Millennium Development Goals, community development and the environment, and rehabilitation after major disasters.

Community and Corporate Philanthropy (through CSR initiatives) in all cultures and societies throughout the world has often sustained social harmony, provided basic needs to families and protected the environment. Organized philanthropy in modern times supports many charitable and social justice causes.

The potential for the development and growth of philanthropy in Asia is enhanced by higher educational levels and economic opportunities, and governments continue to emphasize that they are unable to meet and sustain the social and development needs of their people. Modernization and globalization are eroding communal models of giving. In September 2005, the United Nations said: 'we need companies, foundations, individual philanthropists and social investors to meet the Millennium Development Goals (MDGs).'

Worldwide philanthropic models are undergoing change too. Company portfolios now include social investments and social audits. Consumers are purchasing products from companies that practice ethics and corporate citizenship. Contemporary philanthropy is increasingly organizational in nature. Global challenges as well as factors such as education and economic success are transforming the field of philanthropy. Donors too are concerned about making the world a safer place.

In considering the future of philanthropy in Asia, the question arises: How will 'global philanthropy' affect Asia? Increasing numbers of private banks in Asia have started to offer philanthropic services in direct response to a growing number of clients who want to put something back into society.[24] The role of diaspora philanthropy, e-philanthropy and an enabling legal framework for philanthropy needs to be studied for the further growth and development of this field in Asia.

## Notes

1. WF Ilchman, SN Katz and Edward L. Queen II, *Philanthropy in the World's Traditions* (Bloomington: Indiana University Press, 2009).
2. D Stangis, 'Where Does Philanthropy Fit in the CSR Spectrum?' CSR@Intel blog, 27 July 2007.
3. WF Ilchman , SN Katz and Edward L. Queen II, *Philanthropy in the World's Traditions* (Bloomington: Indiana University Press, 1998).
4. M Liffman, 'Mobilising CSI for Strategic Philanthropy', *Philanthropy Asia Conference KL July* (Asia-Pacific Centre for Social Investment and Philanthropy, 2009).
5. J Fernandez, 'From Charity to Social Investments and Social Justice: Philanthropy in Indonesia' (Centre for the Advancement of Philanthropy: Philanthropy Asia, 2009).
6. Asia Pacific Philanthropy Consortium, 'Investing in Ourselves: Giving and Fund Raising in Asia' (Asian Development Bank, 2002).
7. Ibid.
8. Ibid.
9. Ibid.
10. H Perkins, R Mantle and R Sungthing, 'Giving in Thailand', Fund Raising Opportunities in 2010 (2010).
11. Asia Pacific Philanthropy Consortium, 'Investing in Ourselves: Giving and Fund Raising in Asia' (Asian Development Bank, 2002).

12. D Bonbright (ed. ), 'Philanthropy in Pakistan' , *A Report of the Initiative of Indigenous Philanthropy* (Pakistan: Aga Khan Development Network, 2002).
13. L Vacek (undated) *Corporate Citizenship in Asia Pacific Conference Report*, United States of America, Council of Foundations.
14. J Fernandez and AR Ibrahim, 'A Giving Society? The State of Philanthropy in Malaysia' (Penerbit Universiti Sains Malaysia, 2002).
15. J Fernandez, 'From Charity to Social Investments and Social Justice: Philanthropy in Indonesia' (Centre for the Advancement of Philanthropy, Philanthropy Asia, 2009).
16. Ibid.
17. Ibid.
18. Ibid.
19. TF Ferrell, *Business and society: A Strategic Approach to Social Responsibility* (Boston: Houghton Mifflin Company , 2008).
20. Ibid.
21. Ibid.
22. M Mead and MES Capek, *Effective Philanthropy: Organizational Success through Deep Diversity and Gender Equality* (Cambridge: MIT Press Books, 2006).
23. ME Porter and RM Kramey, ' Strategy and Society: The Link Between Competitive Advantage and Corporate Social Responsibility', *Harvard Business Review*, December 2006.
24. C Piggot, 'Philanthropists Turn to Private Banks to Help Redirect Their Wealth', *The Asian Wallstreet Journal*, 5–7 October 2001, p. 12.

# 2
# Corporate Social Responsibility in India

*Meena Galliara*

## Introduction

The concept of a corporation or an entrepreneur having a social responsibility towards the community has come a long way since the rise of
mercantilism. The pre-industrial era expected mercantile traders to
care not only for themselves but also for members of their guild, the
poor and other needy communities. With the advent of industrialization, the global trade scene witnessed the emergence of corporations
as distinct legal entities that functioned solely for profit maximization
and rejected the proposition that business was responsible for social
welfare. The post-liberalization period expects businesses to adopt the
triple bottom line approach as an inseparable part of their strategy to
attain both shareholder and social value.

India has one of the world's richest traditions of business involvement in social causes for national development. To understand the
current status of Corporate Social Responsibility (CSR) in India, it is
important to map out the CSR format institutionalized by old and
new public and private sector undertakings. Long-established old
private sector industrial dynasties, such as the Birlas[1] and the Tatas,[2]
have integrated the concepts of nation-building and trusteeship long
before CSR became a popular cause. Alongside these are the leading
multinational companies (MNCs) with strong international shareholdings, such as Hindustan UniLever Ltd (HUL),[3] International Tobacco
Company (ITC)[4] and others, where local dynamics have fused with the
business standards of the parent or partner organizations. Public sector enterprises, such as Bharat Heavy Electricals Ltd (BHEL),[5] Housing
Development Finance Corporation (HDFC), National Thermal Power
Corporation (NTPC)[6] and Oil and Natural Gas Corporation (ONGC)

have also incorporated social obligations as an integral part of their business. New generation enterprises like Dr Reddy's Lab,[7] Infosys,[8] Ranbaxy[9] and Wipro Technologies[10] lay greater emphasis on minimizing the negative impacts and maximizing the positive spillover effects of corporate development.

## History of CSR in India

Historically, the philanthropy of Indian businesses is deeply rooted in religious beliefs. Merchants' charity in ancient India took various forms, such as treasury chests for the needy, providing relief in times of famine or floods, provision of drinking water, building temples, water tanks, wells, ponds, supporting schools and so on. Merchants contributed to charities both individually and collectively, through their business and social organizations. At an individual level they gave alms and food to the poor and needy, set up traditional schools (*pathshalas*), constructed night shelters for the poor and travellers, built water tanks and bathing areas (*ghats*), made provision for drinking water during summer, gave access to their private granaries in times of famine, commissioned artists to prepare religious texts and other works of art for temples, provided for dowries and marriage expenses of poor girls and so on. As part of collective charity, a group of families or all the inhabitants of the town would collect voluntary offerings and present them according to different needs of the community, such as health, sanitation, education and other similar aspects of general welfare. There was a strong tradition of charity in almost all the business communities of India and philanthropy has often been used by merchants to gain political power, economic advantage, personal status and honour. The tradition of merchant charity has continued down through the ages, even to present times, where it is still visible among individual businessmen and the unorganized sector.

### Pre-independence period

The arrival of the East India Company in 1620 was a milestone in the history of trade and the wider socio-political environment of India. Over the next 200 years the initial trade and business interests of the East India Company changed into social and political management of the country by the company executives, until 1885 when India came under control of the British crown. The business leaders of the emerging indigenous industry remained rooted in the tradition of philanthropy, which gradually metamorphosed into businesses consciously contributing to social development to liberate India. The period between 1850 and early 1900 witnessed businesses setting up trusts and endowment funds.

The single most important factor influencing business philanthropy in the pre-independence period was the emergence of Mahatma Gandhi as a political and social leader. Gandhiji reinterpreted the traditional concept of 'charity' (*dana*) in his theory of trusteeship, which he held as an ideal to be approximated by business. Founders of business families supported schools, colleges, hospitals, orphanages and the promotion of art and culture. By the 1830s, merchant charity began to change from being largely religious, ameliorative in nature and confined to members of their own community, caste or religion, towards being more secular, more inclusive in terms of caste, creed and community and more oriented towards bringing progress to society through Western-style modern institutions. Though the more enlightened merchants began to diversify their charitable giving in content and intent, they continued the older forms of giving as well.

## Post-independence India

Following independence, India struggled to stand on her own feet through indigenous manufacturing and the creation of jobs. Industries were termed 'Temples of Modern India' and industrialists participated in nation-building programmes by setting up scientific and technical learning institutes. After independence, the need for rapid progress on the part of the government, the people and the business community compelled businesses to contribute more towards social development. Business leaders increasingly engaged themselves and their businesses in social welfare and reform. The emphasis was on vocational and technical training, public health, power and water supply and the Gandhian social reform movements.

The credit for integrating social responsibility with the conscience of business goes principally to business leaders such as JRD Tata, Ramakrishna Bajaj, Arvind Mafatlal and Kasturbhai Lalbhai. As champions of free enterprise, they feared that irresponsible behaviour by the business community would lead the government to encroach on their freedom. They felt that the business community was an essential ingredient of the democratic society and it had a duty not only to create wealth but also to promote the ethical and social goals of the community. Unless the business community fulfilled both these functions, it would not be able to ensure its own survival. In 1965, the Seminar on Social Responsibilities of Business highlighted that the concept of

Social Responsibility was broader than charity. It specified that business social responsibilities comprised:

1. Responsibility towards consumers,
2. Responsibility towards the community,
3. Responsibility towards employees,
4. Responsibility towards shareholders and other businesses, and
5. Responsibility towards the State.

The cumulative result of all these influences was that the business community accepted Social Responsibility as an inherent part of the management of the enterprise itself. The community development and social welfare programme of the premier Tata Company, Tata Iron and Steel Company, began with the integration of the concept of 'Social Responsibility'. The last decades of the twentieth century witnessed a swing away from charity and traditional philanthropy towards designing interventions in the areas of ecology, consumer education, developing rural markets and so on, and directed engagement of business in mainstream development. Many of the old multinationals such as ICI, Hindustan UniLever Ltd and ITC became 'Indianized' and began to feel the same responsibility as the indigenous businesses.

### Liberalization and CSR

Since 1991, with increased foreign direct investments,[11] India has been successful in achieving an annual growth rate of 4 to 8 per cent as part of its reform policies in the market economy. Corporate India, under the influence of increased Foreign Direct Investment (FDI) from Western countries headed towards a 'social market economy with a human face' by incorporating CSR as its main business strategy for creating both shareholder as well as societal value. The Western-driven approach to CSR clearly differentiated between Corporate Philanthropy and CSR. The latter referred to the integration of environmental, social and governance factors into business strategies and operations for attaining business and societal sustainability.

The fundamental objective of these economic reforms was to bring about rapid and sustained improvement in the quality of life of the people of India. Central to this goal was the rapid growth in incomes and productive employment;[12] however, analysts in India argue that the expectations from economic reforms have not been fulfilled, as decline in incomes and increasing unemployment continue unabated. Despite all its growth, in 2009, India ranked 134 out of the 182 countries on the Human Development Index. India's performance in attaining the Millennium Development Goals (MDGs) is mixed, with the country lagging behind the MDG targets, among others, on enrolment for girls in primary schools and elimination of gender disparity in secondary education. High unemployment with inequity in distribution of wealth and opportunity, lower access to and standards of health, education, nutrition, sanitation, safe drinking water and the like continue to remain crucial challenges for India, as for any other developing country. This deprivation also contributes to the increasing incidence of trafficking in women and children and the growing spate of HIV/AIDS and other sexually transmitted diseases.[13]

With India facing a plethora of developmental challenges, and particularly with the State retreating from economic activity, the urgency for the business community to take up wider social responsibilities towards society is growing. Alongside issues related to developing ethical and responsible workplaces and marketplaces, environmental practices to develop sustainable business have also started receiving due attention. Corporate social responsibility emphasizes the responsibility of companies towards the stakeholders as against their earlier focus on profit-making alone. Fears of global warming, the constant exhaustion of natural resources and so on are urging the corporate world to take social initiative with a new perspective.

## Emerging CSR trends

In the past few years, various surveys[14] have been conducted in India by different organizations to understand the perception of CSR among companies and their different stakeholders and to define the drivers and barriers of CSR in India. The 2001 survey of 536 companies across India, conducted by Partners in Change (PiC), revealed that philanthropy is the most significant driver (64 per cent) of CSR, followed by image-building (42 per cent), employee morale (30 per cent) and ethics (30 per cent) respectively.[15] The survey showed that there are several cases of companies in India involved in diverse issues such as health care, education, rural development, sanitation, microcredit, women's empowerment, arts, heritage, culture and the conservation of wildlife and nature, and similar issues.

However, given the economic progress and increase in corporate profits on the one hand and the reality of human poverty and development indicators in India on the other, analysis of the surveys quoted suggests that, though many companies in India have adopted the universal language of CSR, the field seems to be in a confused state. Individual companies define CSR in their own limited ways and contexts, with the end result that all activities undertaken in the name of CSR are merely philanthropy, or an extension of philanthropy. Creating trusts and foundations seems to be a favourite route of CSR practice by Indian companies, but largely such trusts and foundations work at arm's length from the company, preventing CSR from entering the mainstream and the core business processes, thereby limiting CSR to community development only. In nearly all cases, CSR is embedded in the core corporate activity of companies because of company tradition rather than a company strategy, leading to ad hoc and largely CEO-driven CSR policy.

According to the survey, four models of CSR coexist in India:

- The 'ethical model' as suggested by Mahatma Gandhi, where companies voluntarily commit to public welfare[16] and participate in nation-building;
- The 'statist model' propounded by Jawaharlal Nehru, which calls for adopting responsible practices by State interventions in economic activities and protecting stakeholders through legislation;
- The 'liberal model' by Milton Friedman, which discusses CSR being limited to private owners or shareholders;[17] and
- The 'stakeholder model' championed by R Edward Freeman, which calls for companies to respond to all stakeholder needs.

The 2004 PiC survey findings present a marked increase in the number of companies developing and adopting CSR policy as against the earlier survey findings. This may be attributed to an enabling corporate environment that is more conscious of the implications of involvement of business in CSR activities with specific reference to the Indian context. The survey further highlighted the belief that the company's role in CSR activities was directly correlated with its age and turnover, particularly as older companies with greater turnover were more likely to believe in their role in CSR activities. The survey, however, also revealed that Indians are not yet judging companies according to these criteria, and public opinion is still focused on brand quality and reputation of companies. The survey thus confirms a prior finding, by Environics International in 2001, that the demand for CSR is low in India.[18]

The Centre for Social Markets[19] July 2001 survey explored perceptions of and attitudes towards corporate social and environmental responsibility of the modern Indian private sector, covering a wide range of businesses in terms of size, sector and geographical location.[20] The survey report claimed that the government, with unclear policies, ineffective bureaucracy, poor monitoring record, complicated tax systems and poor infrastructure, was the key barrier to CSR in India.[21]

A CSR survey, conducted in 2002 by the British Council and others, revealed that many companies are still steeped in an amalgamation of transition from the trusteeship/ethical model to the Statist Model and highlighted growing recognition among companies that passive philanthropy is no longer sufficient in the realm of CSR.[22]

A survey conducted by Center for Social Markets (2004) highlighted that the primary reason for the changing attitudes of businesses towards social and environmental issues was the pressure exerted by the international business code of conduct and protecting reputations, given that the fundamental public expectation of companies was that they should provide good-quality products at low prices, treat employees well without discrimination, protect the environment, help bridge the gap between the rich and the poor and help in social and economic development.

A comprehensive picture of the state of CSR in India based on the Karmayog[23] 2008 CSR Ratings highlights that 49 per cent of the 1000 companies studied across 35 sectors have not undertaken any CSR activity. The CSR ratings from level '0' (lowest) to level '5' (highest) were measured on two aspects:

1. Steps taken by the company to reduce the negative effects caused by its products and processes on the environment; and
2. Positive steps a company takes using its resources and core competence for the benefit of society. The study highlights that the banking sector is one of the best-performing sectors and CSR initiatives are largely undertaken due to the mandatory regulations on social sector expenditure for PSUs.

The construction sector is one of the sectors with very low CSR activity. Only 10 companies[24] have received a Level 4 rating.

## Contemporary scenario: achievements

In 2007, according to the World Investment Report of the United Nations Conference on Trade and Development (UNCTAD), India has emerged as the second most attractive location for Foreign Direct Investment

(FDI) after China. The private sector today accounts for 80 per cent of investment in the Indian economy, which emphasizes the role of companies in pushing up the Indian economy. The Indian Government's Ministry of Corporate Affairs has recommended that companies should work with the Government to promote inclusive growth.

In the absence of global benchmarks it is difficult to compare the CSR progress of India's private sector with other emerging economies. However, some proxy indicators suggest that companies in India are taking proactive stands in the areas of environmental responsibilities. For instance, 1,250 businesses in India received ISO 14001 certifications. Another broader measure of corporate commitment to Social Responsibility is the UN Global Compact;[25] currently the India chapter has 206 members that have backed the Global Compact.

Given the increasing overseas presence of Indian companies and the expectation that India will become the second largest global economy by 2050, the performance and behaviour of Indian companies are under greater scrutiny than ever before. The Indian private sector, however, is now being managed by executives who have a global understanding and have recognized that the competitive international marketplace increasingly rewards those that go beyond the legal requirements in terms of managing their economic, environmental and social impacts.

As a result, Indian companies investing overseas increasingly practise a sustainable approach to business and undertake sustainability reporting in response to this peer pressure and the competitive international environment. By 2008 12 Indian companies had disclosed their sustainability performance at a global level. Similarly, global carbon credit trading in 2008 was estimated at $5 billion, with India's contribution at around $1 billion. India is one of the countries that have 'credits' for emitting less carbon. The Confederation of Indian Industry's (CII) 'Mission on Sustainable Growth' has set up a code, which was formulated in 2006 and provides consultancy services and technical assistance on social development and CSR. The mission's aims are to promote the reduction of excessive consumption of natural resources and emission of greenhouse gas (GHG). The code started with 23 new signatories, and the total number of code signatories had gone up to 102 by September 2008. Many large corporations are taking up 'green' projects, with the help of the government, to promote the cause of sustainable development.

Indian CSR is now considered as an important part of the movement away from 'rapid-growth, export-oriented, cost advantaged-focused strategies to longer-term, business development initiatives'.[26] In a survey carried out by the Asian Governance Association, which ranks the top 10 Asian countries on Corporate Governance parameters, India has consistently ranked among the top three, along with Singapore and Hong Kong, for the last eight years, but the extent to which Corporate Governance has been able to create responsible and ethical business practices is still debatable.

## Ethical issues and CSR

The twentieth-century business environment in India was driven by the Government, but in the twenty-first century business activities across the world, including India, are governed by a free market economy. In several ways Indian business practices are unique and may give rise to issues pertaining to business ethics that may or may not be compatible with the prevailing Western viewpoint of social responsibility and governance. For instance, Indian business culture puts a premium on favours, friendship and clanship. Friendship is highly valued, whether based on multigenerational family friendships, school friendships, or personal friendships. The Western concept of conflict of interest while doing business does not always mesh well with the Indian value of loyalty to one's group and hence can be branded as a marketplace violation of responsibilities. Hence, there is a great need for understanding the Indian way of doing business and locating areas of interventions for designing responsible and ethical practices to sustain business and society.

As India's private sector goes global, economic crime is emerging as a bigger threat than before. When companies in India expand their reach to other countries, they are exposed to not just 'home-grown' frauds but also frauds prevalent in other markets. According to estimates, India is losing a whopping $40 billion per year because of corporate frauds, which is more than 4 per cent of the country's gross domestic product. According to the KPMG India Fraud Survey Report 2008, India is perceived to be a fraud haven, with over 75 per cent of the respondents to the survey considering undetected fraud as their highest concern. The dual impact of two concerns, the unethical behaviour of employees and the inadequacy of anti-fraud measures, leads to an environment where both inclination and opportunity coexist. This could mean that organizations in India that remain passive in their approach to deal with fraud may be a perfect breeding ground for fraud. Fifty-five per cent of Indian companies in the past two years had reported incidents of fraud, and a 2007 PriceWaterhouseCoopers[27] study indicates that the average direct loss from fraud per company at the global level is $2.4 million, and for India it is $1.5 million. Irresponsible and delinquent work practices of employees are major reasons for financial frauds, and technology has made companies complacent.

With the advent of core banking systems, concurrent audits are not undertaken, which in turn has led to many foreign and local banks being duped. Collusion between employees in such environments can lead to large amounts being siphoned off. Today, almost 80 per cent of data in a company is in electronic form, and technology can be leveraged to commit fraud. The report claims that only 34 per cent of Indian companies have insurance that covers for losses due to fraud, against 45 per cent globally. Industry insiders point to several acquisition deals that have turned sour and resulted in litigation after the acquired company's management failed to meet key conditions. Thirty-four per cent of companies in India reported losses of business opportunities due to the likely payment of a bribe by a competitor, suggesting that business relationships and success may not be determined only on the basis of a product or service quality, efficacy and price. Consequently, employees, business associates and shareholders are negatively affected in the process.

Business visionaries in India feel that the only way to prevent these losses is to have the right policies and the system in place, driven by the right people. Interestingly, many Indian companies do not have an anti-fraud policy and depend on their value framework of integrity, commitment, passion, seamlessness and a code of conduct to drive home the message. The working conditions of staff, specifically in the IT industry, BPOs, construction, mining, textile and manufacturing industries, to a large extent being contractual in nature, are only compliance-oriented. Discrimination against women and vulnerable groups like the handicapped and socially backward groups is evident at workplaces in varying aspects and degrees. Sexual harassment at the workplace, though observed, is seldom reported.

However, companies such as NTPC, Mahindras, L&T, Infosys, Asian Paints, HSBC and a few others have developed significant human resource policies to improve staff productivity at workplace and achieve work–life balance.

Bribery and corruption have all been a regular feature of the Indian black market economy, and are considered by foreign companies as the biggest threat to doing business in India.[28] Bribery and corruption include aspects such as insider trading in the stock market, falsifying export/import documents and evading income tax. The PwC report[29] reveals that as many as 34 per cent of companies believed paying bribes and exercising undue influence have given their competitors an unfair advantage.

In 2009, India was ranked low on transparency (84), meaning high on corruption, by Transparency International.[30] This is a clear indication of the internal business environment. Instances like these create a bad environment and impact the reputation of companies. At another level, they raise significant issues on governance for stakeholders. This is perhaps why old private sector companies in India, such as the Tata Group, Bajaj Group and Birla Group, with long track records of delivering shareholder returns, see their companies enjoy more credibility than the new entrants.

With ethical intellectual capital governing new companies such as Wipro, Dr Reddy's Lab and Infosys, who have a large global workforce, they have developed a 'no tolerance' policy towards any kind of fraud. Wipro has developed a code of business conduct that defines dos and don'ts and tolerance level in the company. Even proxy bribing by vendors or partners is not permitted. Recently Wipro terminated the jobs of 100 employees after it was discovered that these employees had furnished fake resumes in connivance with the external hiring agency. Similarly, a senior employee, who had wrongfully claimed medical reimbursement for a corrective eye surgery, was also forced to resign. Wipro values its policy above all else. The penalty is the same across the company and penal policies are the same: separation.

Dr Reddy's Lab, a US-listed Indian company, adheres to a strict code of business ethics, as it has to contend with the US Foreign Corrupt Practices Act. Not only does it have a Chief Risk Officer and a Chief Ombudsman, but also a whistle-blower policy that is a must-read for all employees. At Dr Reddy's, frauds such as stationery buying and submitting false bills could result in termination.

To improve the internal business practices, regulators in India are becoming increasingly active in identifying and investigating economic crime. For instance, the Competition Commission has been constituted to review antitrust and monopolistic risk prior to large mergers and acquisitions. The Reserve Bank of India has also stepped up enforcement of anti-money-laundering regulations. Similarly, the Foreign Corrupt Practices Act of the US and the adoption of Clause 49 in India have ensured that Indian companies put in place certain measures to help curb economic crime.

## Marketplace practices

The explosive growth and concomitant deregulation of the global economy has produced a myriad of issues in Indian workplaces, marketplaces and environmental practices, which are not sufficiently accounted for by state domestic laws or international legal systems. Among the more abhorrent social problems created and proliferated by the existence of a global economy lacking global regulation is the insidious practice of exploiting child labour because it helps in cutting labour costs. In the global village a premium is placed upon the ethic of profit maximization, where an endless cycle of hosts employ children and internalize the economic benefits of the saved labour cost. The consumers are never given the benefit of these savings. Leading companies such as Monsanto, Gap, Sygenta and others were found to engage child labour through their supply chain. Despite having a supplier code of conduct, these companies have low levels of enforcement because of their indifferent attitude and lack of government regulation. Similarly, multinational drug companies, researchers and institutions are increasingly basing their illegal clinical trials in India, owing to a lack of regulation and accountability, as well as low costs of operation and wide availability of target participants.

Unethical market practices also include cases of land-grabbing. In India there are many limitations on individuals in regards to holding land, money and other properties. At the same time, a company and corporate enterprises can hold large amounts of money, land and other properties. Land-grabbing by the private corporate sector, of both Indian and foreign origin, carried out in the name of so-called 'development' and with the aid of government agencies and state machinery, has become a matter of concern. Forcibly evicting peasants and grabbing their agricultural lands for developing special economic zones amounts to violation of the constitutional and human rights of farmers. Poor rural residents are driven from their lands into the slums. For instance, the Reliance Energy Group (REG) has planned the world's largest gas-based 3,500 MW power plant to be located on agricultural land, not waste or marginal land, at Dadri, Ghaziabad (Northern India). REG has acquired over 2,100 acres of land and is aggressively pursuing the acquisition of 400 more acres in seven villages of Dhaulana, even though experts say 700–800 acres would be sufficient. The 3,500 MW gas-based power generation project is estimated eventually to cost over $100 billion (Rs 10,000 crore). The farmers to whom the lands belong were totally unaware of the 'acquisition' till the foundation stone was unveiled.

## Environmental practices

Many international brands marketing new material such as plastics, food products, packaging or electronics do not bring along systems of waste minimization or management, which they readily incorporate into their Western operations. Take the case of producer responsibility for waste management: many countries in Europe, including Switzerland, Sweden and Germany, by law require companies to collect used cars, television sets, computers and batteries and to dispose of them. It is another matter that much of this is often collected and exported to the South; however, these 'responsible' models work in the given legal and social milieu. The same companies, however, do not show such 'enlightened' behaviour in India, and in fact often resist the setting-up of such systems through their immense lobbying powers with governments. It would be futile to expect CSR to work in such an environment.

A research project commissioned in 2003 by the India Committee of the Netherlands (ICN) and carried out by Consultancy and Research for Environmental Management[31] in The Netherlands and Partners in Change in India, which interviewed Dutch companies and their Indian counterparts along with some stakeholders, concluded that the Dutch companies operating in India practise CSR only partially. Although most of the Dutch multinationals do have a policy or codes of conduct on the issue, their Indian counterparts normally are not engaged in developing CSR policy. The Indian operations of the Dutch companies lack monitoring of the policy implementation, and companies generally do not check that the production in the subcontracting chain follows the internationally agreed labour, human rights and environmental standards.[32]

## Impact of the post-2008 financial crisis and recession

Booz & Co., a global management consulting firm, has released the findings of its 2008 study[33] regarding the impact of the post-financial crisis recession on sustainability-related corporate spending. The study reveals that 'forty percent of respondents said their industries will not be in a position to accomplish as much as they had expected with respect to energy efficiency, the environment and community service. The pull backs will be especially pronounced among transportation and energy companies, with, respectively, 51 percent and 47 percent of respondents in those industries saying CSR agendas will be delayed.

This is disturbing because these industries have larger impacts on the environment and communities. Moreover, there is little correlation between financial strength and optimism about CSR agendas; 28 percent of respondents at financially strong companies said CSR agendas in their industries will be affected by the economic downturn.'[34]

Considering the above examples, corporate responsibility does not seem to be a uniformly globally practised work ethic. It fails to address the irresponsible acts of business organizations and creating more social problems in a country like India.

## Conclusion

Despite the development of Indian CSR from its initial philanthropic focus, there are still cultural influences to modern CSR. The underlying philosophy is that CSR is the responsibility of business to society as a whole. Societal expectations in India are that businesses should be involved in wider issues of societal and national concern while continuing to conduct their business responsibly. Both domestic and global forces encourage a broader understanding of corporate responsibility to develop in India. While some of the impetus may stem from supply chain pressures from international links through trade and investment, there have also been increased governmental and public expectations, as well as corporate involvement in the post-independence drive for social responsibility in India. The historical influence of colonialism, state-planned economic development and the vast disparities of income have created unique local conditions in India. Taking these factors into consideration, there cannot be a single, transferable model of CSR.[35] In this context, CSR in India has a long way to go. Today, CSR in India operates in a political environment that is unfavourably balanced for the consumer, with the corporates dominating the economic and political scene. Even though CSR relates to ethics in business, at this time it seems that this is more a socially and legally enforced practice. The field of CSR in India has yet to emerge from an internalized position of respect for people, nature and the environment. It plays out not as a self-willed moral and ethical self-realized way of being, of the kind Gandhi might have envisaged, but rather as a practice that may have to be socially and legally enforced externally as acceptable behaviour, which an activist organization like 'Greenpeace' may have to ensure, and which State interventions, in the form of stringent compliance mechanisms, will have to enforce.

The aims of CSR in a country like India are to use the market economy to address gaps in income distribution and to help pull people out of poverty, as well as to ensure the sustainability of natural resources. CSR certainly has a potential for becoming a real tool for development – human, social and economic. Indian expectations for the business sector are growing, and include that it must play a wider and more expansive societal role. In addition to providing good-quality products at reasonable prices, companies should strive to govern their companies by adopting ethical practices, making their operations environmentally sound, adhering to high labour standards, reducing human rights abuses and mitigating poverty. Unfortunately in India people are not yet judging companies in the marketplace according to these criteria. Developing such market-oriented pressures could become a powerful lever for change. Only then will CSR in India in the true sense create corporate as well as societal sustainability.

## Notes

1. The Birla Group is one of the foremost business houses in India, headed by the Birla family for generations. The story of the Birla Group goes back to 1870 when Seth Shiv Narayan Birla, belonging to the Marwari community of West Rajasthan, set up a cotton and jute trading business in Pilani, Rajasthan. Today the Birla Group comprises the AK Birla Group of industries and the BK Birla Group of industries.
2. The Tata Group of businesses is one of the socially responsible business groups of India, The leadership of its founder, Jamshedji Tata, who started his first trading business in 1868 and later ventured into manufacturing and allied sectors, considered that the ultimate aim of business is to serve society. The aim of the Tata Group is to improve the quality of life in society by virtue of integrity, understanding, excellence, unity and responsibility. The entire family known as the Tata Group shares these values. Tata's contribution to India's education, science and technology has been widely documented and respected.
3. HUL is India's largest fast-moving consumer goods company, set up in 1931 in India.
4. ITC was incorporated on 24 August 1910 under the name of 'Imperial Tobacco Company of India Limited'. The company was rechristened in 2001 as ITC Ltd, and is currently engaged in a wide range of businesses – cigarettes and tobacco, hotels, information technology, packaging, paperboards and speciality papers, agri-exports, foods, lifestyle retailing and greeting, gifting and stationery.
5. BHEL was set up in the 1950s. Its operations are organized around three business sectors: power, industry – including transmission, transportation and telecommunications – and renewable energy.

6. NTPC, founded in 1975, is engaged in engineering, construction and operation of power-generating plants.
7. Established in 1984, Dr Reddy's Laboratories (NYSE: RDY) is an emerging global pharmaceutical company.
8. Established in 1981, Infosys is a NASDAQ-listed global consulting and IT services company with more than 103,000 employees.
9. Ranbaxy Laboratories Limited, set up in 1961, is currently India's largest pharmaceutical company.
10. WIPRO Technologies is one of the largest IT services companies in India, established in 1980.
11. Cumulative amount of FDI inflows (from August 1991 to February 2009) amounted to US$ 127,460 million (Rs. 554,270 crores).
12. S. Chaudhuri, 'Production and Employment Growth and Decline in Organized Manufacturing in India Since 1991', Paper presented at the International Conference, Beyond the Washington Consensus - Governance and the Public Domain in Contrasting Economies: The cases of India and Canada, 12–14 February 2001, India.
13. ADB, 'Country Strategy and Program 2003-2006' (India: Asian Development Bank, 2003).
14. Some of the prominent surveys include 'Corporate Involvement in Social Development in India' by Partners in Change (PiC), 'Altered Images: the 2001 State of Corporate Responsibility in India Poll' by Tata Energy Research Institute (TERI), 'Corporate Social Responsibility: Perceptions of Indian Business' by Centre for Social Markets (CSM) and 'Corporate Social Responsibility Survey, 2002 India' presented jointly by the British Council, UNDP, Confederation of Indian Industries and PriceWaterhouse Coopers.
15. Partners in Change, 'Third Report on Corporate Involvement in Social development in India' (India: Partners in Change, 2004).
16. A large number of corporate houses and companies in India are doing tremendous work in CSR, including corporate philanthropy. Activities include the area of education, health care services, rural infrastructure, development, community welfare, environment protection, relief and emergency assistance, preserving art, heritage, culture, religious and a host of other initiatives.
17. M Friedman, 'The social responsibility of business is to increase its profits', *The New York Times Magazine*, 13 September 1970.
18. R Kumar, DF Murphy and V Balsari, 'Altered Images: The 2001 state of corporate social responsibility in India poll' (New Delhi: TERI-India, 2001).
19. CSM, 'Corporate Social Responsibility: Perceptions of Indian Business' (Kolkata, India: Centre for Social Markets, 2001).
20. Ibid.
21. K Prakash-Mani, 'Corporate Social Responsibility in the Indian Context' (UK: Sustainability Radar, 2002).
22. British Council, UNDP, CII and PriceWaterhouse Coopers, 'Corporate Social Responsibility Survey, India' (India: British Council, 2002).
23. A leading NGO information portal.
24. ACC Ltd, Ballarpur Industries, HDFC, Infosys Technologies, Jubilant Organosys, Kansai Nerolac, Moser Baer, TCS, Tata Steel and Titan Industries.

25. A set of 10 principles launched by the former UN Secretary-General, Kofi Annan.
26. NK Balasubramanian *et al.*, 'Emerging opportunities or traditions reinforced? An analysis of the attitudes towards CSR and trends of thinking about CSR in India', *Journal of Corporate Citizenship*, March 2005.
27. PwC, The 4th Biennial Global Economic Crime Survey- Economic crime: people, culture & controls (India, 2007) at http://www.pwc.com/extweb/ pwcpublications.nsf/docid/45B0CF98377B0945CA25739200379D15/$file/ GECS_India_report_2007.pdf (accessed 1 June 2009).
28. Transparency International *Global Corruption Report 2009*, D. Zinnbauer, R. Dobson and K. Despota, editors (Cambridge UK: Cambridge University Press, 2009), especially pages 258-61
29. PwC, The 4th Biennial Global Economic Crime Survey- Economic crime: people, culture & controls (India, 2007) at http://www.pwc.com/extweb/ pwcpublications.nsf/docid/45B0CF98377B0945CA25739200379D15/$file/ GECS_India_report_2007.pdf (accessed 1 June 2009).
30. Transparency International India: The Coalition against Corruption, Registered under the Societies Registration Act 1860, *Delhi, Corruption Perception Index Study (2009).*
31. CREM, 'Corporate Social Responsibility in India, Policy and Practices of Dutch Companies' (Amsterdam: CREM, 2004).
32. Ibid.
33. Booz & Company in December 2008 surveyed 828 corporate managers, both in developed markets such as the US and Germany and in emerging markets such as Brazil and India, at http://www.booz.com/ (accessed 25 May 2009).
34. Ibid.
35. Working Document of EU India CSR, 'Comparative analysis of corporate social Responsibility in India and Europe', Working Document of EU India CSR (2001).

# 3
# Social Responsibility Practices of Business Organizations: Bangladesh Perspective

*Dewan Mahboob Hossain*

## Introduction

In recent years, popular theories such as 'stakeholder theory' and 'legitimacy theory' have emphasized the importance of the 'social responsibilities of businesses' in a greater way. These theories are based on the argument that, apart from pursuing the profit-maximizing objective, organizations need to be responsible for their activities in society. Further, the continued operation and success of business activities are dependent on compliance with societal expectations and gaining support for continued existence in society.[1] Stakeholder theory argues that corporations should be accountable not only to shareholders but also to other stakeholder groups, such as employees, consumers, the government, suppliers, interest groups and the public. In general, a stakeholder can be defined as any group or individual who can affect or is affected by the achievement of the firm's objectives.[2] It has been said that:

> ... social responsibility activities are useful in developing and maintaining satisfactory relationships with stockholders, creditors and political bodies. Developing a corporate reputation as being socially responsible through performing and disclosing social responsibility activities is part of a strategy for maintaining stakeholder relationships.[3]

Another related theory is legitimacy theory, which is based on the idea of 'social contract'. Legitimacy theory argues that the business organizations must concentrate on the public as a whole and not just investors. Society will allow business organizations to operate only when the organizations will fulfil the expectations of society. Legitimacy is a condition or status which exists when an entity's value system is congruent with the value system of the larger social system of which the entity is a part. When a disparity, actual or potential, exists between the two value systems, there is a threat to the entity's legitimacy:[4]

> The social contract would exist between corporations (usually limited companies) and individual members of the society. Society (as a collection of individuals) provides corporations with their legal standing and attributes and the authority to own and use natural resources and to hire employees. Organizations draw on community resources and output both goods and services and waste products to the general environment. The organization has no inherent rights to these benefits and in order to allow their existence, society would expect the benefits to exceed the costs to society.[5]

Recently, the impact of businesses on society has become a crucial issue. Business corporations are considered accountable to society for their actions. Businesses are accountable not only to the shareholders but also to a wide range of stakeholders – including business partners, employees, customers, suppliers and the overall community. This view gave birth to the concept of Corporate Social Responsibility.

Businesses operate within the context of a society. They have to procure raw materials, labour and other inputs from society and produce finished products to sell. Businesses exist in an environment surrounded by sociocultural, economic, technological, competitive, legal and political forces. In order to survive they have to adjust to these forces. Just like a member of a community or a citizen of a country, businesses have to abide by rules and ethical considerations so that they do not do anything which is harmful to society. As entities that deal with society and utilize the people and other resources of society, they have duties and responsibilities. In order to perform their task in society, businesses must act as 'socially responsible citizens'.

For a long time scholars have argued about what the responsibilities of a business were. Some, such as Milton Friedman, have argued that there is only one social responsibility of business: to use resources and engage in activities designed to increase its profits, so long as the business engages in open and free competition without deception or fraud.[6] Such scholars argue that businesses have only the commercial responsibilities of generating profit and satisfying shareholder expectations.

Friedman argued that by making discretionary responsibilities, such as making expenditures to reduce pollution, or by hiring the chronically unemployed, the company is spending the shareholders' money for the general interest of society.[7] By bearing the weight of these social costs, the business becomes less efficient. Further, the involvement of businesses in social programs may give business too much power, and some say businesses lack the expertise to manage social problems.[8]

Others, however, do not support this view, and extend the responsibility of the business beyond economic responsibility.[9] Another argument is that companies have two kinds of responsibility – commercial and social.[10] Social responsibilities involve taking on responsibilities as an actor in the society and the community by engaging in activities that go beyond making a profit – such as protecting the environment, looking after employees, addressing social issues and being ethical in trade. According to Carroll,[11] the managers of business organizations have four responsibilities, and these are economic, legal, ethical and discretionary (Table 3.1).

Where these opinions concur is that economic or commercial responsibility is important for the firms in order to survive. But Carroll and Frost disagree with Friedman's argument that economic responsibility is the only responsibility of the organization. There are many arguments for and against whether businesses should perform social responsibilities or not. Griffin[12] explained the arguments in favour of performing social responsibilities in his text:

- Business creates problems (such as air and water pollution, resource depletion) and should therefore help to solve them;
- Corporations are citizens in our society and should not try to avoid their obligations as citizens;
- Businesses often have the resources necessary to solve social problems, as many business organizations often have surplus revenues;
- Businesses are partners in our society, along with the government and the general population.

There is a symbolic affiliation between society and business organizations. At the time of the industrial revolution, the key affair for every business organization was profit maximization.[13] At that time, a business used its actions for the benefit of the stakeholder group who were directly involved with the business, that is, the shareholders or owners (you may want to mention, however, earlier, in the eighteenth century, the rights to incorporate were only granted when the business was to

*Table 3.1* Carroll's four responsibilities of business

| Responsibility | Description |
| --- | --- |
| Economic (must do) | To produce goods and services of value to the society so that the firm can repay its creditors and shareholders. |
| Legal (Have to do) | Government laws that management is expected to obey. |
| Ethical (should do) | To follow the generally held beliefs about behaviour in a society. |
| Discretionary (might do) | Purely voluntary obligations a corporation assumes. Examples are philanthropic contributions, training the hard-core unemployed and providing day care centres. |

be in the best interest of society). But, over the years, the characteristics of businesses have changed: they have become larger and more complicated. Moreover, they have crossed national borders, and as a result they affect global society to a larger extent. Social stances and expectations towards the private sector were also changing. As businesses had to work in the society, businesspeople became more watchful about ethical issues. Moral obligations towards society gained significance. Modern society presents business with immeasurably intricate problems of which it was formerly devoid.[14]

Today businesses live in 'glass houses' and have greater 'public visibility (the extent to which an organization's activities are known to persons outside the organization) in comparison to other institutions in society.[15] Society is attentive to business actions. The rising status of 'social welfare' also spurs businesses to carry out some social responsibilities. Society's new revelation towards the corporate world begot some new views, such as 'Corporate Social Responsibility' (CSR hereafter) and 'social responsibility accounting'. CSR can be described as the voluntary commitment of the business organizations to contribute to social and environmental goals.

Even after so many debates, the concept of social responsibility has remained one of the most talked about issues in the business world for several decades. According to Davis:[16]

There is a call for higher business ethics and more responsible business behaviour. These new expectations reflect what we call a socioeconomic model of business. The socioeconomic model of business is a framework that views business as a subsystem of the society, with a need to satisfy both its economic and social relationships with the society.... The model recognizes that business and society each are part of a total system and therefore are interdependent. Their interdependence requires mutual cooperation and supportive behaviour.... The socioeconomic model sometimes is called the 'social responsibility model' or 'social accountability model.

The socio-economic model of business is highly different from the traditional economic model of business. This difference is presented in Table 3.2.

## Dimensions of social responsibility concerns of business

The notion of CSR has developed rapidly over the last few years in developed countries. As a consequence, companies have developed an extensive range of exercises covering different levels of activities that have an effect on corporate governance, employee relations, supply chain activities, customer relationships, environmental management, community involvement and business operations.

Some argue that consumers, special interest groups and the general public are aware of businesses' impacts on society and demand that firms do more than try to create profit.[17] At present, nearly all managers view social responsibility as a required duty of doing business. Social

*Table 3.2* Economic vs. Socio-economic model

| Economic model: primary emphasis | Socio-economic model: primary emphasis |
| --- | --- |
| Production | Quality of life |
| Exploitation of resources | Conservation of resources and harmony with nature |
| Market decisions | Some community controls on market decisions |
| Economic return on resources | Balanced economic and social returns on resources |
| Individual interests | Community interests |
| Business as a closed system | Business as primarily an open system |
| Minor role of government | Active government involvement |

responsibility provokes many difficult questions for businesses:

- To whom are we responsible?
- How far should we go to satisfy our customers and achieve organizational objectives?
- Will our decisions affect any segments of our society that we have not considered?[18]

Skinner and Ivancevich also state: 'generally we can say that business organizations have an impact on consumers, employees, the environment and to those who invest in the firm' (Figure 3.1).[19]

According to the 2002 Centre for Policy Dialogue (CPD) Report on Corporate Responsibility Practices in Bangladesh,[20] some CSR issues that are followed by many other countries as well as Bangladesh include Sustainable Development, Business Ethics, Human Rights, Legal Compliance, Corporate Governance, Stakeholders' Dialogue, Fair Employment, Health and Safety, Labour Standards, Community Relations and Environmental Responsibilities.

Frost states that CSR can provide opportunities to enhance financial viability for corporations to act as responsible corporate citizens.[21] This opportunity can be realized through:

- Creating a new lens for sourcing new business opportunities and in doing so opening up new revenue sources from entirely new markets in emerging industries.

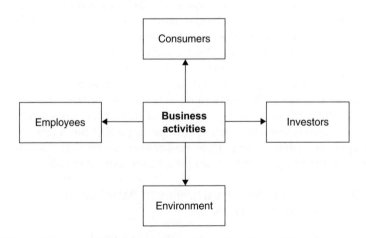

*Figure 3.1*   Social responsibility concerns

*Source*: SJ Skinner and JM Ivancevich, *Business For the 21st Century*, Boston: Irwin, 1992.

- Enhancing company reputation through a more powerful brand and improved stakeholder dialogue.
- Fostering new partnerships between business, government, investors and civil society.
- Strengthening a company's position as an employer of choice.
- Increasing productivity of staff as they derive deeper meaning and value from the work that they perform, contributing to higher levels of morale and employee engagement.
- Influencing positive share market valuation through Global Social Investment.
- Allowing innovation in strategies for leadership development and in particular lifelong learning, diversity and entrepreneurship.
- Gaining more international exposure and affiliations with organizations such as the United Nations.
- Contributing to making the world a better place and achieving long-term sustainability.

In today's business world, social responsibility performance is gaining importance, along with financial performance.

## Objectives and methodology of the study

The main objective of this study is to identify the nature of CSR practices in the corporate sector of Bangladesh. In order to fulfil this objective, a case study method was followed. To identify and analyse the CSR practices in Bangladeshi companies, the cases of some of the prominent companies of Bangladesh are analysed. The organizations examined include Banglalink, Dutch Bangla Bank Limited, Citycell, Unilever, HSBC, Grameenphone and British American Tobacco Bangladesh Limited. Information about these companies was collected through Internet research. Some information was collected by informal interviews with various personnel and staff from these organizations. Some evidence was also collected from newspaper articles. One limitation of case study research is that generalization from a few cases is dangerous because individual situations can be atypical.[22] But, even if situations are not directly comparable, case studies can provide a number of insights and hypotheses that can be used for future research.

## CSR activities of the organizations of Bangladesh: evidence from some cases

This section describes the activities related to CSR practices by the previously mentioned organizations through short case study examples.

To convey all the CSR activities of these big companies in short cases is difficult. The cases prepared, therefore, only cover some instances of CSR practices of these companies. These cases are mainly developed from the information that is provided in the respective websites of these companies.

## Case 1: Citycell

Citycell is the pioneer in mobile phone business in Bangladesh and has performed many CSR activities all over Bangladesh. In 2005, Citycell signed an agreement with the Bangladesh Red Cross Society to carry out a fund-raising program through its Short Message Service (SMS). The funds collected through SMS were contributed to the Bangladesh Red Cross Society for the betterment of citizens. In 2004, Citycell handed over a cheque for Taka 2,500,000 to the then prime minister of Bangladesh for flood relief, and also gave relief to the Rotary Club and sponsored a Saline project to help flood victims. In 2004, Citycell also launched its community program 'Citycell Changing Lives' and made donations to the Society for the Welfare of the Intellectually Disabled (SWID). On 5 December 2004, Citycell donated physiotherapy equipment to the Special Education for Intellectually Disabled Children (SEID) trust. Citycell works for increasing the level of public awareness, providing stickers with the phone numbers of the Police Control Room in order to register traffic complaints faced by commuters using Compressed Natural Gas (CNG) auto rickshaws and taxi cabs. Citycell introduced a media award, which is given to journalists in print and electronic media. Citycell also sponsors a music award with the help of a popular television channel in Bangladesh, 'Channel-i'.

## Case 2: British American Tobacco Bangladesh Ltd (BATB)

BATB is a leading multinational cigarette manufacturer in Bangladesh. In 2001, BATB launched the Youth Smoking Prevention (YSP) program. In 2002, BATB expanded this program by conducting a comprehensive school education program with the help of an anti-tobacco body in 20 schools in Bangladesh. In 2002, BATB also formed a free basic IT education programme (called Dishari) among the rural youth. BATB runs several partnership programs with the universities of Bangladesh. One of these programs is called 'Battle of Minds', which is a talent promotion program. BATB has introduced 'Star Search Program' as an attempt at identifying hidden musical talents in the country. BATB regularly interacts with university students and graduates through its internship programs, job fairs and campus presentations. The organization encourages and motivates its farmers to send their children to school and does not employ child labour in any area of its operations. BATB has also contributed to the country's reforestation drive by implementing a huge reforestation program. It helped in planting trees along roadsides, canal banks and farmers' landholdings and received the Prime Minister's national award for reforestation several times. BATB acknowledges the risk of smoking and supports the right of informed adults to smoke. For this purpose, it distributes consumer leaflets to customers.

### Case 3: Dutch Bangla Bank Limited (DBBL)

DBBL is the first Bangladesh–European Joint venture bank in Bangladesh. It performs CSR practices in the areas of health, education, information technology and disaster management. DBBL was awarded the 2005 Asian CSR Award for its outstanding program on CSR. In September 2006, DBBL donated an amount of Tk. 9.36 crores for the expansion of Ibrahim Cardiac Hospital and research institute. DBBL gave financial assistance amounting to Tk. 18.50 lacs, for the rehabilitation of disabled children in Bangladesh, to 17 NGOs in 2006. In the same year DBBL donated Tk. 15 lacs for purchasing an endoscope machine for the National Medical College Hospital and also distributed medical support to 50 HIV/AIDS patients. In the education sector, DBBL has contributed a significant amount. In 2005, it awarded scholarships to approximately 150 students, including six blind students. In 2006, the organization donated Tk. 15 lacs to Banglabandhu Sheikh Mujib Medical University to purchase academic reference books. In order to select and award better mathematicians in the country, DBBL and *The Daily Prothom Alo* (a renowned daily newspaper in Bangladesh) jointly arranged the Mathematical Olympiad. DBBL also co-organized an IT award ceremony with Bangladesh Association of Software and Information Services (BASIS) in 2005.

### Case 4: Unilever

Over the last four decades Unilever has been operating successfully in Bangladesh. Unilever is renowned as a socially responsible corporation. In May 2006, Unilever's Fair & Lovely Foundation, in a joint effort with the Khan Foundation, helped over 100 underprivileged young women to gain economic empowerment by providing them with IT training. In 2005, Fair & Lovely Foundation initiated a Supplementary Education Programme where 200 women each received a Tk. 25,000 scholarship to support their tertiary level education. In 2004, Unilever's The Fair & Lovely WEALTH programme trained 310 women in nine districts across the country, providing business management skills and practical hands-on training. To give marginalized people access to health care, Unilever worked with an NGO called 'Friendship'. It established a floating hospital to bring essential health services to the char (Small Island) dwellers. Sponsored by its Pepsodent toothpaste, it arranged a bus with modern dental check-up facilities, which enabled professional dentists to visit schools and neighbourhoods. To discover the hidden singing talents in Bangladesh, Unilever launched 'Close-up 1' – a talent hunt programme that received immense popularity and fame throughout the country. Under the name of their famous soap Lux, they have successfully launched the 'Lux-Channel-i Superstar' programme to discover new glamour icons for the Bangladeshi cultural arena.

## Case 5: The Hong Kong and Shanghai Banking Corporation (HSBC)

As in its other countries, HSBC is operating successfully in Bangladesh and conducts important CSR practices. HSBC Bangladesh supports the work of the Acid Survivors Foundation (ASF) in providing medical support and assistance to the victims of acid abuse. HSBC, along with the Department of Environment, placed roadside digital banners at various locations in Dhaka city to raise awareness about World Environment Day and the protection of the environment. In June 2006, HSBC held a day-long environmental programme at Dhanmondi lake area. HSBC contributed Tk. 100,000 to the Gulshan Literacy Program (GLP) School to expand the educational programme of the school. Also in 2006, HSBC, along with the Bangladesh Red Crescent Society, inaugurated the first HSBC Red Crescent Thalassaemia Centre.

## Case 6: Banglalink

Another leading mobile telephone service provider, Banglalink, divided its CSR activities into three subdivisions: environmental responsibilities, economical responsibilities and social responsibilities. Some of the important instances of its CSR practices over the last few years are described here. Banglalink has provided 200 recycling bins in Cox's Bazaar and Potenga sea beaches. The organization has employed 15 men to clean up the Cox's Bazaar Beach every day since November 2006. To reduce air pollution, Banglalink has provided filters in brick factories. It has also performed tree plantation activities in several areas of the country. Banglalink is providing internship opportunities to the students of some of the best universities of Bangladesh. Banglalink is spending money on the construction of bridges and underpasses in the major traffic points of the big cities of Bangladesh. Banglalink is contributing to the construction of roads in rural areas of the country. The organization has also donated money for the development of Zia International Airport, Chittagong port, Mongla sea port and Benapol and Hili land ports. In March 2005, Banglalink arranged a charity concert and donated the money collected to the Bangladesh Protibondhi Foundation, working for handicapped children and disabled men and women.

## Case 7: Grameenphone (GP)

In its official website Grameenphone defines CSR as 'a complementary combination of ethical and responsible corporate behaviour as well as a commitment towards generating greater good in society as a whole by addressing the development needs of the country'.[23] On its website, it also mentions that:

> Grameenphone started its journey 10 years back with a belief that 'Good development is good business'. Since its inception, Grameenphone has been driven to be inspiring and leading by example, when it comes to being involved in the community. At Grameenphone we believe that, sustainable development can only be achieved through long term economic growth. Therefore, as a leading corporate house in Bangladesh we intend to deliver the best to our customers, business partners, stakeholders, employees and society at large by 'being a partner in development.'[24]

Over the years GP has performed many CSR activities throughout the country. The organization mainly focuses on health, education and empowerment. The Village Phone Program (VPP) is one of its most prominent CSR programs. Commencing its operation in March 1997, the VPP is a unique initiative to provide telecommunications facilities in remote, rural areas where no such service was available before. GP places huge importance on education sector development. As a result, it took initiatives to provide access to education, especially for children from disadvantaged backgrounds who might not otherwise have had this opportunity. GP tries to make a positive contribution to the under-privileged community of Bangladesh by helping improve the health perils of the country. Grameenphone has embarked upon a CSR partnership with Grameen Shikhkha, an organization of the Grameen Bank family, to provide scholarships to underprivileged students at various academic levels. In response to the worldwide movement against HIV and AIDS and the Millennium Development Goals[25] set by the Bangladesh Government, Grameenphone is working as a catalyst to unite leaders behind this cause. Grameenphone extended its support to the Acid Survivors' Foundation (ASF) in its effort to rehabilitate the acid victims by providing employment opportunities and skills training. Grameenphone Ltd has signed an agreement with CARE Bangladesh to launch a project titled 'Tathyo Tari' (Information Boat), which is designed to provide necessary livelihood information to the riverine communities of Bangladesh. The main objective of this project is to educate and empower rural communities with necessary and appropriate livelihood information.

### Case 8: Aktel

In recognition of its CSR effort, Aktel is the first among all mobile phone operators to win the 2006 Standard Chartered-Financial Express Corporate Social Responsibility Award. AKTEL has established a tradition of providing scholarships every year to three promising individuals to complete their higher studies at the Multimedia University in Cyberjaya, Malaysia. To provide world-class teaching and learning resources for Bangladeshi professionals, Aktel has joined hands with Chittagong Skills Development Centre (CSDC), Underprivileged Children's Educational Programs (UCEP-Bangladesh), and so on. Aktel has also united with Anjuman-Mufidul-Islam, a 100-year-old civic organization, in distributing bedding and clothing to the underprivileged people of the city, including in orphanages and amongst slum dwellers. Aktel also took the initiative in executing various activities at the recently held Bishwa Estema, the second largest Muslim gathering in the world after Holy Hajj, in which millions of people gathered from different parts of the world to participate in this pilgrimage. Among the initiatives was the provision of primary aids to the pilgrims through free medical check-ups by a team of certified doctors at the Aktel voluntary medical service point. Aktel also served free pure drinking water for the pilgrims of Bishwa Estema.

## Analysis of the evidence on social responsibility practices from the cases

The case studies presented identify that these companies are trying to contribute to CSR primarily in the economic, health and education sectors of Bangladesh. Some important features can be identified from these cases:

- Taking initiatives after natural disasters: the corporate sector of Bangladesh is helping the natural disaster-affected people in Bangladesh.

Natural calamities such as floods and cyclones are common phenomena in Bangladesh, and huge resources are devastated every year as a result. A good number of families lose everything they own. By providing relief to these people, the corporate sector is helping the country.

- Protecting the natural environment: many of these corporations are aiding the protection of the natural environment of Bangladesh. Pollution of the natural environment has become a topical issue and pollution control demands a huge amount of investment. The government will be benefited if the corporate sector continues to invest in the solution of this problem.

- Contributing in education: in a country like Bangladesh where the literacy rate is very low, the involvement of the corporate sector in education can be helpful for the overall development of the country. By providing scholarships to meritorious students, several companies are facilitating the education sector of the country. As well as providing scholarships, the corporate sector is also contributing by arranging talent hunt programmes to discover talented Bangladeshi citizens. They are also performing some programmes where people's awareness about education is growing, and investing in Information Technology Training programmes.

- Working for disabled people: it can be easily identified that the corporate sector is working to help the disabled children, men and women of Bangladesh. Thus it is helping in upholding human rights, which is a relatively ignored issue in Bangladesh.

- Female empowerment: by providing training to this socially deprived section of the community, the corporate sector is helping in the development of human resources and making women more independent. These organizations are also working to raise awareness about acid abuse, which is a significant problem in Bangladesh.

- Contributing to the health sector: the health sector of Bangladesh benefits from the varied activities of the corporate sector. Corporations are working on recent health problems such as HIV/AIDS and are donating to hospitals and non-governmental organizations (NGOs) that work for ensuring the healthcare facilities of the country. Health is a basic need for all human beings. The health sector needs much investment and the contribution from the corporate sector in this area is praiseworthy.

- Cultural development: the corporate sector is becoming involved in Bangladesh's cultural sector. By arranging talent hunt programmes, new cultural talents are exposed to citizens. These kinds of programmes are costly and these organizations are assuming this responsibility.

- Employment creation: unemployment is a serious problem in Bangladesh. By providing internship programs for university graduates, along with various employment opportunities, corporations are contributing to the human resource development of the country.
- Infrastructural development: the corporate sector is also contributing to the infrastructural development of the country by investing in the development of ports and the construction of roads in rural areas.

The common CSR practices in Bangladesh are summarized in Figure 3.2. It has been said that:

> The strategic decision makers at the business, civil or political level must objectively understand the benevolent impact of taking CSR initiatives for balancing the equity position of the people of Bangladesh. The economic landscape, along with a stable political climate, free from foreign intervention, can actually raise the possibility of Bangladesh. If Bangladesh is to join the Asian Tigers in not too distant a future then proper dispensations of CSR and political responsibility become a responsibility – a reality that responsible citizens of Bangladesh must strive toward.[26]

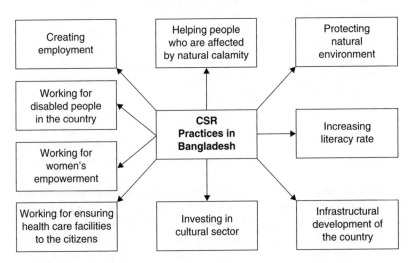

*Figure 3.2*  Main dimensions of social responsibility practices in Bangladesh

These days, the Bangladeshi government is also encouraging the corporate sector to perform social responsibility practices. Recent news reveals the following:

> Finance Adviser Dr Mirza Azizul Islam, on Tuesday, said the government is considering tax exemption on a part of corporate incomes to be spent in discharging Corporate Social Responsibility (CSR). The matter was not included in the budget but there is scope of taking a decision in this regard beyond the budget, he told reporters, following a Dutch-Bangla Bank Limited (DBBL) function at Hotel Purbani.[27]

## Some opposite pictures

Though over the last few years the business sector of Bangladesh has seen a phenomenal growth in social responsibility practices, some contrary examples also exist. This section deals with several news releases over the last few years in some printed media and on the World Wide Web. It can be noticed from this evidence that, though several companies are practising social responsibilities, many business organizations in Bangladesh are not conducting their business in a socially responsible way:

> Lack of effective good governance in Bangladesh has resulted significantly in lack of business ethics and poor CSR culture. In Bangladesh, the private sector seems to focus on earning profits in the short term, ignoring the issue of responsible behaviour and the desirability of earning the trust of the consumers, which are important for the long-term success of their operations. Selling of adulterated low quality products at high prices, cheating in weight and above all, hoarding to reap dishonest profit, all confirm this. In the absence of socially responsible behaviour in the private sector, there is need to enhance capacity building on the part of the state to intervene and implement sanctions effectively to enforce compliance.[28]

In some respects, these organizations demonstrate contradictory behaviour, which goes against the principles of CSR. The article has already described several CSR practices followed by two telecommunication giants, Grameenphone and Aktel. Recently these organizations faced legal action for the illegal use of Voice Over Internet Protocol technology. The following news is extracted from the web site of voip-buzz:

> The country's telecom watchdog fined Aktel Tk 145 crore for its involve-
> ment in the illegal use of VoIP (Voice over Internet Protocol) or call
> termination business. Bangladesh Telecommunication Regulatory
> Commission (BTRC) in a press release said during recent raids by the
> law enforces, Aktel's involvement in illegal call termination business
> was ascertained. Talking to The Daily Star, BTRC Chairman Maj Gen
> (retd) Manzurul Alam said, 'Aktel has already paid Tk 72.50 crore to
> the national exchequer.' Telekom Malaysia International Bangladesh
> (TMIB) is the 70 percent stakeholder of Aktel. Aktel is not alone in
> paying the government compensation. Earlier, country's largest
> mobile phone service operator Grameenphone announced it would
> pay the government Tk 168.4 crore while another major operator
> Banglalink said they would pay Tk 125 crore. The BTRC chairman
> said, 'We hope that no telecommunication operator will facilitate
> any illegal VoIP ventures...No one will be spared if found involved
> in any capacity in the illegal call termination business.' The BTRC
> in a press statement yesterday said international call termination to
> Bangladesh is a licensed service and is currently reserved only for the
> state-owned telephone operator Bangladesh Telegraph and Telephone
> Board (BTTB). Law enforcement agencies and the BTRC started joint
> operations on illegal VoIP operators after this interim government
> took office in January. Aktel, the second largest mobile phone service
> operator in Bangladesh, already made a loss in the third quarter, due
> mainly to the compensation it will pay the government. However,
> Aktel's earnings before interest, taxes, depreciation and amortization
> (EBITDA) fell sharply due to the government compensation.[29]

If Carroll's (1979) social responsibility dimensions are considered, it can
be said that these two organizations have focused on the discretionary responsibilities but have sometimes ignored the legal and ethical
responsibilities.

From several news media, it is also becoming evident that many business organizations are not careful about employee rights, and employee
movement is becoming a common incidence in the country. Some of
the examples are cited here.

### Employee rights violation: example 1

Seventy Bangladeshi factory workers trekked seven kilometers yester-
day, in an attempt to escape from their employer whom they claimed

beat them and deprived them of wages. One of them claimed the group were denied wages of between two and three months. 'When we asked our bosses for our salaries, they beat and kicked us. They treated us like animals and made us work without caring for our welfare'. It is unclear which company the men worked for but they were heading to the Bangladeshi Embassy to request help.[30]

### Employee rights violation: example 2

Tejgaon is home to some of Bangladesh's top garment factories. Garments are Bangladesh's biggest export earners with sales abroad fetching more than nine billion dollars, or three-quarters of the country's total export earnings, in the last fiscal year. But the industry has been hit by a series of protests over low wages and poor working conditions. Sixteen factories were torched and hundreds vandalized last year in the country's worst ever labour unrest. The protests came to a halt late in 2006 when the government, unions and the employers agreed to a 25-dollar monthly minimum wage. The government has issued several warnings to the factories to implement the minimum wage but according to the unions just 20 percent have done so. 'We have conducted surveys in the country's main industrial zones and found that only 20 per cent of the country's some 4000 factories have implemented the minimum wages,' Moshrefa Mishu, president of Garment Workers Unity Forum, said. In the latest warning, the government has said it will take legal action against factories that fail to implement the minimum wage by September 30. The deadline has so far been deferred at least twice.[31]

### Employment of child labour: example 1

There is also evidence of employing and misusing child labour:

> According to a survey conducted by Save the Children, UK, about 10 million children under the age of 18 are involved with different sorts of risky and harmful jobs in Bangladesh, reports the New Age (3 May). The survey found that 24 percent of them are engaged in hazardous work while about 99 percent of child labourers are deprived of having any basic facilities at their workplaces.[32]

There are also examples of employees working in hazardous and dangerous environments:

> At least 21 deaths have occurred this year in Bangladesh's shipbreaking industry along the southern Bangladesh coast, near the

harbours of the port city of Chittagong, making the job of recycling obsolete ocean liners one of the world's most dangerous
occupations. Human rights activists put the blame on the absence
of minimum safety measures and the lack of quick response to
hazards.[33]

Violation of consumer rights on the part of manufacturers is a common phenomenon. Unjustifiable increase in price and providing shoddy,
unsafe and low-quality products are some common practices regarding
consumer rights violation. Some examples can be cited here:

### Consumer rights violation: example 1

The Bangladesh Observer (18 March 2007) reports that since there is
no pricing regulation in Bangladesh, companies usually sell the same
products at different prices, cheating lots of consumers. Although
many companies are using BSTI (Bangladesh Standards and Testing
Institution) certified marks, most of them do not show retail price on
the labels. According to marketing sources, around 90 percent of products, mostly non-essential items, are for sale without having their prices
and manufacturing and expiry dates shown on the labels.[34]

### Consumer rights violation: example 2

In an examination by the Public Health Laboratory of the Government's
Public Health Institute it was found that the germs were beyond the tol-
erable limit in the water of Acme Agrovet & Beverages Limited. Though
the management of this company did not agree with this result of the
examination.[35]

There is also an absence of proper laws and their implementation and
the presence of ample corruption at government level:

In Bangladesh, the non-government members of a technical committee in charge of examining the development scheme of Asia
Energy on Phulbari coalfield have observed in the committee report
that there was no legal basis to allow the company to start mining,
reports the New Age (25 September). The report, which is written by
a 12-member committee headed by M Nurul Islam of the Bangladesh
University of Engineering and Technology, stated that there were
legal loopholes in the original agreement signed with the BHP in
1994 as the royalty rate was fixed at 6 percent despite existing mining rules during that period said it should be 20 percent. The report
also said Asia Energy had proposed mining for 30 years following

open-pit method although the rules did not permit mining for more than 10 years.[36]

If Carroll's four responsibilities of business[37] are considered and compared with the present situation of Bangladesh, it will be seen that on the one hand there is ample evidence that the legal (have to do) and ethical (should do) responsibilities are not performed by many businesses. On the other hand, discretionary (might do) responsibilities are performed by several companies to a greater extent. Through the analysis of the cases and the news items, two opposite pictures came under light. The analysis of these cases identified that, on the one hand, the corporate sector of Bangladesh is performing Corporate Social Responsibility activities in issues such as health, education, natural environment, female empowerment, disability, cultural development and infrastructural development. Almost all these contributions can be considered as discretionary responsibilities. On the other hand, the news items indicated that there is evidence of child labour, human rights violations, low wages, poor working environments, and violation of governmental rules and regulations, among other things. These are either legal or ethical responsibilities.

## Conclusion

In the past, the concept of CSR used to be considered a phenomenon related to developed countries, but this is no longer the case. This study identifies the CSR practices of some organizations dealing in Bangladesh and finds that the corporate sector of Bangladesh is performing CSR activities across a range of spheres. It can be said that the business sector of Bangladesh is trying to aid in the general social problems of the country. These days, almost all the societies of the world are faced with new and complicated social and economic problems. While it remains the responsibility of every government to try to solve its country's problems, in many developing economies poor governments cannot adequately address these problems. In these cases, the corporate sector can help. While the activities of these organizations may help the overall development of the country, the question is whether these discretionary responsibilities are entitled to more importance than the legal and ethical responsibilities. It is a positive sign that the Bangladeshi government is encouraging the corporate sector to perform CSR activities, but it is also important to set and implement proper regulations so that businesses become aware of issues such as employee rights, consumer rights and the environment. It is very important to work for the welfare of society, but it is more important to ensure that the activities of any social unit should not *harm* society in any manner. A greater emphasis on legal and ethical responsibilities can ensure that harm does not occur.

## Notes

1. M Alam, 'Stakeholder Theory', in Z. Hoqu (ed.), *Methodological Issues in Accounting Research: Theories and Methods* (London: Spiramus, 2006).
2. R Freeman, *Strategic Management: A Stakeholder Approach* (Marshall, MA: Pitman, 1984).
3. R Roberts, 'Determinants of Corporate Social Responsibility Disclosure: An Application of Stakeholder Theory, Accounting', *Organizations and Society*, vol. 17, no. 6 (1992), pp. 595–612.
4. CK Lindblom, 'The Implications of Organizational Legitimacy for Corporate Social Performance and Disclosure', Critical Perspectives on Accounting Conference (New York, 1994).
5. Mathews, MR (1993), *Socially Responsible Accounting*, Chapman and Hall, London.
6. M Friedman, 'The social responsibility of business is to increase its profits', *New York Times Magazine*, 13 September 1970, p. 30, pp. 126–127.
7. M. Friedman, 'The social responsibility of business is to increase its profits', *New York Times Magazine*, 13 September 1970, p. 30, pp. 126–127.
8. Ibid.
9. AB Carroll, 'A three dimensional conceptual model of corporate performance', *Academy of Management Review*, October 1979, pp. 497–505.
10. P Frost, 'Corporate Social Responsibility', presented in 2001 Virtual Alumni Summit and published on the Alumni Melbourne website at: http://www.unimelb.edu.au/alumni/ accessed on August 8, 2008.
11. Ibid.
12. RW Griffin, *Management*, 5th edn (India: AITBS Publishers and Distributors, 1997)
13. MNU. Bhuiyan and ASM Anwar, 'Business Ethics for Sustainable Business Development', *Journal of the Institute of Bankers Bangladesh*, Vol. 44–45 (1997), pp. 1–14.
14. K Davis, *Business and Society: Environment and Responsibility*, 3rd edn (New York: McGraw-Hill Book Company, 1975).
15. K Davis, *Business and Society: Environment and Responsibility*, 3rd edn (New York: McGraw-Hill Book Company, 1975).
16. K Davis, *Business and Society: Environment and Responsibility*, 4th edn (New York: McGraw-Hill Book Company, 1980).
17. SJ Skinner and JM Ivancevich, *Business For the 21st Century* (Boston: Irwin, 1992).
18. Ibid.
19. Ibid.
20. Centre for Policy Dialogue, 'Corporate Responsibility Practices of Bangladesh: Results from a Benchmark Study', CPD Occasional Paper Series, Paper 18, CPD, Dhaka, 2002.

21. P Frost, 'Corporate Social Responsibility', presented in 2001 Virtual Alumni Summit and published on the Alumni Melbourne website at: http://www.unimelb.edu.au/alumni/
22. WG Zikmund, *Business Research Methods*, 7th edn (Australia: Thomson South-Western, Australia, 2003).
23. www.grameenphone.com accessed on August 8, 2008.
24. www.grameenphone.com accessed on August 8, 2008.
25. Millennium Development Goals (MDGs) are the goals for international development that are set and agreed by the member states of the United Nations and these goals are to be achieved by 2015. MDGs include issues like ending poverty and hunger, universal education, gender equality, child health, maternal health, combating HIV/AIDS, environmental sustainability and global partnership.
26. Rahman, Z. (2006), 'Corporate social responsibility (CSR) and political responsibility (PR)', *The Daily Star*, 5 November 2006.
27. Source: www.zibb.com (accessed 25 June 2008).
28. KN Haque, 'A business ethic to change the society', *The Daily Star*, 20 August 2007.
29. Source: Bangladesh Fines VoIP Providers, including Grameenphone, from    http://voip-buzz.com/2007/11/11/bangladesh-fines-voip-providers-including-grameenphone/ (accessed 20 August 2008).
30. http://csr-asia.com/index.php?cat=42 (published on 29 May 2008) accessed on August 8, 2008.
31. '25,000 textile workers protest poor wages in Bangladesh', posted on 23 September 2007 in http://www.channelnewsasia.com/stories/afp_asiapacific_business/view/301478/1/.html accessed on August 8, 2008.
32. http://csr-asia.com/index.php?page=2&cat=42 (posted on 9 May 2007).
33. http://csr-asia.com/index.php?page=8&cat=42 (posted on 28 July 2006) accessed on August 8, 2008.
34. http://csr-asia.com/index.php?page=3&cat=42 (posted on 21 March 2007) accessed on August 8, 2008.
35. *The Daily Prothom Alo*, 24 August 2008.
36. http://csr-asia.com/index.php?page=6&cat=42 (posted on 27 September 2006) accessed on August 8, 2008.
37. AB Carroll, 'A three dimensional conceptual model of corporate performance', *Academy of Management Review*, October 1979, pp. 497–505.

# 4
# The Rise of CSR Public Policy in Asia: The Case of Southeast Asia and China

*Joëlle Brohier-Meuter*

## Introduction

Public policy is emerging as an increasingly important component of the Corporate Social Responsibility (CSR) agenda in Asia. For example, in 2005, Chinese president Hu Jintao launched the 'Harmonious Society Policy'. CSR was considered an instrumental tool for achieving the goals of this new policy and marked the start of a series of high-level public CSR activities. In 2005, the Singaporean Ministry of Manpower participated in the launch of the Singapore Compact for CSR, together with the National Trade Union Congress and the main national business organizations. In September 2006, the Minister of Finance of Malaysia officially launched the CSR Framework for Public Listed Companies (PLCs) for the Malaysian Stock Exchange, Bursa Malaysia.[1] The framework was presented as essential for the financial value of companies and for the country's economic performance. The fact that leadership for these pioneering CSR initiatives was taken at high levels shows that CSR was not to be a window-dressing activity in developing and emerging Asia.

After a period of non-engagement by governments, these initiatives were among the first of a series and reflected a significant mindset shift. Asian governments started to consider CSR as a public policy tool, contributing to economic performance (such as investment and market development), social goals (such as poverty reduction and reduction of inequalities) and, to a certain extent, environmental goals.

This chapter will discuss a number of questions arising from these developments, including: what is the current state of engagement of governments in emerging and developing Asia? What initiatives have been taken and how are they characterized? Are there different public policy approaches according to countries? What are the intended goals?

Is impact evaluated? What frameworks for CSR public policy analysis are used by academic and other researchers? What are the specific features of CSR public policies in selected Asian countries with respect to these? What recommendations could be made for the future?

The chapter will provide a brief overview of some frameworks for CSR public policy analysis. It will then analyse CSR public policies in Southeast Asian countries and in China. Finally, it will outline the specific features and achievements of CSR public policies in Asia using the frameworks presented and suggest possible recommendations for the future.

The study builds on two research works. The first analyses the main CSR initiatives in Southeast Asia;[2] the second analyses CSR initiatives in China.[3] Both research scopes include general CSR initiatives but not specific ones. They do not include legal frameworks (except laws referring specifically to CSR). For analysis of legal frameworks with respect to business and human rights, please refer to reports of the Corporate Law Tool Project, undertaken for John Ruggie, UN Special Representative on Business and Human Rights. Country reports are available for China, India, Indonesia, Papua New Guinea and Singapore.[4]

## Research on CSR public policies frameworks – Some key findings

Many Governments across the world have taken steps to promote CSR. These include a broad range of tools and activities. Tools encompass legal provisions, voluntary codes, public–private partnerships, incentives and public bodies' own standards. Among other things, activities target awareness-raising, capacity-building, internal changes in companies, outreach and engagement in international standards, stricter standards and compliance measures. Analysis frameworks demonstrate clearly that, beyond this profusion of CSR public activities, various types of CSR public policies exist that target specific objectives. Thus they allow a better understanding of CSR public policy. We will outline briefly the typologies designed in three key research works.

## The CSR Navigator – public policies in Africa, the Americas, Asia and Europe

The CSR Navigator[5] aims to demonstrate which CSR tools are the best to promote corporate social engagement in a given context and analyses CSR policies of 13 countries from all continents, including three Asian countries: China, Vietnam and India.

The CSR Navigator provides a toolbox analysis, which classifies policy activities according to various criteria (See Table 4.1):

The CSR Navigator builds on the toolbox analysis to propose clusters of countries, presented in Table 4.2.

## Towards greater responsibility – conclusions of EU-funded research[6]

This paper draws on four academic research projects that made recommendations on future CSR public action in Europe. The projects advocate for different recommendations: one recommends a *regulated*

*Table 4.1*  Analysis criteria – CSR public policy instruments and activities – CSR Navigator

| | |
|---|---|
| Field of action | Economics |
| | Politics |
| | Society |
| | Cross-sector cooperation |
| Maturity | First generation (basic activities) |
| | Second (implementing CSR) |
| | Third (stabilizing and spreading CSR) |
| Type of activity | Law |
| | Soft law |
| | Partnering |
| | Incentives |
| | Awareness |
| Field of impact | Corporate Governance |
| | Reporting |
| | Labels/fair trade disclosure |
| | Awards |
| | International standards |
| | Corporate networks implementation/ assessment support |
| | Codes |
| | Public procurement workshops/conferences |
| | Information |
| | Institutionalizing |
| | Local level promotion |
| | Pensions |
| | PPP (public–private partnerships) |
| | Research/education |
| | Monetary support |

*Source*:  CSR Navigator

*Table 4.2*   Country typology – CSR Navigator

| Outspoken CSR countries | Solid CSR countries | Energetic CSR starters | Slow CSR starters with strong philanthropic tradition | Reserved CSR countries |
|---|---|---|---|---|
| Partnering Awareness-raising Range of incentives CSR effectively support broader public policies | Long standing CSR-related public policies Importance of international standards and soft law | High level of consistency in CSR policies Have found appropriate instruments | Can rely on national legislation or on internationally accepted methods | No clear analyses of their needs and no clear policies, apply 'must haves' |
| UK, Sweden | France, Germany | China, South Africa, Vietnam | Egypt, Poland | Brazil, India |

*Source*: CSR Navigator

*CSR approach* building on the fact that many voluntary initiatives have become paralegal. Another advocates a *stimulated CSR regulatory approach*, building on public–private partnerships, incentives and stakeholder dialogue. Two other projects call for policies encouraging a focus on *business internal change* and *strategic processes* and more selective stakeholder engagement. The recommendations also suggest that more attention should be paid to SMEs.[7]

## Public policies on Corporate Social Responsibility: the role of governments in Europe[8]

This research has identified four clusters of countries in Europe according to the following features (See Table 4.3): state-driven versus private sector-driven CSR and wide versus targeted stakeholder participation.

### Some conclusions

These frameworks give insights for sophisticated analysis of CSR public policies. They reflect a shift in analysis from the traditional opposition between legal or hard law and voluntary or soft law to multi-criteria

*Table 4.3* Public policies on Corporate Social Responsibility: The role of governments in Europe

| Model | Characteristics | Member states |
| --- | --- | --- |
| Partnership (state-driven, targeted stakeholder participation) | Partnership and strategy are shared between mostly governmental sectors for meeting employment challenges | Nordic countries + NL: Denmark, Finland, Sweden and Netherlands |
| Business in community (private sector-driven, targeted stakeholder participation) | Soft intervention policies to encourage company involvement in challenges affecting the community through encouraging entrepreneurship and voluntary service | Anglo-Saxon countries: United Kingdom, Ireland |
| Sustainability and citizenship (state-driven, wide stakeholder participation) | Updating of existing social agreement and emphasis on a strategy of sustainable development | Continental: Germany, Austria, Belgium and Luxembourg |
| Agora (private sector-driven, wide stakeholder participation) | Creation of discussion groups for different social actors striving for greater public consensus on CSR | Mediterranean: France, Italy, Spain, Greece and Portugal |

*Source*: Towards Greater Corporate Responsibility – Conclusions of EU-funded research, adapted from Albareda (2007)

analysis of a broad range of various tools. All the activities undertaken by a government are interacting and allow synergy. They form a national approach to CSR. These frameworks are useful for analysing CSR public policies in Southeast Asia and in China. We will use the CSR Navigator tool typology in this chapter.

## Why do governments in Asia engage in CSR activities?

To answer this question, we will give some insights building on two ministerial speeches from Southeast Asian countries and on the link made between CSR and the Chinese Harmonious Society policy.

In a speech delivered at the OECD–ESCAP Asia Conference 'Why Responsible Business Matters'[9] in 2009, Nuanpan Lamsam, Vice Minister,

Thai Ministry of Social Development and Human Security, pointed out that CSR can be effective as a counterbalance to the adverse effects on society of globalization, 'for example unemployment, poverty, household debts and environment problems'. CSR is also seen as essential for company image and reputation, competitive capacity, access to funding, human resources management and, *in fine*, sustainable growth.

In his speech delivered in 2006 for the launch of the Malaysian CSR Framework, the then Malaysian Minister of Finance II, Tan Sri Nor Mohamed Yakcop, pointed out that CSR is key to achieving the Malaysian National Economic Development Plan. He argued that CSR can contribute to ensuring *growth with equity* and achieving *distributional goals*. As part of the policy, companies are encouraged to take part in local economic development, education, capacity-building, environmental sustainability and ethnic diversity in the workplace. In conclusion, the Minister pointed out that CSR helps build the financial value of businesses and is key for attracting financing.

The Chinese government sees CSR as instrumental for the Harmonious Society Policy. The Harmonious Society should be achieved through Scientific Development, which is part of the current Chinese ideological guidance and calls for sustainable development and social welfare. CSR must help in combating the 'disharmonious elements in China', such as the gap between rural and urban development, unequal income distribution, insufficiency of household wealth, ecological degradation and lack of efficient use of resources.[10] CSR is also seen as an important component of companies' competitiveness, as put forward in the CSR Guidelines for State-Owned Enterprises.[11]

These examples illustrate the most common objectives and roles of CSR in emerging and developing Asia:

- Economy: CSR helps a country's economic competitiveness; it can be a business tool for ensuring sustainable growth and may be a condition for attracting investors;
- Social: CSR helps provide a means for allowing corporate contribution to national development and social goals such as poverty reduction and income growth, inequalities and discrimination reduction, and may reduce gaps and tensions between rural and urban development;
- Environment: CSR as part of a low-resource economy can help pollution reduction. China has the strongest focus on environmental CSR.

## CSR public policies in selected Southeast Asian countries: main CSR public initiatives

First of all, it is notable that political action is occurring at the regional level: the Blueprint for the Social–Cultural Community 2009–15 includes a section on CSR (Box 1). This section calls for promotion of CSR and business engagement. It sets the bold objective of designing a national public policy model for CSR or a legal reference instrument. The Blueprint mandates the CSR ASEAN Network with the promotion of CSR. The ASEAN Foundation launched the Network in late 2009. It comprises CSR corporate practitioners.

---

*Box 1*  Blueprint for the Socio-cultural Community – 2009–15 – Section: Promoting Corporate Social Responsibility (CSR)

'C3. Promoting Corporate Social Responsibility (CSR)

29. Strategic objective: Ensure that Corporate Social Responsibility (CSR) is incorporated in the corporate agenda and to contribute towards sustainable socio-economic development in ASEAN Member States.

Actions:

 i. Develop a model public policy on Corporate Social Responsibility or legal instrument for reference of ASEAN Member States by 2010. Reference may be made to the relevant international standards and guides such as ISO 26000 titled "Guidance on Social Responsibility";
 ii. Engage the private sector to support the activities of sectoral bodies and the ASEAN Foundation, in the field of Corporate Social Responsibility;
 iii. Encourage adoption and implementation of international standards on social responsibility and
 iv. Increase awareness of Corporate Social Responsibility in ASEAN towards sustainable relations between commercial activities and communities where they are located, in particular supporting community based development.'

---

Table 4.4 shows Southeast Asia main public initiatives. The Vietnamese government does not appear in this table because it has not undertaken a broad CSR initiative. However, it is active in the field of CSR, with initiatives such as:

- Participation in, or support of, CSR initiatives from business organizations and international donors;
- Upgrading of its laws and standards (labour law, environmental, health and safety standards);
- Capacity-building through the Vietnam Cleaner Production Centre.

Vietnam is classified as an *energetic CSR starter* in the CSR Navigator.

## Analysis of Table 4.4 shows:

## Types of tools utilized

Some governments engage in mandatory provisions, which include specific laws in Indonesia, mandatory requirements, for example in Indonesia and Malaysia, and mandatory CSR investment for tax abatement in the Philippines. Some others use voluntary instruments, such as Singapore or Thailand. Engagement in international instruments remains rather weak. Thailand has the most initiatives referring to international instruments (Table 4.5). In general partnering with stakeholders is still limited, though growing. The Thai government has the best record of partnering across ASEAN. The ASEAN CSR initiative includes a CSR practitioner network, which involves dialogue and participation events.

## Targeted fields of impact

Southeast Asian governments and public actors have initiated CSR activities with different fields of impact. The two most significant trends are provisions for responsible investment and for CSR disclosure.

The Thai Government Pension Fund is an asset member of the UN PRI. A number of other CSR initiatives are set up and/or managed by public financial bodies, including the Thai CSR Guidelines (Securities & Exchange Commission and Stock Exchange); CSR Framework and CSR Disclosure requirement (Bursa Malaysia); CSR investment required by the Board of Investment for companies entitled to tax incentives (the Philippines); and the CSR Institute of the Stock Exchange of Thailand. SRI has recently gained momentum: the Indonesian Stock Exchange launched a SRI index in 2009; Thailand and Malaysia have officially announced their intention to adopt SRI Criteria (Thailand) and to release a SRI Index (Malaysia, possibly Thailand). Singapore is also discussing the opportunity of developing such an index.

CSR disclosure is required by Bursa Malaysia and there are CSR Disclosure Regulations for Public Listed Companies (PLCs). Indonesia has passed a law for CSR Reporting and the Singapore Compact for CSR integrates CSR Disclosure in its awareness and capacity-building activities. CSR promotion and awareness activities by public bodies naturally take place in countries recently engaged in CSR, for example CSR Awards (Thailand, Malaysia) and awareness activities of the Singapore Compact for CSR.

Thailand and Malaysia have designed CSR Guidelines aimed at guiding companies. Thai Guidelines largely refer to international instruments (OECD Guidelines for Multinational Enterprises, UN Global

*Table 4.4*   Southeast Asia's main general public CSR initiatives

| Year | Country/ Institution | Initiative | Type of tool | Field of impact | Reference to international initiatives |
|---|---|---|---|---|---|
| 2005 | Singapore | Ministry of Manpower: participated in the creation of the Singapore Compact for CSR, national tripartite organization for CSR promotion | V, PD | CB, AR, R, II | UN Global Compact, GRI[12] |
| 2006 | Malaysia | Bursa Malaysia: CSR Framework | V | G, BMP | – |
| 2006 | Malaysia | Bursa Malaysia: mandatory CSR reporting for listed companies | M | R, RI | – |
| 2006 | Thailand | Stock Exchange: CSR Awards | V, I, AR | | – |
| 2007 | Indonesia | Law: CSR investment mandatory for companies operating in the natural resources sector | M | BMP | – |
| 2007 | Indonesia | Law: CSR reporting mandatory for Limited Liability Companies | M | R | – |
| 2007 | The Philippines | Board of Investment: registered companies entitled to 6-year tax holiday must implement CSR programmes | M, I | BMP, R | – |
| 2007 | Thailand | Stock Exchange: set up a CSR Institute (CSRI) | V, PD | CB, RI | – |

*Continued*

*Table 4.4*   Continued

| Year | Country/ Institution | Initiative | Type of tool | Field of impact | Reference to international initiatives |
|---|---|---|---|---|---|
| 2007 | Thailand | Thai Government Pension Fund Member of UN PRI | | RI, PS, II | UN PRI, OECD Guidelines for Multinational Enterprises, UN Global Compact |
| 2008 | Malaysia | Ministry of Women, Family and Community Development: Prime Minister CSR Awards | V, I, AR | | – |
| 2008 | Thailand | Ministry of Social Development and Human Security: launched the CSR Centre (promotion of CSR and coordination of CSR activities, including an Entrepreneur's Manual on CSR) | V, PD, AR | CB, G | – |
| 2008 | Thailand | Securities & Exchange Commission/ Stock Exchange: CSR Guidelines | V | G, R, RI, II | OECD Guidelines, UN Global Compact |
| 2008 | Thailand | Department of Industrial Works: Thai Certificate based on ISO 26000 | V | BMP, II | ISO 26000 |

*Source*: adapted from *Overview of CSR Initiatives in Southeast Asia* (OECD, 2009) and using a tool typology based on the toolbox of the CSR Navigator.
*Key*: **Type of tool**: Mandatory, M; Voluntary, V; Partnering/Dialogue, PD; Incentive, I; Awareness-raising, AR; **Field of impact:** Capacity-building, CB; Guidelines, G; Responsible investment, RI; Business management processes, BMP; Reporting, R; Public sector responsible conduct, PS; National Policy, NP; International instruments, II; Impact assessment, IA.

Compact) while Bursa Malaysia CSR Framework does not refer to international instruments but seems focused on country-specific issues.

Other types of impact occur occasionally, such as capacity-building (CSR Institute of the Stock Exchange of Thailand), internal processes and labels or certification activities (Thailand Certificate based on ISO 2600, ASO Award). In general, governments target a rather limited range of impacts. Thailand is the country with the most comprehensive range of fields of impact, as shown in Table 4.5.

## CSR public policy in China

Since 2005 and the launch of the Harmonious Society policy, the Chinese government, with this strong vision, has implemented a broad range of CSR activities.

### Main CSR public initiatives

In 2005, the Company Law was revised and general CSR Guidelines were included.

---

*Box 2* Chinese Company Law - Article 5 of the current version (2005 revision)

'A company must, when engaging in business activities, abide by the laws and administrative regulations, observe social morals and commercial ethics, act with integrity and good faith, accept supervision of the government and the public and undertake social liability.'

---

Other laws supporting better corporate social and environmental behaviour have been passed but are not detailed here. The landmark Labour Contract Law (1 January 2008) can, however, be mentioned, as well as the Law on Prevention and Control of Water Pollution (2008 revised) and the Measures on Open Environmental Information (2008, mandatory disclosure by companies and local governments of pollution exceeding quotas). Table 4.6 shows the numerous CSR public policy activities. Table 4.7 gives some examples of blacklisting, a practice promoted by the state through the Measures (see above).

### Types of tools utilized

Public CSR action includes a wide range of tools:

- Law and guidelines that have a regulatory power;
- Voluntary actions;
- CSR reporting requirements/guidelines;
- Credit and financing subordinated to environmental standards/ performance;
- Some partnering.

*Table 4.5*   Field of impacts of public CSR initiatives in Thailand

| Type of impact | Initiatives (public body) |
| --- | --- |
| Promotion, awareness-raising | CSR Centre (Ministry of Social Development and Human Security) |
| Awards, rewarding | CSR Awards (Stock Exchange) |
| Capacity-building | CSR Institute (Stock Exchange) |
| Guidelines | CSR Guidelines (Securities & Exchange Commission, Stock Exchange) |
| Public sector responsible conduct | Thai Government Pension Fund member of the UN PRI and using OECD Guidelines for Multinational Enterprises and the UN Global Compact in its investment strategy |
| SRI (Socially Responsible Investment) | Process for designing SRI Criteria and possibly a SRI Index (Securities & Exchange Commission, other stakeholders) |
| Support for businesses' internal changes | Thai Certificate based on ISO 26000 (Department of Industrial Works) AIDS-response Standard Organization Thailand (ASO Thailand) / ASO Award (Ministry of Labour, Ministry of Public Health, Thai Coalition against AIDS-HIV) |
| Global strategy and coordination | National CSR policy to be released in 2010 CSR Centre coordinating the public action for CSR |

CSR public policy in China reflects a strong planning style designed for meeting clear objectives. Provisions include law and instructions released through numerous public bodies:

1. Company law including CSR;
2. CSR guidelines – even if these guidelines do not have the status of law, we can assume that they have a regulatory power;
3. Environmental requirements for credit and listing in stock exchange.

In addition to strong planning-style CSR instructions, the Chinese government is making efforts to enforce social and environmental

*Table 4.6*   Main public CSR initiatives in China

| When | Who | Type of tool | Field of impact | What |
|---|---|---|---|---|
| 2004 | SASAC (State-owned Assets Supervision and Administration Commission of the State Council), Tsinghua University's Department of Construction Management | PD | R | Research team on Sustainability Reporting |
| 2005 | Ministry of Civil Affairs | V, I | AR | China Charity Awards. Two categories out of five are concerned with companies: Charity Award for Local Enterprises, Charity Award for Overseas Enterprises |
| 2006 | Ministry of Commerce's Transnational Corporation Research Centre | V | G, R | Draft of 'Guidelines on Corporate Responsibility Reporting for Chinese Enterprises' |
| September 2006 | Shenzhen Stock Exchange | M/V | G, R, RI | Guidelines for Listed Companies on Corporate Social Responsibility (Social Responsibility Instructions for Listed Companies) Includes Disclosure requirement |
| 2007 | China Export-Import Bank (fully owned by the Chinese government, under leadership of the State Council) | | R, O, PS | Public Disclosure of China Export-Import Bank Environmental Policy |

Continued

*Table 4.6*   Continued

| When | Who | Type of tool | Field of impact | What |
|---|---|---|---|---|
| 2007 | State Forestry Administration (SFA), Ministry of Commerce | M/V | G, O | Guidelines on Sustainable Management of Overseas Forests for Chinese Enterprises |
| October 2007 | Shanghai Pudong New Area Government | | IA | Index evaluation of CSR; 60 criteria, referring to ISO 26000 |
| November 2007 | Shanghai Stock Exchange | | RI, IA | Report on Corporate Governance |
| November 2007 | China Banking Regulatory Commission (CBRC) | V | G, RI, II | Recommendations on Strengthening Large Commercial Banks' Social Responsibilities, which require large banks to comply with the 10 basic principles of the United Nations' Global Compact |
| July 2007 | Environmental Protection Bureau of Shandong Province | V | G, R | Corporate Environmental Report Preparation Guidelines for Shandong Enterprises |
| December 2008 | Hong Kong Stock Exchange | V | G, RI | Corporate Responsibility Charter and Carbon Reduction Charter |
| January 2008 | Tianjin TEDA Co (State-Owned Enterprise – SOE), with Shenzhen Stock Exchange | PD, I | RI, IA | Teda Environmental Index of 40 listed companies |

Continued

*Table 4.6*   Continued

| When | Who | Type of tool | Field of impact | What |
|------|-----|--------------|-----------------|------|
| May 2008 | Shanghai Stock Exchange (SSE) | M/V | G, RI | Notice on Strengthening Listed Companies' Assumption of Social Responsibility (Shanghai CSR Notice) |
| May 2008 | Shanghai Stock Exchange (SSE) | M/V, I | G, RI, R | Guidelines on Listed Companies' Environmental Information Disclosure (Shanghai Environmental Disclosure Guidelines) |
| August 2008 | Chinese Academy of International Trade & Economic Cooperation (CAITEC), Ministry of Commerce | M/V, PD | G | Guidelines on Corporate Social Responsibility Compliance for Foreign Invested Enterprises (CSRC) |
| 2008 | Shanghai Stock Exchange (SSE) | I | RI, IA | SSE Corporate Governance Index |
| 2008 | SASAC | M/V | G, R, PS | Guidelines to the State-Owned Enterprises Directly under the Central Government on Fulfilling Corporate Social Responsibilities |

Continued

*Table 4.6*   Continued

| When | Who | Type of tool | Field of impact | What |
|---|---|---|---|---|
| 2008 | SEPA (State Environmental Protection Administration; now Ministry of Environmental Protection) | M, I | RI, C | Green policies for companies: Green Credit (commercial credit restrictions for highly polluting activities), Green Insurance (insurance against corporate pollution), Green Securities (highly polluting companies must pass environmental inspections for initial public offering or refinancing), Green taxation (no tax refund for polluting products) |
| 2009 | China Banking Regulatory Commission (CBRC) | | BMP, IA, RI | Guidelines on Credit Underwriting for Energy Conservation and Emission Reduction |
| 21 July 2009 | Shanghai Stock Exchange (SSE) and China Securities Index Co., Ltd | PD, I | RI, IA | SSE Social Responsibility Index |
| October 2009 | SASAC, CASS (Chinese Academy of Social Sciences) (report writers) | PD | IA | China Top 100 Corporate Social Responsibility Research Report |

*Source*: Adapted from research on CSR Initiatives in China and Europe, China-Europa Forum, to be released in 2010; using a tool typology based on the toolbox of the CSR Navigator.
*Key*: **Type of tool:** Mandatory, M; Voluntary, V; Partnering/Dialogue, PD; Incentive, I; Awareness-Raising, AR (guidelines have been qualified as M/V (Mandatory/Voluntary) because, though they do not have the status of law, they have a strong regulatory value). **Type of Impact:** Capacity-building, CB; Awareness-raising, AR; Guidelines, G; Responsible investment, RI; Business management processes, BMP; Reporting, R; Public sector responsible conduct, PS; National Policy, NP; International instruments, II; Outreach, O; Impact Assessment, IA; Compliance, C.

regulations and instructions. Blacklisting is used for denouncing companies violating laws and standards in the field of environment and also quality and safety (Table 4.7). Heads of companies are exposed to financial sanctions if they are found guilty of environmental degradation. The Supreme People's Court reported 317,000 labour disputes in 2009. Some exemplary court decisions increase dissuasion for not complying with law and standards. For example, no fewer than 21 Sanlu executives and middlemen were tried and condemned in the Sanlu tainted baby milk scandal. A farmer and a broker were sentenced to death, while the Sanlu chairman and three executives received jail sentences – a life sentence for the chairman – and fines.[13]

Another means of enabling enforcement of its CSR standards and regulations is the Green policy of the SEPA (State Environmental Protection Agency), which links access to credit, insurance and listing on Stock Exchange to environmental disclosure and performance.

However, enforcement of corporate social and environmental laws and standards is still a huge issue. Though the Chinese central government is strongly engaged, CSR activities by provincial governments and municipal authorities reveal large disparities. Implementation and enforcement of CSR standards at provincial and municipal levels are key. The Chinese government is therefore using different tools. An original one is the relative liberty of action allowed to environmental NGOS for acting as watchdogs of corporate environmental violations. NGOs such as the Institute for Public & Environmental Affairs, Friends of Nature, Green Beagle and Greenpeace China regularly denounce corporate polluters. A recent example is the report by three of the above-named NGOs on heavy metal discharges by famous electronics companies.[14]

### Targeted fields of impact

Targeted fields of impact are:

1. Change in companies' practices and management;
2. Disclosure;
3. Compliance and enforcement;
4. Blacklisting to encourage compliance;
5. Socially Responsible Indexes and other activities by financial actors (the three Stock Exchanges under the authority of the Chinese government (Shanghai, Shenzhen and Hong Kong) have issued CSR Guidelines for listed companies. Shanghai Stock Exchange and Shenzhen Stock Exchange have launched SRI Indexes);

*Table 4.7*   Some blacklisting activities by Chinese public actors

| When | Who | What |
| --- | --- | --- |
| June 2009 | Shanghai Environmental Department | Published a blacklist of 420 environmental violators on World Environment Day – 5 June 2009 |
| January 2010 | Shanghai Environmental Department | Published a blacklist of 721 companies accused of environmental violations |
| January 2010 | China's General Administration of Quality Supervision, Inspection and Quarantine | Plan announced to blacklist corporate quality violators |
| February 2010 | Guangdong Environmental Protection Bureau | Blacklisted 20 polluting companies for failing to meet water discharge standards (made them public) |
| 2009 | Kunming government | Provision for shutting down businesses not complying with pollution standards. Citizens are encouraged to report on polluting companies and can get financial rewards for doing so. Thus, 43 enterprises in Kunming were shut down for illegal sewage, while 19 companies were forced to clean out 32 production lines not reaching the standards. Reported awards range from RMB 100 to 1,000 yuan. |

*Source*:   CSR Initiatives in China and Europe, Forum China-Europa, to be released in 2010

6. Impact assessment of CSR practices (index evaluation of CSR from the Shanghai Pudong New Area; Stock Exchanges' SRI);
7. Some engagement in international instruments and initiatives (China Industrial Bank (CIB) adopting the Equator Principles; index

evaluation of CSR from the Shanghai Pudong New Area inspired by ISO 26000);
8. Some outreach (i.e. activities by Chinese companies having an impact on other countries) (Export-Import Bank of China Environmental Policy);
9. Awards (limited).

Targeted fields of impact reveal a strong public will for making companies' engagement in CSR effective through guidance and enforcement and for ensuring that CSR generates a real impact through measurement. Public CSR activities encompass diversified fields of impact, demonstrating a relatively sophisticated policy.

## Conclusion

For half a decade, developing and emerging Asia has energetically embarked on CSR public action, catching up after years of very limited – though not non-existent – engagement.

CSR public policies' objectives are in three tiers:

(a) *Social*: poverty reduction, inequalities reduction, contribution to education and to local development;
(b) *Environmental*: increase resource efficiency, decrease waste and emissions releases – these objectives are key for China;
(c) *Economic*: manage inclusion of their economies in globalization; ensure economic competitiveness and investment attractiveness.

Tools used range from mandatory provisions to voluntary action but also, in more and more countries and at various levels, to participatory and partnering initiatives. However, a lack of participatory processes may impede the effectiveness of CSR implementation by not positively engaging the private sector. This has been the case with the Indonesian law on CSR Investment, which was not discussed sufficiently with the private sector and business organizations, according to the latter.[15] Governments are naturally conducting awareness-raising and stewardship activities (e.g. CSR Awards), though this role is shared with NGOs, business organizations and other actors and, except for Thailand, no strong action is taken by public actors. Across most of the countries surveyed, financial institutions are strong CSR drivers. They carry out a relatively broad range of CSR-related activities: Socially Responsible Investment index and criteria, guidelines, CSR disclosure requirement, capacity-building, and so on.

CSR disclosure is another key driver for CSR, with various public initiatives. CSR guidelines are an important field of activity, occurring in several countries (China, Malaysia, Thailand). In China, CSR Guidelines are published in detail by many public actors, from stock exchange to SASAC.

A varied range of impacts are targeted in a patchy manner: capacity-building, awareness-raising and compliance.

Though their national companies (exporting companies, companies invested by global investors screening Environmental Social and Governance (ESG) aspects have long been exposed to international instruments, governments in developing and emerging countries still have only limited engagement in international instruments. Sometimes, international instruments form a basis for defining a country's own standard and are adapted to the local context – for example the Index Evaluation of CSR, from the Shanghai Pudong New Area, and the Thai Certificate, both inspired by ISO 26000.

Impact measurement is conducted by China. Projects involving universities and public bodies are implemented, evaluating performance (the degree to which companies are implementing CSR programmes) and impact (economic, social and environmental indicators). This can be explained by the strong planning–control nature of the Chinese state. Evaluation is beneficial, as it brings insights on effectiveness and efficiency of CSR programmes as well as possible enhancements. Other governments are starting to tackle CSR performance of their companies, mainly through SRI indexes.

Finally, the countries surveyed have various public policy profiles. These range from strong and mandatory, compliance and impact-oriented public action in China, to the voluntary, participatory and partnering Thai style. Malaysia has a mixed style of mandatory and incentive public policies. Indonesia is taking strong regulatory and SRI steps, but probably lacks participation and partnering action.

The following recommendations for CSR public action could be suggested:

(a) More involvement in international instruments and related negotiations. This would help countries:
   – Integrating at government level standards that are already integrated by exporting companies;
   – Gaining international leadership;
   – Having their voice in the future of these instruments;
(b) Widen range of tools used and targeted impacts, with a focus on embedding CSR practices within companies: compliance action, capacity-building, support for internal changes in companies;

(c) Increase focus on Small and Medium Sized Enterprises (SMEs). Good existing programmes and projects could be used as models – like those implemented in Vietnam, Cambodia and China by ILO, aimed at building capacities and upgrading CSR practices in SMEs;

(d) Measure impact of CSR public policies and of CSR implementation within companies. China is taking strong action for the latter;

(e) Achieve regional or subregional coordinated action (ASEAN initiatives a good start);

(f) Develop more compliance and accountability mechanisms, in contexts of rather low civil society activism. China is taking steps with respect to this for pollution control;

(g) Partner with a wider range of stakeholders – this is a good way to leverage public action and make it more efficient, as partners can have complementary expertise and action for complex goals and issues and may provide networks for spreading action;

(h) Formulate national CSR public policies as planned by Thailand and ASEAN.

## Notes

1. Speech of the Malaysian Minister of Finance of Malaysia for the launch Of Bursa Malaysia's CSR framework For PLCS, at http://www.treasury.gov.my/index.php?option=com_content&view=article&id=972%3Alaunch-of-bursa-malaysias-csr-framework-for-plcs&catid=53%3Aucapan&Itemid=251&lang=my (Date accessed 15 September 2010)
2. *Overview of CSR Initiatives in Southeast Asia* (OECD, 2009), at http://www.rse-et-ped.info/IMG/pdf/RBC_Initiatives_SEA_Joelle_Brohier_paper_Rev_May_2010.pdf (Date accessed 5 November 2010).
3. *CSR Frameworks in China and Europe* (China-Europa Forum, 2010). The report can be downloaded at http://www.china-europa-forum.net/bdfdoc-1704en.html (Date accessed 5 November 2010).
4. Available at http://www.business-humanrights.org/SpecialRepPortal/Home/CorporateLawTools (Date accessed 15 September 2010)
5. GTZ & Bertelsmann Stiftung, 'The CSR Navigator – Public Policies in Africa, the Americas, Asia and Europe' (2007) at www.bertelsmann-stiftung.de/csr (Date accessed 15 September 2010)
6. European Commission, *Towards Greater Corporate Responsibility* – Conclusions of EU-funded research (2009) at http://ec.europa.eu/research/social-sciences/pdf/policy-review-corporate-social-responsibility_en.pdf (Date accessed 15 September 2010)
7. Small and Medium Enterprises
8. L Albareda, JM Lozano and T Ysa, 'Public Policies on Corporate Social Responsibility: The Role of Governments in Europe', *Journal of Business Ethics* (2007) at http://www.springerlink.com/content/66l12v7r4ru8tpl3/
9. UNESCAP http://www.unescap.org/tid/projects/csr.asp (Date accessed 15 September 2010)

10. G See, 'Mapping the Harmonious Society and CSR Link', *Wharton Research Scholars Journal* (2008).
11. Ibid.
12. GRI: Global Reporting Initiative.
13. China executes two people for tainted milk scandal, at http://www.3news.co.nz/China-executes-two-people-for-tainted-milk-scandal-/tabid/417/articleID/131150/Default.aspx (Date accessed 15 September 2010)
14. http://www.syntao.com/PageDetail_E.asp?Page_ID=12790 (Date accessed 15 September 2010)
15. The Law has, however, been reconfirmed by the Indonesian government in 2009.

# 5
# The Role of Civil Society: Organizational Drivers of CSR in Asia

*Brian Lariche and Nicole M. Helwig*

## Introduction

This chapter will discuss the role that home-grown and international Non-Governmental Organizations (NGOs) and social organizations have played in the CSR journey of Asia.

The Asian story (excluding the Middle East) of NGOs and CSR includes the role of civil societies in lobbying, such as the campaign against Multinational Corporations (MNC) operations in Myanmar or environmental concerns and Native Customary Rights issues of palm oil cultivation. It also includes non-lobbying interventions, such as the largely successful story of microcredit, especially in Bangladesh. This chapter will document many innovative and previously unpublished cases of several Asian NGOs engaged in eradicating poverty and hunger and addressing issues of health, population, education and human rights. Examples include Magic Bus, DASRA-India, Tenaganita-Malaysia and their programmes working towards development of healthier societies and stronger communities in Asia.

## A few words on civil society in Asia

Civil society in Asian countries reflects the diverse political, historical and cultural contexts of the region. With such variety, it is a difficult challenge to characterize civil society drivers of CSR in an all-encompassing manner. However, a number of subregions are worthy of note: the Middle East, South Asia, South East Asia, nations of the former USSR and East Asia.

Historically, the Arab world has known military regimes, one-party rule and the coercion and repression of civil society organizations. The restriction of publication of Nobel Laureate and women's rights activist Shirin Ebadi's memoirs in **Iran** is notable.[1]

However, urbanization, the expansion of education and access to information technologies, and international development agencies directing aid towards developmental NGOs and municipalities rather than national governments are factors that are now leading to increased public participation.[2] The dissemination of information and coordination of protests during the Iranian elections in 2009 attest to the new power of social networking.[3] In **Jordan**, reforms in the late 1980s and early 1990s leading to multiparty politics and economic liberalization have created a decrease in government services and an increased role of NGOs in providing for social development.[4]

Currently, Queen Rania of Jordan has become an example of a how society can be developed via a partnership that goes beyond just public–private connections and can also involve a ruling royal family. She has made countless public appearances and speeches, advocating enhanced education as the all-important link for bridging gaps, giving people hope and improving lives not only in Jordan but regionally and globally.

One good example of this effort is the 'Madrasati' (My School), a public–private initiative aimed at refurbishing 500 of Jordan's public schools over a 5-year period. This is an excellent example of a national CSR project that has grown from strength to strength and engages all levels of society for the betterment of all.

In **South Asia**, the characteristic of social activism and NGO drivers for legislative change is more developed, especially in **India**. December 2009 marked the 25th anniversary of the Bhopal disaster, and highlighted the campaign that continues to restore the environment and deal with judicial issues as survivors seek compensation.[5] NGOs such as the ChildLine India Foundation and the National Centre for the Promotion of Employment for Disabled People (NCPEDP) are well known for their advocacy work promoting child protection and children's rights, and rights for the disabled, respectively.[6] **Bangladesh** is home to the Grameen Bank and the microcredit revolution, which has been recognized with a Nobel Prize for its founder Mohammed Yunus. The development of the Grameen network demonstrates how civil society endeavours can lead to innovation with respect to established structures, in this case the banking sector.

## Southeast Asia

Events in 2009 revolving around AWARE (Association of Women for Action and Research) demonstrate the awakening of civil society in **Singapore** and its use of social networking. AWARE is a non-profit organization for gender equality founded in 1985.[7] The organization was in the public spotlight following the events of the AWARE AGM of 28 March 2009.[8] Leading up to that meeting, the organization was marked by a steep increase in membership. The AGM was characterized by strong-arm tactics, where 80 per cent of voters were new members, with three times the normal turnout for the voting. The new Executive Committee (EC) took over the organization, which they alleged had become a platform for lesbian issues. This was seen by membership and the public as homophobic and an affront to civil, pluralist and multi-religious society. A website was created to channel and give a voice to those who sought 'to fight for something they believed in whether it was the fate of a women's organization, the importance of ground rules in a secular society or protection of a world view'.[9] Individuals continued the debate on blogs. On 2 May 2009 an extraordinary General Meeting was held, at which the elected EC lost a vote of no confidence.[10] This event has been seen as an eye-opener for the Singaporean public as to the vibrancy of their civil society.

**Malaysia** is a nation with rich civil society participation. With over 100,000 NGOs (albeit more than half are political parties and their branches), the NGOs are an integral part of the fabric of society and serve to fill in the gap of service not borne by the Malaysian Government. Many of these NGOs depend on public and corporate funding to carry out their work. Yet, despite this strong need for corporate support, these NGOs are not afraid to refuse corporate support when it clashes with their ethics and philosophy. In 2008, two women-based NGOs returned almost RM1 million (US$ 330,000) and a quarter of a million (US $85,000) respectively when they were pressured by their members for accepting money from an oil and gas giant that allegedly hired militia that committed crimes against women. This is also reflected in many NGOs refusing to work with companies dealing with alcohol and tobacco.

The People Power revolution in the Philippines in 1986 ended 20 years of rule under Ferdinand Marcos with more than a decade of martial law. It also marked a rejuvenation of civil society, which since 1972 had seen impositions on civil liberties and press freedoms.[11] Non-profit organizations were specifically recognized in the 1987 constitution and numerous laws since have strengthened the sector. Philippine Agenda 21, the nation's reaction to Agenda 21 adopted at the Rio Earth Summit, is the Filipino blueprint for sustainable development and gives civil society a key participatory role to play.[12]

It has been 20 years since the dissolution of the former USSR and yet in **Central Asia** there is much evidence of societies in transition. For example, Uzbekistan is known for human rights abuses, and recent riots in 2010 point to continued political unrest in Kyrgyzstan. On the other hand, Kazakhstan is developing a positive international profile as it accedes to chair the Organization for Security and Co-operation in Europe (OSCE) in 2010.

**In China**, with the opening-up of the Chinese economy, the development of independent, grass roots NGOs has started, whereas before non-profit organizations were strongly tied to government.[13] That said, Paul French of the Ethical Corporation reports on the National Party Congress's continued attempts to retain control over the sector.[14] Furthermore, according to the Asia Pacific Philanthropy Consortium, 'NPOs in China function mostly as philanthropic intermediaries, as foundations are granted more autonomy than other social organizations.'[15] With respect to CSR, there is evidence that both government and academic sectors are encouraging corporate involvement with non-profits.[16]

**In Japan**, a number of events are strengthening civil society organizations (CSOs) and encouraging philanthropy: the Kobe earthquake in 1995 is often quoted as having reinvigorated volunteerism; the economic successes of the 1960s and 1970s and the presence of Japanese countries abroad have led to a rise in corporate giving and CSR, and the 1998 NPO bill supports third sector activities.[17]

It would be interesting to explore a comparison of, for example, the level of awareness of CSR in different Asian civil societies and variances in NGO attitudes towards business and trends in order to identify areas of potential development and collaboration. Additionally, the different rules for the establishment of NGOs and the laws that govern them could be discussed.

It is, however, beyond the scope of this chapter to compare and contrast Asian civil societies and to characterize civil society drivers of CSR on a national or cultural basis. Rather, this chapter examines ways in which specific Asian NGOs engage with businesses, highlighting some unsung success stories and presenting models of innovation.

## Ways civil society engages businesses

In *The Responsibility Paradox*, Davis, Whitman and Zald predict that NGOs will lead global CSR in the areas of human rights and labour, citing the example of the Ogoni people of Nigeria against Shell and Nigerian National Petroleum.[18] In Asia, the cases of Nike in China, Malaysia, Thailand, Indonesia and Vietnam and ExxonMobil in Aceh, Indonesia come to mind. Moreover, numerous well-known NGOs, such as Greenpeace and Amnesty International, have established country offices giving prominence to the actions of their Asian lobbyists.

These well-known cases aside, there are numerous non-lobbying ways through which civil society initiates CSR. Kramer and Kania[19] advocate a new role for NPOs to seek new strategic partnerships with corporations. Specifically, this involves viewing businesses as partners rather than 'villains'; helping corporations set goals for solving social problems; asking corporations for more than just cash donations; and admitting that alliances with businesses can influence their reputations in a positive way.

The examples below present concrete examples of engagement.

### Magic Bus – India

Magic Bus grew from the initiative of one individual into a non-profit organization that aims to have reached 600,000 children by 2012 with its 'sport for development' programmes. It all began when Matthew Spacie, current Magic Bus CEO and rugby player, invited some slum children to join in sport practices. He noticed the benefits that participating in sport had on the children and began a partnership with local NGO, Akansha, forming a group of volunteers. The organization, which began by organizing rugby matches and camping in the countryside for just 50 children, now offers programmes reaching 6,000 children per week.

Magic Bus is a 'vehicle that transports children to a safe and fun place' and has a mission to empower Indian children and youth living in poverty. The programmes reach children aged 7 to 21 across gender lines, castes and religions. Initially focusing on children in the slums of Mumbai, Magic Bus now operates in Delhi, Chandrapur and Medak. Through play, destitute children, street and slum kids, orphans and children of construction and sex workers are guided to develop leadership and life skills enabling them in time to become builders of the community, as well as mentors and possibly staff of Magic Bus themselves.

The team at Magic Bus is comprised of volunteers and staff in both India and the UK and includes professionals from the education, for-profit and non-profit sectors. The organization works with numerous government, NGO and institutional partners and has been particularly innovative in building partnerships with corporations. The organization's focus on sustainable community development and mentorship has led to varied types of CSR interactions.

Corporate partners provide financial and in-kind support and assistance with fundraising. They also sponsor different activities depending on the industry. In addition, their employees volunteer as team leaders and mentors in the children's programmes, serving as role models and integrating Magic Bus goals into the community, and they provide capacity-building training for Magic Bus staff. The commitment from businesses is multi-year and encourages a less philanthropic CSR engagement. In short, Magic Bus provides businesses with opportunities to develop into good corporate citizens.[20]

### Dasra – India

Dasra aims to be a 'catalyst for social change'. Its mission is to educate and enlighten philanthropists and assist and strengthen non-profit organizations; to serve as an intermediary between funders and NPOs; and to 'maximize the investment of social investors and ensure lasting impact for the end beneficiary'.

Dasra activities include conducting needs assessments and strategy-building with NPO partners; facilitating workshops; advising major funding agencies; working on projects for economic empowerment; and mentoring social entrepreneurs.

Dasra comes from the Sanskrit meaning 'enlightened giving' or 'doing wonderful deeds'. Focusing on wealthy individuals and promoting effective philanthropy, Dasra provides a platform for CSR through its education programmes for funders and its mediation between corporate funders and NPOs.

One of Dasra's initiatives is hosting the Indian Philanthropy Forum. The IPF creates a new meeting place for the different actors in development. Upon invitation, philanthropists, private wealth management companies, social entrepreneurs, policymakers and NPO representatives are able to meet to exchange ideas. Further study tours enable donors to learn hands-on about the challenges faced by grass roots organizations and to determine how they can best fulfil existing needs. The IPF also encourages the development of giving circles to pool funds.

Through their Social-Impact programme, Dasra scouts for social entrepreneurs who are given the opportunity to pitch their businesses in person to venture philanthropists and bring their projects to scale. Business leaders are investors who provide management skills and experience through mentorship. Their involvement is again hands-on, which is in stark contrast to the classical philanthropic approach to giving. Working on a longer-term timeline, the aim is to maximize social impact for beneficiaries, much in the same way as an investor wins to maximize on his or her investment.

Dasra participates in events such as 'The Business of Giving', which was held in London by the UK India Business Council Next Generation, and workshops on CSR with the British Business Group and Flourish In India. It also produces Knowledge Sharing Reports to assist effective giving. Dasra was formed in 1999 out of Impact Partners, India's first venture philanthropy fund, and has representation in India, the UK and the United States.[21]

## NVPC – National Volunteer and Philanthropy Centre – Singapore

Established in 1999, the National Volunteer and Philanthropy Centre in Singapore facilitates interactions between non-profit organizations and volunteers. With respect to CSR, it offers numerous services to businesses to foster, in particular, corporate volunteerism.

NVPC staff can assist Corporate Social Responsibility officers to 'tailor an Employee Volunteering (EV) Programme from scratch, or improve upon an existing one, based on (your) organization's interests and strategic objectives'. The organization provides basic information to explain corporate volunteerism and its benefits and to determine what forms of EV are suitable for each corporate partner. It assists with matching with non-profit organizations and has been instrumental in a programme called 'Board Match', which helps link suitable individuals to serve on non-profit boards. The NVPC also advises businesses on corporate giving.

A further initiative is the NVPC annual awards in volunteerism and philanthropy. In particular, they have created a Corporate Citizen Award, which is presented to organizations that 'have demonstrated active corporate citizenship through volunteerism and/or philanthropy, encompassing fundraising and donations (money or in-kind)'. This award serves as an incentive to promote CSR.

In addition, the NVPC provides resources such as publications, of which *An Employee Volunteering Guide* (2007) and *Time, Talent & Treasure: Best Practices in Corporate Giving* (2006) are two examples.

They publish a bimonthly magazine, which publicizes, among other things, corporate activities with NVPC. Finally, their annual conference is a stage for collaboration and exchanges.[22]

## Japan NPO Centre

The Japan NPO Centre was established in 1996 with a mission to strengthen the NPO sector in Japan. Additionally, the centre 'aims for the creation of strategic partnerships between the non-profit sector and the business and government sectors'. These collaborations provide opportunities for businesses to fulfil their CSR policies.

One example is the Nissan–NPO Learning Scholarship Program,[23] launched in 1998. On a yearly basis, students are selected to complete internships at various NPOs. In exchange for successful completion, the students are rewarded with a scholarship. Nissan see this 'as an "investment" in young people who will be responsible for supporting future society'.

Another partnership is with Dentsu.[24] This advertising company organizes seminars given by employees to improve public relations skills at NPOs.

The Japan NPO Centre also created a database of NPOs with the aid of NTT Communications.[25] The NPO Hiroba Database 'enables interested citizens or enterprises to learn about and participate in a non-profit organization, contributing to the development of their activities across Japan', once again creating CSR opportunities.

Another creation of the Japan NPO Centre is a Civil Society Initiative Fund. The fund supports NPO activities and is supported by corporate (among other) donations.[26]

## KEHATI Biodiversity Foundation – Indonesia

Founded in 1994, KEHATI is a non-profit grant-making organization with a mission to 'provide support and resources to facilitate various activities, conservation and utilization of biodiversity in Indonesia on an on-going basis'.[27]

The Foundation created a socially responsible investment index which was launched in June 2009 on the Indonesian stock exchange, an innovative way to recognize the growing focus on sustainable and responsible business and encourage good corporate behaviour. According to Dr Damayanti Buchori, former CEO of KEHATI, the aim is to 'promote best practices in Indonesia and to make the efforts transparent to our international network of responsible investors'.[28]

Additionally, KEHATI created a 'Green Fund' to support eco-friendly corporate activities. Businesses participate through financial support placed into a mutual fund-type investment whereby 50 per cent of the investment return is donated to KEHATI to further its work. In 2010, KEHATI is working towards CSR education and awareness in collaboration with a CSR Academy from Malaysia. This collaboration is hoped to produce a network of CSR practitioners in Indonesia to help develop the field further.

## Tenaganita – Malaysia

Tenaganita is a human and migrant rights organization that works with women workers and migrant workers in Malaysia within the context of a globalized world. What essentially started as a grass roots organization has now blossomed into the focal point for all issues dealing with trafficking and modern-day slavery in Malaysia and the region.

Since its formation in 1991, the organization has grown in leaps and bounds, addressing the various, complex issues of exploitation, discrimination, unequal treatment and violence. It has reached out to the most vulnerable groups, such as sex workers, trafficked women and children, refugees, migrant workers, especially the undocumented, and plantation workers. In 2010, the organization expanded its scope of work to create a new department within the organization titled *'Business Accountability & Responsibility (BAR)'*. Though initially focused on the oil palm industry, it has now expanded to address issues in various industries that employ migrant labour.[29]

## Gawad Kalinga Community Development Foundation – the Philippines

The Gawad Kalinga Community Development Foundation grew out of the activities of CFC (Couples for Christ), a lay Christian community. Members, including GK founder Antonio Meloto, began with projects to alleviate poverty working with youth delinquents in Bagong Silang, Caloocan City, which is the biggest slum of Manila. Officially established in 2003, GK is 'a movement that builds integrated, holistic and sustainable communities in slum areas'.

With a mission to end poverty for 5 million Filipino families by 2024, GK has developed numerous programmes in child and youth development; community-building; the environment; food sufficiency; health; and infrastructure. Other aspects of its work include peace-building and reconstruction (following natural disasters), as well as supporting social entrepreneurship, tourism and township development. With its Building Institutes and 'army of volunteers', the organization has also developed an international presence, with projects in Papua New Guinea, Indonesia and Cambodia. It also lays claim to being a 'global humanitarian movement presently established in major academic, corporate and civic institutions in key cities and provinces around the Philippines and in North America, Australia and Asia'. Projects are planned in East Timor, India and Malaysia.

The organization has a healthy working relationship with corporate partners, as can be seen by the list of trustees, which includes representatives from various companies such as Globe Telecoms, Pilipinas Shell and Olaes Enterprises. Corporate partners are not only Filipino but also from Europe, Canada and the US.

GK focuses on impact beyond corporate philanthropy, highlighting sustainable aims of their projects in poverty alleviation. Long-term partnerships and creative leveraging are sought. However, GK does not lose sight of the benefits to business when seeking partners, and highlights advantages of association through co-branding, developing markets and customer loyalty, and creating a positive corporate image. GK is also engaging corporate players through annual global summits.[30]

### Grameen Bank – Bangladesh

The Grameen Bank and its founder Prof. Muhammad Yunus are synonymous with the microcredit revolution. The insight of Prof. Yunus was to identify what has been called 'financial apartheid'. His recognition of the exclusion of the poor from the traditional banking system has led to innovative models of providing financial services that are now replicated in many parts of the world.[31]

*Innovations of the Grameen Bank[32]*

The Grameen Bank is for the poor and owned by the poor. Borrowers are mostly women and, unlike conventional banks, loans are disbursed without collateral. A supportive social structure is also key: borrowers are arranged into groups of five to encourage behaviours including timely and regular repayment of loans. The Grameen Bank's services have now been extended to include beggars, who receive loans at no interest.

Despite cynical predictions to the contrary, Grameen Bank borrowers have a high repayment rate – a figure that betters rates in conventional banks. Though the bank originally depended on donors, it is now self-financing through deposits. Furthermore, it is a profit-making enterprise.

The Grameen Bank's services began to diversify in 1984 to include housing projects. In terms of other financial products, the Grameen Bank has a loan insurance programme and life insurance; pension funds; scholarships and education loans. The bank also offers micro-enterprise support.

The existence of the Grameen network of organizations, both for-profit and not-for-profit, is a testament to its outreach and impact.

In terms of CSR, the Grameen Bank is an example of a civil society initiative emerging from the academic area to engage the financial sector. As an economist and professor of the University of Chittagong, Prof. Yunus initially focused on improvements in agriculture in the town of Jobra through experimental projects with his students. By working directly with villagers, Prof. Yunus was able to observe that the typical approaches toward social improvements neglected a portion of the population, namely the landless poor. Developing a relationship with the villagers, Prof. Yunus effectively became a mediator who enabled communications and, with time, interactions between communities and institutions (e.g. universities and banks).

It is important to highlight that it was not merely Prof. Yunus's influence as a personality or academic authority that led to success. (Indeed, his image and influence were seen by bank representatives as an argument against expansion to district level, which they felt would not be successful without his direct and personal input in all activities.) In the end, it was proven that the new operational process, once implemented, led to results.

Certain aspects of civil society in Bangladesh enabled the establishment and development of the Grameen Bank. Without freedom of association, the ability of individuals to be proactive, and willingness at levels of government and banking to test new ideas, the experiment of microcredit would not have been nurtured. It is important to note that legal conditions also enabled development, through exceptions being made for the Grameen Bank as it evolved. These connections between different segments of society – civil, business and government – catalysed by grass roots initiatives were fruitful and give hope for the rise of other successful innovations in the area of social development.

Some Grameen Bank figures from March 2010 illustrate the success of the approach.[33] The total number of borrowers is 8.07 million, 97 per cent of whom are women. Grameen Bank has 2,564 branches and works in 81,351 villages with a total staff of 23,133. According to figures available at April 2010, the total amount of loans made by the Grameen Bank is Tk 522.24 billion (US $ 9.09 billion), out of which Tk 463.24 billion (US $ 8.05 billion) has been repaid. The loan recovery rate is quoted at 96.72 per cent. According to an internal Grameen Bank survey, "68 per cent of Grameen borrowers' families of Grameen borrowers have crossed the poverty line. The remaining families are moving steadily towards the poverty line from below".

## Conclusion

The wide and varied landscape of Asia is further reflected in its diverse civil society. From the almost non-existent scenario in the Gulf states, to the state-controlled NGOs in China, to the powerful and influential civil society landscape in South Asia, the various perspectives offer different sorts of influence on the drivers of CSR in the region.

However, it is clear that the rate of change is sure and swift, and Asian NGOs will move towards being influential drivers of CSR within their countries.

## Notes

1. J Chu, '10 Questions for Shirin Ebadi', *Time*, 8 May 2006, at http://www.time.com/time/magazine/article/0,9171,1191820-1,00.html, accessed on April 27, 2010.
2. N Salam, *Civil Society in the Arab World, The Historical and Political Dimensions*, Islamic Legal Studies Program (Harvard Law School, October 2002).
3. M Meyer, 'The Role of Social Media in the Iranian Election', 16 June 2009, at http://directmarketingobservations.com/2009/06/16/the-role-of-social-media-in-the-iranian-election/ accessed on April 27, 2010.
4. S Jara, Working Paper: 'Civil Society and Public Freedom in Jordan: The Path of Democratic Reform', The Saban Centre for Middle East Policy at the Brookings Institution (July 2009).
5. 'Bhopal marks 25 years since gas leak devastation', BBC News, 3 December 2009, at http://news.bbc.co.uk/2/hi/south_asia/8392206.stm, accessed on April 27, 2010.
6. D Bornstein, *How to Change the World – Social Entrepreneurs and the Power of New Ideas* (Oxford: Oxford University Press, 2007).
7. Association of Women for Action and Research (aware), http://www.aware.org.sg/about/overview/ accessed on April 27, 2010.
8. http://www.we-are-aware.sg/2009/05/07/chronology/ accessed on April 27, 2010.
9. Ibid.
10. E-Jay, Ng. 'Josie Lau's team removed and a new leadership at AWARE has been voted in!', Sgpolitics.net, 2 May 2009, at http://www.sgpolitics.net/?p=2885, accessed on April 27, 2010.
11. http://en.wikipedia.org/wiki/Ferdinand_Marcos#Downfall, accessed on April 26, 2010.
12. http://pcsd.neda.gov.ph/pa21.htm#pa21, accessed on April 26, 2010.
13. 'Developing China's Nonprofit Sector', McKinsey Quarterly (August 2006); 'The charity development of Chinese enterprises seriously lagging behind', SynTao.com from ChinaNews.com (14 July 2009) http://syntao.com, accessed on March 25, 2010.
14. Ethical Corporation, *Oxfam under fire from Beijing* (30 March 2010).
15. Asia Pacific Philanthropy Consortium website, Profile: China, http://www.asia-pacificphilanthropy.org/taxonomy/term/30; accessed on March 25, 2010.

16. 'Developing China's Nonprofit Sector', McKinsey Quarterly (August 2006) and 'The charity development of Chinese enterprises seriously lagging behind article', SynTao.com from ChinaNews.com (July 14, 2009).
17. http://web-japan.org/trends96/honbun/tj970207.html and Asia Pacific Philantrhopy Consortium website, Profile: Japan http://www.asiapacificphilanthropy.org/node/59, accessed on: April 18, 2010.
18. *The Responsibility Paradox*, Stanford Social Innovation Review, Winter 2008.
19. *A New Role for Nonprofits*, Stanford Social Innovation Review, Spring 2006.
20. 'Corporate Members for At-Risk Youth', 2005, at http://www.citizenbase.org/en/magic_bus and http://www.magicbusindia.org/ accessed on March 30, 2010.
21. Dasra, http://www.alliancemagazine.org/node/2850, accessed on April 3, 2010
22. National Volunteer and Philanthropy Centre (NVPC), http://www.nvpc.org.sg/pgm/Stack/NVPC_F_Stack_SubPage.aspx?PID=48, accessed on March 28, 2010.
23. Nissan, 'Nissan Begins Tenth Term of the "Nissan-NPO Learning Scholarship Program" -Investing in Young People Through Partnerships with NPOs', 25 April 2007, at http://www.nissan-global.com/EN/NEWS/2007/_STORY/070425-01-e.html, accessed on April 19, 2010.
24. http://www.dentsu.com/csr-env/communication/npo_seminar.html, accessed on April 19, 2010.
25. NTT Communications, *NTT Communications Group CSR Report 2008*, at http://www.ntt.com/csr_e/report2008/social.html, accessed on April 18, 2010.
26. Japan NPO Centre, http://www.jnpoc.ne.jp/English/about/about.html, accessed on April 20, 2010.
27. Kehati, http://www.kehati.or.id/ accessed on April 20, 2010.
28. OWW Consulting, 'First Socially Responsible Investment Index Launched in Indonesia', at http://www.oww-consulting.com/press/first-socially-responsible-investment-index-launched-indonesia.html accessed on April 19, 2010.
29. Tenaganita, http://www.tenaganita.net/ accessed on April 26, 2010.
30. Gawad Kalinga, http://gk1world.com/HomeRedesign, accessed on April 25, 2010
31. M Yunus, *Creating a World Without Poverty: Social Business and the Future of Capitalism* (Public Affairs, 2007), accessed on April 25, 2010.
32. Grameen Bank, http://www.grameen-info.org/ accessed on April 25, 2010.
33. Data source: http://www.grameen-info.org/index.php?option=com_content&task=view&id=26&Itemid=175

# 6
# From CSR Concepts to Concrete Action: Integrated Approaches to Improvement at the Factory Level

*Ivanka Mamic and Charles Bodwell*

## Introduction

The emergence of Corporate Social Responsibility (CSR) initiatives over the past two decades to address voluntary labour, social and environmental issues has been well documented.[1] A myriad of factors have provided momentum to the CSR movement, including the risk of being exposed and receiving bad publicity,[2] reputation risks[3] and arguments for a 'business case.'[4] In the current context of a global economic crisis, this latter factor, the possibility of a positive relation between the voluntary practices adopted by a company and its competitiveness, has become increasingly important.[5] At the same time, it has been well documented that implementing CSR initiatives in the disaggregated supply chains of modern production models is a complex and multifaceted task that requires training and hands-on change management assistance at the factory level.[6] This is particularly the case when it comes to addressing labour issues.

In this chapter we explore some of the results achieved through practical approaches by the International Labour Organization (ILO), the United Nations' specialized agency charged with the responsibility for promoting social justice and advancing decent work opportunities for all, which has assisted companies in Asia in their quest for win-win solutions. The examples highlighted show that it is possible for companies to be more competitive while respecting the core labour rights of workers and operating in an environmentally sustainable fashion. In addition, we will argue that voluntary corporate initiatives are only successful in respecting workers' rights when implemented in the context of coherent labour laws and regulations that are backed up by credible systems of enforcement.

## Role of codes of conduct

The starting point for many companies in taking practical steps to put their voluntary CSR initiatives into practice involves the identification of principles or standards to guide corporate actions. In the case of multinational companies, this commonly involves the development of a Code of Conduct (CoC). Research shows that, due to the increasing number of multi-stakeholder initiatives, which prescribe or predefine a set of core principles for companies to follow, small and medium-sized enterprises (SMEs) are increasingly committing to CoCs or pursuing explicit CSR strategies.[7]

As Prakash Sethi and Oliver Williams[8] have noted, the emergence of and need for CoCs can be traced to two key developments in the latter part of the twentieth century, namely the emergence of globalized market economics and the growth of capitalism. In an area characterized by the absence of highly developed regulatory structures, CoCs reflect an attempt to address the operational challenges of globalization, in which companies are often faced with conflicting legislation and inconsistent enforcement. Essentially forms of self-regulation, CoCs are a tool through which companies try to define and apply performance standards in a range of areas. These are typically social and environmental, as identified by the company and in some cases its stakeholders.

Mamic[9] gives a detailed review and analysis of the various types of CoCs that exist today, their development and application, and notes that today's CoCs are not created in a vacuum but rather against a backdrop of existing laws and regulations. She notes, as others have,[10] that no single template exists to guide companies when it comes to practical integration of CSR ideals into the operational levels of a company. Despite this, based on research conducted on global supply chains, which involved hundreds of interviews with workers, managers, government officials, activists and others, Mamic presents a model of analysis outlining the common elements involved in the transformation of ideas into actions. It is useful to describe the model briefly here in order to put the subsequent discussions in this chapter into context.

As illustrated in Figure 6.1, there are at least four common elements involved in translating CSR ideas into concrete actions. These elements are interrelated and underpinned by the need for dialogue with key stakeholders at all stages. In global supply chains, codes of conduct are

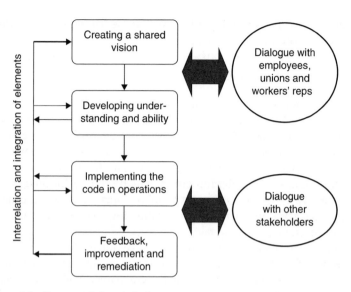

*Figure 6.1*   Framework for analysis

typically instruments applied in a contractual context between the buyer, who has established the code, and the supplier, who agrees to adhere to it.

Such codes can be seen as concrete embodiments of a 'social vision' of the company that has established the code. It has been well documented that the commitment to any principles, including social and environmental standards included in CoCs, generally begins with the development of a vision; a task which must involve top management if it is to be a success. Without top management commitment, even the best-conceived CSR programme stands little chance of success, as has been demonstrated by numerous high-profile examples of the breakdown between the expressed policies and the actual on-the-ground results, including those exposed in October 2000 by the BBC's Panorama programme[11] of the existence of child labour in a factory in Cambodia producing for Nike and Gap products, at a time when both brands had CSR programmes with express standards forbidding the use of child labour. This particular example drew attention to the need not only to have standards but also to communicate and support the standards down the supply chain.

As a starting point, it is essential that this vision is communicated, explained and understood by all those affected by it, namely the employees throughout a company, as well as its suppliers, the suppliers' managers and workers, and others involved in supporting the company's supply chain operations. This can only be achieved through appropriate training, adequate communication and recognition of the fact that this is a continuous, long-term process. Some of the issues that need to be explained include:

(a) What are the objectives of the CSR strategy and resulting CoC policy?
(b) Why it is important in today's marketplace?
(c) What is senior management's vision and long-term commitment to this policy?
(d) How does the CoC relate to the overall objectives of the company?
(e) How is the CoC implemented through the company and its supply chain?
(f) What are the impacts of a CSR policy and CoC on the specific day-to-day activities of individual employees?
(g) And at the supplier level, what will be the impact of the CoC for a particular worker and manager? That is, what does it mean for them?

Practical implementation of a CoC into company and supply chain operations requires a number of steps, such as looking at structures, assignment of roles and responsibilities, and the integration of corporate functions and training so that people have the necessary knowledge and skills to carry out their new tasks. The establishment of feedback, improvement and remediation systems is a critical component of the integration process. This includes the establishment of systems to assure compliance, monitoring and the measurement and reporting of performance of internal groups and individuals, as well as external suppliers. Such information systems, in best case examples, feed into recommendations and assistance with corrective actions and the engagement of stakeholders within all of these components.

A great deal of research and resulting literature has been devoted to understanding these last two elements of the framework, and an in-depth discussion is beyond the scope of this paper. However, it is important to acknowledge that the last two decades have witnessed an evolution in the practical implementation of CSR initiatives, particularly in the case of globalized supply chains. Multinational companies and others actively engaged in this field have recognized that the first stage of 'compliance and policing' models of CSR, in which one company or organization assumes responsibility for inspecting, policing and advocating change, typically to the supplier factory, have not been successful.[12] Notwithstanding this, some countries, such as Indonesia and Malaysia, have attempted to legislate for CSR.[13] The practical implications of such legislation remain to be seen, particularly in light of the fact that such legislation simply adds yet another layer of standards for companies to try to comply with and governments to try to police. One foreseeable challenge rests with the actual implementation and administration of the legislation in countries where labour inspectorates are weak, corruption is endemic and workers are often not empowered or represented. In such cases a voluntary approach, one requiring commitment from both buyers and suppliers, will have a crucial role – resulting in the need for capacity-building, partnerships and training in order to have a positive impact on working conditions.

The shift from a policing approach to one of training, capacity-building, and increased partnerships between buyers and sellers is evident throughout Asia. This transition has been aided by programmes delivered through organizations such as Business for Social Responsibility (BSR) and Social Accountability International (SAI) , as well as through programmes from international organizations, including the ILO. At the same time, research shows that there is a great variation in the penetration of CSR among countries in Asia. Chambers et al.,[14] in their comparative study of CSR reporting in seven Asian countries, conclude that both local firms and those that operate internationally follow broadly similar CSR objectives, but that multinational firms are more likely to engage in CSR based on partnerships with both local stakeholders and other stakeholders and NGOs like BSR or SAI. Furthermore, they argue that the process of globalization, together with the institutionalization of corporate norms through codes of conduct and supporting processes, is in fact a key driver of CSR at the enterprise level.

Locke et al.[15] argue that what is necessary, particularly with regard to improving performance relating to labour issues in voluntary initiatives, is a shift to a commitment-oriented approach based on joint problem-solving, sharing of information and best practices. Such an argument is supported by the programmes delivered by the ILO over the past decade: training programmes and technical assistance focused on increasing dialogue, fostering the development of partnerships and improving performance at the factory level. The rest of this chapter is devoted to examining some of the results that have been achieved by the ILO in its programmes and to better understand the approach and methods used in helping to address labour issues at the enterprise level.

## Transformations at the factory level

As has been noted, the initial models adopted in integrating voluntary initiatives into corporate practices focused on compliance with standards, either legal or voluntarily adopted such as those in a CoC and assurance of the same through monitoring and reporting, typically via a series of audits. This approach led to a mushrooming of CSR audit companies and helped identify the problems that existed, but did little to analyse the root causes of these problems, often resulting in limited sustainable change in practices being adopted at the factory level. The recidivism rate of factories in terms of breaches of labour standards such as payment of minimum wages or limitation of excessive overtime hours was very high.[16] This was particularly true in the case of factories based in developing countries, where there was limited managerial capacity, worker expertise and understanding of human resource management. Furthermore, these challenges were aggravated by limited understanding of and compliance with national labour laws and regulations, inadequate occupational safety and health, working conditions and basic social protections for workers, poor worker-manager relations and limited support of trade unions and true dialogue within factories.[17]

At the start of the new millennium the ILO sought to address these challenges with a series of factory-based training programmes designed to bring about long-term, sustainable changes in practices adopted by companies. As will be argued, these programmes have had impressive results not just in the labour field but also with regard to environmental concerns, which are increasingly being seen as an integral component of all production. The ILO's Better Work, Sustaining Competitive and Responsible Enterprises and CSR in the Chinese textiles sector programmes are all based on a methodology put forward in the successful demonstration models of the Factory Improvement Programme (FIP), core elements of which have been adopted in these other factory-level training programmes.

The FIP approach differentiated itself from other approaches being adopted in four key ways:

(a) Approach – it specifically involved both workers and managers and asked for joint solutions to be developed for factory-level issues.

(b) Integrated methodology – it addressed labour relations, working conditions, productivity, quality, environmental and other issues together and had clear linkages between them.

(c) Scope – the focus was on providing hands-on, change management assistance within the factory, rather than solely on training.

(d) Intensity – there was a long-term commitment to working with the factory over an extended period of time in order to bring about change rather than a one-off factory audit resulting in a checklist of changes to be undertaken.

The structure of this new approach to addressing labour issues at the factory level can be seen in Figure 6.2.

Typically workers and managers of participating factories participate in group training, after which an 'improvement team' of both workers and managers is formed. Following the training, a series of visits by experts to the factory helps this improvement team identify areas of improvement and provides recommendations supporting changes that need to be made. To the highest degree possible, factories' improvement

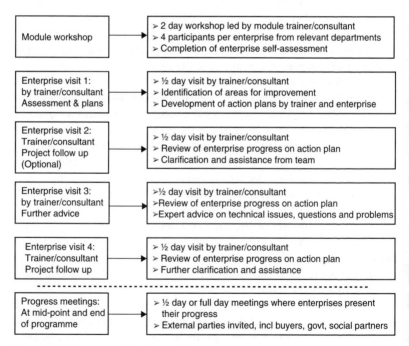

*Figure 6.2*  Structure of the factory improvement programme

teams should drive the process, building ownership, commitment and increased capacity to continue such joint problem-solving following the programme. Assistance is given with developing baseline criteria in order to monitor and measure improvements, analysing root causes and working together to identify and implement required solutions in a multitude of areas as outlined above. Given management's orientation towards focusing on the bottom line, initial changes often focused on 'quick wins' or 'low hanging fruit' that would bring about assured results and increased managerial commitment, while helping demonstrate (as outlined below) the value of worker commitment and broad-based continuous improvement.

The remainder of this chapter is devoted to looking at some case studies that illustrate the results achieved through the FIP at the factory level.[18]

## Case A: Increased worker involvement

Haprosimex ('Hapro') is a large, modern garment factory producing garment products for export to the United States and European Union for a range of customers including Nike, Gap and Columbia Sportswear. Employing 1,800 workers, Hapro was well accustomed to abiding by international CoCs requiring compliance with certain social and environmental principles as well as the need to meet high quality standards. One frequently imposed requirement by customers was an end-line defect rate of 8 per cent, and at the start of the FIP the end-line defect rate was 7.93 per cent. However, the end-line defect rate imposed by one buyer, namely Nike, was 1 per cent, and Hapro recognized that if it were to obtain future orders from Nike it would have to take action to meet this goal.

One obstacle faced by Hapro was that quality control was only conducted at the end of the production line, and as such was the responsibility of workers assigned to the task at that time. Workers throughout the process paid little attention to in-line quality, as this was not seen as their responsibility. Consequently, nearly completed products often had to be redone completely due to the late detection of defects.

The problem was further compounded by the fact that quality issues were considered to be the responsibility of a supervisor rather than the responsibility of both workers and management. Supervisors were charged with the responsibility for communicating quality standards to workers, and this was generally done via verbal announcements. With no written guidelines for workers to follow, there was a high risk of workers misunderstanding or neglecting to follow the quality standards.

The FIP project team recognized that the issue of high defect rates was potentially a broader problem than one relating only to quality. The need to redo production would have a knock-on effect on, for example, working hours, resulting in the company's non-compliance with both the CoC standards and the quality standards. As such, it was recommended that a number of actions be taken, including the following:

(a)  Better communication with workers through the provision of written summaries in Vietnamese so that they could understand the technical requirements with regard to quality;
(b)  Worker training to discover defects and take preventative actions to avoid them;
(c)  Introduction of in-line quality control and random quality checks to discover and solve problems early in the process; and
(d)  Regular meetings with the participation of all workers to discuss ways to improve performance and solve problems that may arise.

These recommendations were taken up by the factory, and 9 months after commencing the FIP the factory had an end-line defect rate of 1 per cent. The impact of this was significant for the factory, not only in terms of improving financial performance but also in terms of their social performance.

The changes that took place in the Hapro case could not have been undertaken without the involvement of the Human Resource (HR) department. The need for HR development, in terms of building managerial capacity and understanding the critical role and value of their workers, is a core component of the FIP approach.

## Case B: Critical role of HR

Hiep Hung is a private, medium-sized garment company employing approximately 1,000 employees engaged in the production of mosquito nets and embroidery products for both the Vietnamese and international markets. At the commencement of the FIP programme, the company did not have a systematic salary structure for the various groups of workers. The salary system was a piece-rate system which had not been updated for 3 years and did not follow the market. This meant that the company was in a situation of not meeting the basic requirements regarding the payment of minimum wages, something generally required by CoCs.

As a result of participating in the FIP training on HR management, the managing director of the company revised the entire salary system for Hiep Hung. The piece salary rate was increased by 25 per cent, exceeding even the workers' desired goals, with this and other changes leading to an increase in per-worker productivity. The effect of these changes was immediate: the average salary of workers increased by 60 per cent in the mosquito net department and by 33 per cent in the embroidery department, both of which were increases due to the combined effect of increased piece-rate payments and the resulting increases in worker productivity, all over the course of 9 months.

Importantly, the salary increase also had a knock-on effect on worker commitment and productivity, which would help the company obtain new buyers and meet the requirements of existing buyers.

As can be seen in this example, improved dialogue and worker involvement can result in benefits not just to workers but also to the company itself, resulting in a win-win situation for both management and workers, as highlighted in the following case.

## Case 3: Increased productivity leading to increased salaries

Chien Tang is part of a large, Vietnamese, state-owned corporation that has ten factories and almost 3,000 workers. The factory predominantly produces clothes for international customers based in the United States, the European Union and Japan, with a small proportion (approximately 5 per cent) being sold domestically.

At the commencement of the FIP, productivity in Chien Tang was low due to inefficiencies in production input, poor production planning and the physical layout of the production lines, as well as poor communications between workers, supervisors and managers. The production lines had been organized in such a way that workers were required to be involved in several production processes, affecting the workflow negatively and thereby reducing productivity rates.

With guidance from the ILO's FIP experts, the factory decided on a number of actions, including:

(a) Undertaking a reorganization of the production lines and adding lead times to the production process;
(b) Establishing better communication means between departments with a view to avoiding shortages with regard to material supply;

(c)  Changing the production lines so that workers could focus on only one production process, for example by merging lines for complex processes;

(d)  Reporting and communicating on productivity performance and goals.

These changes were carried out by Chien Tang, resulting in significant improvements in productivity in a number of workshops. For example, one workshop reported an improvement of 35 per cent over the course of the programme. Importantly for workers, this workshop also reported an increase in salaries as a direct result of the improvements in productivity. Salaries in the workshop increased by 32 per cent.

This example highlights the interconnectedness of company performance from an economic perspective as well as from a social perspective. Increasingly, it is being seen that the environmental perspective must and can be addressed at the same time as the other pillars of sustainable development. As was demonstrated by the FIP, cleaner production that focuses on improving energy efficiency and reducing waste can often be a relatively easy entry point for companies to start addressing some of the environmental challenges that they are confronted with.

## Case 4: Improved financial, social and environmental performance

Viet A Power is a medium-sized enterprise employing approximately 150 workers. Established in 2001, the factory produces electric steel poles and control panels predominantly for domestic consumption in Vietnam, largely for the national electric company.

In terms of physical design, the factory plant had an iron roof and was lit by 80 lamps, the primary use of electric power in the factory. Despite the high number of lamps, the lighting was still inadequate for workers to properly see what they were doing. At the same time, the electricity costs for the lamps were extremely high.

As a result of the FIP, Viet A replaced sections of its roof with transparent composite materials allowing the entry of natural sunlight. This not only led to a better working environment for workers but also resulted in an 80 per cent decrease of electricity costs for the company, predominantly due to the fact that the electric lamps had to be used for only a few hours per day.

## Lessons learned

The cases above highlight some of the results that can be achieved through collaborative models of engagement in which workers are involved and seen as core to the implementation process. Increasingly this approach is being adopted when it comes to addressing voluntary CSR issues.

At the same time, it must be acknowledged that it can be challenging to obtain the buy-in of factory management, particularly during times of economic crisis such as the 2008–10 financial crisis. This is the typical challenge faced by companies all over the world that are accountable to shareholders on a short-term basis. It is a challenge that is amplified in the case of SMEs, which typically have less capital to invest in undertaking necessary changes, and one that the ILO has explicitly acknowledged and attempted to address in its programmes.

The ILO's integrated approach to addressing social and environmental issues, whether under the banner of the Factory Improvement Programme[19] or the FIP-based modular training programme of the ILO's Better Factories Cambodia project, has been under implementation in Asia since 2002. Focused mainly on export sectors, often in factories located in export processing zones, this approach seeks to develop the capacity of local service providers and ILO constituents to support their ILO country programme objectives. In the course of these last 8 years a number of lessons have been learned, lessons which point the direction for such work in the future.

First, it is clear that there is a strong and positive relationship between good labour and environmental practices as well as workplace relations and competitiveness issues centred on quality and productivity. A central tenet of the ILO's work on integrated enterprise-focused programmes has been that those closest to the point of production are best suited to understanding how to improve a particular operation. This is not revolutionary – rather it is the basis of much of what has taken place in terms of quality control and the TQM movement over the last 50 years. It is, however, something that has often been overlooked by management in rapidly expanding export sectors. Yet this point has important implications for working conditions, workplace relations, communications and problem-solving in these sectors. For example, with workers in a crucial position for implementing continuous improvement, the most effective approach is to value such workers, involve them in organizational improvement efforts, gain their commitment and ensure their development. The ILO and others concerned with both labour and environmental practices should continue efforts to demonstrate environment-labour-competitiveness linkages to sometimes doubtful managers and their supervisors, who often believe that only with a firm hand can their workforces be pushed to increase output and quality.

Related to this last point, that of direct linkages between each of these areas, it is clear from implementation of FIP and its results at the enterprise level that this integrated approach works. Based on the ILO's assessment of results, over 50 per cent of the factories taking part witnessed major changes in operations, with over 20 per cent going through a process that could be termed 'transformative'. External reviews have found similar and often dramatic results. In factories participating in such programmes, relations were improved, health and safety was clearly much better, the productivity and quality often saw dramatic improvements, workers' wages were higher, and in general the factories were in a much stronger position to participate in the global economy – and create needed jobs.[20]

This success can be credited to a number of factors, the first one being related to enterprise-level capacity-building. The combination of training and in-factory assistance provides enterprises with a process of handholding needed to implement what are often seen as uncertain changes to operations. Other factors that can be seen as supporting the success of FIP and related programmes include: the institutional support given to continuous improvement by the establishment of a factory-level improvement team chaired by a person determined to implement change and with the power to support decisions; and the presence of some external pressure, typically a client who demands higher performance in terms of both bottom-line issues (quality/price) and compliance with labour or environmental standards.

Of course, not all factories have made great progress through participation in these programmes, and not all partner institutions were well suited to providing this sort of integrated support. The ILO has found that selection of factories, local counterparts, service providers and experts to take part in the programme is a primary driver of results, both good and bad. Factories of varying levels have taken part, including some that were quite well managed at the start of a programme and others that were in extremely poor shape. Across the spectrum, in small operations and large, factories have made good progress, but only when top management at the factory was committed to change and supportive of the FIP intervention. Similarly with service providers, when they were committed to implementing the ILO's approach, with an eye toward developing their service offering rather than just benefiting from support payments under ILO projects, then they were much better suited to run the programme successfully. As this integrated approach is increasingly accepted, consideration of local counterparts, their capacity and the role they will play in project implementation requires attention.

Related to the last point, of institutional sustainability of an integrated programme, linking labour and environment issues to competitiveness practices with direct support to enterprises has been and will continue to be a challenge. Such sustainability depends on creating the capacity of local institutions to provide services on a cost-recovery basis while managing the operation of the overall programme. In turn, it requires that the services provided by the local institutions are seen by enterprises in the business community as worth the cost of their participation, in terms of time, money and commitment. To date, none of the ILO programmes based on the FIP model have achieved this level of sustainability at the institutional level in terms of the full programme. This is not to say that some level of sustainability has not been achieved. This integrated approach to enterprise improvement has expanded internally at the ILO, most notably in the modular training component of the large Better Work programme of the ILO and the International Finance Corporation. In India, the Ministry of Micro, Small and Medium Enterprises has built its lean manufacturing programme based largely on the work the ILO did under FIP in Faridabad, and will hopefully reach tens of thousands of workers and hundreds of factories. With wide coverage of the approach, its reach has hopefully included a change in understanding of factory-level improvement that will benefit a wide variety of consultants, institutions and eventually the factory floors of Asia.

## Looking ahead

All of this said, neither the integrated approach promoted by the ILO, nor the capacity-building model focused on enterprises as advocated by some researchers, provides a solution for all problems. While there is a clear linkage between good relations, and working together, and competitiveness, the linkage is less clear with respect to core labour rights, including freedom of association and the right to collective bargaining.

In many of the export-oriented sectors of the developing world producing for developed world markets, there is little or no trade union
presence. While this is sometimes due to the nature of the sectors –
which are sometimes quite informal – it is also frequently due to hidden
and in some cases explicit hostility towards workers' unions. In such
an environment, the respect for such rights cannot be addressed solely
at the factory level but requires a much more systemic and regulatory
approach.

Export processing zones are of particular concern. The ILO has
worked with a variety of factories that operate under special export
rules, sometimes within a delineated physical space (the zone itself)
and other times under special rules, if not explicitly under the law,
then implicitly by the way the law is applied. When the export
processing zones are located within physical areas, trade union
organizers are typically denied access, making organization that
much more difficult. At the same time, the government may provide
guidelines for operation in the zone that vary from national law,
making organizing difficult. This again is something that cannot be
addressed in a direct factory-level programme like FIP and requires
a regulatory approach, one that can, of course, be implemented in
conjunction with FIP.

These earlier points have had a common theme, the need to complement any factory-level programme based on voluntary action
with the strengthening of the regulatory environment and its ability to support labour standards. Voluntary initiatives, whether implemented under CSR programmes, compliance standards like SA8000,
multinational compliance programmes, or national-level compliance
programmes, are not a replacement for the effective implementation
of a coherent set of labour laws, backed up by a credible system of
enforcement with involvement of tripartite institutions. Without
this regulatory framework, there will always be factories that benefit
from abusive labour and environmental practices, whose management believe they can save money or make greater profits by illegal
treatment of staff or dangerous operations. For such operations the
business case is not the answer; it may, in fact, argue for the abuse of
workers, the employment of children in dangerous conditions, or the
lack of support for workers' rights. In such cases we can see that the
need for well-developed labour and environmental regulation, with
the regulatory apparatus to support it, will be with us for some time
to come.

# Notes

1. UNRISD 'Voluntary Approaches to Corporate Responsibility: Readings and a Resource Guide' (Geneva: NGLS, 2002). (NOT FOUND IN TEXT)
2. N Klein, *No Logo* (New York: Picador, 2002).
3. J Bebbington, C Larrinaga and JM Moneva, 'Corporate Social Reporting and Reputational Risk Management', *Accounting, Auditing and Accountancy Journal*, vol. 21, issue 3 (2008), p. 337.
4. S Waddock, C Bodwell and S Graves, 'Responsibility: the New Business Imperative', *Academy of Management Executive*, vol. 16, no. 2 (2002), pp. 132–48; D. Vogel, *The Market for Virtue: the Potential and Limits of Corporate Social Responsibility*, (Washington D.C.: Brookings Institution Press, 2005).
5. A Carroll and KM Shabana, 'The Business Case for Corporate Social Responsibility: A Review of Concepts, Research and Practice', *International Journal of Management Reviews*, vol. 12, issue 1 (2010), p. 85.
6. Mamic, 'Managing Global Supply Chain: The Sports Footwear, Apparel and Retail Sectors', *Journal of Business Ethics*, vol. 59, no. 1/2 (2005), pp. 81–100.
7. R Welford and S Frost, 'Corporate social responsibility in Asian supply chains', *Corporate Social Responsibility and Environmental Management*, July 2006, vol. 13, issue 3 (2006), p. 166; H Jenkins, 'Small Business Champions for Corporate Social Responsibility', *Journal of Business Ethics*, vol. 67, no. 3 (2006), pp. 241–56.
8. P Sethi and O. Williams, *Economic Imperatives and Ethical Values in Global Business: The South African Experience and International Codes Today* (Boston: Kluwer Academic Publishers, 2000).
9. I Mamic, *Implementing Codes of Conduct: How Businesses Manage Social Performance in Global Supply Chains* (Geneva: Greenleaf/ILO, 2004).
10. P Utting, 'Rethinking Business Regulation: From Self-Regulation to Social Control', UNRISD Programme Paper TBS-15, October 2005.
11. http://news.bbc.co.uk/2/hi/programmes/panorama/970385.stm, accessed on November 6, 2010.
12. R Locke, M Amengual and A Mangla, 'Virtue out of Necessity?: Compliance, Commitment and the Improvement of Labour Conditions in Global Supply Chains', MIT Sloan Working Paper No. 4719–08 (Cambridge: MIT, 2009); D O'Rourke, 'Smoke from a Hired Gun: A Critique of Nike's Labour and Environmental Auditing in Vietnam as Performed by Ernst & Young,' report published by the Transnational Resource and Action Centre: San Francisco, 10 November 1997, at www.corpwatch.org/trac/nike/ernst/
13. S Frost, 'Comparative Overview of CSR in Asia: Issues and Challenges', ADBI conference paper (2007) at http://www.adbi.org/conf-seminar-papers/2007/10/24/2374.csr/
14. C Chambers, W Chapple, J Moon and M Sullivan, CSR in Asia: *A seven country study of CSR website reporting* (Nottingham, UK: International Centre for Corporate Social Responsibility, 2005).
15. R Locke, 'Rethinking Compliance: Improving Working Conditions in Global Supply Chains'. *Perspectives on Work*, vol. 13, no. 1, Summer (2009), pp. 3–5.

16.  I Mamic, *Implementing Codes of Conduct: How Businesses Manage Social Performance in Global Supply Chains* (Geneva: Greenleaf/ILO, 2004).
17.  C Bodwell, 'Factory Improvement Report: Final Report of the Chief Technical Advisor' (2007), unpublished.
18.  The full details of the case studies referred to here can be found in the ILO's Final Report on the FIP Pilot Programme in Vietnam published in 2005.
19.  ILO, 'Factory Improvement Programme: Final Report Pilot Programme in Vietnam' (2005).
20.  See, for example, the joint ILO / US Department of Labour assessment of the initial Sri Lanka FIP implementation (http://www.ilofip.org/Documents/LMPDevalreport.pdf). This independent evaluation indicated that 'participation in the project had led to changes in workplace communication and labour-management dialogue, reductions in labour turnover, absenteeism, quality defects, average cost/minute and increased levels of productivity.' Similar results were found following FIP implementations in Vietnam and India.

# 7
# Social Partnership Industrial Relations in PT Hero Supermarket, Indonesia

*Magdalene M. Kong*

## Introduction

Economic globalization has brought intensified challenges, increased competition and rapid changes in the way companies, and in particular large multinational corporations (MNCs), do business. Correspondingly, this has a tremendous impact on the global labour market and on how workers work. At the same time, this is matched with a brewing global consciousness of the need to address the mounting pressures and the effects of a global economy. On the one hand, market deregulation and capital mobility have weakened the bargaining power of workers, and on the other hand the rise of international civil society movements has created new social forces assisting general labour movements.[1] One such result of this new social movement unionism is the campaign on Corporate Social Responsibility (CSR). This movement calls for a social scrutiny of corporate powers to fill the governance gaps left by governmental retreat from international issues of corporate responsibility in defence of weaker members in the international economy, such as women, children and workers in developing countries.[2] Integral to the ongoing civil society movements to protect workers' rights is the increasing participation of developing countries.

CSR first came into public discourse in the global South when some MNCs adopted Codes of Conduct on social responsibility in their host countries. As part of the adherence to these Codes of Conduct, local firms are called to report on their companies' contribution to the local community, including labour-related issues. Despite these trends, the policies and practices on codes of good conduct and CSR have largely been confined to MNCs in Europe and North America. As such, critical scholars and union activists have remained sceptical about the partnership approach and CSR campaigns.[3] They argue that CSR is no more than another public relations ploy targeted at customers in the global North rather than a genuine interest in protecting workers in the South.

Indeed, a range of CSR programmes have been undertaken by various MNCs, and many such initiatives have been subject to harsh public scrutiny concerning their real and hidden motives. In addition, many of the CSR initiatives across Europe and North America are more often related to issues other than labour market issues (for instance, environmental issues and philanthropic activities). Given the bleak picture of the context, content and actual results of Corporate Social Responsibility, this paper attempts to draw positive experiences and lessons from the case study of PT Hero Supermarket in Indonesia to elucidate the approach of social partnership industrial relations in the practice of CSR. Although this is a single case study, this model of partnership industrial relations, arguably the most fundamental component of the debate on CSR, has now influenced some other retailers in the country to emulate the practice and approach to labour-management relations. There is, therefore, a glimmer of optimism for the future of CSR in Asia.

## Corporate social responsibility in Asia

Social movement unionism and its CSR campaign are usually associated with local forms of mobilization. This type of labour movement goes beyond the usual tool of 'going on strike' to develop community coalitions and grassroots worker mobilization. It frames the issues in term of social justice rather than material interests of workers alone.[4] As a core discourse of social movement unionism, CSR emphasizes the participation of respective stakeholders in regulating corporation's activities. From the normative view, a corporation is not just an economic entity but also a social actor. Besides making profits and obeying market principles, following social norms and respecting community's interests are also key criteria for business activities (Archie, 1999).[5] From the pragmatic view of government leaders, the engagement of civil society in checking corporate power has been supported by many governments in developed countries and international agencies such as World Bank (WB) and International Monetary Fund (IMF). Self-restraint by corporations and initiatives to regulate corporations from civil society groups could thereby help relieve government's burden, compatible with the trends of cutting public spending, minimal governments and neoliberal economic policies.[6]

While the majority of CSR programmes take place in more developed economies, the subject of most CSR policy debates has been over labour and workers in developing countries. Yet, CSR has not yet been in the centre of the agenda of Asian trade unions or the general public. The absence of local stakeholders' participation and public awareness has resulted in a pessimistic picture of the application of CSR in Asian countries. Labour issues, if acknowledged, are often restricted to basic employment criteria – non-discrimination and equal opportunities – and many companies do not commit to guaranteeing freedom of associations and promoting workers' education.

In developing Asia, there is also an absence of the powerful consumer lobbies that have prompted the rise of CSR initiatives in the West. Industrialization and economic growth policies in developing countries still rely on cheap, submissive and obedient workers.[7] A case study in Indonesia revealed that business leaders believed improving working conditions according to CSR practices was only suitable for rich countries.[8] Existing literature has not made any study on the participation of labour groups in the construction of CSR discourse in Asia. This lacuna may tentatively hypothesize the absence of a strong civil movement to raise public awareness about labour-related CSR in the region.

Across Asia, the practice of CSR varies according to either economic or civic development. Within the same industry, the practice of CSR is more common and companies tend to commit to their codes of conduct (COCs) more often in the developed countries of Asia, including Japan, South Korea and Hong Kong. CSR is not a common practice in developing Southeast Asian countries. There are, however, the exceptions of Singapore and India, which arguably demonstrate that the level of economic development alone is not a sufficient condition for better practice of CSR. Singapore ranks low in term of fair wages and working time in Welford's survey and does not have close partnerships between corporations and civil groups.[9] On the contrary, corporations in India are recognized to comply better with CSR principles in term of reporting labour practices, initiating COCs and maintaining partnerships with labour and civil groups.[10] Arguably, India has a more vibrant civil society and has a strong commitment to freedom of labour association in comparison with other Asian countries at the same level of economic development, and with Singapore, which is richer but whose civil society is under tighter political control. This confirms the theoretical conception of CSR as the result of social partnership embedded in civil society networks.

In terms of sectors, CSR is most widespread in the garment, footwear and toy manufacturing industries. This is mainly due to the fact that these sectors have received more public attention in the global North, and a number of international civil groups campaign on behalf of workers in developing countries, many of whom are in Asia.[11] The rarity of CSR policies in other sectors does not mean that working conditions are not problematic. In Asia, the agriculture and the services sectors employ the largest working population. However, it is also in these sectors that workers are most invisible to international CSR campaigns, as products of the service sector are usually consumed at the local market.

The underdevelopment of CSR practice in Asia is an outcome of Asian production structures and the general nature of global movements on CSR. Developing economies in Asia are mainly engaged in low value-added manufacturing activities. As Asian economies compete for Foreign Direct Investment (FDI), the fluid mobility of capital puts companies in a better bargaining position than trade unions and governments, with the powerful threat of simply closing down their factories and moving elsewhere.[12] Furthermore, enforcement depends on the ability of corporations to discipline the labour practice of their contractors. Most factories in Asian developing countries are second-tier contractors, and the distant relationships between corporate headquarters and their contractor factories makes it more difficult for corporations to monitor the practices of their contractors.[13]

A main reason for this distanced relationship, and also a critical problem of CSR in Asia, is the lack of Asian stakeholders' participation in the CSR global movements. The practice and effectiveness of CSR in Asia largely depend on the support and campaigns of civil movements in Western developed countries. This leads to a related problem: sectors that are visible to international public and receive international advocacy have more CSR policies and CSR applications than less visible sectors. There are few spillover effects from CSR practice into the Asian economies as a whole. CSR is not tailored to local needs, and many workers in other industries do not benefit from CSR movements.[14] Another problem resulting from the lack of Asian participation is the scepticism of Asian workers and civil groups about the potential benefits of CSR.

In spite of these current limitations, CSR is still a potential tool for labour movements in Asia. First, most codes of conduct include the clauses on ILO Conventions and the UN Global Compact, which recognize the association rights of workers, as their benchmarks. Workers can use these Codes to demand collective bargaining with their employers. Second, the availability of numerous CSR frameworks ratified by MNCs means that local stakeholders can require the applications of these international initiatives in local markets. This requires the efforts of CSR activists to raise local public awareness about these CSR policies and to campaign for their application. Most importantly, the non-conflictual approach of CSR movements can be a useful means to facilitate the development of new unionism in post-democratized Asian societies. In these societies, the lack of sociopolitical mechanisms to mediate industrial relations hurts not only business interests but also the short-term and long-term welfare of workers. The case of Indonesia, analysed below, is an example of this problem.

A common weakness of both Western practitioners and researchers is their top-down perspective when they approach labour problems in Asian countries. They tend to assess the nature of CSR in Asia from the starting point of large CSR campaigns in the West. A result of this view is their picture of CSR practice in Asia as doomed. Not only is there a gap between initiating CSR (in developed countries) and CSR implementation (in Asian developing countries) but there is also little prospect of closing that gap. As aforementioned, the complexity of production networks restrains the communication between CSR initiators and implementers. Nevertheless, the case study below will demonstrate that complexity is not necessarily a disadvantage of the CSR movement. The understanding of how CSR can contribute to labour movements in Asia requires a more bottom-up-oriented approach. Thus, the case study of Indonesia's Hero Supermarket aims at introducing a different view, accumulated from the field experience of Asian practitioners.

## Brief background on Indonesia and the labour movement: trade unionism in a weak civil society

Indonesia shares many features with other Asian countries in the area of labour politics. The developmental authoritarian state before 1997 left a legacy of fragmented unionism.[15] At the same time, the priority on fast growth and policies to attract foreign investment has made workers' rights underrepresented, if not marginalized. Although the democratization process following the fall of Suharto's regime in 1997 (Reformasi) opened the social space for the development of trade unionism in Indonesia, the legacy of Suharto's regime still cast a shadow over the functioning of labour movements in particular and of civil society in general. After experiencing three decades of political suppression, the organizational capacity of Indonesian labour unionism was weak and highly fragmented. The disperse membership and the extremely large numbers of trade unions diminished the authority and bargaining strength of unions.[16] Though civil society has vigorously developed, its horizontal linkages to the state and the business society have not yet completely opened. The government welcomed the non-governmental sector and encouraged community initiatives to improve the community's capacity to solve their own problems, but is sceptical about the 'ultra democracy' of civil society. On the other hand, civil groups, and especially labour, are also suspicious of the state. While the post-Suharto government continued to prevent the politicization of labour movements, labour groups themselves guarded against being a tool for political and electoral manipulation.[17]

Due to the fragmentation of labour movements and the lack of trust in society, social partnerships looked impossible in Indonesia. Thus, despite support from international donors, existing institutions for social dialogues did not function well. Tripartite cooperation was ad hoc and often broke down, because compromises between labour and management were few and far between, and the government found difficulties in being an effective mediator. The absence of effective mechanisms for social dialogues and conflict resolution mechanism resulted in a high rate of industrial disputes in Indonesia (see Table 7.1).

As such, labour's interests are also hurt by uncompromising labour movements and stalemates between workers and employers. Fundamentally, labour movements aim at not only short-term material interests for workers but also institutionalizing their negotiations with employers. Organizational guarantees ensure the representations of labour interests in business decision-making. Only by reaching stable institutional arrangements can workers and employers avoid risks in the future.[18] Furthermore, compromise and self-restraint from both workers

*Table 7.1*   Data on strike demands nationwide 2000–5

|  | 2000 | 2001 | 2002 | 2003 | 2004 | 2005 |
|---|---|---|---|---|---|---|
| Number of strikes | 273 | 194 | 220 | 161 | 125 | 96 |
| Normative demands | 176 | 142 | 120 | 112 | 80 | – |
| Other demands | 376 | 300 | 312 | 290 | 255 | 184 |

*Source*: Unpublished data from the General Director of Industrial Relations and Labour Insurance, The Ministry of Manpower, Jakarta[19]

and employers are the prerequisites for the construction of negotiation institutions. The state also plays a key role in taming industrial conflicts and coordinating the institutionalization of industrial negotiations.[20] Thus, without a conflict resolution mechanism, Indonesian labour movements could hardly achieve fruitful outcomes.

## Case study of PT Hero supermarket: social partnership industrial relations as an approach to CSR in PT Hero supermarket

The development of the social partnership model analysed here presents a different picture of CSR practice in Asia. The practice of CSR in Hero Supermarket, Indonesia is truly 'local product' in the sense that it is self-sustained by the nurturing of social partnership between an international firm and local stakeholders, rather than relying on top-down pressure from Northern customers or the supervision of the firm's headquarters. Yet, this does not mean that the making of social partnership in Hero Supermarket is separated from the global social movement of unionism. Indeed, the involvement of UNI Global Union – Asia and Pacific (UNI Apro), a global trade union – has been a key bridge-builder in the relationship between the union and the management of Hero Supermarket, thereby demonstrating how international networks of civil groups can empower local stakeholders. The success of the social partnership model in Hero Supermarket and its impacts on the emerging tripartite in Indonesia is also an interesting case of how the bottom-up social partnerships approach can initiate changes within a local social system. Hero, one of the subsidiaries belonging to the pan-Asian retailer group Dairy Farm International,[21] is the third largest employer in the retail sector and the oldest supermarket chain in Indonesia. Problems at Hero Supermarket (Hero) prior to 2003 were typical examples of the lack of effective dialogue and conflict resolution mechanism in industrial relations.

Following the start of Indonesia's Reformasi, Hero employees formed a union in 1997. One year later, the union was affiliated to ASPEK, a federation union in the services sector affiliated to UNI Global Union (UNI). After the Asian financial crisis of 1997, employment relations in Hero were especially strained. A large number of employees were laid off as a result of the crisis, while others barely survived, with real income diminished dramatically due to an 80 per cent inflation rate. As a response to the harsh economic realities, trade unions, including the Hero union, frequently organized strikes or mass demonstrations outside Hero's head office. The management saw workers' strikes as immediate threats to their business and repeatedly abused or verbally intimidated the workers. In response, workers would stop customers from entering the stores. Hero's management and the union tried to settle their conflicts, but negotiations were trapped in 'traditional' tit-for-tat disputes. Moreover, the Hero union was poorly prepared for such communications. The union did not have a clear agenda and took an uncompromising approach, with negotiations ending in a deadlock.

The build-up of past failed negotiations, coupled with the 2002–3 SARS pandemic, brought the labour-management relationship to an all-time low. Through the Hero Union's affiliation to Aspek Indonesia, this matter was brought to the urgent attention of UNI Apro to call for solidarity support and mediation. The request for intervention by UNI Apro was not an easy or short-term process, given the socio-economic-political-historical context of post-regime Indonesia. In addition to the need to advocate the rights of workers, it was also crucial to turn the deadlock in Hero's industrial relations full circle and to institutionalize a long-term, sustainable and meaningful labour-management relationship that would benefit all stakeholders of the company. This was the basis of the UNI Apro approach to social partnership, wherein both corporate and union are empowered with their respective rights and their social responsibilities.

The adoption of the CSR approach in building social partnership comprised three phases:

## 1. Mediation through participation of regional union and management networks

Tapping into the regional and global network of UNI, a meeting was set up between the then Chief Operations Officer (COO), Ian McLallan, the National Secretary of Shopping, Distribution and Allied Employees Union (SDA) Australia and Joseph de Bruyn President of UNI Apro. This was due to the trade union work of SDA being familiar to Ian McLallan. In response to the Hero union's request, UNI Apro decided the right course of action was to have a discussion between the COO of Hero and the UNI Apro President.

Following that, the Regional Secretary of UNI Apro, Christopher Ng, communicated the mediation process to the holding company, Dairy Farm International, and met up with the Head of Human Resources, Chan Kah Fai, from the South Asian headquarters based in Singapore. With the strong support of the then Regional Director of Dairy Farm, Michael Kok,[22] this helped in institutionalizing a mechanism to improve management-union relations at Hero.

## 2. Changing organizational behaviours

Despite the mounting pressures and disputes confronting the company, both the HERO union and management, and in particular the human resource department, agreed that an amicable settlement had to be reached. For this to happen, both parties agreed that representatives of the union and the human resource department would participate in a week-long, outward bound, team-building training workshop organized in cooperation with UNI Apro. This neutral platform for gathering of the labour-management was part of the strategy to improve communication and build mutual understanding within the company. Through such interactions, the union was able to appreciate the difficulties and limits faced by management on a day-to-day basis, as well as the conditions on how union requests are processed and accommodated. Meanwhile, management realized the importance of breaking the vicious cycle of resisting the union, and gravitated to empathizing and looking into creative ways to accommodate the workers' requests. This training workshop marked the milestone for open and honest communication within the organization.

> This was the initiative that arose out of the discussions between Michael Kok, Chan Kah Fai and Christopher Ng. They felt that this would be an avenue for everyone to gather together to think of a resolution. This has proved to be very successful.
>
> (Noertjahja Nugraha, former Director of Human Resource at Hero)

The union started to pick up techniques and skills on how to conduct itself during negotiations in order to have a fruitful discussion with the management. Instead of simply making demands at the boardroom, the union now prepares data and facts. On the other hand, the management reciprocated by providing union leaders with information to reveal the realities of the operation of the business and the company's plan, thereby involving the union in the execution of its organizational strategies. These candid and honest dialogues gave the union and workers an enhanced understanding of the company that they belonged to and also instilled a deep sense of responsibility towards their work and organization. As mentioned by the General Chairman of Hero Union:

> The current situation in Hero is that fluid communication and deliberations between the union and the management is conducted

before making certain company decisions. Not only has relationships improved at the general level, interpersonal relations among individuals in the company has also improved substantially. Employees, middle and top management employees no longer feel segregated but instead are now much more open to casual conversations at the shop floor.

(Rusdi Salam, General Chairman, Hero Supermarket Union)

The effectiveness of the CSR social partnership approach shown in this case was seen when all parties transformed their respective behaviours. The organization built a new sense of common purpose and aligned all business actions to this purpose. After 10 years of ups and down in their relations, Hero union and management started to enjoy a cordial working relationship. The union trusted management's way of handling the matter and was patient for policy changes, understanding that the company policies took time to be implemented, especially when a public listed company such as Hero is also responsible to its shareholders. The union's strategies became more flexible and constructive. Instead of being concerned with only their immediate interests, Hero employees engaged in sharing responsibility and addressing the business challenges faced by the organization, attempting to achieve a 'win-win' solution. Therefore, from a game of 'equivalent retaliation', management-union relations at Hero transformed into 'reciprocal cooperation'. Two prominent examples of this reciprocal cooperation were the increase in wages, the staff allowance in 2008 and the recent efforts to deal with the shrinkage problem.

As mentioned, a key demand of Hero employees was an increase in wages matching the high rate of inflation. The union proposed an increment of 12 per cent to their wages, which was pegged to the company's performance and took into account the inflation rate. Management's position was to ensure that Hero's business was viable in the long run. Hence, despite agreeing that employees' wages would be raised, they could not promise the 12 per cent increment, because Hero had only just made a profit after many years of struggling and Hero shareholders would not accept this proposal. Eventually, Hero's management and union agreed to a compromise. Wage increment would be done on a proportionate basis. The lowest-wage worker would enjoy the full 12 per cent increment, and the percentage increase in wage would decrease for workers earning higher wages. In total, the package paid out by the company would add up to no more than 8 per cent.

The pay-offs from wage bargaining depend on the degree of patience that a player has. A more patient player can sustain negotiations longer into the game and gain more of the available rewards.[23] Many studies from labour movements in developed countries have shown that drastic action, such as a strike, makes firms very impatient, and hence they lose bargaining power if the strike is widespread. In contrast, poverty among workers can make them impatient to go back to work and not achieve desirable bargaining outcomes.[24] Players are patient only when they commit to negotiation more than any other means of bargaining, that is, strikes, and they see the credibility of the other players.

The partnership model thus ensured commitment and credibility in the bargaining between Hero's management and the union, so that both sides could achieve agreeable outcomes. Over the long term, Hero workers requested that their salaries increased at least to match the pace of the continuous rise in consumer prices. In this situation, the union adopted a gradual method. It explained the difficulties to Hero management and asked for an increase of the meal allowance from Rp4,000 to Rp5,000. It kept following the deliberations on wage increases until 2008. By early July 2008, after a twofold increase in profit for the second quarter, Hero management decided to double the staff discounts from 5 per cent to 10 per cent. Moreover, all employees were rewarded with a week's bonus for their contribution to Hero's growth. Management also expanded the staff religious holiday discount budget from 1.5 million to 3 million rupiah and from 3 million to 6 million rupiah. All these measures were indirect measures of wage increments to help workers cushion themselves from the impact of economic inflation in the country. Due to this bargaining, Hero management were able to maintain harmonious relations with their employees, and at the same time boosted employee morale.

In return for the management's responsiveness to employee demands, the Hero union cooperated with the management in solving the shrinkage problem. Shrinkage is the most serious problem facing the retail industry in Indonesia.[25] The Hero union signed a Memorandum of Understanding with the management to further their commitment in dealing with this issue. The union persuaded its members not to engage in unethical practices, and actively cooperated with the Loss Prevention Division to investigate cases in which employees were found stealing or manipulating company data. The union's cooperation helped Hero to reduce the shrinkage in seven out of eight targeted supermarkets.

It should be noted that, during this course of changes, UNI Apro kept an important supporting role. Although UNI Apro had stepped back from the bridge-building role to allow the organization's industrial relations to grow between the partners, it was still a supportive mediator, ready to assist when problems arose.

### 3. Anchoring CSR through partnership approach

In order to have harmonious employment relations, employees and employers need to institutionalize their bargaining mechanism so that cooperation rather than confrontation is sustainable in the long run. Institutionalization is reflected in two mutually reinforcing aspects of behaviours. Certain behavioural patterns constitute the organization's norms and values. These norms give meanings for behaviours and shape the objectives of the organization. At the same time, the organization also needs some concrete, tangible adjustments in its structure and needs formal rules to discipline actors' behaviours. Changes in Hero's employment relations have been in the process of being institutionalized in these aspects.

The commitment of Hero's top management to sustain the employment partnership is elucidated through their efforts to construct Hero's new organizational culture of communication. In particular, the CEO of Hero Supermarket, John Callaghan, has been especially enthusiastic in building up the communication culture, preferring an open-door, face-to-face interaction with the management team and inculcating the organizational culture into management trainees. In the area of formal structure, Hero formed the Labour Management Corporation (LMC) to bridge the trade union and management in 2008. The LMC helps ensure the continuity of dialogues and the representation of labour interests in business decision-making.

## Lessons for CSR in Asia

When emerging from the social movement of unionism and the rise of international civil society, CSR can offer a new approach to the transformation of employment relations. Rather than using the traditional tactic of confrontational class positions, this model offers an alternative for unions and employers to engage in dialogues and work out win-win solutions. However, dialogues are fruitful only when union and employer consider each other as equal respected partners. Partnership requires employment relations to be embedded in supportive networks of civic relations, so that employees and employers are bound by trust and mutual responsibilities.

The practice of CSR is still in its infant stage in Asia but promises a new way for the development of unionism. The current limitation is due to the fact that most CSR movements originate in the global North, with little involvement of Southern stakeholders. The case of social partnership at Hero supermarket and its contribution to the development of the Indonesian sectoral tripartite shows that local unions and civil groups can adopt a CSR approach to engage in cooperative relationships with employers and the state in the interests of labour and society.

The success of Hero's partnership model has several implications for the international social movement of unionism:

First, it demonstrates how the transnational labour networks can benefit local actors. Hero's partnership is a 'local product', but the making of that final product involves the participation, at least in the initial stages, of the transnational network in which the Hero union and management are located. The involvement of UNI Apro and its connections to other international stakeholders prove this point. Support mobilized from multiple levels of this network empowers local labour in bargaining with the management. It should also be noted that the existing international network does not necessarily generate international support or international awareness of the issue.

One lesson from the Hero experience for trade unionism in Asia is the importance of coalition-building between multiple stakeholder groups at a national and international level. Not only do these coalitions bring material support and resources to the labour unions and other social movement groups involved; they are also aimed at strengthening the collective legitimacy of such coalitions, as well as creating greater propensities in mobilizing public support. As such, they have had to open up to new organizing strategies and varied constituencies and recognize the benefits of material and symbolic gains.[26]

Second, the project at Hero and its impacts on the ongoing improvement of Indonesian labour relations give an example of using a CSR approach to solve industrial disputes. Starting from the grass roots level, the behaviours of employees and employers improved, and they have now become agents of change within the Indonesian labour system. Although it will take time to see whether this is a powerful enough agent for new labour industrial relations to emerge, there are positive signs of a different conception of labour positions in Indonesia. At least, trade union members in APSEK have been recognized as partners of the state and employees in various sectoral social dialogue forums, such as the recent formation of the Indonesian Sectoral Tripartite Body for Commerce and Telecom sectors.

At the 2009 signing of the Concluded Collective Bargaining agreement (CBA), the ceremony was attended by the then Minister of Manpower and Transmigration, Dr Ir Erman Suparno, as an endorsement and recognition of the contributions of the union-management to the Indonesian economy and society. This deep-seated recognition went as far as the naming of a union community in Jakarta, comprising the streets 'Jalan Hero Union', 'Jalan UNI Global' and 'Jalan SDA'.

Using the case study of Hero Supermarket, this paper has attempted to illustrate that a CSR approach via social partnership industrial relations can be a model for companies and communities to emulate. The partnership between employers and employees can facilitate the development of a more meaningful trade unionism in the Asian context. The role of the state should not be ignored. Social changes are sustainable when the state recognizes the social partners and acknowledges that they have a formal position within the political decision-making process. The introduction of a partnership model here is just one view that constructive social activism can assist in the functioning of the state. Where the state has not yet been an active mediator and social memories of suppression and unrest are strong, the role of external genuine social actors in assisting with trust-building efforts is desirable and necessary for the creation of an eventual tripartite institution.

## Notes

1. M Hanagan, 'Labour Internationalism: An Introduction', *Social Science History*, vol. 4, no. 27 (2003), pp. 485–499.
2. U Beck, *Risk society: Towards a new modernity* (London: Sage, 1992).
3. R Braun and J Gearhart, 'Who Should Code Your Conduct? Trade Union and NGO Differences in the Fight for Workers' Rights,' *Development in Practice*, vol. 1–2, no. 14 (2004), pp.183–196.
4. S Lopez, *Reorganizing the Rust Belt: An Inside Study of the American Labour Movement* (Berkeley: University of California Press, 2004).
5. Archie B. Carroll, "Corporate Social Responsibility Evolution of a Definitional Construct" *Business Society*, September 1999, vol. 38 no. 3, pp. 268-295.
6. J Sayer, 'Confrontation, cooperation and cooptation: NGO advocacy and corporations', in B Rugendyke (ed.), *NGOs as advocates for development in a globalizing world* (New York: Routledge, 2007).
7. M Prieto-Carrón, P Lund-Thomsen, A Chan, A Muro and C Bhushan., 'Critical perspective on CSR and development: what we know, what we don't know and what we need to know', *International Affairs*, vol. 5, no. 82 (2006), pp. 977–987.
8. M Kemp, *Corporate social responsibility in Indonesia: Quixotic dream or confident expectation* (Geneva: United Nations Research Institute for Social Development, 2001).

9. W Chapple and J Moon, 'Corporate social responsibility in Asia', *Business and Society*, vol. 4, no. 44 (2005), pp. 415–441.
10. W Chapple and J Moon, 'Corporate social responsibility in Asia', *Business and Society*, vol. 4, no. 44 (2005), pp. 415–441.
11. D Vogue, *The market for virtue: the potential and limits of corporate social responsibility* (Washington DC: Brookings Institute Press, 2005).
12. M Kemp, *Corporate social responsibility in Indonesia: Quixotic dream or confident expectation* (Geneva: United Nations Research Institute for Social Development, 2001).
13. S Barrientos, 'Mapping codes through the value chain: from researcher to detective', in R Jenkins, R Pearson and G Seyfang (eds), *Corporate responsibility and labour rights. Codes of conduct in the global economy* (Sterling, VA: Earthscan Publications, 2002).
14. R Lipschutz, 'Sweating it out: NGO campaigns and trade union empowerment', *Development in practice*, vol. 14, nos.1–2 (2004), pp. 197–210.
15. J Benson and Y Zhu, *Trade unions in Asia: an economic and sociological analysis* (London: Routledge, 2008).
16. B Kelly, *Promoting Democracy and Peace through Social Dialogue: A Study of the Social Dialogue Institutions and Processes in Indonesia* (Geneva: International Labour Organisation, 2002).
17. M Ford, 'Economic unionism and labour's poor performance in Indonesia 1999 and 2004's elections', in M Baird, R Cooper and M Westcott (eds), *Reworking work* (Sydney: Association of Industrial Relations Academics of Australia and New Zealand, 2005).
18. P Buchanan, *State, capital and labour* (Pittsburgh: University of Pittsburgh Press, 1996).
19. H Juliawan, 'Extracting labour from its owner: Private employment agencies and labour market flexibility in Indonesia', *Critical Asian Studies*, vol. 1, no. 42 (2010), pp. 25–52.
20. A Przeworski and M Wallerstein, 'Structural Dependence of the State on Capital', *American Political Science Review*, vol. 83, no.1 (1988), pp. 11–29.
21. At 31 December 2009, the Group and its associates operated over 5,000 outlets, employed over 76,000 people in the region and had total annual sales exceeding US$8 billion. The Group operates supermarkets, hypermarkets, health and beauty stores, convenience stores, home furnishings stores and restaurants under well-known local brands. Dairy Farm International Holdings Limited is incorporated in Bermuda and has its primary share listing in London, with secondary listings in Bermuda and Singapore. The Group's businesses are managed from Hong Kong by Dairy Farm Management Services Limited through its regional offices. Dairy Farm is a member of the Jardine Matheson Group (http://www.dairyfarmgroup.com/global/enquiry.php (accessed 17 March 2010).
22. Michael Kok has since then been appointed as the Group Chief Executive of Dairy Farm (http://www.dairyfarmgroup.com/people/committee.htm (accessed 17 March 2010).
23. A Muthoo, 'A Non-Technical Introduction to Bargaining Theory', *World Economic Journal*, April (2000), pp. 145–166.
24. M Wallerstein, 'Wage-Setting Institutions and Pay Inequality in Advanced Industrial Societies', *American Journal of Political Science*, vol. 43, no. 3 (1999), pp. 649–680.

25. Shrinkage refers to the loss of products between point of manufacture or purchase from supplier and point of sale.
26. J Stillerman, 'Transnational Activist Networks and the Emergence of labour Internationalism in the NAFTA Countries', *Social Science History*, vol. 27, no. 4 (2003), pp. 577–601.

# 8
## Consumers and CSR in Asia: Making Sustainability Easy for Consumers: The New Opportunity for Corporate and Societal Innovation

*Cheryl D. Hicks and Fiona Hovenden*

It is in the interest of businesses to protect their future by helping customers to adopt sustainable lifestyles and behaviour. To do this, businesses need to make sustainable products and services easy to buy and affordable, and without compromise on performance. They also need to take a full life-cycle approach on product design, production, use and through end of life, but also to leverage the power of consumers by applying a deep understanding of how people think and what motivates different people to act.

The growth of national GDPs and the consumer classes in Asia presents a unique opportunity to positively impact global consumption patterns by demonstrating new models of success in sustainable living and by encouraging corporate innovation that improves people's lives as well as society.

This chapter will review recent findings in consumer trends, behaviour shifts and sustainable lifestyles and will make the case for the opportunities for Asian companies in understanding the critical links between CSR, sustainability and triggers to behaviour change. We will draw on the recent work on sustainable consumption and sustainable lifestyles from The World Business Council for Sustainable Development (WBCSD) and approaches to linking the knowledge of sustainability and consumer behaviour as the new opportunity in corporate and societal innovation from social innovation groups, Collective Invention and The Idea Factory.

## The role of consumers in addressing global challenges

Consumers have tremendous power to address global challenges and to influence the social responsibility of corporations. The daily actions and lifestyles of consumers and citizens are seen as a key driver in addressing the development needs of billions of people around the world and to enabling radically more eco-efficient solutions.[1]

There is new thinking globally about the importance of addressing the rising demands for global resources and lifestyle choices that are currently having profound impact on global consumption patterns. In past decades the focus for CSR and sustainable development solutions has been to address the issues of resource supply, conservation and adaptation, as well as the sourcing and production methods of companies. We have seen a shift in recent years to a recognition that exists amongst leading global companies, who have said that:

> ... efficiency gains and technological advances will not be sufficient to bring global consumption to a sustainable level; changes will also be required to consumer lifestyles, including the ways in which consumers choose and use products and services. There is a need for business to play a leadership role in fostering more sustainable levels and patterns of consumption through current business processes such as innovation, marketing and communications and by working in partnership with consumers, governments and stakeholders to define and achieve more sustainable lifestyles.[2]

The Worldwide Fund for Nature (WWF) suggests that we, the consumer, are a major part of the problem. 'Demand for resources now exceeds the planet's capacity to replenish its "natural capital" by about 30%. If global consumption continues at the same rate, by the mid-2030s we will need the equivalent of two planets to maintain our lifestyles.'[3]

## The product life cycle and the consumer use phase

The findings of manufacturing companies have revealed that consumers can also be a large part of the solution. They have found that the way in which consumers choose, use and dispose of products is just as important as how a product is sourced, manufactured or transported. In

order for managers to understand where the most significant improvements can be made, or where consumers can help to address current
demand for resources, there must first be a deep understanding of the
full life cycle of products and the sustainability impacts and opportunities for improvement at each stage.

A clear example is that of the companies making laundry detergents.
As illustrated in the Figure 8.1, the life-cycle assessments revealed that
the consumer use phase of the product life cycle of laundry detergent
was by far the most energy use intensive, due to the fact that, historically, laundry detergents required hot water to achieve superior performance in the washing of clothes.

The importance of the use phase of the product life cycle tends to
apply in particular to products that require significant energy inputs
during the use phase, such as cars (via fuel) and dishwashing detergents (via hot water), as well as light bulbs and electronics (via electricity). Services and communications also have significant impacts during
the use phase. For example, when end use of its products is taken into
account, the information technology industry could be said to account
for 2 per cent of global carbon emissions.[4]

Deeper understanding of the impacts and opportunities along
the full product life cycle helps companies to innovate the process and achieve significant improvements. In the case of the

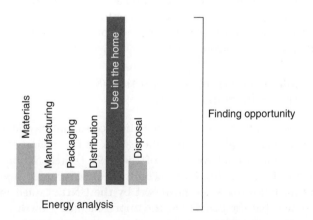

*Figure 8.1*    Company product energy usage from life cycle perspective

*Source*: http://www.pg.com/en_US/images/content/sustainability/sustainability_img finding
oppurtunity.gif accessed November 4, 2010.

laundry detergent, sustainability and the key issue of reducing energy consumption drove innovation to develop active ingredients that allow clothes to be washed in cold-water temperatures, while maintaining superior washing quality. This innovation, washing at cold temperatures, has proved to be a significant improvement in the environmental impact of this product and other 'like' products such as dishwashing detergents.

In order for this innovation to be optimized, the consumer must first choose that product over others and the consumer must also remember to set the washing machine to a low temperature.

Recent findings in consumer behaviour trends show consistently that the majority of consumers will not change their behaviour for the environment alone. They will change their behaviour when they see an immediate benefit for themselves, their families or their community – and they will not compromise on quality, price or convenience. In the case of laundry, consumers chose the laundry detergent that washed clothes in cold water and remembered to set the dials of their washing machines to cold temperatures because it also saved them money on their water heating bills and did not compromise on the cleaning performance of the clothes.

There are business opportunities in the efficiencies gained and sustainability impacts minimized by having a deeper understanding of product life cycles, but also in having a deeper understanding of the motivators, influencers and triggers that bring about change in human behaviour. Companies around the world see this as the next phase of business intelligence. Understanding how to make sustainable living and choices easier for people will be the area of opportunity for successful companies in the next decades.

## Sustainable production, consumption (SCP) and demand side management

The business case for sustainable production, consumption and demand side management in global corporations took its first major step in the CSR movement around the time of the 1992 United Nations Earth Summit in Rio de Janeiro, Brazil. The issue of SCP gained significant momentum following a special report by the UNDP, issued in 1998, which stated that the benefits of the unprecedented growth in global consumption in the twentieth century had been badly distributed, leaving a backlog of shortfalls and gaping inequalities, particularly in terms of the strains on the environment and on the poor.[5]

Sustainable Consumption and Production (SCP) is an attempt to reconcile the increased demand for goods and services that respond to basic needs and bring a better quality of life, while minimizing the use of natural resources, toxic materials and emissions of waste and pollutants over the life cycle, in order not to jeopardize the needs of future generations. Materials, Water and Energy are the three key elements.

Sustainable Production concerns the supply side, focusing on the economic, social and environmental impacts of production processes. Sustainable Consumption addresses the demand side, focusing on consumers' behaviour, their choices and their use of goods and services.

In Asia, major challenges also concern the region's increasing energy consumption leading to rising greenhouse gas emissions. Increased adoption of SCP can lead to improved energy efficiency in the life cycle of our products, preventing climate change.[6]

In the last two decades, many companies have been able to reduce the impacts of their operations by employing eco-efficiency mechanisms and applying life-cycle management techniques to products.[7] Companies have seen tangible cost savings in doing so, and therefore have found that sustainable production approaches also make good business sense.

Today, there is increased importance on linking production with consumption – the way in which products and services are selected and used – to address current unsustainable consumption patterns revealed in population growth estimates for the next decades. The population and the consuming global middle class are expected to double by 2030, with most growth in current emerging economies such as those in Asia.[8]

From a business perspective, sustainable consumption is a meaningful concept only in the broader context of a sustainable marketplace and relies on three things: the development of sustainable products, processes and business models; the use of marketing communications and other means to enable and encourage consumers to choose and use products more efficiently; and the removal of unsustainable products and services from the marketplace (such as joint initiatives with retailers and authorities). These three concepts can be called 'sustainable innovation', 'choice influencing' and 'choice editing'.

## The business case

In 2008 the WBCSD articulated the business case for sustainable consumption. Their report, *Sustainable Consumption Facts & Trends: From*

*a business perspective,*[9] signalled a shift in the nature of companies'
approach to the sustainable consumption agenda from the introduction of niche products and services to the embedding of sustainability principles into the core business model. The report articulates that
business can play an important role in fostering sustainable consumption by delivering sustainable value to society and consumers, helping
consumers to choose and use their goods and services sustainably and
promoting sustainable lifestyles that help to reduce overall consumption of materials and resources.

The WBCSD report grouped business action on sustainable consumption into three main categories of business opportunity:

- INNOVATION – Business processes for the development of new
  and improved products, services and business models are shifting
  to incorporate provisions for delivering maximum societal value at
  minimum environmental cost.
- CHOICE INFLUENCING – The use of marketing communications
  and awareness-raising campaigns to enable and encourage consumers to choose and use products more efficiently and sustainably. From
  a business perspective, choice influencing refers to a partnership
  between business and the consumer, which extends from sustainable production and design of products through to their selection,
  use and disposal.

'In order for technological innovations to succeed, companies are
often required to spot opportunities at an early stage and to implement effective marketing strategies. Even then, it can take a considerable amount of time for mainstream consumers to adopt new
technologies. Toyota says that this was the case with hybrid cars,
which enjoyed widespread consumer uptake approximately a full
decade after the introduction of the technology. Other industries
share similar stories. The challenge ahead then is to narrow the gap
between innovation and consumer demand.'[10]

- CHOICE EDITING – The removal of 'unsustainable' products, product
  components and services from the marketplace in partnership with
  other actors in society. Choice editing refers to the decisions that
  directly control the impacts of consumption. Consumer groups and
  policymakers tend to prefer choice editing as an effective approach
  to changing consumer behaviour and achieving goals to have only
  the most sustainable products available in the market. Businesses

edit choice by controlling elements of their supply chain or by eliminating product components that pose a risk to the environment or human health.

## The case for deeper links between CSR, sustainability and behaviour

Recent work with global companies on approaches to address current unsustainable consumption patterns has shown that product design, life-cycle and consumer communication strategies have not been enough to realize the large-scale societal shifts that will achieve sustainability. This chapter makes the case that this is because we are just starting to understand the critical links between what we know about our natural behavioural habits and what we need to achieve environmental sustainability. This will be a vast opportunity space for businesses in the future.

Richard Thaler and Cass Sunstein describe in their recent book, *Nudge*, that 'everyday we make decisions on topics ranging from personal investments to schools for our children to the meals we eat to the causes we champion. Unfortunately, we often choose poorly. The reason is that being human we all are susceptible to various biases that can lead us to blunder. Our mistakes make us poorer, less healthy, (and have a negative impact on the planet). By knowing how people think, we can design choice environments that make it easier for people to choose what is best for themselves their families and their society. Thoughtful choice architecture can be established to nudge us in beneficial directions without restricting freedom of choice.'[11]

In many companies there is a current disconnect between those working on CSR and sustainability and those looking at behaviour – such as consumer behaviour trends and marketing. Marketing departments are seldom asked to give input on the sustainability of a product or a CSR strategy and the CSR department rarely gets asked to give input into a marketing or brand campaign.

Most CSR and sustainability professionals approach sustainability from an environmental engineering or related skill set. The engineer, similarly to the economist, applies the principles of science and mathematics to develop economical solutions to technical problems,[12] whereas most marketers approach the consumer with a social science approach of anticipating the needs and wants of consumers and then providing a solution that satisfies them.[13]

It has been found that managers are just now realizing that anticipating the needs and wants of consumers can drive CSR and sustainability and that complementary sustainability can drive innovation. Participation in the global dialogue on SCP with global governments via the United Nations Environment Programme revealed a similar phenomenon: in other words, the people discussing SCP in governments come from sustainable environmental departments or ministries and not from consumer affairs.

As a result, sustainably designed products, which have been created efficiently in the production process and designed for optimal efficiency in their use phase, are often being left on store shelves or not being used by the end consumer in the proper manner. At the policy level, some environmental policies have had unintended negative consequences because human behaviour was not considered in the development of the policy.

People prefer products and services that improve their lives. There is an urgent need for products and services that make sustainability easy and transparent for the consumer, hyper-efficient through collaboration and innovation in value chains and resilient by applying understanding of human behaviour motivations and triggers.

However, people are also diverse, with differing needs, motivations and triggers. The global population will not change behaviour or lifestyles homogeneously. Influencing change requires a deep, or particular, understanding of human behaviours and cultural legacies. People will react differently to the lifestyle changes needed to enable living well within one planet for all: some people will naturally connect with messages about sustainability and maybe even become leaders or advocates; others might reject any suggestions that require inconvenient or undesirable changes to their current lifestyles. Some will not see how changes benefit their life or the lives of those in their immediate community and will therefore feel excluded from the change needed.

Leading companies are now realizing that anticipating the needs and wants of consumers is also important to CSR and sustainability, and therefore an area for new business opportunity. Applying a deeper understanding of human behavior to sustainability could be the missing link to unlocking consumer, and citizen power to help us achieve sustainable development.

## What we know about behaviour change and findings for triggering sustainable lifestyles

### Understanding needs and motivations

Immediate information about what consumers are currently buying is important but does not tell us enough about why people buy and what would help them to change their consumption habits. Therefore we need to understand what products and services mean to people and what needs they fulfil. This information may act as a design blueprint, helping us – consumers, citizens, businesses – to work together to develop more sustainable ways to fulfil those needs.

In a preliminary research project conducted by Collective Invention last year, talking to consumers from across the globe about their lives generally and then about sustainability, we identified four key areas of motivation:

a. The desire to build a better world and leave a legacy of improvement for the future; ability to delay gratification (Legacy Builders)
b. The desire to protect and conserve, maintaining the best of the past, protecting it for the immediate community (Stewards);
c. The desire to maximize pleasure and personal gratification above all else and to accept no compromise (Pleasure Seekers);
d. The desire to be taken care of and to avoid decisions or choices (Escapists)

Understanding different types of consumers may help corporations design products and services that better address consumers' growing concerns. Adding knowledge of sustainability in this process creates a new opportunity for business to drive product and process innovation and to advance broader societal innovation.

## What sustainability means to consumers

The concept of sustainability and related ideas of sustainable living and a sustainable future also show slight nuances of interpretation around the world.

For Asian, European and American interviewees in our study, sustainability meant some variation of 'Living with minimal impact on the earth'. This included things like minimizing the use of non-renewable resources, thinking about purchases in terms of whether they were really needed, how they would be disposed of and recycling.

The Asian interviewees also included nuances of economic sustainability. Some talked about economic sustainability first and the importance of the viability of national economic development, for example. This is also part of the message that businesses bring to the debate about sustainability – without an economically viable sustainable future, the possibilities for living well, within the resources of one planet, are remote. *[Sustainability means] maintaining stuff. Like buying a house: you can't just think of what you pay for the house, you have to think of renovations ... the hidden costs (Female, Asian, 20s).*

Another benefit of discussing the economic aspects of sustainability is that it allows more people into the global debate. Many of our interviewees had a sense that sustainability is some kind of specialized endeavour. Much of the popular debate around sustainability focuses on the science, for example of climate change, and on technology, such as what kinds of technologies can we invent to get ourselves out of this? However, it is also true that sustainability is about the ways in which people live their lives. Because science is a fairly exclusive practice throughout the world, any impression that sustainability is a specialized science-based discipline risks increasing people's sense of alienation from it and of decreasing their sense of agency.

## Change

We are also, increasingly, beginning to understand the process of change – the ways in which individuals change and the ways in which groups change. One of the great contributions of the psychotherapeutic disciplines in the latter half of the twentieth century has been the understanding that individuals develop an internal logic about the ways in which the world works, based upon early taught values, life events and information from the external world. The latter particularly tends to be filtered through the system of values. Understanding this logic allows us to avoid the inevitable surprise that no one acts like a so-called 'rational agent' all the time and in all situations. But, when the internal logic is understood, actions and choices make sense and can be addressed in terms of the needs they fulfil.

We can extrapolate this to the ways in which groups change in the following ways:

(a)  Taught values = cultural norms
(b)  Life events = national or cultural group history
(c)  Information from the external world

Change, for individuals and groups, often occurs when significant trauma undermines and demands a reformation of the value system. For change to occur without that, several key things have to happen.

### Initiating change

Changes proposed have to fill the individual's needs. Therefore, if a consumer currently has a certain kind of lifestyle focused on pleasure and feelings of success, new products and services will only be adopted if they at least maintain and ideally enhance pleasure. A drop in performance or perceived status will not be accepted.

Old behaviours need to be unlearned. If a new product or service is clearly better than the old one and fulfils the same need, then the unlearning of old behaviours is less of an issue. This is why driving a hybrid will be easier for most Western consumers than beginning to bicycle, or taking public transport. However, where new behaviours are needed – such as attending virtual meetings rather than face-to-face meetings, for example – they work best when phased in, so that new behaviours are learned in a non-critical way and old behaviours gradually reduced.

Unknown changes need space. If behaviour change is needed but the new options are not yet clear, or if they cannot dovetail gradually with old behaviours, then people need to make space for change. This requires a difficult transition, since old behaviours tend to be very persistent, and suggests why things like retreats, conferences and vacations are helpful in initiating changes.

*Maintaining change*

Positive reinforcement or feedback is critical. This allows people to keep connecting change to things that are important to them.

One change at a time: Recent research has also suggested that individuals trying to make changes that are not obviously more pleasurable than the previous options should not try to make more than one kind of change at a time.

*Triggers for behaviour change*

Many recent reports on consumer buying patterns show that when it comes to buying 'green' products the majority of people fall into the category of not likely to buy 'green' or respond to messaging about sustainability.

To understand why there has not been global consumer demand for sustainable products, we can look back to the varying needs and motivations identified by each segment.

- People with a strong desire to build a better world and leave a legacy for the future (Legacy Builders) will always or almost always buy green because they have the ability to delay gratification in favour of 'big picture' goals such as those of sustainability.
- People with a strong desire to protect and conserve (Stewards & Nurturers) will regularly buy green because they are committed to sustainability, the environment and better lives for their communities and families. However, Stewards will make trade-offs; for example, if they don't find a

sustainable option they will settle for a less sustainable one rather than trying harder. Nurturers' purchases are more likely to be affected by access and by price because their values, while similar to those of the Stewards, are more impacted by context and perception. This refers to the finding that Nurturers often have a lower level of agency and therefore will be less ambitious in 'making' sustainable happen.

- People with a strong need to be taken care of and to avoid decisions or choices have (Escapists) have no active interest in buying green and will only do so if it is the default option. This is because Escapists do not see the 'big picture' and do not see the immediate benefits of buying green for themselves, their families and community.
- People with a strong desire to maximize pleasure and personal gratification (Pleasure Seekers) cut across most populations, which suggests that the importance of instant gratification is a dominant attribute of most people – they may regularly buy 'green' by shopping in 'Whole Foods', or buying locally produced organic, artisan-produced goods, but only because these things bring pleasure and cachet and not because they are green.

This example illustrates how a deeper understanding of the needs, motivations, influencers and triggers of people can help companies inform innovation processes to make sustainability, sustainable product choice and sustainable living easier for people and, in turn, better for societies.

## Conclusion

### Opportunity for Asia – innovation that links CSR, sustainability and human behaviour triggers

The Idea Factory (TIF) in Singapore has a long history of working with Asian businesses on innovation. It says that, with some exceptions, Asian businesses' approach to innovation tends to follow that of Western businesses. 'Asian businesses often wait to see the innovations that are most successful in western or multinational companies and then apply the learnings to their business context.'[14] TIF says that the same is generally true for Asian businesses in their approaches to CSR and sustainability.

It is in the interest of Asian businesses to protect their future by helping customers to adopt sustainable lifestyles and behaviour. The findings from Western businesses and multinationals are indicating that the success of businesses in the future hinges on making sustainability easy for consumers and by applying a deep understanding of human behaviour, motivators and triggers as the new opportunity for corporate and societal innovation.

## Notes

1. WBCSD, *Vision 2050: The new agenda for business* (2010).
2. WBCSD, *Sustainable Consumption Facts & Trends: From a business perspective* (2010).
3. WWF, *Living Planet Report* (2008).
4. WBCSD, *Sustainable Consumption Facts & Trends*.
5. UNDP, *Human Development Report: Special Report on Sustainable Consumption* (1998).
6. SWITCH Asia: http://www.switch-asia.eu/ accessed July 2, 2010.
7. WBCSD, *Sustainable Consumption & Production from a business perspective* (1997).
8. WWF, *Living Planet Report* (2008).
9. WBCSD, *Sustainable Consumption Facts & Trends: From a business perspective* (2008).
10. WBCSD, *Sustainable Consumption Facts & Trends* (2008).
11. R Thaler and C Sunstein, *Nudge: Improving Decisions About Health, Wealth and Happiness* (2008) Yale University Press; 1st edition (April 8, 2008).
12. http://www.bls.gov/oco/ocos027.htm, accessed March 8, 2010.
13. http://en.wikipedia.org/wiki/Marketing
14. Interview with Nicholas Lee, The Idea Factory Singapore, March 2010.

# 9
# Responsible Tourism in Asia
*Rod Allan A. de Lara and Arno Thöny*

## Development of responsible tourism and social responsibility

One could say that modern tourism in Asia rose from the ashes of wars. This adds both colour and controversy to its history. Although war is bad for tourism, it did in fact advance the production of aircraft, which led to the development of modern commercial airplanes that would later be used to transport millions of tourists all over the world. In fact, the first modern passenger aircraft, the Boeing 247, was developed from a modified bomber plane that was customized from among the huge surplus of planes that were left at the end of the First World War. The advent of modern passenger aircraft marked the dawn of commercial aviation and subsequently tourism.

In Asia, the development of tourism was not spontaneous and smooth. In the early days, tourism was dominated by military personnel who used the Philippines, Thailand, Hong Kong and other Southeast Asian countries for R&R (Rest and Recreation), giving rise to sex tourism, which flourished during and after the Second World War. This trend continued during the Korean and Vietnam Wars, where R&R camps set up by soldiers recuperating from the front lines created commercial spots for exploitative tourism-related activities to thrive (Truong, Thanh-Dam, 1990).[1]

This gave tourism a repressive image that would later trigger xenophobia among Asian populations and ideological conflicts between the East and West.

## Growth trends

Until the 1980s, tourists from Europe and America dominated the global travel market, but in recent years tourist arrivals in the Asia-Pacific region have been steadily increasing at an astonishing rate of 13 per cent per annum; double the global average of 6.5[2] per cent, and slowly eating into the market share of Europe (see Figure 9.1).

East Asia and the Pacific are expected to receive a sizeable portion of the global travel market by 2020 with 397 million tourists. Together with the Middle East and Africa, East Asia is forecast to grow at a record rate of over 5 per cent per year, compared with the world average of 4.1 per cent[3] (see Table 9.1).

## Tourism in Asia

In many Asian countries, the expansion and growing significance of tourism as an economic contributor has caused it to compete with other industry sectors and influence national development policies. Today, the tourism sector is a key driver for social and economic growth and a major source of income for low-income countries, such as Cambodia, Vietnam and Laos, and virtually all lower-middle-income countries, such as Thailand, India, China, the Philippines and Indonesia. In Southeast Asia alone, tourism is estimated to employ 4.2 per cent of the population and contributes 11 per cent of the region's GDP[4] (see Table 9.2).

The economies of several areas in Asia, particularly Bali, Phuket, Pattaya, Chang Rai, Chang Mai, Penang, Melakka, Cebu, Hongkong, Macau and Singapore, flourished because of tourism, transforming their economies from agriculture-based to tourism-based. With rising

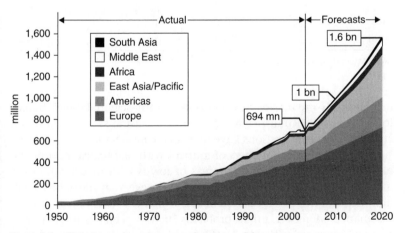

*Figure 9.1*   Global travel market growth rates and forecasts
© UNTWO, 9284401010

*Table 9.1*   Global travel market growth rates and forecasts

|  | 2009 | Forecast 2010 |
| --- | --- | --- |
| World | −4% | 3% to 4% |
| Europe | −6% | 1% to 3% |
| Asia and the Pacific | −2% | 5% to 7% |
| Americas | −5% | 2% to 4% |
| Africa | +5% | 4% to 7% |
| Middle East | −6% | 5% to 9% |

© UNTWO, 9284401010

*Table 9.2*   Asian tourism economic size and employment

| Travel and tourism income % of GDP 2009 | | Travel and tourism employment % of population | |
| --- | --- | --- | --- |
| Country | % | Country | % |
| Indonesia | 7.8 | Indonesia | 3.0 |
| Thailand | 14.7 | Thailand | 6.2 |
| Malaysia | 12.3 | Malaysia | 4.5 |
| Philippines | 8.7 | Philippines | 4.2 |
| Vietnam | 13.1 | Vietnam | 5.8 |
| Singapore | 7.3 | Singapore | 3.9 |
| Cambodia | 17.5 | Cambodia | 7.5 |
| Brunei Darussalam | 11.5 | Brunei Darussalam | 5.9 |
| Burma | 6.5 | Burma | 2.7 |
| Laos | 10.8 | Laos | 3.3 |
| **Total** | **11.0** | **Total** | **4.2** |

*Source*: WTTC (2009)

income levels and increasing urbanization, intra-regional travels in Asia to less developed countries with significant natural sceneries and rich cultural heritage attractions have increased considerably.

The influx of large numbers of tourists, with high-consumption and high-waste habits, into natural areas or towns with inadequate waste management infrastructure has disrupted the everyday life of host communities and destroyed ecosystems on which residents relied for their sustenance. Moreover, urban problems such as overcrowding, congestion and increased vehicular traffic in cultural and heritage-rich towns and cities like Georgetown, Melaka and Intramuros Manila have caused tremendous damage to many historical monuments and exposed these structures to the destructive elements of pollution, thereby reducing the visual appeal and structural integrity of these historic buildings. Thus, the pressure of managing the problem of large tourist numbers in historic cities with fragile built environments is becoming a pressing concern. Although the state of tourism as a pillar of economic development differs among Asian countries, there is a general consent on its importance for national development.

## Sustainability of tourism development

In the early stages of tourism, the social and economic effects were not fully understood or even visible. As a result, discourse on sustainability and social responsibility did not emerge until the 1990s, when the negative impacts from tourism became apparent. At that time, it was almost impossible to ignore or even dispel the dangers of tourism. A surge of social and economic reform soon followed, beginning with the Rio (Earth) Summit in 1992 that provided international policy guidelines for sustainable development, otherwise known as 'Agenda 21'.

Since the Rio Declaration in 1992, many sovereign states remain committed to working towards international agreements on adopting development systems that recognize the indivisible relationship between the economy and its surrounding social and ecological environment. But the approach to which sustainable development is achieved, or even interpreted, varies across regions and cultures worldwide, despite the existence of international conventions that prescribe a broad set of policy guidelines to attain sustainability. While the rationale of sustainability is universally accepted, the concept of a universal strategy for sustainability is generally rejected, particularly in Asian societies, who view these international standards as primarily developed for and by Western interests. Moreover, these global policy guidelines have also been thought of and criticized as capitalist and modernist in thinking, which does not suit the prevailing communist/socialist and conservative ideologies of many Asian societies. For this reason, many Asian policymakers are less inclined to rely on these established social and environmental standards. The same resistance is seen with regard to the concept of Corporate Social Responsibility (CSR), which was initially perceived as a novel Western concept. Although this is no longer true, as CSR continues to gain global acceptance, the challenge of defining it within the context of a particular social system remains a complex task.

This is even more complicated in culturally and economically diverse regions such as Asia.

CSR and Sustainable Tourism share a common narrative: both evolved as a response to the inequities and damage of contemporary development approaches. They practically evolved at the same time and confronted similar issues with respect to gaining global recognition.

The movement for Sustainable Tourism was formalized in 1996 with the ratification of the UNWTO's *Agenda 21 for the Travel and Tourism Industry*, which contained policy prescriptions similar to the *Rio Declaration* in 1992. The UNWTO's Agenda 21 gave rise to new 'Alternative Forms' of tourism, such as Green Tourism, Ecotourism, Special Interest Tourism, Quality Tourism and Alternative Tourism, which at that time was dominated by mass tourism.

Although early practices of sustainable tourism centred on protecting the environment, making it easily distinguishable from CSR, the recent incorporation of the social and community aspects of growth into the grand scheme of tourism development practically made it synonymous with CSR. More importantly, the expansion of the concept of sustainable tourism gave rise to a new generation of development strategies founded on the management of tourism's triple bottom line – economic, social and ecological goals – whose central goal is not to increase the size or capacity of the tourism sector but rather to equitably distribute the benefits of tourism. These offshoot strategies include community-based tourism, pro-poor tourism and responsible tourism.

## Developing responsible tourism

With the growth of tourism in Southeast Asia, the need to be aware of the dynamics of tourism, the development process and the consequential impact on the region and its people has become more apparent. In Asia, however, many governments have been so preoccupied with wrestling to establish political control and stability in government that there was little room to address the socio-economic and environmental problems of the country.

The concept of social responsibility is not new to Asia; it is a fundamental part of the Asian culture to contribute a portion of one's wealth to society. The extent to which social and environmental issues emerged, however, differs greatly from the concerns that had to be addressed before the economic boom of the past four decades, in which the tourism industry has played an ever greater economic role and hence has been a contributor to sustainable growth.

To address some of those 'modern' social and environmental issues, Asia was looking towards the European Model of CSR: a movement that began in the 1990s, as a way to advocate awareness of the way a business manages its impact towards the society within which it operates and its stakeholders (EU Commission on CSR, 2007).[5] In that context, tourism development was strongly influenced by global players in the travel trade with a focus on a primary global and regional strategy. As antiglobalization movements emerged in the 90s, the phrase 'think global, act local' slowly shifted attention towards the local community and stakeholders. Focusing on the local content of operation led to CSR activities that had earlier been embraced by other industries.

Responsible tourism is a collection of organizationally driven development strategies that incorporate global ethics in tourism and sound management practices to bring about positive social, economic and environmental change for all its stakeholders. For tourism operators, it means offering tourists rewarding holiday experiences while improving the quality of life for residents of host communities, conserving the natural environment and protecting the social and cultural heritage of tourist destinations.

## The Asian dilemma of governance

Ethics are the foundations of Responsible Tourism. Although these concepts are regarded as a 'Universal Good', there have been attempts in recent years to reject 'global ethics' on the ground that many of the values espoused therein are held by Western countries but are not shared by Asians.[6] On the contrary, many also believe that these conflicts are not as profound and threatening as often portrayed by many Asian governments, who incidentally define and pronounce these so-called Asian values in the first place. For this reason, Western scholars often denounce these Asian values as fictional, biased, politically engendered and exploited by Asian governments in order to perpetuate themselves in power or improve their bargaining leverage with Westerners. Sometimes tourism is used by governments as a propaganda tool to instil national ideals and convey subliminal messages consistent with the ideologies of ruling political parties.

The economic miracle of the Newly Industrialized Economies (NIEs) of Taiwan (R.O.C.), Hong Kong (R.O.C.), Singapore and South Korea, plus China, Japan and India, legitimized Asian political and social systems, which are often described as authoritarian and having long-standing

traditions of respect for family and social structures. Of course, authoritarianism is less profound in the governments of Japan, India and South Korea, but the inclusion of China in the list of emerging economies, not to mention its growing influence in Asia and the world, overshadows liberal democracy as an alternative system of public governance in Asia. In summary, the dominant political ideologies in Asian countries assert a strong influence on its tourism development policies, as well as in defining 'social contracts' among the stakeholders of tourism. In turn, these established social contracts will have direct implications for tourism management practices.

## Confucianism and implications for tourism management

Although Asia does not have a single coherent set of values, Confucianism has long been recognized by the West as the ethos of value systems of Asians, particularly that of the 'Far East'. This is partly based on three reasons: first, because Confucian philosophy has never been part of mainstream Western dogma; second, because of the Chinese Diaspora and the economic success of Chinese immigrants throughout the region; and, third, the widespread influence in Asia of Buddhism, Taoism and Animism, which are closely associated with Confucianism. But, more importantly, the precepts of CSR and Responsible Tourism are intrinsic to Confucian traditions and perfectly conform to its basic tenets, namely Goodwill, Protocol, Filial Piety, Balance and Harmony as illustrated in Table 9.3. Furthermore, CSR and responsible tourism enhance the spirit of Confucianism by translating its philosophical beliefs into practical management techniques.[7]

## Social and moral imperatives of CSR and responsible tourism

Immanuel Kant's moral philosophy describes humans as more than just physiological and sociopolitical beings driven by physiological and social self-preservation, but also as moral beings with predispositions to do what is morally good (and naturally avoid evil). Kant also argues that humans do not aspire to live solely on a moral pedestal, for all human dispositions are innately good, whether or not these instincts are driven by selfish motives or humans' animalistic nature. Of course, it is equally essential that the attainment of these selfish desires conform to universal moral principles.

*Table 9.3* Comparative principles of leading fields of thought

| | Comparative principle | |
|---|---|---|
| **Confucian philosophy** | **Corporate Social Responsibility** | **Responsible tourism development / Management practices** |
| Goodwill/Humanity | Philanthropy<br>Supporting outreach programmes<br>Sponsoring social development projects<br>Making social and economic contributions to the general public<br>Caring for public health, safety, environmental issues, and other concerns related to the general welfare of the public | Promoting mutual understanding and respect between people and societies, with an attitude of tolerance and respect for diversity of religious, moral and philosophical beliefs<br>Advocating pro-poor tourism development strategies<br>Tourism as a vehicle for individual and collective fulfilment |
| Protocol (Rules of proper conduct) | Respect for national/ international standards, conventions and guidelines<br>Adhering to laws and regulations, and to formal and informal rules on fair competition<br>Following corporate governance and code of corporate ethics<br>Respect for social structures, social systems and norms of communication | Broad community consultation and participation of residents and community leaders in tourism planning and development<br>Featuring authentic, aesthetic and unique rituals and other traditional practices<br>Respect for tourists' symbolic gestures and greetings, such as using appropriate greetings, protocols on seating arrangements, gift-giving practices and negotiation etiquettes when welcoming guests<br>Establishing a code of practice consistent with local culture and values<br>Respect for social and cultural diversity |

Continued

*Table 9.3* Continued

| | Comparative principle | |
| --- | --- | --- |
| Confucian philosophy | Corporate Social Responsibility | Responsible tourism development / Management practices |
| Filial piety / Loyalty | Advocating social responsibilities towards employees; and, in turn, fairly demanding that employees perform their duties and responsibilities towards the company/ organization<br>Cultivating a culture of righteousness and moral duty and responsibility<br>Fostering a culture of mutual loyalty and respect among people within the organization | Respecting traditional family values and practices, as experienced in homestays and other culture and nature-based tourism<br>Observing the principle of devolution and decentralization of authority to the lowest level |
| Balance | Taking precautionary approach to social and environmental challenges<br>Adopting a 'Triple Bottom' approach to performance evaluation, that is, Social, Ecological and Social Objectives | Equal emphasis on the social, ecological and economic development aspects of tourism<br>Setting guidelines for tourism assessment, monitoring impacts and limits of acceptable changes in the social, ecological and economic environment<br>Promoting social, cultural and ecological conservation/protection and preservation through ecotourism and other rural tourism products<br>Endorsing alternative forms of tourism<br>Maintaining biodiversity |

Continued

*Table 9.3* Continued

| Confucian philosophy | Comparative principle | |
|---|---|---|
| | Corporate Social Responsibility | Responsible tourism development / Management practices |
| Harmony | Promoting multi-stakeholder initiatives<br>Creating synergistic outcomes through open and honest communication and well-intentioned goals that serve the interest of all stakeholders<br>Acknowledging social responsibilities towards competitors and markets<br>Advocating diversity management practices | Attaining mutually beneficial alliance between tourists, host communities and the environment<br>Respecting and understanding social, cultural and religious diversity<br>Managing tourists and host community's expectations and experiences |

The propensity of humans for malevolence is not justified by their animalistic nature and sociopolitical desires alone but by the order of priority in which human beings place these needs (to the detriment of moral laws) for the purposes of achieving their individual and social goals.[8] In other words, selfish motives driven by economic, social or political interests are not negative *per se*, as long as they are achieved within the parameters of moral laws or prescribed social values and norms. In view of these arguments, it holds that humans and their institutions are inclined and voluntarily bound by moral duties that serve the interest of the common good. Hence, CSR is intrinsically rooted in the social and moral imperatives of humans and human organizations, which also means that compliance to 'do the right thing' is instinctive and second nature to all humans and human institutions.

On the contrary, malevolent acts that deviate from social norms do occur; but, from a normative perspective, many sociologists believe that these problematic acts are not always voluntary but determined by factors, such as sociopolitical environments, that compel an individual to deviate from established rules. It follows that, given the choice, individuals would normally choose to adhere to social norms rather than to deviate from them. Thus, it can be said that the 'free choice' of individuals and organizations not 'to do the right thing' or to purposely adopt unethical business practices is caused by weak sociopolitical systems that fail to advocate universal principles of human rights (*a universal good*) and to promote the general welfare of society.

The same reasoning applies when explaining many of the failures and inequities of tourism, and why tourists and tourism operators alike are more likely to commit amoral activities by breaching established codes of conduct in places where laws are lacking or are weakly enforced. Fortunately, these systemic failures can be addressed with proper policy interventions, legislative support and law enforcement.

## Challenges of CSR and responsible tourism in Asia

At the outset, CSR was misconstrued as primarily philanthropy-focused, involving donation drives for photo opportunities with a clear intention to seize publicity. Slowly, this perception is changing due to the inescapable and undeniable problems confronting societies today that are visibly caused by people's collective choices and actions towards development.

Most visible and much talked about are environmental concerns over the destruction of natural habitats on land and in the sea. Tourism is directly competing against the monoculture of plantations and industrialized fishing to keep pristine forests, jungles and coral reefs intact, while at the same time damage to the environment is caused by the ever larger influx of tourists. Recognizing the importance of tourism led to a greater willingness to accept and implement environmental protection programmes throughout the Asian region.

The tourism sector is likewise guilty of massive displacement of human settlements and deprivation of livelihood, caused by infrastructure developments in rural communities containing fishing or farming villages, where people are often evicted from their homes simply because they are in the wrong place at the wrong time. For many developers, these communities have little perceived use or value in a tourism setting and must therefore give way for development. In some fortunate cases where relocation is offered as a compensation for being evicted, these resettlements are situated in locations where the people cannot practise their traditional (and only known) livelihood. On the contrary, perhaps, the least visible and talked about issue regarding tourism development is the ongoing social structural change that is affecting the supply and demand for human resources.

As economies shift from being agricultural to become industrialized and service-oriented, there will be a mismatch between available jobs and existing skills in the labour market. This is a problem, because the service paradigm in Asian tourism has been traditionally dependent on cheap labour sourced from a labour market that is highly protected and regulated by laws. Furthermore, the presence of highly organized, highly demanding and sometimes militant labour groups in many Asian countries makes it difficult for industry players to maintain productivity and to keep labour costs down. While the system rightfully protects employees, it provides little incentive or flexibility for businesses to improve their competitiveness. Over the next decades the pressure to reduce labour cost, while maintaining good service standards, will be among the top priorities of many hospitality establishments.

While tourism is known to create jobs and improve living standards, uncontrolled development can ruin the lives of people and destroy whole communities, leaving long-lasting scars on both the natural and social environments that may take years to heal. Hence, despite its often virtuous pretence, tourism is not as innocent and chaste as it looks, and is equally accountable for a number of social injustices and environmental problems prevailing in many popular tourist destinations, particularly in less developed countries.

Since tourism is highly dependent on natural resources, the inability of tourism to sustain the social and ecological viability of its surroundings endangers its survival as an industrial/commercial entity. Therefore, 'Responsible Tourism' is no longer just a question of conscience, but more importantly a matter of survival as well. This change towards a more responsible approach to development is precipitated by three key factors.

First, the market has changed significantly; tourists are more vigilant and aware of social, cultural and environmental issues confronting residents of host communities. This is partly because of advances in information technology (the Internet) that spread news and information around the world and the growing influence of civil societies. For example, tourists and tour companies have been known to stay away from countries that have poor human rights records and those that adopt forced labour on tourism projects (UNEP, 2002).[9] Thus, tourist destinations that adopt good practices will definitely gain market advantage.

Second, sound environmental practices are known to reduce energy and water bills and improve the quality of the destination's surroundings, while enhancing the overall experience of tourists. Eventually, this will promote the destination's image through 'word of mouth', which is the most credible source of marketing information when selling intangible or experiential products such as tourism.

Finally, for business owners and tourist operators, attaining a symbiotic and synergistic relationship with host communities promotes industrial peace and enhances service delivery to guests.

## Tourism and child prostitution

Perhaps of all the inequities of tourism, few (if any) can be more morally reprehensible than Child Sex Tourism. It is difficult to accurately assess the gravity of the problem in terms of the total number of child prostitutes or the social and economic cost of child sex tourism, because the sex trade remains unregulated and poorly reported in many countries, particularly in Asia. The International Labour Organization (ILO) estimates that the 'Sex Trade' in Southeast Asia, in countries like Indonesia, Malaysia, the Philippines and Thailand, accounts for between 2 and 14 per cent of national income, and that child prostitution makes up half of those figures.

In addition, UNICEF estimates that as many as 2 million children are affected worldwide, but are mostly concentrated in developing countries in Asia and Central and South America, many of which are also popular tourist destinations, such as Thailand, Cambodia and Costa Rica. Most sex tourists are adult males from industrialized countries. The lucrative capacity of the sex trade, plus the influence of various socio-economic factors such as globalization, the feminization of migration, the widening income gaps between rich and poor countries and, of course, the growth of the tourist industry, fuelled the explosion of this undesirable consequence.[10]

In 1990, during a tourism-based consultation in Thailand, when the extent of the problem of child prostitution in many Asian countries was first exposed, the 'End Child Prostitution, Child Pornography and Trafficking of Children' (ECPAT) was formed to end commercial sexual exploitation of children. ECPAT consists of more than 80 members in over 75 countries around the globe. In 2006, ECPAT, with the support of UNICEF and the UNWTO, established the 'Code of Conduct for the Protection of Children from Sexual Exploitation in Travel and Tourism' to guide tourism operators in the fight against child sex tourism. The signatories of this document commit themselves towards the following goals:

(a)  Incorporating the protection of children and fight against child exploitation in their policy documents and standard operating procedures
(b)  Providing training to staff to fight child exploitation
(c)  Educating tourists

(d) Putting pressures on tourism suppliers by including a clause against child prostitution in their contracts with hotel chains, tour agencies and airlines

(e) Collaborating and sharing information with key individuals, NGOs and other civic groups to raise awareness of local peoples in child tourism destinations.

## Gender equality

Achieving gender equality and empowering women are essential to combating poverty and sustaining social, political and economic development. But, to do this, a number of constraints that inhibit women's participation in mainstream economic activities need to be addressed, particularly those related to social and cultural bias that has no firm moral foundation, factors that continue to discriminate against women in workplaces.

While tourism is known to employ a higher proportion of women than other industry sectors (46 per cent compared with 34–40 per cent in other sectors), the quality of jobs available to women remains low and the majority of work is in traditional female roles such as housekeeping, waitressing and cleaning. There is also evidence to suggest that women receive disproportionately lower wages than men – approximately 79 per cent of the wages of their male counterparts for the same position and status. Nonetheless, the tourism sector remains an important source of employment for women.[11]

## Sociocultural challenge

Mass Tourism has put peoples' culture, heritage and environment under siege, supplanting conservation/protection initiatives with consumption-based development strategies that threaten the survival of host communities' cultural and natural resources. Ironically, the tourism sector, which heavily depends on these resources, has done little to promote the conservation and protection of these unique and non-renewable resources. Tourism has succumbed to the pressures of growing 'consumerism'. Regrettably, tourism does not see consumerism in a more contemporary sense – as related to consumer empowerment – but sees it in a more anachronistic view, which supports the idea that increased consumption is economically and socially good.

Believing this to be true, many developing countries have designed strategies to rapidly boost their sluggish and ailing economies with activity-based forms of tourism, whose success depends on mass-market retailing. This has led to a systematic depletion of our natural resources and erosion of social cultures and values, basically consuming the very foundation on which 'nature and culture-based tourism' is built upon. As seen in countless cases, mass tourism strategies disastrously over-whelm the destination's carrying capacity, which not only puts the site's long-term viability in doubt but also gradually and permanently erases the cultural identities of peoples and communities.

As many issues can be addressed by the tourism industry itself, sensi-tizing the general population as a protective measure against abuse and exploitation requires government intervention. This is desirable in the education sector. Sex education is a taboo in many Asian societies, and environmental and social issues are merely touched on. Education reforms need to address those issues, however sensitive, in support of society, to reduce social woes gradually and from within the society. Sustainably developing tourism for the next generation and the decades to come also requires that the private sector reaches out to educate its workforce and the community in support of the government on those very same issues.

## Notes

1. Thanh-Dam Thruong Sex, Money and Morality: Prostitution and tourism in Southeast Asia, London. Zed Books (1990).
2. UNWTO (2009), http://www.unwto.org/facts/menu.html
3. WTTC (2009), *Economic Impact Data and Forecast*, www.wttc.org/download. php?file=http://www.wttc.org/bin/file/original_file/final_league_table-saug09.xls
4. M Hitchcock, VT King and MJ Parnwell, *Tourism in Southeast Asia* (London: Routledge, 1993).
5. EU Commission on CSR, ec.europa.eu/enterprise/csr/index_en.htm
6. A Cramer and J Prepscius, 'Creating a sustainable future', vol. 2, no. 3 (2007); P Yu, *Bioethics and Asian Cultures Asian Bioethics in the 21st Century*, The Hong Kong Polytechnic University, Eubios Ethics Institute (2003).
7. C Arcodia, *Confucian values and their implications for the tourism industry*, School of Tourism & Leisure Management (2003).
8. JS i Borras, 'Evil, Freedom and Responsibility: An essay on Kant's moral phi-losophy', *Richmod* [Richmond?] *Journal of Philosophy*, 4 (Summer 2003).
9. United Nations Foundations (2002), '*Sustainable Tourism – turning the tide*' Towards Earth Summit 2002, Briefing Paper: Economic Briefing No. 4.
10. S Song, *Global child sex tourism: Children as tourist attractions*, Youth Advocate Program International Resource Paper, YAP international (2003).
11. A Pritchard, N Morgan and C Harris, 'Gender posed: The people behind the postcards', in: *Tourism and gender embodiment, sensuality and experience* (Oxford: CABI Publishing, 2007), pp. 219–34; UNIFEM, 'Tourism offers opportunities for women workers but new problems emerge', in: *Riding the Wave of Tourism and Hospitality Research* (CAUTHE, 2009), pp. 5–8.

# 10
# Corporations and CSR in Asia: Sustainability As the Future Driver of Corporate Innovation and Entrepreneurship

*Cheryl D. Hicks and Kevin Teo*

Sustainability and Corporate Social Responsibility (CSR) departments in global and national businesses are relatively new. Most CSR and sustainability functions have been created in companies only in recent decades and have gained the most significant growth and momentum post-millennium, following the Johannesburg Summit on Sustainable Development in 2002. The CEOs of leading multinational corporations have said recently that the businesses that will lead in the next decades will be those whose business models directly address the world's most pressing challenges, such as climate change, global resource management, economic empowerment, demographic shifts and lifestyles. The World Business Council for Sustainable Development (WBCSD) has said that this shift will require sustainability-driven innovation, which will define the next agenda for business.

Social businesses such as The Body Shop and Ben & Jerry's ice cream are considered the pioneers of a new wave of entrepreneurs that put ethical and social considerations at the core of their businesses and product offerings in the 1970s. Today, there are vast networks of social or sustainability entrepreneurs around the world, demonstrating that sustainability-driven innovation and entrepreneurship are not only plausible but are in fact already being revealed in increasing numbers globally. Organizations such as Ashoka, the Schwab Foundation, the Skoll Foundation and Volans are working with these entrepreneurs to scale their innovations, address market and societal failures and play a major role in the next agenda for business. Volans' co-founders,

John Elkington and Pamela Hartigan, call this uprising 'The Power of Unreasonable People', taking inspiration from George Bernard Shaw's quote 'The reasonable man adapts himself to the world; the unreasonable one persists in trying to adapt the world to himself.'

This chapter will review the recent evolution of CSR, sustainability and business and will make the case for the opportunity for Asia to set the new rules of the game and lead the world in social and sustainability entrepreneurship that drives corporate innovation into the future. We draw upon the experience from our work with the leading global companies of The World Business Council for Sustainable Development and the extraordinary entrepreneurs in the Volans network.

## The role of business in addressing global challenges

Corporations have always had responsibilities to the societies and communities in which they are licensed to operate. Historically, businesses have seen their role in society as contributors to improved quality of life for many through job creation, skills training and the provision of desired goods and services. However, in 1972 the first United Nations Conference on the Human Environment in Stockholm, Sweden raised new questions about who should be held responsible for the earth, the management of its resources and the environmental degradation that was becoming increasingly evident.

By 1992, at the Earth Summit in Rio de Janeiro, Brazil, the world's NGOs and many governments had decided that corporations should be held accountable for their impacts on the environment and that they should in turn accept more of the responsibility for environmental clean-up efforts (where governments had previously been left with the burden). At this same time The Brundtland Commission report, *Our Common Future*, had recently been published and a new concept, sustainable development, was launched in an effort to discuss the environment and development as one single issue.

As a result, corporations started to ask themselves new questions about their changing role in society and their responsibilities for sustainable development. The World Business Council for Sustainable Development was founded at this time, in the early 1990s. It sought to provide a platform for global businesses interested in formulating the business case for sustainable development and drawing the boundaries for their responsibilities for the environment and other societal issues.

## The business case

CSR and business action on sustainable development need to make business sense. Global businesses have found a strong business case for the corporate responsibility for people and planet. They have found cost-saving opportunities from implementing resource efficiency measures (coined by the WBCSD as eco-efficiency), opportunities for increased access to capital by being seen as a superiorly managed company by the investment community, and opportunities to gain market share, competitive advantage and access to new markets by providing improved information to consumers and engaging in dialogue with stakeholders.

## The case for innovation

From the Rio Summit in 1992 to the World Summit on Sustainable Development in Johannesburg, South Africa, in 2002, there were substantive shifts in thinking amongst governments and NGOs regarding the role of business. At the Johannesburg Summit, corporations went from being the main source of the world's major challenges to the expectation that business holds the key to the solutions. For the CEOs of global businesses at the time, this declaration by global governments and NGOs came as a rather large surprise and led leading businesses to discuss what the role of business would be in tomorrow's society. In 2006 a group of global CEOs from the WBCSD came out with this statement:

> We believe that the leading global companies of 2020 will be those that provide goods and services and reach new customers in ways that address the world's major challenges – including poverty, climate change, resource depletion, globalization and demographic shifts.
>
> If action to address such issues is to be substantial and sustainable, it must also be profitable. Our major contribution to society will therefore come through our core business, rather than through our philanthropic programs.

In recent years international organizations and the media have started to label this shift in business thinking as moving from the old industrialized and even knowledge economies to the green economy. The United Nations Environment Programme (UNEP) defines the green economy as substantially increased investments in economic sectors that build on and enhance the earth's natural capital or reduce ecological scarcities and environmental risks. These sectors include renewable energy, low-carbon transport, energy-efficient buildings, clean technologies, improved waste management, improved freshwater provision, sustainable agriculture and forest management, and sustainable fisheries. These investments are driven by or supported by national policy reforms and the development of international policy and market infrastructure. These investments and policy reforms provide the mechanisms and the financing for the reconfiguration of businesses, infrastructure and institutions and the adoption of sustainable consumption and production processes. Such reconfiguration leads to a higher share of green sectors contributing to GDP, greener jobs, lower energy and resource-intensive production, lower waste and pollution and significantly lower greenhouse gas emissions. It can also assist in the reduction of persistent poverty through targeted wealth transfers and new employment, as well as improvements in access and the flow of ecosystem goods and services to the bottom of the economic pyramid.

The CEO co-chairs of the WBCSD's Vision 2050 study state that the pathways to sustainable development and the transformation to the next economy will bring massive opportunities for innovation: '...to do more with less, to create value, to prosper and to advance the human condition...many of these opportunities will be in emerging markets'.

Some companies are known for being savvy to shifts in markets and industries. For example, Japanese automotive giant, The Toyota Motor Company, has in the past applied its expertise and innovations in production line manufacturing of automobiles to sewing machines, and is now known for innovating the automobile industry from cars to sustainable mobility. The oil and gas industry has evolved to become the energy industry, and, for instance, the former British Petroleum, a British oil and gas company, now refers to itself as BP (beyond petroleum), an energy company.

These shifts are already gaining momentum with forward-thinking companies that have seen an opportunity for an old economy innovation or innovative process to be applied to an emerging green economy industry. This has been the case with Henkel, known to many German households as a leading maker of household consumer goods. In performing life cycle analysis (LCA) on its products, Henkel found that its unique innovation in adhesive technologies could have significant positive impact on climate change. Henkel's lightweight natural ingredient adhesives can be used to significantly reduce the weight of products in the transportation, electronics, aerospace, metal, durable goods, consumer goods, maintenance and repair and packaging industries, resulting in significant efficiencies in the use of $CO_2$, critical for addressing climate change. Henkel has made the strategic decision to grow the adhesive technologies portion of its business.

Eskom, a South African electricity utility company, generates approximately 95 per cent of the electricity used in South Africa and approximately 45 per cent of the electricity used on the African continent. Eskom states that it is focused on improving and strengthening electricity generation, transmission, trading and distribution throughout Africa. In this way, Eskom's business is critical to enabling the improvement of the lives of many Africans currently living without power and therefore limiting their access to the basic needs of water, sanitation, safe storage and preparation of food. Eskom is actively developing renewable energy investments, which will in turn help to achieve sustainable development goals in the region.

In Asia, Infosys, an Indian company and provider of technology-enabled business solutions, announced in 2007 that the company had reorganized its business units to anticipate changes in the global IT Industry. Infosys believes that, to win, companies must address the shifts of the 'Flat World', flattened by forces of globalization, changing demographics, ubiquity of technology and regulatory compliance. Infosys further articulates that countries must focus on education to develop a skilled labour force, and is proactively developing human capital with the aim of lifting people out of poverty, increasing employability through the transfer of skills, and enabling participation in the IT revolution.

## The case for market incentives

The private sector cannot address major global challenges alone. The challenges of global climate change, environmental degradation, poverty alleviation, sustainable lifestyles and corruption are systemic challenges that are highly dependent on the systems in which they operate. One extremely important system for incentives and deterrents is the global financial system. The ripple effect of impacts in one part of the financial system has been evident in the past 2 years, with the damaging effects of the credit crisis being felt around the world.

We have learned in this short history of CSR that the technological and societal changes needed to address current global challenges such as climate change, global population growth and increasing resource constraints are more urgent than we once thought. Transitioning to the green economy will also need the support of the global capital markets.

Market incentives need to be updated and aligned with the future goals of sustainable development. One way to redirect capital flows towards the future vision for sustainable development would be to make the capital markets more effective and efficient in integrating environment, social and governance (ESG) factors into the valuation of companies. With these market incentives, companies and entrepreneurs directly addressing global challenges would be rewarded with increased access to capital, and businesses that are inhibiting sustainable development would be punished by the markets and incentivized to innovate.

Important links between the capital markets and enabling sustainable change are being explored. Including CSR and sustainability as part of company valuations is becoming important to both companies and the investment community.

In 2008 and 2009, the WBCSD and the United Nations Environment Programme Finance Initiative (UNEP FI) conducted a study that brought together corporate CSR and sustainability managers with SRI investment managers in six global markets (including Asia) to explore how to accelerate the change needed to value sustainability in the capital markets. The driver of this study came from approximately 200 corporate members of the WBCSD and the approximately 200 financial institutions and institutional investor members of UNEP FI, who 'believe that a company's management of ESG factors, as well as a company's leadership on sustainable development are at the core of business today and therefore need to be considered by the capital markets. Both organizations believe that ESG factors can be financially material and can enhance long-term sustainable company value'.

The study recommends that, to include sustainability in corporate valuations, companies should focus on three main improvement areas:

1. Draw clear links between the management of ESG issues, sustainability, financial performance and strategy. Companies rarely explicitly link their management of sustainability issues or how sustainability is driving innovation in the company to financial performance or outlook for investors. This is needed if investors are to reward that company directly addressing global issues.
2. Standardize the disclosure of quantitative ESG data. Companies may provide a CSR or sustainability report outlining their corporate strategy. However, this seldom includes how their strategy and performance against their goals compares with their competitors in the

sector. This is needed if investors are to determine the sustainable value of one company over another, reward the leaders and incentivize improvement among the laggards.

3. Formalize a communication process for qualitative ESG data. Currently CSR and sustainability performance data are typically collected by investment managers in the form of a questionnaire. However, the questionnaires do not allow companies to include material qualitative information. This qualitative data is not 'user-friendly' for the mathematical models of investment advisors and managers. This study found that, when companies outlined the importance of that qualitative information to the financial performance, short or long-term outlook of the company, it influenced the investment decision-making of investment managers. Companies need to be bolder in helping investment managers to understand the material importance of CSR and sustainability management information.

From a purely financial point of view, the concept of corporate sustainability is attractive to investors because it aims to increase long-term shareholder value. A growing number of investors are now convinced that sustainability is a catalyst for enlightened and disciplined management and, thus, a crucial success factor for corporations to show superior performance and favourable risk/return profiles.

In Europe, associations representing the financial services industry are lobbying their governments for legislation that requires more detailed corporate disclosure of ESG data. 'It is increasingly understood that financial statements capture less than 20% of corporate risks and value creation potential, with the balance deriving from intangible factors such as human capital and resource efficiency. ESG data are relevant, material information that investors should have and increasingly want as a means to better gauge longer-term risks and opportunities. It is therefore important that companies provide an overview of all major risks and detail the most important ones.'[1]

The Association for Sustainable and Responsible Investment in Asia (ASrIA), a non-profit membership association dedicated to promoting corporate responsibility and sustainable investment practice in the Asia-Pacific region, states that: 'There is no one roadmap for implementing responsible investment policies, only a set of tested tools and strategies which have increasing relevance to Asian governments seeking to encourage sustainable growth. Over the next decade, we expect to see significant policy developments across Asia to address climate change, ecosystem destruction, pollution and a range of associated social impacts. Together with important infrastructure needs, these policies will have significant impacts on the investment climate (in Asia).'

In order to facilitate the investment choices of investors and asset managers, market mechanisms such as Sustainability Indexes, linked to global and national stock exchanges, are selecting the company stock titles that show superior performance and risk/return profiles inclusive of environmental, social and governance impacts. On a global scale, companies with superior performance inclusive of sustainability performance indicators can be found in indexes such as the Dow Jones Sustainability Indexes or FTSE4GOOD Indexes.

The World Federation of Exchanges (WFE) notes in its 2008 report that several stock exchanges – many of them in emerging markets – are adopting proactive commercial strategies in response to growing investor interest in ESG issues and global sustainable development challenges. In Asia, many exchanges have taken initiatives to raise issuing companies' awareness and to promote or require better transparency and disclosure on ESG-related performance and risk factors.

In Malaysia, Thailand and China, the emphasis has been on promoting CSR concepts, including the publication of annual CSR/Sustainability reports. Bursa Malaysia, the Shenzhen Stock Exchange and the Shanghai Stock Exchange all offer CSR guidance and training programmes for listed companies. The Taiwan Stock Exchange has revised its Corporate Governance Best-Practice Principles for Listed Companies in 2006 to include ESG. The National Stock Exchange of India has held Forums on Responsible Investment for institutional investors and Indian company CEOs.

In 2009 Korea launched the Dow Jones Sustainability Index (DJSI) Korean Index with the aim of tracking the sustainability leaders among South Korea's 200 largest companies by free-float market capitalization. In its first year 41 sustainability leaders in Korea have been selected. The Korea Productivity Centre (KPC), a partner in the development of the Korean Index, cites that investor interest and company interest in the Sustainability Index in Korea have grown significantly in its second year due to the increased awareness that the index has enabled in the Korean market. The Korean Index follows a trend of national sustainability indexes, which began with the Johannesburg Sustainability Index in South Africa and the Bovespa Index in Brazil.

There is a market incentive for companies to more closely manage, report and continuously improve their CSR performance benchmarked against their competitors. According to Swiss-based sustainability investing group, Sustainable Asset Management (SAM), who also manage the analysis for the DJSI family of indexes, 'sustainability leaders generate better performance and thus higher returns for shareholders than companies that pay little or no attention to sustainability criteria.' From 2001 through 2008, 'the annual share performance of sustainability leaders exceeded that of sustainability laggards by 1.48 percentage points.' SAM Indexes further states that: 'The international recognition enjoyed by the DJSI makes the prospect of index membership an important incentive for participating companies. It enhances both their reputation and their appeal to sustainability investors, offering them access to an additional pool of capital.'

The United Nations Principles for Responsible Investment (UN PRI), a global initiative with over 750 institutional investor signatories (51 signatories in the Asia-Pacific region) representing over $18 trillion in assets and focused on mainstreaming the consideration of environmental, social and corporate governance issues within investment decision-making, has said that: 'to enhance ESG behaviors and disclosure by companies, a number of PRI signatories are asking how exchanges can assist them in promoting transparency and good corporate practice.' The PRI signatories, representing some 15 per cent of global capital markets, are required to adhere to six principles, including actively seeking ESG disclosure from their investee companies. Sustainability Indexes provide the due diligence and disclosure investors are seeking.

'The global financial crisis convinced many investors and policymakers of the urgent need to promote better risk management, good governance and enhanced transparency to protect long-term returns. Any moves to improve corporate disclosure on ESG issues are likely to benefit exchanges through enhancing both the reputation of markets and the investability of the companies traded on them.'[2]

These examples of the movement of global and national stock exchange towards increased disclosure of ESG issues provide useful case studies for Asian markets seeking to accelerate CSR amongst corporations in the region.

There is also a future opportunity to extend these market incentives to the social businesses and entrepreneurs building the pathway to societal innovation for sustainable development. For example, private investors such as high net worth individuals (HNWIs) and Family Foundations are becoming increasingly interested in seeking investments that combine the idea of using profit-seeking investment to generate social and environmental good. This type of direct investment in entrepreneurs and social businesses is being called impact investing, and new reports show that it is moving from the periphery of activist investors to the core of mainstream financial institutions. The term 'impact investing' was coined by a group of investors gathered by the Rockefeller Foundation in 2007 as a way to define investments that seek to address inefficient markets and market failures.

A 2009 study by the Monitor Institute, a California-based think tank focused on helping innovative leaders develop and achieve sustainable solutions to significant social and environmental problems, found that impact investors want to move beyond 'socially responsible investment', which focuses primarily on avoiding investments in 'harmful' companies or encouraging improved corporate practices related to the environment, social performance, or governance. Instead, they actively seek to place capital in businesses and funds that can provide solutions at a scale that purely philanthropic interventions usually cannot reach. This capital may be in a range of forms including equity, debt, working capital lines of credit and loan guarantees. Examples in recent decades include many investments in microfinance, community development finance and clean technology.

The 2010 World Wealth Report, produced annually by French-based financial services consulting firm Capgemini and US-based wealth management firm Merrill Lynch, shows the highest level of growth in high net worth individuals and their fortunes in the Asia-Pacific region, with Asia-Pacific's HNWI population reaching 3 million individuals in 2009, matching that of Europe for the first time. Asia-Pacific wealth rose by 30.9 per cent to $9.7 trillion, surpassing the $9.5 trillion in wealth held by Europe's HNWIs. Asia-Pacific HNWI wealth is expected to grow by 8.8 per cent per year until 2018, in spite of a 14.2 per cent decrease in the high net worth population.

This 'perfect storm' of corporations' focus on sustainability-driven innovation, investor interest in accelerating market incentives for sustainable businesses, trends in more detailed requirements for corporate sustainability disclosure from stock exchanges and high net worth investors seeking increased 'deal flow' of social and sustainable businesses provides a unique opportunity for Asia's growth market to demonstrate that the next agenda for business is indeed one of sustainable business.

The next section will provide a short history of social entrepreneurship and sustainable business, with a case study that shows how sustainable business is being scaled in Asia.

## The role of social entrepreneurs and SMEs in shaping CSR and the vision for a sustainable future

In the documentary 'Food Inc.', Gary Hirschberg, founder of organic food company Stonyfield Farms, shows the interviewer the rows of organic producers setting up their stalls at an organic food fair. 'When we started this fair, we only had one row of stalls, now we have a whole convention centre of them,' Gary muses. 'The major Food and Beverage companies are not walking, they're running to these stalls to make deals and attempt to acquire them.' Stonyfield Farms is a testament to the rising tide of consumer demand for organically produced farm products, driving up the market values of other companies that have championed the organic movement. 'Food Inc.', incidentally, was produced by Participant Productions, which is also credited with producing 'The Inconvenient Truth' and is owned by Jeff Skoll, founder of the Skoll Foundation for Social Entrepreneurship.

In 'The Power of Unreasonable People', Pamela Hartigan and John Elkington describe social entrepreneurs as sharing the same characteristics as all entrepreneurs – namely, they are innovative, resourceful, practical and opportunistic. However unlike 'regular' entrepreneurs, what motivates many social and environmental entrepreneurs is not doing the 'deal' but achieving the 'ideal'. And, because the ideal takes a lot longer to realize, these entrepreneurs tend to be in the game for the long haul.

We have read inspiring stories about social entrepreneurs like Gary with Stonyfield Farms, John Mackey with the US-based organic food retailer Whole Foods, and Anita Roddick with The Body Shop, UK-based natural beauty products company. We applaud their heroism and tenacity, and numerous business school case studies on leadership and entrepreneurship revolve around their strong adherence to the social mission underpinning each of these organizations and the consistent values that run from the boardroom all the way down to the store-fronts. Muhammad Yunus, founder of the Grameen Bank, a bank in Bangladesh with specialized financial services for the poor, and Nobel Peace Prize winner in 2006 (together with the Grameen Bank), has become the chief advocate of social businesses, sparking waves of interest around related themes such as Conscious Capitalism.

Universities all around the world are responding to a rapidly growing interest in social entrepreneurship, and this is also evidenced by an increasing array of social business plan competitions. There is tremendous energy to be harnessed given this interest. We will do greater justice to the social entrepreneurship movement by not diverting this energy towards launching more social enterprises, but rather by focusing on launching businesses that incorporate lessons on Corporate Social Responsibility from successful social enterprises. The differences between a social enterprise – an organization created to achieve a social mission, operated in a financially sustainable manner – and a financially sustainable business practising social responsibility are subtle. The concept of social enterprises has become fashionable, but also potentially overplayed in today's context, whereas focusing on CSR might in fact reap greater dividends.

Ashoka's motto – 'Everyone a Changemaker' – says it best. Bill Drayton, Ashoka's founder, had earlier estimated that there would be one social entrepreneur for every 10 million citizens. Since the late 1990s, Ashoka's strategy through its Youth Venture programme started promoting a broader entrepreneurial mindset among youths, to become active and empowered citizens in anything they pursued. According to Bill, 'society cannot significantly increase the proportion of adults who are Changemakers and who have mastered the necessary and complex underlying social skills until it changes the way all young people live.' Building upon this, the lessons that we take away from social entrepreneurs should not be about launching the next social enterprise, but rather to inform how we think and function as engaged everyday citizens and employees.

The success stories of social entrepreneurs that inspire and motivate us are indicative of a survivorship bias; behind every Grameen Bank that makes it to the headlines lie many failed ventures. Launching a commercial enterprise is already difficult enough; layer on top of this the challenges of selling to market segments with reduced purchasing power (e.g. bottom of the pyramid strategies), with a workforce that is less than 100 per cent productive (e.g. work-integration social enterprises that hire persons with disabilities) and operating businesses in developing world business environments to serve a social mission with poor governance and the odds of success get diminished significantly. Stonyfield Farms, in selling organic products that we now take for granted to be deemed healthier than 'regular' products, spent 9 years making losses to deliver their message.

Corporate Social Responsibility has its fair share of critics, who see it as window dressing, typically implemented as an afterthought. This is hardly surprising, because a successful CSR strategy requires either significant top management buy-in, or to have elements of itself embedded in the organization from the beginning. You could argue that many social enterprises have had their CSR strategy (or at least most of it) built into their mission and values system since they were born.

The small business sector in the United States economy accounts for more than half of all private sector employment – 60 million – and generates more than half of non-farm private gross domestic product (GDP), amounting to US$6.92 trillion. If we agree that the small business sector represents the lifeblood of an economy, then instilling CSR practices within this sector ought to be seen as the most bankable social investment available. Hence the 'long-tail' of social impact lies not in inspiring the creation of more social entrepreneurs but rather in working with sole proprietors and small businesses to inculcate a set of values that have made accomplished social entrepreneurs successful and noteworthy.

There are many CSR standards that a business can align itself with and they comprise an alphabet soup of GRI – The Global Reporting Initiative,[3] B-Corp[4] and ISO14001 – The International Standards Organization,[5] to name a few. Helping the small business sector become acquainted with these standards should be an incremental process, as to become fully compliant with all facets of a given standard could simply be too much for a small business to manage.

As an example of promoting gradual adoption of CSR practices, SPRING Singapore – the enterprise development agency that supports the small and medium enterprise sector in Singapore – and Singapore Compact for CSR – the local chapter of the UN Global Compact – have come together to promote and increase the adoption of ISO14001 recommendations within the small business community in Singapore.

In a September 2008 Inc. article, Meg Hirshberg, the wife of Stonyfield Farms founder, recounts how she went through 25 years of toil and sweat with her husband, delivering her first two children on the farm and at several junctures even wishing that Stonyfield Farms would fail, so as to end their misery. After Stonyfield Farms' astounding success, however, Meg is grateful that they have reached the light at the end of the tunnel and that Stonyfield Farms is now generating annual sales of $330 million after Danone, the French food company, made a major investment in the company.

It is these stories of the Stonyfield Farms of the world that will continue to fuel our passion and motivate us towards greatness. But it will be in the domain of small businesses, at 60 million employees and $6.92 trillion of annual revenue, that gradual shifts in business practices towards increasing social responsibility would result in significant impact on society and the environment.

In our vision for a sustainable future many of these small businesses will 'grow up' to become the next market leaders, like Stonyfield Farms or Body Shop, and leaders of the new agenda for business.

The social entrepreneurship movement, working also to promote broader adoption of CSR practices among small businesses, could trigger a tipping point where social and sustainable businesses become the dominant businesses in the market.

## Entrepreneurship and CSR in Asia

Social entrepreneurship is also gaining momentum in Asia. Volans, a think tank and consultancy focused on the business of social innovation, was first established in London and Singapore in 2008 and works globally with entrepreneurs, businesses, investors and governments to develop and scale innovative solutions to financial, social and environmental challenges.

Here we outline one example of entrepreneurship in action in Asia. It is the story of entrepreneurs who identified a market failure, created a strategy to overcome the issue and developed a new partnership model to achieve significant societal impact in the region.

## Producing societal changemakers through strategic combination of training and CSR goals

Employee volunteerism is a traditional CSR activity for many companies. According to a 2009 survey by 'The Committee to Encourage Corporate Philanthropy', 94 per cent of corporations had a formal employee volunteer programme – a steady increase from 81 per cent in 2004. Furthermore, 49 per cent of the corporations in the 2009 report invested in international volunteerism programmes, reflecting a more global outlook on community engagement, as well as a desire to connect these programmes across cultural and geographical boundaries.

This should translate into rich opportunities for social impact. Although significant resources are committed towards employee volunteer programmes, the extent to which these programmes have sustainable social impact is unclear. One analysis is that, like the case of corporate grant-making, corporate volunteerism suffers from a disproportionate emphasis on the quantity of activity, rather than its potential impact. Rather than simply trying to 'do more', consciously matching the core competencies of the corporate volunteer with the critical needs of the community partner is one way to improve outcomes achieved. Also, it makes good business sense to connect volunteer or community engagement programmes with training or human capital development needs of the corporation.

In 2005, PricewaterhouseCoopers (PwC) launched the Developing Responsible Leaders (DRL) programme in partnership with the Singapore International Foundation. DRL includes a significant leadership development component, whereby senior executives within the firm are handpicked for coaching skills training and are provided with personal renewal through community service. It ran for two consecutive years (with community service carried out in Bhutan and China, respectively) and successfully provided its participants with much personal growth. Nonetheless, something was still missing. As senior executives with deep industry knowledge and experience, the participants felt that their skills could have been more fully tapped and leveraged to render greater impact on the community.

Being familiar with the developments of the social enterprise sector, Leng Lim of Pivotal Leadership, an organizational development consultancy, who was the executive coach in the initial DRL trips, identified a compelling opportunity for PwC to partner with social enterprises, in response to a desire to deliver greater impact given the project team's capabilities.

Seeking out experts in the field of social innovation, Pivotal reached out to Volans to discuss this concept. The idea of the partnership was to link PwC's participants to social entrepreneurs who could also benefit from the professional expertise of PwC executives to advance their social businesses. Besides attaining a training objective, the partnership would also help PwC achieve its goal of greater societal impact by working with social entrepreneurs to grow social businesses.

Following consultations with PwC, Pivotal and Volans identified Hagar International as a potential partner for the DRL program. Hagar is a social enterprise based in Cambodia that serves the needs of women and children directly affected by violence, abuse and trafficking.

Founded in 1994 by Pierre Tami, Hagar started operations in Phnom Penh by providing shelter services to abused women and children. Over the years, Hagar launched several social businesses that would provide jobs for the women and older children coming out of the shelter, as well as generating a small surplus to support the shelter operation. Hagar's social businesses are professionally managed to high standards; as an example, Hagar Catering serves the staff can-teens of five-star hotels and the American Embassy in Phnom Penh, Cambodia.

Having established itself in Cambodia, Hagar began exploring plans to replicate to Vietnam, Laos, Afghanistan and India (Mumbai). Given the international and complex nature of this replication plan, profes-sional service input was required around control systems, corporate governance and taxation. These needs were well matched to the core competencies of PwC, and Hagar's expansion also presented an oppor-tunity for PwC to align its global corporate responsibility programme with priorities in various parts of Asia.

As part of putting together the DRL project, management staff from PwC, Hagar and Volans met on a planning trip in Phnom Penh to dis-cuss and confirm the scope of the upcoming project. Specific focus was put on aspects of the project that could fully utilize the skill sets of the project team, namely in the areas of tax, audit and business advisory. Through this planning trip, the framework for the 2-week project was mapped out and the PwC project team continued communicating with Hagar by phone and e-mail to assemble the necessary documentation to best prepare for the project ahead of arriving in Cambodia.

The implementation phase of the project kicked off in September 2009, with members of the DRL team converging from Singapore, China and Hong Kong. The team was introduced to Cambodia's dark history through a visit to Toul Sleng, where prisoners of the Khmer Rouge were tortured before being shipped off for execution at the Killing Fields. They also experienced the challenging reality of a typical Cambodia through visits to urban slum areas organized by Cambodian Living Arts, a local charity with the mission of preserving traditional perform-ance arts. With this context, the DRL team set out to work with Hagar on a few different assignments, engaging with Hagar's various business units over the course of 2 weeks.

A key objective for the DRL team, aside from addressing the needs of the social enterprise, is to focus on the personal development of the team members. To accomplish this, Pivotal wove a coaching programme into the daily activities for the team and utilized the rich variety of experiences and challenges of the day as points of learning.

Over the 2-week project period, the DRL team not only contributed in excess of 500 man-hours of expert-level consultation on tax, audit and business planning but also discovered many new things about them-selves and laid out plans for subsequent personal development after the project. Conversely, Hagar was not merely a receiver of pro-bono input from the DRL team but was also able to reciprocate by providing unique opportunities for the team to touch the lives of Hagar's beneficiaries.

Overall, there was a strong sense of a collective win from the corporate and social enterprise stakeholders in this collaboration. PwC continues to run the DRL programme, with an eye towards future partnerships with social enterprises, and Hagar is well on its way to expanding its operations to other parts of Asia.

In this case, corporate trainees were harnessed to become societal changemakers. PwC fulfilled its leadership development and global CSR goals. Social entrepreneurs in Asia received needed management training from PwC. As a result of the partnership, both parties were able to achieve their societal vision – and, in doing so, have advanced societal change in multiple countries in the region.

This new way of working and collaborating provides an interesting model for the next agenda for businesses that are seeking to lead in the future.

## Conclusions: opportunity for Asia – setting new rules of the game

There is a significant opportunity for growing Asian markets to redefine success in the future economy, where sustainability and CSR drive corporate innovation and entrepreneurship, and markets reward and incentivize sustainable businesses.

In the new millennium a global consensus is emerging on the need for significant shifts in the ways of working, governing and living. There is a growing recognition that we will need a new set of solutions to manage the complexity of the trade-offs that will be required to transition from the old economy to a new economy that supports sustainable development. There is also a broad belief that these new solutions already exist and are starting to be revealed on a local scale in communities around the world.

Growing networks of social entrepreneurs and indexes of sustainable businesses are demonstrating that many of these solutions have been developed already, often by 'unreasonable' people with the sole objective of improving the lives of themselves, their families and communities – these are the new generation of entrepreneurs, and they may hold the key or hyperlink from the old economy to the new economy that will enable the sustainable future.

There is an opportunity for Asia to take the lead in scaling up these solutions as the foundations of the new economy at a critical time of growth and opportunity for change.

It will be tempting to accept easy wins that will not achieve transformational change and that pull Asia backwards into growing the 'old economy'. For this we should remember:

> We cannot expect to solve any complex problems from within the same state of consciousness that created them (Albert Einstein)

> We need 'to help ensure that we are not battling to meet 21st century challenges with, at best, 20th century decision making systems.' (His Royal Highness the Prince of Wales)

## Notes

1. European Social Investment Forum (EUROSIF), Public Policy Position Paper related to Sustainable and Responsible Investment (SRI), April 2009. http://www.eurosif.org/images/stories/pdf/eurosif_public_policy_position_paper_2009.pdf accessed 30 June 2010.
2. www.unpri.org/sustainablestockexchanges09 accessed June 2010.
3. www.globalreporting.org, accessed 2 July 2010.
4. www.bcorporation.net, accessed 2 July 2010.
5. www.iso.org, accessed 2 July 2010.

# 11
# The Growing Risk of Climate Change: Implications and Strategies for Asian Companies and Economies

*Ruth Yeoh*

> The greatest security threat we face as a global community won't be met by guns and tanks...It will be solved by investment in the emerging techniques of soft power – building avenues of opportunity that will lead to a low carbon economy.
>
> Margaret Beckett, former UK Foreign Secretary
> Foreign policy address at the British
> Embassy in Berlin, October 2006.

## Introduction to global warming: the hard facts

Mankind has historically had a voracious appetite for resources, brought on by the Industrial Revolution and ongoing civilization. Every year, there is an Ecological Debt Day or Overshoot Day, which measures the point at which the consumption of resources exceeds the ability of the planet to replace them. From this day on (in 2009 it was 25 September) until the end of the year, humanity will be in ecological overshoot, building up ever greater ecological debt. What is alarming is that it gets earlier every year.

NEF policy director Andrew Simms explains: 'In a market economy, the only constraints on what we consume are what we may legally buy and what we can afford. The result is, as the great environmental economist Herman Daly warned, that we end up treating the planet as if it were a business in liquidation. If you were managing a business, you would be considered grossly negligent if you had no idea of your assets or cash flow. Yet this is how we manage our environmental resources.'

So how does all this relate to global warming? Global warming is caused by the expanding emission of greenhouse gases (GHGs) caused by human activities – and a vast majority of GHGs are from carbon dioxide ($CO_2$: 83 per cent; methane: 8.8 per cent and nitrous oxide: 6 per cent), according to Eurostat. $CO_2$ concentration in the atmosphere has shot up by 30 per cent since 1800 and is expected to double within this century. The rich industrialized countries emit almost half of the world's carbon dioxide, and the International Energy Agency (IEA) has forecast that power generation and transport in developing economies could drive $CO_2$ emissions to 40 billion tons by 2030 if current consumption habits continue (see Figure 11.1).

Most scientists agree that global temperatures are likely to rise between 2 and 6 degrees Celsius by the end of the century from the burning of fossil fuels for power generation (the biggest contributor of emissions at 24.5 per cent, with coal being the biggest contributor among sources of power) and transport (13.5 per cent of emissions) – and this would cause disasters such as floods and famines to worsen, putting millions at risk. Deforestation (18 per cent) is the second biggest source of emissions.

In addition to the implications of a rise in global average temperatures, secondary effects include rising sea levels and an increase in extreme weather patterns. In some regions, damage from climate change has become grievously visible, with stronger hurricanes, floods and disintegrating ice sheets testament to its merciless severity. Other consequences will include a decline in overall biodiversity. There are also implications for agriculture and food security, in which as little as a 1 degree Celsius temperature rise produces a 161 kilometre shift in temperature zones, with a shift in agricultural belts decreasing food production where it is most needed and escalating food scarcity to record levels. Loss of human lives, however, will be most significant in least developed nations.

## Global warming: a clear global risk

Climate change may well be the greatest threat and challenge of our generation, presenting strains on the environment, the world economy and individual businesses. It will have both negative and positive implications for global economies, and businesses must regard climate change as a clear example of risk whereby long-term planning is one such solution to mitigate its potentially irreversible effects. According to a recent International Energy Agency (IEA) report, carbon dioxide

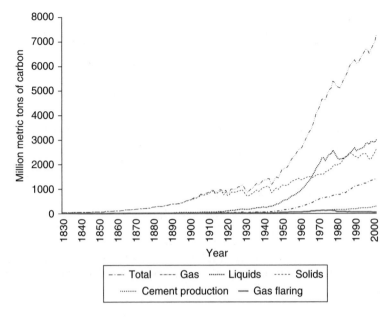

*Figure 11.1*   Growing $CO_2$ emissions

The Energy Information Administration (EIA) estimates global $CO_2$ emissions will rise by 75 per cent from 2003 to 2030. Emissions increased by 2.5 per cent per year from 2000 to 2002, mostly from developing nations.

*Source*: Carbon Dioxide Information Analysis Centre (CDIAC) http://cdiac.ornl.gov/ and United Nations Environment Programme (UNEP) http://www.unep.org/.

emissions and oil demand will continue to grow rapidly over the next 25 years, and this worrisome trend is likely to worsen, extending this outlook beyond 2030 (see Figures 11.1 and 11.2).

The *World Economic Forum* recently published its *Global Risks 2006 Report*, which assesses today's global risk landscape. It identifies four key risk scenarios, drawn from an extensive list,[1] and illustrates the different forms that global risk will take in the decade ahead. Risks whose probabilities are high in the short term include oil price spikes and localized terrorist incidents, for which companies and governments are reasonably well prepared. Climate change features as a **long-term environmental risk** whose impact is potentially very severe, next to influenza pandemics and outbreaks. Organizational risks can be considered as a subset of the various global risks, and these are highlighted in Figure 11.3. Here, the risks presented by climate change are interrelated with other key risks, from storms and environmental degradation to regulation and the future of long-term energy prices.

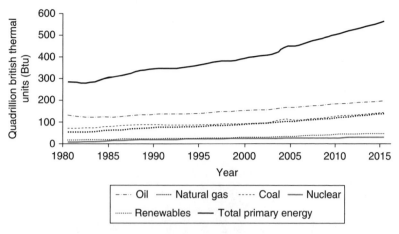

*Figure 11.2*   World primary energy consumption

World primary energy consumption by fuel type (quadrillion British thermal units, Btu) is shown for the years 1979 to 2005, with demand forecasts up to 2015. Asia accounts for three-quarters of growth.

*Source*: International Energy Agency (IEA) http://www.iea.org/, EIA, International Energy Outlook 2006.

The report admits there is still uncertainty as to how climate change risks will manifest, although one thing is clear: 'rises in sea levels, gradual temperature shifts and intensifying weather patterns have the potential to impact heavily on both society and the global economy and are increasingly well understood as risks to business.'

A growing body of scientific evidence indicates the seriousness of the long-term challenge of climate change, as it may potentially become irreversible, with many regions near to, or already at, breaking point. Climate change is therefore a growing threat to international security and the world economy. Involvement and cooperation between sectors and governments will be a strong determining factor in reducing this risk.

## Key energy and environmental challenges in Asia

Asia is currently at a crossroads when it comes to climate change. One need only travel to haze-filled Southeast Asia, be stuck in a gridlock in Jakarta, breathe in the polluted air in Beijing and contract bronchitis in Hong Kong to experience the full furore of climate change. A *Time Asia*

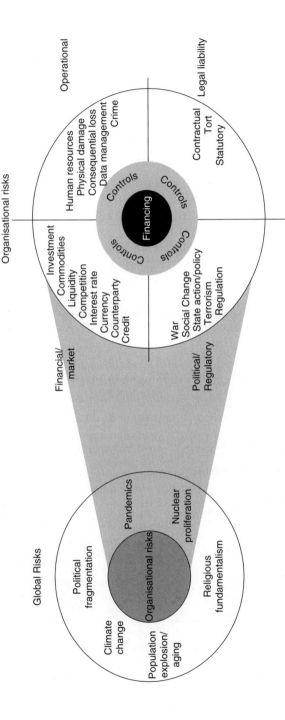

*Figure 11.3*    The risk spectrum

*Source:* HF Kloman, 'Rethinking Risk Management', Geneva Papers, July 1992;[2]

HF Kloman, *Risk Management Reports*, March 1998[3]

(2006) article summarizes Asia's dilemma as one in which 'the forces damaging the environment are the same ones that drove the economic miracle that has lifted more than 270 million Asians out of poverty in the past 15 years.' Rapid industrial expansion in many Asian countries – combined with rising affluence – has led to an increasing need for energy.

By 2020, the region will require nearly 5.6 billion tons of oil equivalent per year – more than double what it consumed in 1997. This trend can be said to be neither economically nor environmentally sustainable (see Figure 11.2). This great demand for energy cannot be sufficiently met by conventional fossil fuel sources such as oil, coal and gas, and the problem is exacerbated by soaring oil prices (as most Asian countries are oil importers). This is driving governments to pursue more balance in the fuel mix, which will see growth in the renewable energy sector, natural gas consumption, wind energy, nuclear power and the advance of oil substitutes such as the biofuels ethanol and biodiesel.

Figure 11.4 shows the constraints and possible solutions (through a combined strategy of leadership and cooperation) of renewable energy development in Asia.

| Constraints | Solutions |
| --- | --- |
| Limited awareness on alternative energy options | Leadership with intention to: |
| Lack of reliable data to undertake specific projects | Gradually expand the share of renewable energy in overall consumption |
| Poor or no research and development base | Promote integrated use of various energy forms |
| No commercial business models | Develop decentralized renewable energy systems for use in rural areas |
| Inadequate access to latest Renewable Energy technology | |
| Limited financial resources | Create a level playing field for renewable energy through various support mechanisms |
| Lack of supporting policies and necessary regulations | Overcome the inherent bias and distortions in energy policies favouring fossil fuels |
| Limited institutional set-up | |

*Figure 11.4*  Constraints and possible solutions of renewable energy development in Asia

*Source*: World Council for Renewable Energy (WCRE) http://www.wcre.de/en/index.php

## Sustainability

To make sustainability happen, Asia needs to balance the conflict between two competing goals of ensuring quality of life and living within the limits of nature (keeping in mind the world is already in ecological red). In light of these major challenges, the ADB has identified the following strategies (see Figure 11.5) for developing Asia:

1) *Energy Efficiency*: Huge prospects remain for improving energy efficiency, which is notoriously low in many Asian countries. In China, for example, GDP is expected to quadruple by 2020, whereas commercial energy supply will only double. Energy intensity will, therefore, need to be halved over the next 15 years.

2) *Energy Diversification*: Alternative and renewable energy sources will increase in the next 20 years from an average 8–10 per cent today to almost 18–20 per cent. This will, however, depend on the implementation of conducive policies, reduction of fuel and coal subsidies and stronger incentives for renewable and clean energy to tap large hydropower, biomass, solar and wind energy sources.

3) *Climate Change*: According to the International Energy Agency (IEA), US$16 trillion of energy investments will be needed through 2030, including US$4–5 trillion in Asia over the next 15 years, to be mostly financed through capital market resources and public-private partnerships. More emphasis on low-carbon technologies is needed to mitigate the possible negative impact of these investments on the world's climate. Since the 1980s, Asia's share of GHG emissions has already soared from less than one-tenth of global emissions to nearly one-quarter of the world's total.

*Figure 11.5*   Three strategies for sustainable development in Asia

*Source*: 'Key Energy Trends and Challenges in Asia', Statement of the Asian Development Bank (Philippe Bénédic, Resident Director General, European Representative Office), OECD Forum 2006: Balancing Globalisation, 22–23 May 2006, Paris.

It is imperative that Asia's energy production and consumption become more sustainable to ensure the security of Asia's oil and gas supplies and also its environment. True, economic growth will provide more jobs and benefit economies. However, increased production and consumption will also bring damaging consequences for the environment. Increased logging activities, sprouting factories, power plants and the increasing frequency of dumping chemicals in rivers are contributing to the region's environmental degradation. The conflict between economic growth and environmental protection is intensifying at a frighteningly exponential growth rate.

However, this is not to say that the journey to sustainability will be impossible. The argument here is that economic growth, which is responsible for much of Asia's environmental disaster, can also bring about its recovery. At one stage, Japan was one of the worst polluters the world has ever seen – today, Japan has cleaned up its act and Tokyo has become one of the world's cleanest megacities, thanks to stricter laws, tougher enforcements and growing environmental consciousness, especially among the younger generation.

Sustainable green growth, policies and improved environmental technology, together with innovation, will help developing Asia become efficient in decreasing its pollution and improve its environmental management.

Crucially, energy-efficient technologies used today are far superior to previous technologies. However, Asia must seriously commit to investing in environmentally friendly policies and technologies in order to instigate positive change.

## The policy arena in Asia

It seems that the only logical solution to balance the budget and end ecological overshoot would be to demand less of the planet. Much will depend largely on global initiatives and international policies. Renewable energy policies can play a role by:

- redirecting resources,
- increasing the speed of innovation and research development,
- and increasing public awareness.

Experience in Europe and the US has shown that favourable government policies can be a strong catalyst for the development of alternative energy. Thus, governments in Asia are implementing policies encouraging or mandating alternative energy investment. Coupled with strong economic growth and growing Asian environmental issues, the prospects for meaningful growth in alternative energy investment and manufacturing in the region are good. China and India, already among the world's top 10 countries for wind turbine installation, seem to have significant growth potential, and in most other places the outlook is promising – Korea stands out with its aggressive plans for photovoltaic (PV) cells. The Clean Development Mechanism (CDM) of the Kyoto Protocol for reducing GHG emissions, together with non-binding international partnerships such as the Asia-Pacific Partnership for Clean Development and Climate (the US, Australia, China, India, Japan and Korea) could also fuel investments in Asia by providing an additional

*Table 11.1*   Clean energy incentives by country

| Country | Feed-in tariff | Renewable portfolio standard | Tax reductions or credits | Public loans/ financing |
|---|---|---|---|---|
| China | • a | | • | • |
| Hong Kong | | | | |
| India | • a | • a | • | • |
| Indonesia | • | | | |
| Korea | • | | • | |
| Malaysia | • | | • | |
| Philippines | | | • | • |
| Singapore | | | • | • |
| Taiwan | • b | | • | • |
| Thailand | • | • | | |

*Note* (a):  Many states have policies but there is no overall national policy.
*Note* (b):  Currently drafting legislation.
*Source*: Goldman Sachs, Renewables 2005: Global Status Report, Industrial Technology Research Institute (Taiwan), Energy Commission (Malaysia).[4]

---

For developing countries in Asia, the CDM offers the following opportunities:

- it can attract capital for projects that assist in the shift to a more prosperous but less carbon-intensive economy;
- it encourages and permits the active participation of private and public sectors;
- it can be an effective tool of technology transfer if investment is channelled into projects that replace old and inefficient fossil fuel technology or create new industries in environmentally sustainable technologies; and
- it can help developing countries define investment priorities in projects that meet their sustainability goals.

---

*Figure 11.6*   How the CDM can help developing countries in Asia
*Source*: 'Establishing National Authorities for the CDM: A Guide for Developing Countries', 2002[5]

potential revenue stream to further enhance project economics (see Figure 11.6).

Conventional power generation using coal or gas is often more cost-competitive than alternative energy; hence the latter needs to be either financially supported or mandated to stimulate installation. It can be observed that many Asian governments are starting to provide incentives for alternative energy:

## Why invest in solutions to climate change?

Renewable energy is the fastest-growing energy sector in terms of percentage annual increase and has potential in terms of responding to global environmental, economic, safety, social and sustainability goals. Factors such as new markets opening up, growing environmental concerns, company savings via carbon credits and less resistance from environmental lobby groups towards nuclear power and uranium mining have fuelled the popularity of alternative energy.

Renewable energy is becoming big business, attracting some of the world's largest companies, including Sharp, Siemens, General Electric and Royal Dutch Shell. Market leaders championing renewable energy in 2004 included China in solar hot water, Germany in solar electricity, Brazil in biofuels and Spain in wind power. The fastest-growing energy technology is grid-connected solar photovoltaic (PV), which grew in existing capacity by 60 per cent per year from 2000 to 2004. Other renewable energy power generation technologies include biomass, geothermal and small hydro, which are mature and growing at more traditional rates of 2–4 per cent per year.

The costs of renewable energy technology have been shown to fall with increased investment and capacity expansion; therefore it can be anticipated that the cost of renewable energy will drop below that of fossil fuel (see Table 11.2).

## The renewable energy investment potential in Asia

There is huge growth potential for renewable energy in Asia. Renewable energy investment comes from a wide range of public and private sources and there is a growing belief that renewable energy is a serious business opportunity. Multilateral lending agencies such as the Asian Development Bank, as well as a number of countries such as Germany and Japan, are pouring expenditure into renewable energy projects in Asia.

Investment flows are being aided by two things: technology standardization and growing acceptance and knowledge by financiers at all scales, from large wind farms to microfinancing. More and more Asian countries are emphasizing alternative energy sources and introducing new regulations to promote them, with companies in these

*Table 11.2*   Costs of renewable energy compared with fossil fuels and nuclear power

| Technology | Current cost (US cents/ kWh) | Projected future costs beyond 2020 as the technology matures (US cents/kWh) |
|---|---|---|
| Biomass energy: | 5–15 | 4–10 |
| Electricity | 1–5 | 1–5 |
| Heat | | |
| Wind electricity: | 3–5 | 2–3 |
| Onshore | 6–10 | 2–5 |
| Offshore | | |
| Solar thermal electricity (insolation of 2,500 kWh/m² per year) | 12–18 | 4–10 |
| Hydroelectricity: | 2–8 | 2–8 |
| Large-scale | 4–10 | 3–10 |
| Small-scale | | |
| Geothermal energy: | 2–10 | 1–8 |
| Electricity | 0.5–5.0 | 0.5–5.0 |
| Heat | | |
| Marine energy: | 12 | 12 |
| Tidal barrage | 8–15 | 8–15 |
| Tidal stream | 8–20 | 5–7 |
| Wave | | |
| Grid-connected photovoltaics, according to incident solar energy (insolation): | 50–80 | ~8 |
| 1,000 kWh/m² per year (e.g. UK) | 30–50 | ~5 |
| 1,500 kWh/m² per year (e.g. Southern Europe) | 20–40 | ~4 |
| 2,500 kWh/m² per year (most developing countries) | 40–60 | ~10 |
| Stand-alone systems (inc. batteries), 2,500 kWh/m² per year | | |
| Nuclear power | 4–6 | 3–5 |
| Electricity grid supplies from fossil fuels (inc. R&D) | 2–3 | Capital costs will come down with technical progress but many technologies largely mature and may be offset by rising fuel costs. |
| Off-peak | 15–25 | |
| Peak | 8–10 | |
| Average | 25–80 | |
| Rural electrification | | |
| Costs of central grid supplies, excl. transmission and distribution: | 2–4 | Capital costs will come down with technical progress but many technologies already mature and may be offset by rising fuel costs. |
| Natural gas | 3–5 | |
| Coal | | |

*Source*: ICCEPT 2002[6]

areas needing more capital requirements. Hedge funds are also eyeing opportunities in the sector, and UK-based environmental organization Trucost and the Association for Sustainable and Responsible Investment in Asia (ASrIA) have released a major Asia-oriented report investigating the carbon emissions of major regional corporations, to encourage institutional investors to take into account the environmental impacts of the companies they invest in.

Major investments have already taken place: in August 2006, the World Bank brokered the largest ever GHG contract, which will see Asian and European organizations paying two Chinese chemical firms US$1 billion to reduce $CO_2$ emissions by 19 million tons a year.

Another interesting phenomenon is the listing and acquiring of companies. Seven renewable energy companies in Asia-Pacific have conducted public equity issues in the past 2 years. Suzlon Energy of India, which develops turbines and blades for wind-power generators, conducted its US$344 million Initial Public Offering (IPO) in October and SunTech Power Holdings of China priced its successful US$455 million IPO in December 2005. The Renewable Energy Exchange Asia was also launched in Singapore, sponsored by the Renewable Energy and Energy Efficiency Partnership (REEEP). The REEEP focuses on the development and support of legislative and regulatory frameworks that accelerate the marketplace for renewable energy and energy efficiency, with the purpose of the Exchange to act as a 'matchmaker' between investors who cannot find bankable projects and developers who cannot find cash for their ventures. Since its launch in June 2006, it has arranged meetings between proponents, interested parties and potential investors for more than 20 projects, from biodiesel plants to small hydroelectric projects in Southeast Asia.

## Strategies for Asian companies

Businesses nowadays are becoming more environmentally conscious, spurred by the government to adopt measures to practise sustainability and driven by the possibility of saving money. Being green has most certainly become a moral issue, as well as being 'fashionable', with companies on a quest to improve their images by 'looking good' environmentally. However, it should be noted that this strategy is more than good environmental stewardship – it can also safeguard a company's share price in the short term and create a long-term competitive advantage for those companies willing to take it seriously.

There is evidence that managers and companies are now being rewarded for being green, with banking analysts awarding 'brownie

*Table 11.3*   Asian government renewable energy targets

| Country | Stated targets |
| --- | --- |
| Australia | 9,500 gigawatt-hours (roughly extra 2% of total energy) to be sourced from renewable energy annually by 2010. |
| China | Rmb1.5 trillion (US$184 billion) to be invested in renewable energy sources by 2020, under the 11th Five Year Plan (FYP). Renewable energy to be 10% of electric power capacity by 2010 (expected 60 GW); 5% of primary energy by 2010 and 10% of primary energy by 2020. Wind power to comprise 5,000 MW by 2010 and 30,000 MW by 2020. |
| Hong Kong | 1% and 2% of electricity to be supplied from renewable energy by 2012. |
| India | Renewable energy to be 10% of added electric power capacity during 2003–2010 (expected 10 GW). Wind power to generate 5,000 MW by 2012 (likely to be reached before 2009). 12% of overall energy to be sourced from renewables by 2012. |
| Japan | Utilities to source 1.35% of total electricity from renewables by 2010, excluding geothermal and large hydro Renewable Portfolio Standard (RPS). 3,000 megawatts (MW) from wind by 2010. |
| Korea | Renewable energy to be 5% of total energy by 2010 and 8.5% by 2012, from 2% in 2004. |
| Malaysia | Renewable energy to provide 5% of electricity generation by 2005, equal to between 500 MW and 600 MW of installed capacity, backed by Fuel Diversification Policy (2001) and Small Renewable Energy Program (SREP). Under the Ninth Malaysia Plan (9MP), this was modified in 2006, with new targets to achieve 350 MW of installed capacity by 2010 (30 MW on peninsular Malaysia and 50 MW on Sabah). |
| Philippines | Renewable energy to provide 4.7 GW total existing capacity by 2013. |
| Singapore | 50,000 m$^2$ (~35 MWth) of solar thermal systems to be set in place by 2012. |
| Thailand | Renewable energy to contribute 8% of total primary energy by 2011 (excluding traditional rural biomass). |

*Source*: Macquarie Securities, Goldman Sachs, BCSE, Earthscan, Asia Money[7]

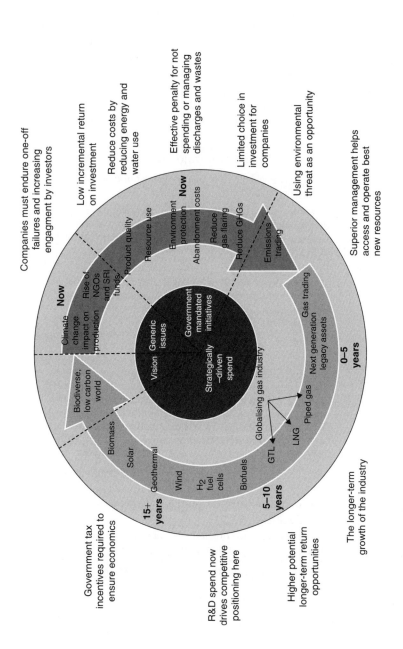

*Figure 11.7* Drivers of strategic vision towards a low-carbon future

*Source:* Sir David King, Chief Scientific Advisor to HM Government, London, UBS Conference: 'Global Action to Control Global Warming', February 2006.

points' in the form of good ratings to shining examples in the industry. Regulatory compliance under the Kyoto Protocol is the primary motivation for emission reductions in Europe and Japan, and it could impact on developing economies in Asia sooner rather than later.

So what can Asian companies do to capture low-carbon opportunities and profit at the same time? Figure 11.7 illustrates the cycle of strategic vision for a low-carbon and biodiverse future.

What must be done immediately is that companies must be ready to:

- endure one-off failures and increase their level of engagement with investors;
- face low incremental return on investments;
- reduce costs by reducing energy and water use;
- implement effective penalties for not spending or managing discharges and wastes;
- reduce GHG emissions.

Future drivers will include:

- using environmental threat as an opportunity;
- superior management, which will help access and operate best new resources;
- increased Research and Development spend (which is anticipated to drive competitive positioning within the next 5–15 years);
- Government tax incentives to enhance project economics.

Over the next 5 to 15 years, the way in which a company manages its carbon exposure could create or destroy shareholder value. Managers who fail to respond to calls for more transparency and better planning will face greater public censure and charges of breach of duty. They may even find the share price of their companies discounted in capital markets. Since 2005, leading American corporations such as General Electric and Wal-Mart have pledged strong efforts to limit their emissions. Executives now are not only hoping to improve public relations but fear future lawsuits for causing damage, not wanting their companies to be caught off guard by emission regulations and suspecting their profits could tumble from a loss in competitive advantage due to the effects of climate change. Powerful investors, from state pension funds to Wall Street firms such as Goldman Sachs, are also weighing in on global warming risks before investing in a company.

To analyse the strategies Asian companies must adopt, a good starting point will be to assess the various industries and their sensitivity to carbon limits.

Potential 'losing' companies will be those whose production generates many GHGs, particularly carbon dioxide. Coal and petroleum industries, the airline industry, auto manufacturers and logistics companies that make or rely on products that generate $CO_2$ will need to be wary. Electric utilities industries are also facing pressure, as most rely heavily on coal-fired generation. However, some utility companies are expressing increased interest in GHG trading and other market-based mechanisms, believing the blow of emissions limits could be softened by using economic mechanisms instead of a rigid regulatory regime.

Potential 'winning' companies, on the other hand, are a diverse group. Beneficiaries of emissions limits will be renewable energy companies, the biofuels industry, diversified technology companies, and engineering and environmental firms that have the potential to assist companies with liabilities to reduce their $CO_2$ emissions.

Regardless of sector, however, companies that implement energy efficiency and energy-saving programmes will see increases in profit while at the same time meeting their climate targets. Motivations for corporate and institutional actions include:

- reducing costs and improving profitability;
- risk mitigation to hedge against uncertainty;
- developing a competitive advantage via early action;
- regulatory positioning via voluntary 'early action';
- developing new products and markets.

In particular, the strategies Asian companies can adopt on climate change through incorporating these measures include emission reductions such as energy efficiency improvements, cogeneration (generation of heat and power) projects and fuel-switching. It is noteworthy that early action in this area can enable companies to implement such projects effectively through testing, evaluating and improving the technologies and practices being used.

- Emission accounting, auditing and reporting
- Development of an internal baseline
- Market screening of carbon offset markets: internal/external carbon trading and hedging
- Enabling new technologies

- Creating new low-carbon products and services for the ever discerning consumer

## Corporate environmental reporting

Accounting, corporate environmental reporting, carbon footprints and tracking systems are rising areas of development, whereby companies must learn to account for the carbon dioxide emitted from or consumed by their business. These methods also involve and educate staff on the risks and options related to climate change and gain significant competitive advantage. Larger companies can, for example, establish an internal GHG programme to help meet their $CO_2$ emissions targets. Management consulting firm McKinsey is further helping financial analysts to develop global reporting standards to facilitate rating of companies. For example, in Europe's utility sector, several new variables make it possible to measure carbon emissions against production or revenue – two areas that are gaining exposure are the carbon factor of the production portfolio and the revenue/profit exposure per carbon profile.

Furthermore, companies should engage in corporate environmental reporting for the following motives, as outlined by the ACCA (2002):

- Risk management – mitigating risks in terms of financial, legal and reputation implications
- Marketing strategy – public image and brand enhancement such as through receiving environmental and sustainability awards
- Legal needs – to keep in pace with or anticipate regulations
- Competition – to get ahead of or stay with competitors
- Ethics – individual commitment; commitment to accountability and transparency
- Accounting requirements – in compliance with financial reporting requirements and providing a link between financial and environmental performance/reporting
- Investors' interests – demands of green (ethical) investors
- Employees' interests – attracts right staff from the labour market
- Value-add reporting – to add value to corporate reports and communicate to wider range of stakeholders, addressing their environmental concerns
- Certifications needs – to indicate compliance with ISO14000 and other environmental regulatory guidelines

Companies must, however, note that uncertainty about future regulations is the biggest risk in the carbon equation, as executives often need long-term assurances on credits and emission levels to encourage them to plan for expensive capital investments. Both the Kyoto Protocol and EU Emissions Trading Scheme (ETS) have set initial goals, but it is uncertain what will happen thereafter.

What is certain is that management leadership is necessary to steer Asian firms towards a brighter and cleaner future, with well-managed firms in all sectors and industries ideally using the challenge of global climate change to stimulate innovation and improve business activities through unifying their business performance and environmental goals. It will be the quality of a firm's management and its strategy to adapt to future carbon limits that will determine its success, helping to make it a 'winner' while delivering shareholder value. Asia can most certainly lead the way, as we have seen with the example of Japan and its positive transformation to a clean energy zone.

## Greening our growing company in Asia: YTL Corporation, Malaysia

> It is imperative that developments are sustainable for our own economic welfare otherwise we are cursing future generations with our negligence as we are now cursed by previous generations of political and business leaders that did not pay attention to sustainability...
>
> Tan Sri Dato (Dr) Francis Yeoh,
> Managing Director, YTL Corporation[8]

The YTL Corporation is one of the largest companies in Malaysia, listed on the Kuala Lumpur Stock Exchange, and, together with its four listed subsidiaries, has a combined Market Capitalization of almost RM19 billion (US$5 billion). The company, listed in 1985, has also had a secondary listing on the Tokyo Stock Exchange since 1996.

YTL Corp. is one of the largest independent power producers in Southeast Asia (see Figure 11.8). As one of Malaysia's leading integrated infrastructure conglomerates, it owns and manages regulated assets with long-term concessions globally, employs over 6,200 people around the world and currently serves over 10 million customers worldwide. Its key businesses include: utilities, high speed rail, cement manufacturing, construction

SINCE 1955

## ENVIRONMENTAL RESPONSIBILITY

### The YTL Group's Environmental Vision

We are fully committed to being a responsible corporate citizen. Energy plays an essential role in ensuring quality of life for people everywhere, for us and for future generations. Supplying energy reliably is critical to helping people maintain and improve their standard of living. However, this brings with it significant challenges – for example, the very real threat of climate change means that we need to continue to provide and deliver energy in a way that minimizes the impact our emissions have on the environment. We recognize the importance of sustainable development, taking account of the impact of our operations on society and understanding the dire consequences of global warming.

## Energy Saving and Resource Conservation

### Water & Sewerage Services

Wessex Water, our subsidiary in the UK, operates under a stringent set of environmental directives and regulations with a key long term goal of becoming a sustainable water company. Wessex Water's comprehensive programme to achieve this goal has ensured that all compliance rates for drinking water, sewage treatment and bathing water have not only been met but are amongst the best in the United Kingdom.

### Issues to Incorporate in Sustainable Development

| Finances | | | Finances |
|---|---|---|---|
| Water resources<br>sewage treatment and effluent quality<br>sludge reuse<br>emissions to air<br>ecosystems and biodiversity | health and safety<br>terms and conditions, rewards and motivation<br>training and skills<br>internal communication | | |
| ENVIRONMENT | STAFF | | |
| CUSTOMERS AND COMMUNITIES | INFRASTRUCTURE | | |
| drinking water quality<br>customer services and operational impacts<br>work with regulators and other interests<br>security and emergency planning<br>community work<br>affordability | specifications for new assets<br>equipment and process materials<br>condition of existing assests<br>capacity and service delivery | | |

*Source*: Wessex Water; Striking the Balance Report: Introduction[9]

*Figure 11.8* Continued

## Property Development

In our Sentul project, we made the decision to maintain a 35-acre green lung in the heart of Kuala Lumpur as a park for the use of our residents because we believe that this will enhance the quality of life of the people who buy our properties. We have adopted this philosophy throughout all our current residential property developments. We have placed the focus on reducing the number of units in favour of maintaining a balance between nature and development and have adopted building and design techniques that make the most of natural sunlight and improve airflow to reduce the need for artificial light and air-conditioners.

Wessex Water's operations centre, hailed   The majestic Kuala Lumpur Performing   Sentul park                   Lake Edge in Puchong
as one of the greenest offices in Europe   Arts Centrein in Sentul Park

## Express Rail Link

YTL Corp is a major shareholder of Express Rail Link Sdn Bhd - a railway development company which was awarded a concession on 25 August 1997 to finance, design, construct, operate and maintain the KLIA Ekspres, KLIA Transit and other ancillary activities related to railway services.

The fleet consists of twelve state of the art, high speed trains which have no direct emissions of pollutants and have 'built in' energy savings by design. We acknowledge that environment friendliness does not end with the trains. There is an Energy Saving Programme for trains that was implemented in 2003. Drivers were trained to operate the trains using energy saving techniques, which ERL Maintenance Support Sdn Bhd (E-MAS) named the 'MAKAN' principle:

• Make sure that trains are switched off during stabling
• As much driving as possible in coasting mode
• Know to brake early and with not more than 40% braking force
• As much as possible using the electrical brake
• No traction effort more than 80%

## Climate Change

We recognize the impact of global warming and climate change on our community, not just locally but globally. We regard climate change as a clear risk and have taken measures to reduce Green House Gas (GHG) and noxious emissions in all our activities, from our utilities and cement manufacturing plants to property and hotel operations.

The YTL Group is constantly searching for innovative ways to encourage energy saving and to minimize the risk and glaringly visible effects of climate change. We therefore anticipate our future projects to integrate technology, policy and

*Figure 11.8*   Continued

positive action to steer our company towards being not only clean and green but also secure, in trust for future generations.

## Water & Sewerage Services

Climate change awareness and carbon management have been at the forefront of Wessex Water's developments. Its environmental impacts – for example, quantities of water taken from the environment, effluent released into rivers, re-use of sludge and greenhouse gas emissions (mainly carbon dioxide and methane) – are closely monitored through environmental regulation. Tighter environmental regulation has consequently benefited the water environment more. Wessex's carbon dioxide emissions are now lower than in 1990 because of technological advancements enabling the carbon content of an average kWh of electricity from the national grid to be lower.

However, its energy consumption has climbed through increase of sewage treatment to meet environmental regulation. The company's carbon dioxide emissions, 95% of which came from consuming energy, have increased significantly in the last few years and plans are now underway to reduce these emissions. The Royal Commission of Environmental Pollution published a report in 2001 that lobbied for a 60% decrease in carbon dioxide emissions from energy use by 2050 to avoid escalating damage to the earth's environment.

## Climate change and carbon management at Wessex Water

*Emissions Forecast*

| Reduction of Emissions | | |
|---|---|---|
| | Carbon Dioxide | Carbon Dioxide and Methane Combined |
| What we emitted in 1997 | 101,108 tonnes | 168,224 tonnes |
| What we would need to emit in 2050 (60% less than 1997) | 40,423 tonnes | 67,312 tonnes |
| Annual reduction needed from 1997 levels | 1,145 tonnes | 1,904 tonnes |
| *Source*: Wessex Water; *Striking the Balance Report*; 'Climate change and carbon management'. | | |

*Figure 11.8 Environmental Responsibility* of YTL Corporation – selected excerpts adapted from YTL Corporation Bhd, Corporate Social Responsibility Report 2006

Source: *Environmental Responsibility* of YTL Corporation, selected excerpts adapted from YTL Corporation Bhd, Corporate Social Responsibility Report 2006.

contracting, property development, hotels and resorts and technology incubation.

YTL Corporation's strategy of providing world-class services at very competitive prices, together with its innovation vision, has led directly to its recording a compounded annual growth rate in pre-tax profits of 55 per cent over the last 15 years and an enviable track record of creating shareholder value. The company's strategy has also resulted in it and its subsidiaries accumulating numerous international awards in the process.

YTL Corporation and its subsidiaries ('YTL Group') reports on its sustainability measures and initiatives, published in its yearly Sustainability Reports. The report combines both Corporate Social Responsibility (CSR) and environmental reporting (ER), and the company is one of only a handful of companies that have taken initiatives to pioneer CSR and ER in its home country of Malaysia – the rationale being that there is conventional wisdom in businesses that companies can no longer afford to be socially and environmentally irresponsible. A recent study showed that companies will benefit not only from being socially responsible but also from being able to demonstrate convincingly that they are socially responsible through communicating to stakeholders their commitment to, and record on, CSR. YTL believes that effective Corporate Social Responsibility can deliver benefits to its businesses and, in turn, to its shareholders.

YTL Corp.'s statements on corporate governance and internal control are also included in a separate section of its Annual Report. YTL Corp.'s Sustainability Reports are also publicly accessible in the 'Investor Relations' section at their corporate website at http://www.ytl.com.my accessed on 2 August 2010.

## Conclusion

The research presented in this chapter has shown a remarkable picture of the accelerating momentum, commercial viability and policy initiative of sustainability and renewable energy in Asia. The goal is sustainable development, whereby society should adopt a policy of sustainable development that allows society to meet its present needs while preserving the ability of future generations to meet their own needs.[10] Concern is placed on the rights of future generations and the 'triple bottom line' of economic prosperity, social equity and environmental protection.[11]

From a business perspective, the focus should be the creation of long-term shareholder value by recognizing that corporations are dependent on licences provided by society to do business. If businesses choose not to comply with sustainable development policies, society can enforce compliance through imposing additional government regulation and control.[12]

Overall, the time has come to think beyond traditional precepts of power politics and beyond positions dictated by short-term interests – a new era of Green Power has arrived, bringing with it a surge of entrepreneurs, innovators and new entrants. Asian companies and economies will need to adapt and innovate quickly in the new low-carbon environment, for the sake of Asia's security in energy, food production, water and health, if it is to survive the extreme effects of climate change.

---

*Four key strategic imperatives for asian companies*

1) *Adaptation is necessary and unavoidable*
   So why adaptation? There are six reasons why adaptation is necessary:

   Climate change cannot be avoided
   Anticipatory and precautionary adaptation is more effective and less costly than forced last-minute fixes
   Climate change may be more rapid and pronounced than current estimates suggest, and unexpected events, as already witnessed globally, are more than just possible
   Immediate benefits can be gained from better adaptation to climate variability and extreme atmospheric events (for example, with the hurricane risk, strict building laws and better evacuation practices will need to be executed)
   Immediate benefits can be gained by removing maladaptive policies and practices (for example, building on flood plains and vulnerable coastlines)
   Climate change brings opportunities as well as threats

2) *Embrace renewable energy*
   The case for renewable energy is on the rise. Ideally, a combination of improved energy efficiency and alternative energy is a solution to global warming. It must be noted, however, that, from the environmental and safety perspective, carbon capture methods (the storage of $CO_2$ either underground or in the ocean) are not technically proven to be secure, however helpful this would appear to be in the short term.

3) *Change energy use and mix through innovation*
   It is now not a question of whether we will use oil, coal and gas but rather *how* we will use them less – and through cleaner and greener methods, of course! Replacing our energy infrastructure over the next 50 years is expensive but not prohibitive. Power generation through renewable sources at the point of use should be an imperative!

4) *Remember the 3 'Is'*
   The 3 'Is' that Asian firms and economies should keep in mind are:
   **Implementation** – because, without effective policies at the national, regional and local level, the *Kyoto Protocol* and other such policies will fail.

---

> ***Improvement*** – because companies and governments have the necessary means to adapt and evolve to changes which will involve new insights, developments and circumstances.
> ***Innovation*** – because this will require substantial inputs in terms of money, time, energy and creativity.

## Notes

1. World Economic Forum, at www.weforum.org, accessed on 2 August 2010.
2. HF Kloman, 'Rethinking Risk Management', Geneva Papers (July 1992).
3. HF Kloman, *Risk Management Reports* (March 1998).
4. Goldman Sachs, *Renewables 2005: Global Status Report*, Industrial Technology Research Institute (Taiwan), Energy Commission (Malaysia).
5. 'Establishing National Authorities for the CDM: A Guide for Developing Countries' (2002).
6. Imperial College Centre for Energy Policy and Technology (ICCEPT, 2002). http://www3.imperial.ac.uk/icept/publications/workingpapers.
7. Macquarie Securities, Goldman Sachs, BCSE, Earthscan, Asia Money.
8. 'Tan Sri Dato' (Dr) Francis Yeoh, Managing Director, YTL Corporation.
9. Wessex Water publishes a yearly sustainability report reporting on environmental indicators and sustainability issues. The water company's *Striking the Balance* 2006 report, which provides a wealth of information on these important areas, can be accessed at its website: http://www.wessexwater.co.uk/strikingthebalance2006/ accessed date 2 August 2010.
10. Gro Harlem Brundlandt, *Our Common Future* (Oxford University Press, 1987).
11. M Whittaker, 'Emerging "triple bottom line" model for industry weighs environmental, economic and social considerations', *Oil and Gas Journal*, 20 December 1999.
12. John R Fanchi, *Energy in the 21st Century* (World Scientific, January 2005).

# 12
# CSR Initiatives for Green Buildings: Perspectives of Hong Kong Financial Institutions

*Paul Boldy and Lisa Barnes*

## Background

High carbon emissions from buildings are causing Hong Kong's air quality to diminish.[1] Massive amounts of energy are used by buildings,[2] and Financial Institutions (FIs) are among the largest occupants of commercial building space in Hong Kong. As a consequence, FIs are well placed to reduce building-related power use and mitigate the environmental damage caused by it. This chapter focuses on the demand side for environmentally friendly building options, where pressure is beginning to form.[3] Eight Hong Kong-based FIs are interviewed to find out their perspectives on initiatives for green buildings. The findings show that FIs are very serious about environmental CSR and it has become a normal part of doing business in the banking sector.

## Introduction

Buildings consume over 40 per cent of the world's electricity,[4] and in Hong Kong building-related consumption is far greater, with estimates ranging from 70 per cent[5] to 89 per cent.[6] This results in increased $CO_2$ emissions, leading to a large carbon footprint and bad air quality.[7] Financial Institutions (FIs) are a major contributor to the Hong Kong economy, as they are a major employer and the city is seen as being a major finance hub. As a consequence FIs are major occupiers of building space in Hong Kong, and hence whatever they can do to reduce their carbon footprint should have a beneficial effect on energy usage and $CO_2$ emissions.[8]

Many FIs have embraced Corporate Social Responsibility (CSR) and since 2005 there have been benchmarking exercises to gauge best practice.[9] Davies argues that the adoption of CSR as a key way that a bank does business is critical in moving forward in an industry in which CSR is increasingly seen as a competitive advantage.[10] Tipgos and Keefe point out that all stakeholders need to be taken into account.[11] CSR is therefore being adopted as a method of conducting everyday business[12] and forms part of Triple Bottom Line (TBL) reporting.[13] Nonetheless, it also has its critics.[14]

In Hong Kong, FIs are an important part of the economy[15] and there are numerous FIs based there.[16] Their actions are important to reduce the city's $CO_2$ emissions and carbon footprint. Ranged against these are the city's landlords and owners, many of whom are Chinese Family Companies who do business based on a Chinese cultural model,[17] that is to say, 'in a harmonious way'. This business model is supported by the Government, but there is limited state regulation or leadership in this area.[18] By contrast, international practices show government taking the lead and being a key driver of change.[19]

Against this backdrop it has become increasingly important for tenants on the demand side to be forceful in demanding green building features from landlords.[20] Most recent research has been focused on the supply side, that is, those who build or own buildings and have to be encouraged to build in green features. Jones, Lang, LaSalle and Core Net[21] identified that the owners were not moving fast enough to meet demand, and a 'Circle of Blame' had become established, in which everyone blames each other for the lack of space built to green building standards. Several 'break-options' to this model were proposed by Lorenz[22] to promote green buildings, but this was supply side-focused only. This chapter will focus on the break-options from a demand side perspective and will examine how tenants could be a driver of change for the promotion of sustainable green buildings in Hong Kong.

## The literature

Most of the $CO_2$ produced in Hong Kong comes from buildings, principally office buildings. These are mainly in densely populated areas and were designed in times of low-cost energy and low awareness of climate change. Studies show that developed countries produce up to 40 per cent of $CO_2$ from the operation of their buildings. In Hong Kong this figure is estimated at between 70 per cent[23] and 89 per cent,[24] illustrating a clear need to focus on reducing building-related $CO_2$ levels. The Financial Services sector and its associated businesses, such as lawyers and accountants, are tenants in many of these buildings. Given their global nature, these businesses tend to work around the clock and hence are a major source of $CO_2$, principally from their high use of energy. FIs could therefore have a major effect in reducing Hong Kong's $CO_2$ emissions by reducing their energy use.

FIs also represent one of Hong Kong's major sources of employment.[25] It is for this reason that the financial sector was selected for this study. Given that the major FIs occupy many of the largest buildings in the city and that energy usage is one of the major causes of pollution, FIs can contribute much to its reduction by adopting policies to reduce energy use within their occupied space. FIs were among the first corporations to measure their carbon footprint, and to produce plans and targets to reduce it, especially in the areas of energy, water and waste management. This approach also supports their stance on CSR, sustainability and the focus on the Triple Bottom Line (TBL) and how this affects their method of operating.

According to the Hong Kong Monetary Authority's statistics (2009) there were 145 Licensed Banks, 27 Restricted Licensed Banks, 28 Deposit Taking Companies and 85 Representative Offices of Foreign Banks active in Hong Kong at the end of December 2008. The sector employed over 80,000 people, which is indicative of the importance of Hong Kong as a leading financial and banking centre in Asia. Generally 'banks are the backbone of the global economy, providing capital for innovation, infrastructure, job creation and overall prosperity.'[26] That this is certainly the case in Hong Kong provides the motivation for this study.

CSR came to the forefront of corporate and academic thinking in the early 1960s, partly as a result of the views of Nobel Laureate Milton Friedman, who took the view that business's only goal was to earn maximum profit for its owners. This was seized upon as being too singular a notion of how business works and that, by contrast, business had many more stakeholders and, as a consequence, more responsibilities than just profit. This was given further credence by examples of the social failure of business: for example, the poison gas disaster in Bhopal in 1984, in which the local subsidiary of Union Carbide, a huge US chemical corporation, employed lax safety procedures, thereby causing a leak at its plant that proved deadly to local inhabitants. This gap between company profit and the greater good was further highlighted by the problems at Enron, WorldCom and Tyco International, where the balance of power had shifted to top management. The consequent detachment from shareholders led to misuse of management positions for their own, rather than the owners', gain. To combat this there was a swell of opinion that 'business has a social responsibility to its stakeholders and to society at large, advocating that top management should use the vast economic power of business to promote social goals such as cleaning the environment, urban renewal and equal opportunity.'[27]

Regulations such as the Sarbanes–Oxley Act passed by the US Congress in 2002 aimed to prevent this happening again, but, as recent events have shown with the subprime crisis, even if regulation is in place it does not mean that the regulators themselves will be vigilant.

This detachment of management from shareholders caused much debate, with some academics supporting shareholders' increased voice in the running of their company,[28] while others saw it as futile given the voting rights of the management group.[29] Others wondered if it would be counterproductive given the short-term views of shareholders, especially institutional shareholders.[30]

Arguments were also advanced to demonstrate that share prices often rose as a result of good CSR practices.[31] However, others found there to be little relationship between CSR and financial performance.[32] Given the bull market of the past few years it is hard to say whether there is a significant correlation between the two, but, given the cost of setting up a good CSR system, it will be interesting to see what happens in a bear market, and this will provide a useful area of further research.

Much of the work on CSR has focused on how financial returns can be safely managed in a way that meets all stakeholders' needs. However, there are other areas to take into account, such as sustainability and care of the environment. These areas are quite recent and many of the definitions of the key terms, such as carbon footprint, sustainability and CSR, are still debated. The issues of measuring concepts and benchmarking them are in their early days.[33] The Triple Bottom Line (TBL) approach is examined, with the key literature originating from Europe, USA, Australia as well as a growing volume from Asia. This will give a global picture of how the issue of reducing $CO_2$ is being tackled, compared with the methods being used in Hong Kong.

Notions from the literature review lead to the following research question:

*How important is CSR to your Institution and how is that reflected in obtaining and maintaining buildings to the highest green standards?*

## Method of enquiry

The research issue under consideration depends heavily on how people understand the issues facing their companies and the effect they can have in working from a tenant's point of view with a landlord. It is clear that 'rich data'[34] is required, so a qualitative method has been adopted. Also the subject matter is relatively new, and as such a qualitative approach is to be taken to gather meaningful information that will enable a significant depth of understanding.[35]

The use of a qualitative approach tends to rely on verbal analysis rather than statistical analysis.[36] We conducted a semi-structured interview on a face-to-face basis with eight FIs in Hong Kong who are major occupiers of office space in the city. The use of in-depth interviews in light of time and cost restrictions allowed us to collect large amounts of information in terms of people's perceptions quickly[37] from relatively few people.[38] Interviews, particularly in the banking sector, are more generally successful in gaining information than other methods such as surveys.[39]

In order to gain as wide a range of participants as possible, the membership list of the Banking Association of Hong Kong was used as a basis for selection. Financial Institutions were selected by purposive sampling in order to give a global view of sustainable green buildings and to avoid a more insular sample that would arise from just selecting Hong Kong banks.

The selected Institutions owned or leased a lot of office space in Hong Kong, around 5,289,500 sq. ft. They were therefore well placed to give informative answers on their landlords and the issues they were facing while trying to ensure that their Institution's green goals were achieved.

Nine interviews were carried out. Two were carried out by phone due to business travel. One company had two responsible people to interview in order to obtain all the data required from the eight Institutions. Interview was selected as the means of data gathering rather than mail questionnaires, which give an unsure response rate and less opportunity for participants to fully explain their positions as well as to add other issues not included in the interview plan. Two areas of interest that were added as a result of this approach were carbon offset payments and the ability of real estate professionals to advise on green buildings.

Apart from background information, six questions were asked, in relation to: (1) the company's approach to CSR, (2) the role of senior management, (3) CSR targets, (4) results measurement, (5) the role of the Company Real Estate (CRE) department and (6) how CSR achievements are rewarded. It is hoped that the information will help answer research Question (RQ) 1:

*How important is CSR to your Institution and how is that reflected in obtaining and maintaining buildings to the highest green standard?*

Question 1 asks: what is the FI's overall approach to CSR? This will be used to triangulate their answers with their websites and other activities and to judge their commitment to CSR. Question 2 seeks to gauge the level of support within the FI for CSR and the level of senior management involvement. Question 3 asks who sets the CSR targets, while question 4 asks how they are measured. Both these questions seek to find out how central CSR is to an organization in terms of the importance it attaches to CSR and whether it forms part of the Key Performance Indicators (KPIs) of individuals or groups. Question 5 is trying to find out how important the CRE department is to a FI being able to achieve its CSR goals. As this group controls the buildings, and thus a large part of a FI's carbon footprint, its actions are vital to achieve CSR goals in this area. Question 6 looks at how CSR goal achievement is rewarded across the company. This seeks to see whether there is a relationship between bonuses or awards and the goals that are achieved and will provide some indication as to the importance of CSR goal achievement within a FI.

## Data analysis

### Interview group

Nine interviews were carried out in total with employees of eight different FIs. One Institution had two senior managers who looked after this area, so both were interviewed for completeness.

### Background data

In order to give an overview of the participants and their companies, some descriptive data were collected about themselves, their company and their department.

The participants had educational backgrounds ranging from school leaver qualifications and attending night school through to Master's Degrees in Business Administration and Environmental Management. Only one person had attained a recognized qualification in green buildings and sustainability (this was the LEED accreditation), which is perhaps a fair indication of how new this area is.

*Table 12.1*   Level of education

| Education | Total | Percentage |
|---|---|---|
| High school certificate | 3 | 33.3 |
| Higher school certificate | 1 | 11.1 |
| Diploma/Tafe certificate | 1 | 11.1 |
| Bachelor's degree | 2 | 22.2 |
| Master's degree | 1 | 11.1 |
| Postgraduate studies | 1 | 11.1 |
| Total | 9 | 100 |

*Table 12.2*   Participants' position within the company

| Position | Total | Percentage |
|---|---|---|
| Team leader | 3 | 33.3% |
| Middle manager | 2 | 22.3% |
| Senior manager | 4 | 44.4% |
| Total | 9 | 100% |

*Table 12.3*   Length of employment

| Institution | Years of employment |
|---|---|
| FI 1 | 3 |
| FI 2 | 3.5 |
| FI 3 | 1 |
| FI 4 | 3 |
| FI 5i | 6 |
| FI 5ii | 5 |
| FI 6 | 3 |
| FI 7 | 0.75 |
| FI 8 | 16 |
| **Average** | **4.5** |

All of the participants held senior positions within their organizations, either being Head of Department or holding Senior Vice President or Regional roles.

Their span of employment in their current company varied from as little as 8 months to 16 years. However, the person with the shortest tenure had previously worked for 10 years in Asia in a similar capacity for another FI. Most of the group had been with their employer for 3 years, with most of that time spent in their current role. One area of interest observed was that, out of the nine people interviewed, eight were Caucasian (four Australian and four British) and only one was local to Hong Kong. All were male.

## Summary of information

The FIs came from different countries and included Institutions from USA, China, Australia, Europe, Japan and Hong Kong. This sample was chosen in a purposive manner so as to get as wide a view as possible of how FIs approach sustainability and green buildings in Hong Kong. The size of the FIs differed greatly, with the smallest having under 2,000 employees while several of the others had over 300,000 globally. Paradoxically, the smaller Institutions tended to have more

*Table 12.4*   Summary of information

| Country of origin | Full Time (F/T) Employees | Operating revenue 2008 | Space in Hong Kong – Leased (square ft) | Space in Hong Kong – Owned (square ft) |
|---|---|---|---|---|
| British/ Hong Kong | 315,000 | US$6.5 billion | 400,000 | 1.6 million |
| Chinese | 1,400 | HK$164 million | 80,000 | 20,000 |
| USA | 320,000 | US$20 billion | 844,449 | Nil |
| German | 80,000 | (Euro 3.85 billion) | 270,000 | Nil |
| Australian | 35,000 | A$3.3 billion | 45,000 | Nil |
| British | 75,000 | HK$13.9 billion | 1,000,000 | Nil |
| Japanese | 24,000 | (JPY708 billion) | 250,000 | Nil |
| Hong Kong | 8,000 | HK$6.5 billion | 390,000 | 390,000 |

employees situated in Hong Kong than the larger ones, and this could be ascribed to the level of focus the smaller Institutions had on the China market as opposed to Asia-Pacific as a whole. Turnover likewise varied greatly, with figures ranging from USD 20 billion profit to losses of a similar scale brought about by the subprime exposures of some of the Institutions in the sample.

When participants were asked about the amount of space their Institution occupied in Hong Kong and the proportion leased and owned, the answers gave an insight into the different real estate strategies being utilized. Outside the Hong Kong Institution, all the foreign Institutions save for one leased all of their space in Hong Kong, and this was the case whether it was a fully let headquarters building or just a few floors. The non-Hong Kong International Institution owned 75 per cent of its space, for historical reasons. The amount of space occupied ranged from 100,000 sq. ft to over 2 million sq. ft. The local Hong Kong Institution also leased 50 per cent of its space requirement, but this was mainly attributed to its larger branch network, as its Head Office building was owned.

### Corporate Social Responsibility (Research question 1)

This research question was: *how important is CSR to your institution and how is that reflected in maintaining buildings to the highest green standard?* This question was broken down into six parts and was designed to see how CSR was driven, measured and rewarded in the institutions and what part the CRE department played.

### Companies' approach to CSR

When asked about their company's approach to CSR, all answers were in the affirmative and they were all supportive of the concept. Some of the larger groups were investing a lot of time, effort and money in this area, often directed globally from head office. One executive said, 'we live sustainability, it is not just a marketing tool' (FI 1); another pointed out 'CSR is a component of responsible business practice, it is part of running a good business' (FI 5i). One of the smaller institutions stated: 'the bank seeks to adopt the highest standards of CSR in terms of ethics, corporate governance and its interaction and contribution to the community' (FI 2).

Many of the groups pointed to the fact that they publicly post their goals and results on their websites and include them in their CSR reports as evidence of their commitment to CSR. One group, though, had only fairly recently (within the last 2 years) begun to take CSR seriously but were now investing in the area. As one aspect of this they had put into place a global sustainability policy, although this was narrow in its focus, zeroing in on energy and not taking a broader environmental approach. This, however, was becoming wider as their experience of this area grew.

To sum up the approach to CSR, one executive put it this way: 'if you are in the business of banking and finance, then to deliver these you must include CSR as part of the offering'(FI 5i).

### Role of senior management

The role of senior managers in the CSR process was unanimously seen as being supportive. In most cases it was indeed driven from the 'C' office, that is, CEO, CFO and COO. Each institution interviewed had a strong supporter in Hong Kong who drove the CSR strategy through either committees or special teams. In one large institution targets form part of senior management's annual performance criteria, and this was seen as being cascaded down through the organization in time. In another, the CEO 'has a personal interest in sustainability and green initiatives so the culture and philosophy is driven from the very top' (FI 2). However, one executive mentioned that senior management did not drive the CSR process and it was 'difficult to know who did in such a large organization' (FI 3), although in this group both Marketing and Corporate Communications were active to ensure newsworthy stories were published on a regional level and the Regional Head would not do anything without considering the impact of CSR.

### Target-setting

The setting of targets for CSR performance in the company was mainly set at board level, then cascaded down to be implemented at regional and local levels, creating a 'top-down approach'. This contrasted with one large institution that set the targets locally, then sent them to the Head Office to be consolidated into a global plan, a 'bottom-up approach'. What was interesting here is that a global consulting firm was involved in making sure the targets were reasonable and was responsible for the annual audit and inclusion in the Sustainability Report. Another institution went even further and had outside experts set the targets, as 'the experts provided the background proposal that was then debated and approved' (FI 5i). Only one institution at this stage had not set specific targets due to its late adoption of the CSR approach. This group came from a country that is very well advanced regarding sustainability, but it had taken time to appreciate the importance of CSR to its business. This area of target-setting for sustainability and CSR targets is worthy of further research to see which approach is most effective: top-down, bottom-up or external.

## Measurement of CSR

When asked how CSR results are measured, there was a diverse set of answers. At one end of the spectrum institutions were audited by external groups: ' the results form part of the Triple Bottom Line accounting of the bank' (FI 1) and are posted on their websites. Two Institutions took another path by developing databases that covered $CO_2$ emissions across the global organization focusing on energy, water and waste. These were consolidated into environmental databases, which in one case were benchmarked against the World Resource Institute Ratings. Another group took measurement to a deeper level to 'also include the supply chain and sustainable sourcing in... [their] ... sphere' (FI 7). At the other end of the spectrum there was no measurement in place, or in the case of a smaller Institution they were treated as 'soft targets'. As one executive remarked, 'CSR results are not really measurable unlike regulatory issues that are black or white, they are included in personal objectives under the section for core values' (FI 2).

In some ways the institutions at the non-measurement end of the spectrum could be accused of 'greenwashing' their product, that is, using sustainability and CSR claims that are not backed up by measurable action. In fairness, the size of the institutions at the measurable end are large and they have commensurate resources to devote to this area, whereas the smaller ones do not.

## Role of the Corporate Real Estate (CRE) department

The CRE group in every Institution interviewed were very passionate and positive in their contribution to helping their Institution achieve their CSR goals. As one executive said, 'property is one of the key areas that contributes to our targets and results' and 'has the controls and influence to significantly reduce the bank's impact across the organization globally' (FI 1). Another was of the opinion that the CRE team focuses on the direct environmental impacts, which are electricity, water consumption, waste and $CO_2$ emissions.

Many of the Institutions pointed out that the CRE group is responsible for the areas that produce most of the $CO_2$ emissions, and several of the Institutions had goals either to significantly reduce their emissions or to achieve carbon neutrality within a given time. They therefore had the task of ensuring that they controlled their area of responsibility well.

Energy was the area of most focus. One executive said 'that anything relating to the firm's Carbon Footprint involves the CRE department as it relates to energy, purchase of materials and products and any fit outs or new buildings' (FI 5ii). This has focused some Institutions into putting criteria into place when new buildings are being sought because 'CRE needs to know what is the environmental rating (if they have one) and the landlord's view towards waste' (FI 7). This unanimous forceful viewpoint gives support to the fact that the CRE group are intent on ensuring that they are located in the best buildings possible to meet their CSR sustainability goals.

### Rewards for CSR achievement

The rewards for achieving CSR goals differed markedly across the Institutions, and only two tied their achievements against Key Performance Indicators (KPIs), which in turn were translated into cash bonuses. The cash bonus, as one executive explained, 'is paid on the overall performance then rolls into the business unit then into the organization as a whole' (FI 5i). Other institutions took a middle path, where success was rewarded in terms of recognition for the efforts and awarded with prizes. 'Nothing in this case went into the bonus packet and it is seen as being inappropriate as it is everyone's efforts' (FI 6). Another in the same position said 'that the reward for achieving CSR targets is mainly aspiration and is used as a marketing tool for employee recruitment and retention' (FI 4).

Half of the institutions did not reward CSR achievement at all. This question gave the most diverse answers of the section and split the Institutions into three camps: 'bonus,' 'recognition' and 'no-reward'. The latter Institutions were all Asian-based, perhaps demonstrating that they are lagging behind their Western-focused peers in this area. This would make sense in light of the view that 'there is clear variance across the globe in the pace at which sustainability is becoming a critical CRE issue.'[40] Asia lags behind Europe and the USA significantly at this stage, and their reward and recognition systems seem to show this to be the case.

### Website triangulation

As part of the corroboration of the interview answers from the eight Institutions, the websites of each of them were reviewed to see what they said about CSR and sustainability. This forms part of the triangulation process to give the research findings more validity, and because an

*Table 12.5* Corporate Social Responsibility

| Institution | Who sets targets for CSR? | How is achievement rewarded? |
| --- | --- | --- |
| FI 1 | By country – consolidated in London | Bonus for senior management – not for teams yet |
| FI 2 | CEO | N/A |
| FI 3 | CEO's office | Bonus |
| FI 4 | Board level | Aspirational / Employee retention + attraction |
| FI 5 | Outside experts | Terms in KPI |
| FI 6 | Board | Prizes |
| FI 7 | No formal target | N/A |
| FI 8 | gm executive office | It is not |

external source is used it is more reliable, although it could be described as within method, since the web site is controlled by the Institutions. This is viewed as not being as good as between methods, such as third party sources (Jick 1979, Johnson 1997).[41] However, as most of the groups are using an independent accredited green building rating system, this gives another level of corroboration that is truly third-party.

All eight websites were reviewed and all eight fully supported what the Institutions had said, even to the stage where two of the eight had already pre-warned the researcher that they did not have sustainability reports or CSR reports on their websites. Some of the Institutions had links to separate sites that covered their CSR and sustainability efforts. These websites included their sustainability and CSR reports as well as listing their targets and progress against them. They also showed all the efforts that they were making in the communities they served. One of the two Institutions with no CSR or Sustainability Reports had highlighted that their CSR work was mainly on tree-planting and giving volunteer time to the communities, and their website had a page depicting this.

The only Institution not to have anything at all on its website pertaining to CSR or sustainability was the Hong Kong Institution. During the interview the executive had made it clear that this Institution was very low-key as it was a Chinese family-run business, and, although they had very impressive environmental credentials and were committed to sustainability, their website reflected none of this. This is to a large extent typical of a Chinese family business in Hong Kong, but in a very competitive market represents a lost marketing and brand-building opportunity that the others seem to have seized.

It is clear that all of the FIs interviewed are trying to deliver on their CSR goals with regards to sustainability. It appears that the Asian institutions are lagging behind their Western counterparts when it comes to publicizing their work, but this is not surprising, given that CSR and sustainability is a Western-driven agenda. However, the Asian groups have realized the importance of this area and are working from the basic level such as tree-planting, controlled use of lights and so on.

## Comments on the findings

### CSR adoption

It was clear from the research findings that all of the Institutions were very committed to CSR, that is, to being seen to be good corporate citizens and achieving results under their Triple Bottom Line (TBL) of People, Planet and Profit. The findings here disagree with the sceptical view that saw TBL as being a fad and a marketing tool paying lip service to areas that were difficult to quantify.[42] In fact, the findings whole-heartedly support Davies (2006), who saw CSR as 'becoming critical to the success of global business'.[43] In the words of one executive from the findings, 'if you are in the business of banking and finance, then to deliver these you must include CSR as part of the offering'(FI 5i). The findings also supported the view that to ignore green buildings would result in public relations problems.[44]

It seems that CSR has moved on considerably since Norman and MacDonald (2003),[45] as now several of the Institutions had the goal of becoming carbon-neutral in the coming years, and one had already achieved this. This carbon neutrality cannot be purchased off the shelf; it takes a huge amount of investment and change to be able to do this, and the findings point to increased momentum in this area. The realization that $CO_2$ is a major cause of climate change[46] has been taken on board by the Institutions, as evidenced in these findings.

### Setting of CSR goals

The CSR goals were set and fully supported by senior management (normally from the 'C' level of CEO, COO, CFO) and this was mainly from the Head Office. This is important, as it ensures that the standard of the country where the Head Office is situated becomes the global standard. This supports the view that CSR standards should be adapted to global best practice in each country and not just implemented to local standards.[47] This top-down approach was the norm.

However, one of the Institutions took a different approach to setting goals for CSR and adopted a bottom-up approach: targets were set locally and consolidated globally, and then these targets were independently verified by an outside consultancy group. Another Institution had an outside group set the targets for them. This shows how seriously this area is being taken and how a wider holistic approach is being taken.[48] This appears to be a new approach in Hong Kong.

## CSR benchmarking

One of the arguments based around the fact that the TBL is difficult to measure[49] is proven by researchers[50] who have had difficulties of this nature when trying to develop a tool to enable stakeholders to effectively audit a corporation from their CSR activities. Benchmarking has been used as a model, while only taking into account external issues to do with lending and so on,[51] and has also included internal factors such as energy, water and waste.[52] Benchmarks were set up so FIs could compare each other's performance.

The findings, however, show that the Institutions measured their results in many ways, including the use of benchmarks, but not those of their 'brother' institutions[53] but independently, either by external auditors or by developing databases focusing on energy, water and waste on a global basis. These were then benchmarked against the World Resource Institute Ratings.

This demonstrates that measurement of the TBL is becoming a reality, as Profit is measured by acceptable accountancy techniques, Planet by a number of environmental techniques (although not yet standard across all groups), and People by acceptable Human Resources ratios. The movement in measurement of CSR targets has been rapid and ongoing, in disagreement with Norman and MacDonald (2003) and Strandberg's (2005) viewpoint.

## CRE department's involvement in CSR

The CRE department is key when it comes to an Institution being able to achieve its CSR goals. Energy is one of the key areas that require focus if an Institution is going to reduce its carbon footprint.[54] This is because energy used within buildings accounts for between 40 and 50 per cent of global energy consumption.[55] This is of particular concern in Hong Kong, where brightly lit malls and skyline and over-reliance on air conditioning mean that up to 89 per cent of all electricity is used in its buildings.[56] Fellows (2006) identified that energy was a major contributor to carbon emissions in Hong Kong and criticized government for not taking a more hands-on approach.[57]

It is in this area that the CRE Department has particular focus. The findings show that the CRE groups are responsible for areas that produce most of the $CO_2$ emissions. This is all the more so as many of the Institutions questioned had goals either to reduce their carbon footprint significantly or even to go completely carbon-neutral, and this is not possible without major changes in how energy is used. Every Institution mentioned the steps they were taking to reduce emissions, from changing light bulbs, reducing lux ratings and putting in more energy efficient chillers and lifts to taking a holistic view of any new building to be occupied by the use of external criteria. This criterion is provided by the rating techniques such as LEED, HK BEAM and Green Star. Landlords need to be aware that this movement will not go away and they will need to take this into account in their new builds and retrofits in future. In fact, one Institution said that at present energy was their only CSR goal.

### Rewards for CSR achievement

Although no general literature was found that directly looked at what rewards corporations gave to their staff for successful achievement of CSR targets, the question was included for completeness, as what gets measured gets done and what gets done is usually rewarded. In this case, while only three of the Institutions gave cash bonuses, others were moving down this path. In the main the Institutions rewarded their staff by anything from prizes to recognition in the staff news sheet. The rewarding culture appears to be Western-dominated, as the Asian-based Institutions did not offer any rewards at all to their staff. This is not surprising and is consistent with the findings of the Jones Lang LaSalle/ Core Net Survey 2008 survey, showing Asia lagging behind the USA and Europe in all aspects of sustainability.

While staff were or were not rewarded, the literature did cover the rewards that corporations could expect for adopting good sustainable CSR policies in terms of their share price. While research had shown that 'value driven CSR outperforms non CSR peers'[58] in the Dow Jones Sustainability Index, the participants did not mention share price accretion as being part of the reason they were taking CSR and sustainability so seriously; indeed, quite the opposite, as some of these Institutions saw CSR as becoming 'business as normal' and key to running a good business. Of course a well-run business should create added wealth for its stakeholders, and this in turn should lead to positive recognition and share price movement. The fact that several of these Institutions were striving for carbon neutrality/reduction perhaps shows that in Hong Kong they are trying to improve the bad air as their key 'reward'.

## Conclusion

Research Question: *How important is CSR to the Institution and how is that reflected in obtaining and maintaining buildings to the highest green standard?* The findings showed that all of the Institutions, whatever their level of sophistication and development with regard to CSR strategies, fully support occupying and maintaining green buildings. The majority of the institutions (six) had their CSR strategies posted on their websites and had clear targets to meet. Those that did not have them on their websites said that they would only occupy buildings that were sustainable and non-polluting. Targets were set from the top in all Institutions except one. This one set targets locally, but these, once consolidated at Head Office, were fully endorsed by the CEO.

Each Institution took CSR very seriously, and it is clear that FIs in Hong Kong do not see CSR as giving them a competitive advantage; rather, it is a key component of being in the banking business and has become an integral part of how they operate.

The top officers of each Institution supported the CSR strategy or direction, and the results were measured and in three cases were rewarded by cash bonuses to employees. The CRE department was seen as being critical to each Institution's efforts to achieve its CSR targets, as buildings cause the greater part of their carbon footprint and much of this is within the CRE's control. This is the reason why the Institutions tend to occupy only those buildings in Hong Kong that are owned by responsive and green-minded landlords, as in this way they can achieve their CSR goals. Overall, CSR is seen by FIs in Hong Kong as being integral to doing business.

## Notes

1. Business Environmental Council (BEC), *Living under blue skies* (April 2005, December 2006).
2. Reed and Wilkinson 2005, Chan, Qian and Lam 2009.
3. AJ Nelson, 'Globalization and Global Trends in Green Real Estate Investment', *RREEF Research*, vol. 64 (September 2008); Fischer, Loh, Lawson and Chau 2008.

4. T Beyerle, *Green buildings, green washing and future green values*, DEGI Research – Real Estate Focus (2008).
5. Business Environmental Council, *BEAM – Green Building Labeling* (2008).
6. HW Chan, QK Qian and TL Lam, 'The market for green building in Developed Asian Cities – the perspectives of building designers', *Energy Policy*, vol. 37 (2009).
7. A Fischer, C Loh, A Lawson and J Chua, *Urban Transformers: High-Performance buildings clean up* (Hong Kong: CLSA Blue Books, October 2008).
8. A Fischer, C Loh, A Lawson and J Chua, *Urban Transformers: High-Performance buildings clean up* (: CLSA Blue Books, October 2008).
9. O Weber, 'Sustainability Benchmarking of European Banks and Financial Service Organizations', *Corporate Social responsibility and Environmental Management*, vol. 12 (2005), pp. 73–87.
10. M Davies, 'Standard Chartered CEO: Responsible for More Than The Bottom Line – Companies That Recognize Corporate Social Responsibility Will Be The Successful Global Companies of Tomorrow', *The Banker* (1 January 2006), p. 1.
11. MA Tipgos and TJ Keefe, 'A Comprehensive Structure of Corporate Governance in Post-Enron Corporate America', *The CPA Journal*, vol. 74, no. 12 (2004), pp. 46–51.
12. S Persram, M Lucuik and N Larsson, 'Marketing Green buildings to Tenants of Leased Properties', Canada Green Building Council (August 2007).
13. AJ de Francesco and D Levy, 'The Impact of sustainability on the investment environment', *Journal of European Real Estate Research*, vol. 1, no. 1 (2008), pp. 72–81.
14. W Norman and C MacDonald, 'Getting to the Bottom of "Triple Bottom Line"', in press, *Business Ethics Quarterly* (2003); C Strandberg, 'The Future of Sustainable Finance', Thought Leaders Study (2005).
15. DG Cogan, *Corporate Governance and Climate Change: The Banking Sector* (2008) A CERES Report, Coalition for Environmentally Responsible Economics (CERES), Boston, US.
16. Hong Kong Monetary Authority, at www.info.gov.hk/hkma/eng/statistics/msb/index (2008) accessed on 21 January 2009.
17. G Hofstede, 'National Cultures in four dimensions', International Studies Management Organization, vol. 13 (1983), pp. 46–75; L Lai, K Chau, D Ho and F Lorne, 'A "Hong Kong" model of sustainable development', *Property Management*, vol. 24, no. 3 (2006), pp. 251–271.
18. A Fischer, C Loh, A Lawson and J Chau, *Urban Transformers: High-Performance buildings clean up* (CLSA Blue Books, October 2008); HW Chan, QK Qian and TL Lam, 'The market for green building in Developed Asian Cities – the perspectives of building designers', *Energy Policy*, vol. 37 (2009).
19. T Iwami, 'The "advantage of latecomer" in abating air-pollution: the East Asian experience', *International Journal of Economics*, vol. 32, no. 3 (2005), pp. 184–202; AJ Nelson, 'Globalization and Global Trends in Green Real Estate Investment', *RREEF Research*, vol. 64 (September 2008); T Beyerle, *Green buildings, green washing and future green values*, DEGI Research – Real Estate Focus (2008).
20. AJ Nelson, 'Globalization and Global Trends in Green Real Estate Investment', *RREEF Research*, vol. 64 (September 2008).

21. Core Net (2007).
22. D Lorenz, *Turning the Vicious Circle of Blame into Loops of Feedback and Adaptation – a Holistic Approach*, Global Property Sustainability Survey, RICS Economics (May 2009).
23. Business Environmental Council, *BEAM – Green Building Labeling* (2008), p. 1.
24. HW Chan, QK Qian and TL Lam, 'The market for green building in Developed Asian Cities – the perspectives of building designers', *Energy Policy*, vol. 37 (2009).
25. Cogan (2008).
26. Cogan (2008).
27. MA Tipgos and TJ Keefe, 'A Comprehensive Structure of Corporate Governance in Post-Enron Corporate America', *The CPA Journal*, vol. 74, no. 12 (2004).
28. TA Thompson and GF Davis, 'The Politics of Corporate Control and the Future of Shareholder Activism in the United States', *Corporate Governance: An International Review*, vol. 5, no. 3 (1997), pp. 152–9; M Trachuk, 'The Challenges and Opportunities of Shareholder Activism', *The Osler Outlook* (Fall, 2007).
29. K Kelleher, 'A Proxy battle: Shareholders vs. CEOs', *CorpWatch* (13 June 2006), at www.corpwatch.org/article.php?id=13716
30. S Deakin and S Konzelmann, 'After Enron, An Age of enlightenment?', *Organization*, vol. 10, no. 3 (2003), p. 583; R Fisman, R Khurana and M Rhodes-Kropf, 'Can Shareholders Be Wrong?', *MITSloan Management Review* (Fall 2005).
31. M Lopez, A Garcia and L Rodriguez, 'Sustainable Development and Corporate Performance: A study based on the Dow Jones Sustainability Index', *Journal of Business Ethics*, vol. 75 (2007), pp. 285–300.
32. T Kennedy, J Whiteoak and T Ye, *A Comprehensive Analysis of the relationship between ESG and Investment Returns*, State Street global Advisors, Active Equity (November 2008).
33. Cogan (2008).
34. A Bryman, *Social Research Methods* (Oxford: Oxford University Press, 2008).
35. D Carson, C Gilmore, C Perry and K Gronhaug, *Qualitative Research in Marketing* (London: Sage, 2001).
36. D Grace, 'Critical Variables in Child Care Services Switching: Contrasting Consumer and Staff Perceptions', Honours Thesis, Griffiths University, chapter 2 (1999).
37. C King, *Exploring the role of employees in the market orientated strategy of brand management to achieve superior organizational performance*, Griffith University, chapter 3 (2004).
38. RY Cavana, BL Delahaye and U Sekaran, *Applied business research: Qualitative and Quantitative Methods* (Australia: John Wiley & Sons Australia, Ltd, 2001).
39. M Arden, *Reforming the Companies Act – The Way ahead*, J.B.L. (2002), p. 579.
40. Jones Lang LaSalle, *Results of the 2008 Core Net and Jones Lang LaSalle global survey on CRE and sustainability*, Jones Lang LaSalle and Core Net Global (2008).
41. Johnson, R. Burke 1997, *Examining the Validity Structure of Qualitative Research, Education*, Vol. 118, no. 2, pp. 282-292.

42. W Norman and C MacDonald, 'Getting to the Bottom of "Triple Bottom Line"', in press, *Business Ethics Quarterly* (2003); C Strandberg, *The Future of Sustainable Finance*, Thought Leaders Study (2005).
43. M Davies, 'Standard Chartered CEO: Responsible for More Than The Bottom Line – Companies That Recognize Corporate Social Responsibility Will Be The Successful Global Companies of Tomorrow', *The Banker* (1 January 2006).
44. Persram, Lucuik and Larrson (2007).
45. W Norman and C MacDonald, 'Getting to the Bottom of "Triple Bottom Line"', in press, *Business Ethics Quarterly* (2003).
46. A Fischer, C Loh, A Lawson and J Chau, *Urban Transformers: High-Performance buildings clean up* (CLSA Blue Books, October 2008).
47. S Zyglidopoulos, 'The Social and Environmental Responsibilities of Multinationals: Evidence from the Brent Spar Case', *Journal of Business Ethics*, vol. 36 (2002) p. 141.
48. AJ de Francesco and D Levy, 'The Impact of sustainability on the investment environment', *Journal of European Real Estate Research*, vol. 1, no. 1 (2008), pp. 72–81.
49. W Norman and C MacDonald, 'Getting to the Bottom of "Triple Bottom Line"', in press, *Business Ethics Quarterly* (2003).
50. R Morimoto, J Ash and C Hope, 'Corporate Social Responsibility Audit: From Theory to Practice', *Journal of Business Ethics*, vol. 62 (2005) pp. 315–25.
51. O Weber, 'Sustainability Benchmarking of European Banks and Financial Service Organizations', *Corporate Social responsibility and Environmental Management*, vol. 12 (2005), pp. 73–87.
52. O Schmid-Schonbein and G Oetterli, 'Sustainability performance measurement and reporting in financial institutions' (2005), E2 Management Consulting Inc. Opportunities in the Pearl River Delta.
53. O Weber, 'Sustainability Benchmarking of European Banks and Financial Service Organizations', *Corporate Social responsibility and Environmental Management*, vol. 12 (2005), pp. 73–87; O Schmid-Schonbein and G Oetterli, 'Sustainability performance measurement and reporting in financial institutions' (2005), E2 Management Consulting Inc. Opportunities in the Pearl River Delta.
54. O Schmid-Schonbein and G Oetterli, 'Sustainability performance measurement and reporting in financial institutions' (2005), E2 Management Consulting Inc. Opportunities in the Pearl River Delta.
55. K Giljohann-Farakas and G Pfeiderer, *Green Buildings, greenwashing and future green values*, DEGI Research – Real estate Focus (October 2008).
56. HW Chan, QK Qian and TL Lam, 'The market for green building in Developed Asian Cities – the perspectives of building designers', *Energy Policy*, vol. 37 (2009).
57. R Fellows, 'Sustainability: a matter of energy?', *Property Management*, vol. 24, no. 2 (2006).
58. F van Dijken, 'Corporate social responsibility: market regulation and the evidence', *Managerial Law*, vol. 49, no. 4 (2007) p. 141; M Lopez, A Garcia and L Rodriguez, 'Sustainable Development and Corporate Performance: A study based on the Dow Jones Sustainability Index', *Journal of Business Ethics*, vol. 75 (2007), pp. 285–300; van Dijiken (2007).

# 13
# Practical Ethics and Carbon Finance

*Wilfred Walsh*

## Introduction

The issues surrounding the debate about climate change and what to do about it add up to a 'perfect storm' of complexity, uncertainty and doubt. They involve subtle matters of science, engineering, economics, accounting, politics and ethics – each of which can itself be relied on to provide a rich vein of confusion and disagreement whenever matters of substance and wider interest are discussed. This confluence of complexity might simply be an intellectual curiosity if it were not for the fact that decisions of monumental importance need to be made, and made quickly.

This chapter takes a pragmatic, somewhat personal, look at the problem and asks why the climate change debate got to be so tortuous, how opposing sides became so entrenched and how we might resolve this problem and avoid other ones like it. To the extent that this article aims to be pragmatic, relevant ethical considerations are construed as being purely emergent properties of macroeconomics. If we allow this, then ethics, in the context of climate change, is just shorthand for collective thinking on the largest scale, over the longest time that may be practically considered. If ethical thinking is good for anything, it must surely provide guidance in matters such as the avoidance of catastrophic events that have, at some level of probability, the potential to completely disrupt the civilization within which those ethics apply.

The philosopher Alasdair MacIntyre once suggested that the intransigence of so many ethical issues today is due to the fact that our entire ethical structure is inappropriate to its contemporary context.[1] If the above characterization of ethics can be entertained, at least metaphorically, then I argue below that climate change changes our context in a new way. I will also suggest that a necessary condition for dealing with new-context problems, of which climate change is just an early example, involves improvement to our education systems.

## The scientific issue

Global warming by definition touches on the whole planet, so it's no wonder the subject is complicated. To make unambiguous statements of fact about the matter – scientific statements – we need to break the problem down into manageable pieces. Scientists do this by looking at the big picture, making reasonable assumptions and then applying the known laws of physics and chemistry in limiting cases. Following this approach, we can consider planet Earth to be a more or less solid sphere, surrounded by a more or less gaseous atmosphere. The whole planet is bathed in solar radiation consisting of a range of wavelengths peaking somewhere near the optical and infrared.

Well-understood laws of physics tell us that there will be a balance between the radiation absorbed by the planet and the radiation emitted

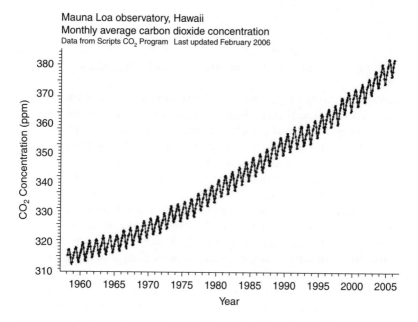

*Figure 13.1*  Carbon dioxide concentration of earth's atmosphere as measured at Mauna Loa 1958–2006, as for figure 13.5

*Source*: Scripps Institute of Oceanography, NOAA ESRL

by it. We also know that adding certain easily detectable greenhouse gases such as carbon dioxide to the atmosphere will slow the rate of infrared radiation emitted and therefore lead to a net warming. Figure 13.1 shows several decades' worth of measurements of such gases.[2]

Given that over 80 per cent of global energy demand is satisfied by burning fossil fuels of one form or another, the origin of the carbon dioxide increase seen in Figure 13.1 is hardly mysterious. Indeed, the veracity of the equation: *atmosphere + greenhouse gases + sunlight = warmer atmosphere*, first articulated in print in 1827, was considered settled by about 1900.[3] In other words, for most scientists, the alleged debate about anthropogenic global warming is a long-solved and therefore rather uninteresting question in elementary planetary atmospheres. Just as a meteorologist won't want to talk about the weather on any particular day, an astronomer may be ambivalent about the effects of the greenhouse effect on any particular planet. The intricacies of climate change caused by the energy added by solar radiation are, for the astronomer, someone else's problem. What *is* known, with a high degree of certainty, is that an increase in atmospheric carbon dioxide concentrations like that observed in Figure 13.1 is certain to eventually lead to an increase in the annual global atmospheric temperature, exactly as observed and shown in Figure 13.2.[4]

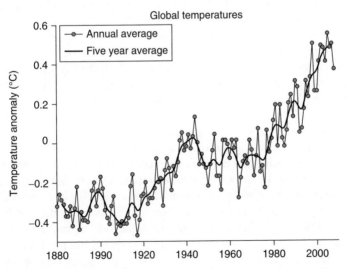

*Figure 13.2*  Measured changes in global temperatures from 1880 to 2005
*Source*: IPCC.

What is perhaps most remarkable about all this is the number of people who deny these simple facts, the vitriolic nature of their denials and the extent to which their bad-faith arguments about the whole issue receive coverage in the mainstream press without critical review. Although many of the precise details of climate change science constitute current areas of research and are hence somewhat uncertain, the basic physical scenario leading to potentially catastrophic future global warming is well understood and has been for over a century. So why are we even arguing about it?

## The political issue

In a democracy, political events are influenced by public opinion. Therefore, citizens interested in living in a democratic society that is structured to do what is in some sense the 'right' thing, or at least that can preserve itself, need to understand matters that may affect the general societal well-being. From the point of view of public policy, 'well-being' appears currently to be defined as that outcome which optimizes the macroeconomic health of the society, but more on that later.

Global warming predictions are based on computer modelling. Despite their inability to predict small-scale, local detail, these models deserve attention for the fact that they have, over the past 25 years, correctly predicted the overall warming trend in both direction and magnitude. Some scientists estimate that unchecked global warming could make much of the Earth's surface uninhabitable.[5] Yet significant numbers of voters deny that global warming is an issue at all. As a result, many democracies find themselves in a policy gridlock that appears to scientists convinced of the dangers to be both bizarre and deeply troubling.

Perhaps the scientific data are simply not convincing enough? To assess this claim we need to know something about the standards of scientific datasets that lead to progress of ideas.

Consider Figure 13.3, showing Edwin Hubble's original 1929 data relating the velocity of recession of a galaxy to its distance: evidence for the expansion of the Universe.[6] This scatter plot was one of the key pieces of evidence that developed the remarkable belief that the Universe is expanding and originated in an event now known as the Big Bang. When Einstein saw Figure 13.3 he remarked that changing an equation in his General Theory of Relativity (to explain the pre-Figure-13.3, apparently non-expanding, Universe) was 'the biggest blunder of his life'. I'll leave it up to the reader to decide the extent to which the positive correlation claimed on the basis of this plot is convincing.

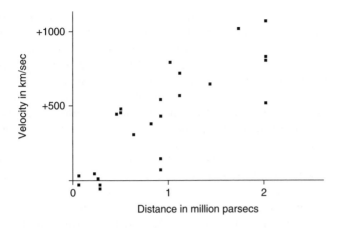

*Figure 13.3* Edwin Hubble's 1929 data showing the relationship between a galaxy's recession velocity and its distance. This plot was instrumental in establishing that the Universe is expanding.

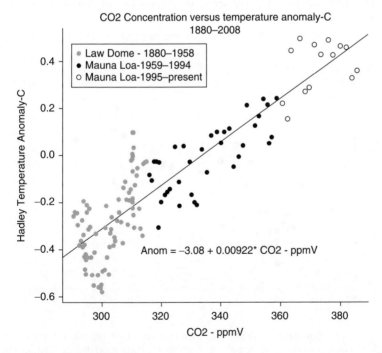

*Figure 13.4* Carbon dioxide concentration (x-axis) against temperature anomaly (y-axis), as formatted in figure 13.5

*Source*: chartsgraphs.wordpress.com

Figures 13.4[7] and 5 show scatter plots like Figure 13.3, but in these plots the data is the relationship between atmospheric carbon dioxide concentrations and average global atmospheric temperatures. The plot in Figure 13.4 shows the data for 1880–2006, while Figure 13.5 shows the data over the past 400,000 years. The measurement of and the relationship between carbon dioxide concentrations and temperatures are both complex and involve other phenomena, so a perfect correlation is not expected. However, it is perhaps instructive to compare the apparent correlation in Figure 13.3 with those in Figures 13.4 and 13.5.

It is clear that a certain level of familiarity with the data presented and quantitative judgment is required to make sense of any of Figures 13.3, 13.4 and 13.5. To judge the validity of scientific data requires the reader to have some idea of the nature of scientific progress, the limits to scientific knowledge and the criteria by which scientific claims may be assessed. Nevertheless, it is remarkable that the tentative effect shown in Figure 13.3 (from which Hubble initially derived a key parameter wrongly by a factor of 10) set the wheels in motion for one of the greatest scientific discoveries. The strength of the effect shown in Figure 13.3 is in fact fairly typical of the level at which much cutting-edge science occurs: scientists are adept at recognizing patterns in data and assessing

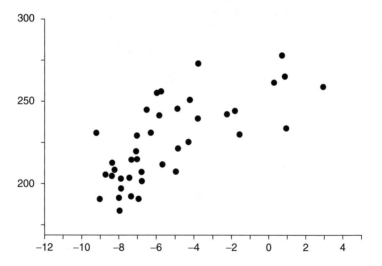

*Figure 13.5* Atmospheric carbon dioxide concentration (ppm), averaged over 8,000 years (y-axis) vs. temperature anomaly in degrees celsius (x-axis) for the past 400,000 years

*Source*: Publishing Network for Geoscientific & Environmental Data, doi.pangaea.de

their significance. While it is too much to ask the general public to be able to perform such assessments, it is surely not too much to ask that the phenomena manifest in Figures 13.1 and 13.2 be accepted as real.

Some non-trivial level of intellectual sophistication is required to absorb quantitative information and draw conclusions from it. Over time, public debate aided by an unbiased, professional and civic-minded media may correctly identify and highlight the critical issues. But what if a crisis occurs and we do not have the luxury of leisurely debate?

The question then arises, in a modern democracy, what level of sophistication is it reasonable to expect of the media and the voting public? Perhaps the question needs to be, what level of sophistication is *demanded* of citizens if a modern democracy faced with complex, technology-driven challenges is to survive? At the very least, this is a question that must be considered when planning our education systems.

It is probably fair to say that, while many people would agree that Figure 13.4 shows a stronger correlation than Figure 13.3, few people would feel comfortable articulating their reasons for believing assertions based on either plot. Whether or not the Universe is expanding towards heat death is a matter we can comfortably leave to the astronomers for another gigayear or two. But whether or not our planet is warming at a dangerous rate is a pressing matter that may require urgent – within a couple of voting cycles – action. If the voting public is not equipped to decide what to do and scientific results are not accepted by policymakers, then what happens if irreversible global warming occurs? Does the ethical imperative lie with scientists to more forcefully point out what for them is the painfully obvious? Or does our society need to acknowledge that in a technological future, where our actions have planetary consequences, we all ought to understand the relevant issues deeply enough to act on them in an informed way?

## The economic issue

One of the less controversial ethical doctrines is that we can only suffer a moral obligation to do something if it is possible to do it: 'ought' implies 'can'. In terms of dealing with climate change, this boils down to whether the economic costs of dealing with climate change are justified in some way. Can a market-based approach solve the climate change problem without creating worse problems? If so, what should that approach be? An extensive literature has debated these points, with national-level reviews commissioned by the UK and Australian governments providing policy-level reasoning.[8] The Nobel-prize-winning economist and columnist Paul Krugman has recently provided a lucid summary of the issues,[9] where he points out that surveys of economic models conclude that proposed US legislation would reduce the projected average annual rate of growth of gross domestic product between 2010 and 2050 by 0.03 to 0.09 percentage points, and this would leave the American economy between 1.1 per cent and 3.4 per cent smaller in 2050 than it would be otherwise. The effect on other countries is generally considered to be less than in the USA, which is a highly developed economy and an expensive place to make radical changes.

There are several problems with the economic arguments about how to deal with climate change. Like the scientific predictions, economic predictions are based on models. But economic models are much less constrained than scientific models and do not have the history of successful predictions that climate models do. Particularly acute problems for economic models are how to determine the structure of the climate change market mechanism and over what timescale it ought to be applied. The former point generally revolves around whether the best approach is a carbon tax, which provides market certainty regarding the climate mitigation costs, or cap and trade systems, which can provide certainty in emissions reductions but not in cost. The latter point raises contentious ethical questions about the value we place on the quality of human life, and indeed which people's (current or future generations) benefit deserves greatest consideration by the models.

The subtleties of economic models impinge on societal ethics, since the workings of economies, no matter how efficient or close to ideal they may be, do not and cannot address questions of right and wrong, quality of life, or what is good for the very long-term health of the environment. As Krugman says: '....efficiency isn't everything. In particular, there is no reason to assume that free markets will deliver an outcome that we consider fair or just.'[10]

An especially important deficiency of economic models, recognized by some economists, is the difficulties that the models have with extremely rare but extremely devastating events.[11] One school of thought has it that even the remote possibility of extreme events (e.g. much of Earth becoming too hot to support human civilization) is so grave that enormous weight ought to be placed upon them.[12]

## The ethical issue

The level of vitriol in the climate change debate today is remarkable. It would appear to deny Cartesian or transcendental assertions about the self-evidence of certain truths, or that there are principles and concepts, inherent to our reasoning, that no rational mind can deny. Perhaps it is a symptom of an inappropriately tolerant and inclusive world view: one in which there is no certainty, merely approximations and conjectures, in the Popperian sense, whose veracity is at all times to be considered contingent or temporary yet more or less equally deserving of consideration. The resulting denial of anything approaching certainty is pure poison when it comes to democratic political action.

One reason why our collective confusion and the resulting political paralysis matters is not just that global warming is a serious problem now and one that may get much worse, but that this is just one of many new problems that ever more technologically driven societies will need to contend with. It is in the nature of these new problems that they will involve technologies, timescales and consequences impossible to address with our current – manifestly inadequate – social and political institutions. It is in the nature of these problems that certain aspects of them will only be apparent to citizens with sufficient familiarity with those technologies that caused them and the complex systems (economies, ecosystems, or important subunits thereof) on which they depend.

In democratic societies, ever more sophisticated and educated voters will be necessary if there is to be any hope of rational political outcomes. A more technologically oriented society needs to be a more educated and more reflective society as well. This adds a modern dimension to the classical notion of virtue and its opposition to subsequent distinctions between a person's intrinsic moral worth and his ability to act in a morally correct way. As McIntyre put it, '...for Kant one can be both good and stupid; but for Aristotle stupidity of a certain kind precludes goodness'.[13]

In one sense, we are fortunate that the climate change problem is characterized by fairly long timescales. Writers such as the futurist Ray Kurzweil and astronomer Martin Rees have suggested that the apparently incessant increase in the rate of technological change is our greatest existential threat.[14] Kurzweil and Rees postulate that ever more rapid advances in technologies (microbiology and weaponry, for example) will outstrip our ability to control them and that it is only a matter of time before a disastrous combination of destructive force and malevolence or bad luck occurs. If they are even close to being right, then we will need not just highly sophisticated – probably global – administrative responsive capabilities but also the capacity to act extremely quickly, perhaps within days or hours. It is difficult to see how we can ever get ourselves organized enough to put such systems in place without a vastly improved general understanding of the technologies from which these future risks, if real, will devolve.

Globalization adds numerous complications to this picture. The increasingly integrated nature of the world's economies, and hence value systems, can only make the path to moral consensus even more tortuous. As the astronomer and writer Carl Sagan put it: 'We've arranged a global civilization in which most crucial elements profoundly depend on science and technology. We have arranged things so that almost no one understands science and technology. This is a prescription for disaster. We might get away with it for a while but sooner or later this mixture of ignorance and power is going to blow up in our faces.'[15]

## Notes

1. A MacIntyre, *After Virtue* (Notre Dame, IN: University of Notre Dame Press, 1981).
2. See, for example, CD Keeling, RB Bacastow, AE Bainbridge, CA Ekdahl, PR Guenther and LS Waterman, 'Atmospheric carbon dioxide variations at Mauna Loa Observatory, Hawaii', *Tellus*, vol. 28 (1976), pp. 538–51; KW Thoning, PP Tans and WD Komhyr, 'Atmospheric carbon dioxide at Mauna Loa Observatory 2. Analysis of the NOAA GMCC data, 1974-1985', *Journal of Geophys Research*, vol. 94 (1989), pp. 8549–65.
3. J Fourier, 'Mémoire Sur Les Températures Du Globe Terrestre Et Des Espaces Planétaires', in *Mémoires de l'Académie Royale des Sciences*, vol. 7 (1827), pp. 569–604; S Arrhenius, 'On the Influence of Carbonic Acid in the Air upon the Temperature of the Ground', *Philosophical Magazine and Journal of Science*, series 5, vol. 41 (1896), pp. 237–76.
4. S Solomon, D Qin, M Manning, Z Chen, M Marquis, KB Averyt, M Tignor and HL Miller (eds), *Contribution of Working Group I to the Fourth Assessment Report of the Intergovernmental Panel on Climate Change* (Cambridge, United Kingdom and New York, NY, USA: Cambridge University Press, 2007).
5. N Bostrom and MM Irkovi, *Global Catastrophic Risks* (USA: Oxford University Press, 2008).
6. E Hubble, 'A relation between distance and radial velocity among extragalactic nebulae', *Proceedings of the National Academy of Sciences of the United States of America*, vol. 15, no. 3 (1929).
7. Chart from: http://chartsgraphs.wordpress.com/2009/08/13/excel-chart-misrepresents-co2-temperature-relationship
8. N Stern, S Peters, V Bakhshi, A Bowen, C Cameron, S Catovsky, D Crane, S Cruickshank and S Dietz, *Stern Review: The economics of climate change* (HM Treasury, 2006); R Garnaut (editor)., *The Garnaut climate change review: final report* (Cambridge University Press, 2009).
9. P Krugman, 'Building a green economy', *The New York Times* (5 April 2010) at http://www.nytimes.com/2010/04/11/magazine/11Economy-t.html

10. P Krugman, 'Building a green economy', *The New York Times* (5 April 2010).
11. N Taleb, *The black swan: The impact of the highly improbable* (New York: Random House Inc., 2007).
12. ML Weitzman, 'A review of the Stern Review on the economics of climate change', *Journal of Economic Literature*, vol. 45, no. 3 (American Economic Association Publications: 2007), pp. 703–24.
13. A MacIntyre, *After Virtue* (Notre Dame, IN: University of Notre Dame Press, 1981).
14. A Schopenhauer, 'Superintelligence and Singularity', *Science Fiction and Philosophy: From Time Travel to Superintelligence*, (Blackwell: 2009), p. 201; A Gorman, 'Review of our Final Hour: A Scientist's Warning: How Terror, Error and Environmental Disaster Threaten Humankind's Future in this Century – on Earth and Beyond by Sir Martin Rees', *Journal for the Study of Religion, Nature and Culture*, vol. 10, no. 3 (2007), p. 407.
15. C Sagan, *The Demon-Haunted World: Science As a Candle in the Dark* (USA: Ballantine Books, March 1997).

# 14
# Sustainable and Responsible Investment in Asia

*Geoffrey Williams*

## Introduction[1]

The global financial crisis and ongoing concerns about climate change have placed the spotlight on new styles of investment that are socially responsible and environmentally aware. Recent worries about man-made environmental disasters, life-threatening product safety standards and poor corporate governance have been a driver of 'Socially Responsible Investment' (SRI) in Europe and North America, and similar concerns are now growing in Asia. As in the West, these are accompanied by wider interest in the social and environmental impact of corporate activity, both positive and negative, and the extent to which these can be influenced or controlled by investors.

## What is SRI?

> Sustainable and Responsible Investment (SRI), also known as Socially Responsible Investment, is investment which allows investors to take into account wider concerns, such as social justice, economic development, peace or a healthy environment, as well as conventional financial considerations.
>
> Association for Sustainable and Responsible Investment in Asia (ASrIA)[2]

SRI funds try to deliver two forms of return for investors: first, financial returns based on standard financial analysis that match or exceed returns on conventional investments and, second, social and environmental benefits that add wider value from investment decisions in addition to the returns to investors.[3]

SRI funds also try to produce more stable returns by tracking and mitigating sources of risk within portfolios, such as poor corporate governance or bad environmental management. By identifying non-financial sources of risk, SRI investors try to manage the overall risk profile of their investments and reduce or remove exposure to companies that face current or future problems on environmental, social and governance (ESG) issues.[4]

For this reason SRI is closely linked to Corporate Social Responsibility (CSR) and environmentally sustainable management. Companies with good CSR programmes or well-managed sustainability strategies can signal to prospective investors that they are aware of ESG risks and opportunities and are taking them into account in their day-to-day management.[5]

From an economic perspective SRI addresses externalities, which are the costs or benefits that arise from company activities that are not compensated by the market mechanism. Most often this means that companies that cause harm to communities or the environment do not pay the costs. As a consequence, the full environmental and social impact is not reflected in their profits, dividends and share prices. SRI can help investors address externalities by making positive economic decisions that take into account not only financial but also non-financial management of costs, risks and opportunities. Externalities are a form of market failure, and in this respect SRI can be viewed as a partially market-based solution, which can be a complement to or a substitute for regulatory interventions.

SRI covers all types of investments, including direct share-ownership, unit trusts and mutual funds, hedge funds, venture capital, private equity investments, private and national institutional pension funds, corporate and country bonds, sovereign wealth funds and endowment funds for universities and charitable organizations. It also includes Community Investing and investments in Social Enterprises on a smaller scale.

Ethical Investment, which includes faith-based financial products such as Syariah-compliant investments, is also a key component of SRI, especially in Asia. Some investors also refer to RI or 'Responsible Investment', which is considered to be more objective and mainstream in contrast to many SRI approaches that may include subjective considerations such as values and ethics in their portfolio selection.

## Integration of ESG into the investment choice

While there are many forms of SRI, general investment styles have emerged over time. These have become more sophisticated as our understanding of the link between ESG issues and financial returns has developed.[6]

From an investment perspective SRI makes sense for a very straightforward reason – good management of ESG issues leads to good financial performance and adds shareholder value. Two premises underpin this hypothesis. One approach uses comparative valuation. A company like British Airways, with ongoing strike action due to complex employee relations, is seen as having greater investment risk than, for example, Singapore Airlines, which has a record of well-managed human resources. Downtime due to industrial action reduces revenues and incurs costs for solution efforts and these in turn have an impact on profits.[7]

The second approach uses option values. Clean-technology companies with low-carbon products that consumers increasingly prefer are expected to have better future business value than companies that pollute the environment and face carbon taxes, emissions penalties or consumer disfavour. For example, the Shenzhen-based company BYD (Build Your Dreams) transformed from an industrial components manufacturer into a next-generation automotive company with the launch in December 2008 of the world's first mass-produced, plug-in hybrid vehicle, the BYD F3DM. This transformation was based in a large part on existing expertise in mass production of industrial batteries. The option value of mass hybrid production in China and overseas attracted huge interest from SRI Funds, and, as a sign of the mainstreaming of ESG opportunities, the international financier Warren Buffet's Berkshire Hathaway spent $230 million to acquire a 10 per cent stake in BYD Auto's parent company.[8]

In addition to these two approaches, standard valuation methodologies such as the discounted cash flow valuation (DCFV) method can be easily adapted to gauge the current value of future profits adjusted by ESG factors. In simple terms, the DCFV method states that good management of ESG leads to increased profits with reduced risk, as shown in the simplest form in Figure 14.1.

The key is to identify ways in which good management of ESG issues can add value. From a revenue perspective, the Body Shop, for example, sells products that are similar to those in most other cosmetics stores. However, people are prepared to pay a higher price for Body Shop products because of its recognized environmental and socially responsible supplier rules and its policy of prohibiting animal testing. This produces a price premium. In Asia an example of a similar business model can be found in the Truly Loving Company (TLC) in Malaysia.[9]

On the cost-side, companies that manage their energy consumption efficiently are able to reduce greenhouse gas emissions (GHG) and at the

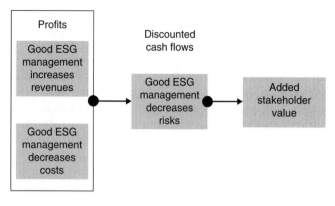

*Figure 14.1*   The simplest SRI schematic
*Source*: OWW Consulting (2010)

same time cut their energy bills. These lower costs translate positively to the bottom line.

ESG risk considerations also offer opportunities for added-value in portfolio management. For example, companies with good corporate governance avoid the risks that hit Satyam in India in 2009 or Transmile Berhad in Malaysia during 2007.[10] Companies that manage their environmental systems properly avoid the risk of clean-up costs and fines for pollution such as those that hit BP due to the Gulf of Mexico disaster, or the widespread condemnation of Bakrie Brothers in Indonesia for various environmental and social issues.[11] Companies that look after their staff, their customers and the communities in which they work avoid strike action and consumer boycotts. Well-managed ESG can also help companies build good stakeholder relationships through CSR programmes that enhance their brand and reputation and translate into better business performance.

Put simply, higher prices and lower costs give better profits both now and in the future, and well-managed ESG issues help to lower commercial risks so that profits are more sustainable in the long term. This all adds value for shareholders as well as creating benefits for society and the environment.

## ESG and ethical screening

The earliest and still the most common forms of SRI use portfolio screening, which is the inclusion or exclusion of shares in investment portfolios for ethical, social or environmental reasons.[12] Investors can use screens to exclude unacceptable shares from their portfolio, such as companies involved in tobacco or animal testing or those associated with human rights abuses. They can also use positive screens that are proactive in selecting companies with good social and environmental performance. Common examples include companies producing and using low-carbon technologies, which contribute to more environmentally sustainable economic development. Many investors use ESG ratings from specialist research organizations to compare company performance across a range of issues such as corporate governance, environment and supply-chain issues. Shares are then selected on a 'best-in-class' basis so that the overall portfolio contains the best performers relative to the available market by screening out underperformers.

## Engagement, active management and divestment

SRI fund managers have also become more active, especially large institutional investors such as pension funds. Through shareholder engagement, for example, investors aim to use their shareholdings to improve the ESG performance of companies. They can influence management performance positively by raising issues of concern with CEOs and investor relations managers to promote responsible management practices. Alternatively, they can put pressure on companies through voting against bad ESG practices at Annual General Meetings (AGMs). In extreme cases investors may even divest of companies that underperform on ESG issues and encourage other investors to do the same.

In January 2010, for example, the Teachers Insurance and Annuity Association – College Retirement Equities Fund (TIAA-CREF) divested of major oil and gas companies in Asia in response to their activities in the Sudan. TIAA-CREF is one of the largest financial services companies in the United States, with just under $400 billion in assets under management (AuM).

TIAA-CREF targeted five Asian companies, PetroChina, CNPC Hong Kong, Oil and Natural Gas Corporation, Sinopec, and PETRONAS, all of which have links with the Government of Sudan through their exploration and production concessions in that country. TIAA-CREF stated that it would divest of those that refused to acknowledge the genocide in the Darfur region and engage in a productive dialogue to confront it. TIAA-CREF's final decision to divest rested on a number of factors, including the seriousness of concerns about Sudan among TIAA-CREF's stakeholders, the success of the engagement with target companies and the calculation that divestment would not have a significant impact on the financial performance of TIAA-CREF's portfolios.

After meeting with each of the companies through its shareholder engagement process, TIAA-CREF concluded that there had been insufficient progress. On 31 December 2009 TIAA-CREF sold its holdings in PetroChina, CNPC Hong Kong, Oil and Natural Gas Corporation and Sinopec across all its funds and accounts.

In explaining the action, Roger W Ferguson, Jr, TIAA-CREF's Chief Executive Officer, said: 'Our decision to sell shares in these companies culminated a three-year effort to encourage them to end their ties to Sudan or attempt to end suffering there.' The benefits of positive engagement were also highlighted when he explained: 'We have not divested from PETRONAS, which has acknowledged our concerns and engaged in dialogue about how it might address them.'[13]

## Other forms of SRI in Asia

A common form of SRI in Asia is Islamic Finance and Syariah-compliant financial products. The Global Market in Islamic Finance is estimated at US$822–950 billion by the end of 2009 and expected to exceed US$1 trillion during 2010.[14] Syariah funds apply ethical screens excluding various forms of business and requiring various types of business practices, such as avoiding interest in financial transactions. Asia is a leading centre for Syariah-compliant finance and Malaysia takes a large share of the global market, estimated at 10.5 per cent of the global total. Malaysia is also the world's leading issuer of Islamic bonds and the third largest Syariah market in the world by AuM, after Saudi Arabia and Iran.[15] The recent collaboration between the Bahrain Stock Exchange and Bursa Malaysia has the potential of strengthening this market by building new forms of financial products that are attractive to non-Muslims as well as Muslims.

Another form of SRI common in Asia is Community Investing, which is also called Philanthropic Investment.[16] This form of investment is often associated with Social Enterprises and is a way of supporting particular causes or activities through financing, investment or loans. Community investing such as microcredit and revolving loan schemes and new online forums such as Kiva.com allow easier access to this market for even the smallest retail investor. Some of the best known examples of Community Investing, such as Grameen Bank of Bangladesh, originated in Asia and are now replicated around the world.

Community Investment often tolerates financial returns lower than the market rate. This allows them to achieve a specific 'social return' from their investment as a primary target. Unlike making a donation, cause-based investors or the social finance organizations investing on their behalf require, at a minimum, that the original value of the investment is returned by either repayment (for loans) or trading (for shares). Grameen Bank is a good example that illustrates the potential of community investment. The bank provides small loans, 90 per cent of which are to women and 100 per cent to people classified as very poor. The repayment rate is regularly around 98 per cent.[17]

A new extension of this form of SRI aims to allow direct investment in Social Enterprises. The Singapore-based Impact Investment Exchange (IIX), for example, is developing a system to provide a regulated trading platform for securities issued by sustainable for-profit and not-for-profit social enterprises in Asia. Investment in social enterprises is expected to provide a liquid and transparent market where social enterprises can raise capital for expansion and enhance their social and environmental impact while investors can also achieve good financial, social and environmental returns.[18]

## How big is SRI?

Sustainable and responsible investment is supported by the world's major institutional investors. Estimates of the size of SRI funds vary but it is likely that at least US$5 trillion is managed using SRI criteria globally.[19] A report in 2009 by the International Finance Corporation estimated that around US$300 billion was held in sustainable equity investment in emerging markets at the end of 2008, including around US$40.8 billion in Asia. In 2007 OWW Consulting estimated Asian SRI equity-based funds to be around US$33.2 billion, which represents a 23 per cent increase over 2 years.[20] The total AuM in Asian SRI appears to have been damaged by the effects of the 2008 financial crisis. Private sector SRI in Korea is estimated to have fallen by 10.8 per cent from February 2008 to April 2009 and total SRI AuM in Japan may have fallen by as much as 45.1 per cent by the end of 2008 compared with the previous year.[21] The most recent estimates by OWW Consulting put the total AuM figure at around US$50 billion by mid-2010.

This is just the tip of the iceberg, since, apart from share market-based investment, other forms of SRI are large and growing. Syariah-compliant funds in Malaysia are estimated at around US$86.3 billion at the end of 2009, of which US$62 billion is in Islamic Banking assets and around

US\$24.2 billion in other forms of Islamic Finance. Islamic Banking represents around 15.4 per cent of Malaysia's banking assets.[22] Indonesia, the world's largest Muslim country, accounts for a much smaller share of Islamic funds, estimated at around US\$3 billion.[23]

Non-faith investment in ESG issues also takes more direct forms. In March 2010 the international Climate Investment Fund (CIF), a collaboration of international development banks and the World Bank, endorsed direct investments in clean-technology projects in Indonesia, Thailand, Philippines and Vietnam worth US\$13.6 billion in total.[24] In April 2010 around US\$5 billion in investments in Indonesian Geothermal projects was announced at the World Geothermal Conference in Bali.[25] In the private sector Fortis Investments has raised US\$1.2 billion for its China Green Fund between December 2009 and February 2010. For governments, too, investment in SRI is high on the agenda. Japan announced a US\$5 billion loan fund in March 2009 for developing countries investing in solar power and other green technologies.[26] In June 2010, the Norwegian Government announced US\$1 billion in initiatives in Indonesia to protect biodiversity among plantation owners.[27] This is in addition to a US\$4 billion multilateral fund under the REDD Plus programme for Reducing Emissions from Deforestation and Degradation announced in July 2010.[28] Looking forward, a report in February 2010 by the Swiss international finance house Vontobel Asset Management, which launched its own successful Asia (excluding Japan) Responsibility Fund in 2008, estimated that SRI assets under management in Asia could rise to between US\$1.5 and 4 trillion by 2015.[29]

In terms of SRI Funds, a study by OWW Consulting drawing on various sources estimated that there were around 466 SRI Funds in Asia by mid-2010.[30] These are summarized in Table 14.1 and include 262 equity-based funds and 197 faith-based funds, mainly Syariah Funds in Malaysia. In addition there were seven hedge funds, and not counted in the overall total are a number of international funds with an undisclosed Asia segment. The largest number of non-faith SRI funds is in Korea, followed closely by Japan. In the former case government pension fund investments and incentives have been a key driver of SRI. Hong Kong also features strongly, although this is largely as a trading centre for overseas funds rather than a source or initiator of SRI-focused investments.

Information available from the ASrIA SRI Funds portal allows us to plot the growth of SRI in Asia in terms of the number and type of funds over time. These are shown in Figure 14.2.[31] The earliest fund identified was the ASM Investment Services Berhad 'Dana Al Aiman' Syariah

*Table 14.1*   Sustainable and responsible investment funds in Asia

| | SRI funds[a] | Faith-based[b] | Country total |
|---|---|---|---|
| China | 3 | 0 | 3 |
| Hong Kong | 56 | 1 | 57 |
| Japan | 71 | 0 | 71 |
| Korea | 73 | 0 | 73 |
| Taiwan | 17 | 0 | 17 |
| Singapore | 27 | 8 | 35 |
| Malaysia | 5 | 146 | 151 |
| Indonesia | 4 | 39 | 43 |
| India | 2 | 1 | 3 |
| Thailand | 2 | 1 | 3 |
| Vietnam | 2 | 0 | 2 |
| **Segment total** | **262** | **197** | **459** |
| Asia hedge funds | | | 7 |

[a] Includes Private Equity Funds and SRI Pension Mandates; [b] Mostly Syariah Funds.
*Source*: ASrIA SRI Funds Portal (2010), KoSIF (2009) and OWW Consulting (2010).

fund established in Malaysia in 1968, followed by the Amanah Saham Kedah Berhad 'ASM Syariah Money Market Fund' established in 1969. The first non-faith funds identified were the Hong Kong Axa Wealth Management 'Framlington Health Fund', established in 1987, and the Taiwan Jupiter Investment Management Group Limited 'Jupiter Ecology Fund', established the following year. The main period of growth took place after 2000, and within 10 years from that date non-faith SRI Funds had grown more than 10-fold from 22 to 252. Faith-based funds had grown more than eight times, from 24 to 197.

## Promoting responsible investment (RI) in Asia and around the world

The growth of SRI in Asia is part of a global trend towards integration of ESG issues into investment decisions. The United Nations-backed Principles for Responsible Investment (PRI) are a key driver of this movement. The PRI were developed by a group of leading international

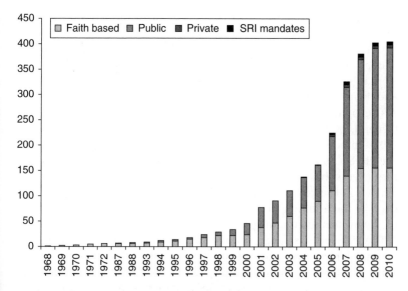

*Figure 14.2* The growth in SRI funds in Asia
Source: ASrIA Funds Portal (2010) and OWW Consulting (2010)

institutional investors to reflect the importance of ESG issues in current investment practices. By mid-2010 the organization had around 720 signatories with an estimated US$18 trillion of AuM globally.[32]

Signatories to the PRI commit to six principles and aspire to:

1. incorporate ESG issues into their investment analysis and decision-making processes,
2. be active owners and incorporate ESG issues into ownership policies and practices,
3. encourage appropriate disclosure on ESG issues by the entities in which they invest,
4. promote acceptance and implementation of the Principles within the investment industry,
5. work together to enhance the effectiveness of implementation of the Principles, and
6. report on their activities and progress towards implementing the Principles.

Although the PRI is voluntary, becoming a signatory represents a clear public commitment and demonstrates support from top-level leadership to considering ESG issues. The principles are not prescriptive but provide a selection of possible ways for investors to incorporate ESG issues into mainstream investment decision-making and ownership practices. Different investors adopt different approaches but with a similar purpose: to take into account ESG issues and to use investment and ownership practices to address them positively.

The process was convened by the then United Nations Secretary-General, Kofi Annan, and coordinated by the UN Environment Programme Finance Initiative and the Global Compact. Since its launch, the PRI Secretariat, which administers the six principles and the signatory events, has emerged as a powerful organization in its own right, and the PRI Secretariat, headed by Executive Director James Gifford, has become the leading global focal point for the sustainable and responsible investment community.

The PRI has a strong presence in the Asia-Pacific, which has the second largest regional membership after Europe, as shown in Table 14.2, but, excluding Australia and New Zealand, Asian membership is only slightly larger than South America. At the start of 2009 the PRI held a series of important events at the Stock Exchanges of Indonesia, Singapore and Thailand and with the sovereign wealth fund of Malaysia, Khazanah Nasional. Other events were also held to bring together insights from major international SRI funds and local stakeholders and investors. Engagement in Asia continued during the year with events in Indonesia, Malaysia and Singapore and also in China. In India, where CSR and SRI are gaining momentum, the PRI organized a major event with the National Stock Exchange for companies and investors in 2009. In September 2010 a joint PRI event with UNCTAD and the UN Global Compact was convened in China, focusing on sustainable stock exchanges. The collective work of the PRI complements that of local SRI advocacy groups such as ASrIA and KoSIF – the Korean Sustainability Investment Forum.

## Promoting SRI through Asian stock exchanges

Stock exchanges in Asia are increasingly promoting CSR and ESG management as part of their overall programmes to develop and deepen share trading in the region and to help investors to gain access to the information they need to make sustainable investment decisions. In fact, most of the initiatives are focused on listed companies directly rather than on investors. The general aim is to raise awareness and encourage companies to address ESG issues and improve reporting and

*Table 14.2* Signatories to the UN principles for responsible investment (Global and Asia)

| Global | Asset owners | Investment managers | Service providers | Total |
|---|---|---|---|---|
| Europe | 109 | 171 | 53 | 333 |
| Asia-Pacific | 46 | 90 | 30 | 166 |
| North America | 28 | 78 | 29 | 135 |
| South America | 18 | 18 | 9 | 45 |
| Africa | 2 | 21 | 6 | 29 |
| International | 1 | 1 | 5 | 7 |
| Middle East | – | 1 | 4 | 5 |
| Total | 204 | 380 | 136 | 720 |

| Asia-Pacific | Asset owners | Investment managers | Service providers | Total |
|---|---|---|---|---|
| Australia | 31 | 51 | 16 | 98 |
| New Zealand | 9 | 11 | – | 20 |
| Japan | 3 | 10 | 1 | 14 |
| South Korea | 1 | 7 | 6 | 14 |
| Hong Kong | – | 2 | 2 | 4 |
| Thailand | 1 | 3 | – | 4 |
| Singapore | – | 1 | 2 | 3 |
| India | – | 1 | 1 | 2 |
| Malaysia | – | 1 | 1 | 2 |
| Vietnam | – | 1 | 1 | 2 |
| Indonesia | 1 | – | – | 1 |
| Oceania | – | 1 | – | 1 |
| Pakistan | – | 1 | – | 1 |
| Asia-Pacific | 46 | 90 | 30 | 166 |
| Asia | 6 | 28 | 14 | 48 |

*Source*: UNPRI (2010) http://www.unpri.org/signatories/ accessed on 2 August 2010

transparency. Often these programmes are accompanied by regulatory changes, but mainly they focus on awareness events, training and awards programmes.

## Stock exchange SRI Indices

An increasingly common way for Asian stock exchanges to address SRI issues is through the promotion of SRI Indices. To create an SRI Index the ESG performance of listed companies is assessed. The criteria for inclusion in a sustainable index vary across ESG aspects, but in general only top ESG performers are included in an index. The development of SRI Indices can contribute to the promotion of SRI and raise companies' awareness of sustainability management. Investors who are interested in long-term sustainable companies can use the index as a guide in making investment decisions, and it also helps well-performing companies to be properly recognized in the capital market.

Demand for SRI Indices in emerging markets is growing, as they are seen as a way of minimizing risk and ensuring sound long-term performance of stocks in markets where general company information may be poor. Following this trend, the Indonesian Stock Exchange, Korea Exchange, the National Stock Exchange of India, Shanghai Stock Exchange and Tokyo Stock Exchange are currently offering SRI Indices to investors. A number of other exchanges, such as the Stock Exchange of Thailand, are currently in the process of evaluating such indices.

## Examples of SRI Indexes in Asian stock markets

The Korea Exchange SRI Index consists of companies that demonstrate outstanding performance in an assessment over a range of ESG issues. It is a market capitalization index with 70 components. Inclusion in the index depends on initial selection criteria covering assets and liquidity and on a formal ESG assessment. This assessment is conducted by Korea Corporate Governance Services (KCGS) and Eco-Frontier, a leading Korean SRI assessment service provider.

The S&P ESG India Index comprises 50 of the best-performing stocks of the top 500 Indian companies by market capitalization that are listed on the National Stock Exchange of India. Companies are benchmarked by ESG parameters, which are translated into a scoring system and ranking of each company against its peers. The top 500 companies are subject to a screening process giving them a qualitative score based on ESG disclosure in the public domain. The quantitative score is combined with a qualitative score for the top 150 companies. In addition, liquidity is used as a threshold for inclusion in the index, so that stocks should have traded a minimum of Rs 12 billion in the last 12 months. India Index Services & Products Ltd (IISL), a joint venture between National Stock Exchange of India Ltd and CRISIL Ltd, acts as the index's calculating agent.

The Shanghai Stock Exchange (SSE) Social Responsibility Index comprises the top 100 stocks from the SSE Corporate Governance Index ranked by 'Social Contribution Value per Share' (SCVS), which is a measure of spending on social and environmental issues. The SSE Social Responsibility Index is designated to reflect performance of stocks with good performance in Social Responsibility.[33] 'A-class' shares in the SSE Corporate Governance Sector with their Corporate Social Responsibility Reports disclosed are eligible for inclusion in the index. Constituents are selected based on the average daily trading volume of at least 20 per cent and SCVS. The top 100 in the ranking list in terms of the social contribution value per share are included in the SSE Social Responsibility Index.[34]

The Tokyo Stock Exchange TOPIX 1000 CSR TSE started to incorporate the element of CSR into the calculation of 'TOPIX 1000 Float'. Domestic companies listed on the TSE first section with highest market capitalization and liquidity are eligible for the Index. Inclusion is based on a screening incorporating CSR elements provided by The Good Bankers Ltd and Mitsubishi U&F Research & Consulting Co Ltd. The 1000 best-performing stocks are then included in the Index.

One successful example of SRI can be seen in the SRI-Kehati Index on the Indonesian Stock Exchange (IDX) in Jakarta. The SRI-Kehati Index is a collaborative project between Yayasan Keanekaragaman Hayati Indonesia (The Indonesian Biodiversity Foundation – Kehati) and IDX, launched on 8 June 2009 by Professor Dr Emil Salim, former Minister for the Environment in Indonesia.

The Index Universe starts with all listed companies on IDX. Financial screens are applied to remove small companies with a market capitalization below Rupiah 1 trillion (approximately US$100 million) and companies with low share availability, that is with a free-float ratio below 10 per cent. Companies must also have a positive Price/Earnings (PE) Ratio.

A set of ESG criteria agreed to by Kehati, IDX and their stakeholders is then applied. Exclusion screens are used for companies involved in pesticides or chloride-organic chemistry, genetically modified organisms, nuclear power, severe violations of labour and human rights, armament

Pergerakan LQ45 Indeks dan SRI-KEHATI Index
1 January 2007 - 29 January 2010

*Figure 14.3*   SRI index performance: the Indonesia SRI-Kehati Index
*Source*: OWW Consulting (2010)

and weapons, tobacco, alcohol and pornography. A further screen is also applied to exclude companies of concern for other reasons, such as corporate governance issues that arise or remain unresolved during the selection period.

The remaining companies are then rated by OWW Consulting, using international ESG criteria, customized for Indonesian laws. These cover corporate governance, environment, human rights, labour practices, community investment and business behaviour related to suppliers and customers. This produces a SRI-Kehati Index candidate list for scrutiny by an independent committee, which has sole responsibility of selecting 25 constituents which are 'best-in-class' when compared with their peers.

The limit of 25 was chosen to make membership of the index competitive, and it does not necessarily imply that only 25 companies are considered responsible. Membership of the SRI-Kehati Index has become a source of pride for companies, which are now beginning to improve their sustainability performance in order to enter the index and maintain their position. This was an important motivating factor behind the project, which was highlighted by Prof. Dr Emil Salim in his launch speech.[35]

The financial performance of the SRI-Kehati Index has been impressive, even through the worst financial crisis since the Great Depression, as shown in Figure 14.3. From the baseline set in January 2007 to January 2010 it had grown 52.8 per cent, compared with 33.8 per cent on the benchmark LQ45 Index.[36] During the period of the financial crisis, stocks on the SRI-Kehati Index proved more resilient, falling 62.1 per cent compared with 66 per cent on the LQ45. Since the end of the crisis the SRI-Kehati Index has grown 168.2 per cent trough-to-peak compared with 146.9 per cent growth seen in the conventional index.

The SRI-Kehati Index hit a number of important milestones in its first 12 months. First, the fact that it was launched successfully shows that SRI has an important role to play in emerging markets in Asia and is not just for rich, developed economies. Second, the outperformance of the SRI-Kehati Index relative to the conventional benchmark demonstrates that SRI can be a successful investment style in its own right. Third, two new SRI funds have been established by Mega Capital and Bahana Securities using the SRI-Kehati Index, which allows institutional and retail investors easy access to sustainable investment products. Fourth, the SRI-Kehati Index is backed by online information sources and training programmes. These help companies improve their sustainability management and help fund managers and shareholders understand ESG investment styles and how they work in practice. Finally, it offers a real example for other stock exchanges to follow and will hopefully show them the value of creating SRI Indices across the region.

## Challenges and opportunities

Some challenges exist that should be addressed urgently to take advantage of the growth potential for SRI in Asia. These fall into three broad groups: first, to establish which ESG issues are important in Asia and which add or subtract value; second, to build Asian SRI capability; and third, to increase ESG disclosure amongst Asian companies.

## Materiality

The determination of whether any particular issue is material for investment purposes is a balance between the concerns of major stakeholders and the impact on specific industries or businesses. This poses a particular challenge for SRI in Asia, especially when Western investors are concerned about issues that are of less urgency to Asian stakeholders.

This is particularly true when it comes to the pivotal balance of environmental and social issues. For example, the issue of climate change is clearly an important issue for the Western SRI Community and for investors generally. In Asia, while climate change is seen as important, it is not afforded the urgency that many Western observers often demand.

In the run-up to the Copenhagen Summit in December 2001, for example, the Indian Prime Minister Manmohan Singh commented that: 'What we are witnessing today is the consequence of over two centuries of industrial activity and high consumption lifestyles in the developed world,' but added: 'It is the developing countries that are the worst affected by climate change.'[37]

The UCLA economist Deepak Lal has described what he calls 'the Western obsession with curbing carbon emissions' as 'wicked and also economically foolish'.[38] This is a strong view, but is a position taken in a milder form by many countries in Asia, including the largest, China and India, and also smaller countries. It articulates a concern that Western domination of the global discussion on climate change has weighed the balance against economic and social development in favour of assertive environmental responses.

In fact, environmental issues are often not considered as urgent a priority in Asia as they appear to be in the West. They are therefore not as material an issue for Asian companies as for their Western counterparts. Indeed, in Lal's analysis, curbing carbon emissions to meet Western targets would have devastating effects on Asian economic and social development. He concludes that: 'For India it would mean not only reversing the current trends in poverty alleviation but a vast increase in the numbers of the poor who would otherwise be pulled out of poverty.'[39]

This dichotomy between Western and Asian priorities on climate change versus socio-economic development was seen as a major cause of the widely perceived failure of the Copenhagen process. In turn it raises the question of whether Western-type environmental SRI will gain traction as a driver of SRI in Asia or whether growth in Asian SRI will be slower due to a seeming lack of materiality for socio-economic development by the Western SRI community.

Similar concerns exist regarding corporate governance (CG) issues, especially since Asian CG systems often differ significantly from

Western models.[40] In order to address these questions, the Western SRI community are challenged to understand material issues for Asian stakeholders and identify the value drivers from socio-economic as well as environmental investments. This may not be a challenge that they choose to take up.

## Mandates, management and mezzanine infrastructure

One of the main drivers of SRI in Europe and North America has been the active involvement of Asset Owners (AOs), especially large pension funds such as the Universities Superannuation Scheme (USS) in the UK, the Norwegian Pension Fund in Europe and CalPERS in the USA. By introducing SRI criteria when issuing investment mandates to Investment Managers (IMs), large institutional AOs can require IMs to adopt ESG considerations in various forms ranging from screening to active ESG integration. They can also be instrumental in active engagement, since they hold and deploy investment funds in large volumes.[41]

As a consequence, institutional AOs have helped the development of ESG integration not just in their own investments but also among IMs who have developed SRI capability to bid for competitive fund mandates. This in turn has also supported a mezzanine infrastructure of specialist Service Providers (SPs) focusing on ESG ratings, governance monitoring, proxy voting, SRI product design and other forms of materiality research.

In Asia, by contrast, the SRI infrastructure across AO SRI mandates, IM SRI specialists and ESG SP companies is very thin. This can be seen in part from the number of PRI signatories in Asia-Pacific outside Australia and New Zealand:

- Only six Asian institutional Asset Owners (AO) are signatories of the PRI, and three of these are in Japan
- Only 28 Investment Manager (IM) signatories are from Asia, fewer than 10 per cent of the 380 SRI IM signatories worldwide
- Only 14 specialist Research & Service Providers (SP) out of 136 are in Asia

Taken together, this presents a picture of a severely underdeveloped SRI industry concentrated in Australia, Korea and Japan. To a large extent the investment industry will 'follow the money', and it is likely that if major AOs introduced ESG criteria and SRI mandates then this would provide a key driver of change. The Government Pension Funds in Korea and Thailand have begun important initiatives in this regard, but their counterparts in Hong Kong, China, Singapore, Malaysia and Indonesia have yet to follow suit.[42]

## Measurement and monitoring

A third issue holding back SRI in Asia is company disclosure on ESG issues. For some this is by far the most important barrier to SRI in the region. Financial markets need this information to measure and monitor ESG performance and to create new SRI Funds. Companies in Asia have a mixed record on writing clear CSR and Sustainability Reports that meet international standards such as the Global Reporting Initiative (GRI-G3) Guidelines. A number of regional regulatory bodies in Asia, such as in Malaysia and Indonesia, have introduced reporting requirements for listed companies, but compliance and enforcement are still patchy. In neither case are the GRI-G3 Guidelines required and there is no requirement for third-party verification or assurance.

An alternative, more popular indicator includes ESG assessments of various forms made for SRI indices such as the National Stock Exchange in India and Shanghai Stock Exchange in China, which are following the example of Indonesia in using SRI Indices to help drive sustainable and responsible investment. These indices often draw on local research companies such as OWW Consulting in Indonesia or Eco-Frontier in Korea, which offer large databases for this purpose. The variety of approaches taken, including, for example, the SSE Social Value per Share measure, reflects both the difficulty of obtaining ESG indicators from companies and a lack of agreement about how such indicators should be collated and interpreted. This is an ongoing debate, which has yet to reach a conclusion.

On environmental performance, the global Carbon Disclosure Project (CDP), which is managed by ASrIA in the region, aims to encourage greater transparency on emissions and environmental management.[43] Nonetheless, while efforts are being made to improve transparency, a great deal more needs to be done in order to ensure that the potential benefits of applying SRI in Asia are fully realized.

## Conclusions and the future

Despite some important limitations, SRI in Asia has a strong foothold and many people are optimistic about its future growth potential. The momentum generated by SRI funds in Europe and North America is now spilling over into Asian markets, where new opportunities and high returns offer manifold options for fund growth. Overseas SRI fund managers are already developing new Asian strategies that will put SRI in Asia onto a new trajectory. At current growth rates SRI in Asia is estimated to match that in other markets within 5 years. This is a tremendous prospect and one that is likely to be exciting and challenging in equal measure.

## Notes

1. I would like to thank Narina Mnatsakanian, Head of Global Networks, Recruitment and Emerging Markets Work Streams and Elliot Frankel, Communications Manager at the Principles for Responsible Investment for useful comments on the early drafts of this article. A shorter version of this article appears in *Social Space 2010* published by the Lien Centre at Singapore Management University. The editors of *Social Space* offered invaluable help in preparing that article.
2. There are various definitions of SRI, but the ASrIA approach is reasonably representative of the approach in Asia; see http://www.asria.org/portal/sri/intro?expand_all=1 accessed on 2 August 2010.
3. Useful references to SRI can be found in R Sullivan and C McKenzie (eds), *Responsible Investment* (Sheffield, UK: Greenleaf Publishing, 2006); MJ Kiernan, *Investing in a Sustainable World: Why GREEN is the New Color of Money on Wall Street* (New York, NY: AMACOM, 2009); or C Krosinsky and N Robins (eds), *Sustainable Investing: The Art of Long Term Performance* (London, UK: Earthscan Publications, 2008).
4. Ibid.
5. Ibid.
6. An early discussion of various forms of SRI can be found in R Sparkes, *Socially Responsible Investment: A Global Revolution* (London, UK: Wiley, 2003).
7. It is estimated that strikes cost British Airways around £43 million in its early stages as part of total losses of £531 million at May 2010; see http://www.bbc.co.uk/news/10135112. The strikes also caused loss of passenger numbers; which fell by 14.3 per cent in May 2010 compared with the previous year; see http://www.bbc.co.uk/news/10229033
8. See http://en.wikipedia.org/wiki/BYD_Auto and the BYD website at http://www.byd.com.cn
9. The full background on TLC can be found at their website: http://www.thetrulylovingcompany.com
10. The Satyam scandal in 2009 is described at http://en.wikipedia.org/wiki/Satyam_scandal. It has largely been settled but at great cost to the company. The Transmile Berhad issues of 2007 are discussed at http://en.wikipedia.org/wiki/Transmile_Air_Services#Incidents_.26_accidents and http://biz.thestar.com.my/news/story.asp?file=/2007/5/18/business/17769064&sec=business

11. There are many complaints against Bakrie & Brothers and related companies such as PT Bumi Resources: see, for example, http://www.asiasentinel. com/index.php?option=com_content&task=view&id=1472&Itemid=226 on the impact on the Indonesia Stock Exchange of Bakrie environmental disasters in Indonesia and http://www.biofuelwatch.org.uk/docs/BakrieStudy. pdf on indigenous rights.

12. See, for example, Sparkes (2003) ibid.

13. See full text, 'TIAA-CREF Statement on Former Holdings in Companies with Ties to Sudan', New York, 4 January 2010 at: http://www.tiaa-cref.org/public/about/press/about_us/releases/pressrelease313.html

14. Estimates in the *Banker* magazine placed pure Syariah-compliant assets at US$822 billion at the end of 2009 (http://www.payvand.com/news/09/ nov/1122.html) and an alternative definition by Moody's Investor Services estimates US$950 billion by end 2009 (http://www.todayszaman.com/tz-web/news-207150-105-islamic-finance-assets-could-reach-5-trillion.html). Both studies estimate global Syariah AuM will exceed US$1 trillion for 2010, and Moody's estimates growth to US$5 trillion within a decade.

15. See http://www.payvand.com/news/09/nov/1122.html and coverage in Malaysia's National News Agency Bernama at http://web7.bernama.com/ finance/news.php?id=326660

16. See, for example, the ASrIA Philanthropic Investment Portal http://portal. asria.org/philanthropic_investment/

17. See the Grameen website at http://www.grameen-info.org/ or background information and discussion at http://en.wikipedia.org/wiki/Grameen_Bank

18. See the Impact Asia Exchange website at http://www.asiaiix.com/

19. The European Social Investment Forum (EuroSif) estimated €2.7 trillion in European SRI Funds in 2008 (European SRI Study 2008: http://www.eurosif. org/publications/sri_studies) and the US Social Investing Forum (SIF) estimated US$2.7trillion in the US in 2007. New surveys for both organizations are expected in 2010.

20. 'Gaining Ground: Integrating environmental, social and governance (ESG) factors into investment processes in emerging markets', International Finance Corporation, Washington DC (March 2009) and OWW Consulting SRI Newsletter (November 2007).

21. See 'SRI in Korea 2009 Report' by Korea Sustainability Investment Forum (KoSIF) and Nikko Asset Management 2009 presentation to TBLI Conference, Tokyo.

22. As reported by Bernama at http://web7.bernama.com/finance/news. php?id=326660

23. Ibid.

24. Country Investment Funds (CIF) of the Clean Technology Fund (CTF) of the Climate Investment Fund (CIF): http://www.climateinvestmentfunds. org/cif/pf_2010_pressrelease_03_19

25. See the report in the Jakarta Post: http://www.thejakartaglobe.com/home/ billions-in-geothermal-deals-in-bali/371678

26. Japan Bank for International Cooperation (JBIC), Establishing 'Leading Investment to Future Environment(LIFE)' Initiative: http://www.jbic.go.jp/ en/about/news/2008/0323-01/index.html

27. See the Jakarta Post story at http://www.thejakartaglobe.com/columns/ norwegian-agreement-offers-the-best-deal-for-indonesias-forests/383842

28. See the Jakarta Post story on the REDD Scheme at http://www.thejakar-taglobe.com/home/rich-nations-pledge-4-billion-to-stop-deforestation-indonesia-agrees-to-moratorium/387151. The REDD Funds cover a number of emerging markets including some outside Asia.
29. F Paetzold, *Sustainable Investing in Asia: Uncovering Opportunities and Risks*, Zurich, Switzerland: Vontobel Asset Management, http://www.vontobel.com/en/about_vontobel/sustainability/publications/
30. 'Responsible Returns: SRI performance in Asia', OWW Consulting (2010).
31. The data is available at http://portal.asria.org/sri_fund/. The date of the fund's launch was not reported for many funds and has been uncovered from other sources. The start date of three funds remains unidentified; hence the total number of funds shown in Figure 14.2 is 407 from ASrIA's estimate of 410 Asian SRI Funds. Any errors are the responsibility of the author.
32. Refer to http://www.unpri.org/
33. http://static.sse.com.cn/sseportal/webapp/ennew/queryindexIntroduction Act?indexName=&indexCode=000048
34. http://static.sse.com.cn/sseportal/en_us/ps/home.shtml
35. See further details at: http://www.asria.org/news/press/1244602812/print
36. The LQ45 is an index of 45 companies with the highest level of liquidity that are the most tradable in terms of number of shares available in the market: http://www.duniainvestasi.com/bei/prices/stock/LQ45
37. The comments came in a press statement in July 2009 in the pre-Copenhagen position period; see the Bloomberg article at http://www.bloomberg.com/apps/news?pid=newsarchive&sid=aqr.54wsxvmI for example.
38. See the *Business Standard* article of 25 August 2009 at http://www.business-standard.com/india/news/deepak-lal-spikingroad-to-copenhagen/367985/ reproduced on Deepak Lal's UCLA website http://www.econ.ucla.edu/lal/busta/busta0809.pdf
39. Ibid.
40. See, for example, J Roche, *Corporate Governance in Asia* (London, UK: Routledge, 2005) and X Jia and R Tomasic, *Corporate Governance and Resource Security in China: The Transformation of China's Global Resources Companies* (London, UK: Routledge, 2009).
41. See, for example, *The Time to Lead is Now: The Adoption of ESG Analysis by Asian Government Pension Funds* (Hong Kong: ASrIA for the Asian Development Bank, 2009) at http://www.asria.org/publications
42. In his 2006 Budget Speech the then Malaysian Prime Minister, Abdullah Badawi, announced that the Malaysian Employee's Provident Fund (EFP), the country's largest asset owner, would introduce CSR criteria into its investment mandates. This was in line with the new CSR Reporting require-ments for listed companies introduced at the same time. As at mid-2010 no public announcement or commitment by EPF has been made.
43. See, for example, the ASrIA CDP Portal at http://www.asria.org/portal/cdp/introduction.

# 15
# Sustainable Investing in Asia: Uncovering Opportunities and Risks

*Falko Paetzold*

## Introduction

Economically, emerging Asia[1] is a success story, where superlatives and strong growth are common. To expand the network of highways and railways, USD50 billion was spent in 2009 alone. Fuelled by fundamentally strong economic growth and ample savings, demand for all kinds of goods will continue to explode in the region, where currently only 50 out of 1,000 citizens can afford a car. However, the same is true of the severe negative environmental, social and governance (ESG) effects that accompany such rapid growth. Emerging Asia's economic rise feeds off the inherently unsustainable system pioneered by the West since industrialization – extensive, fossil fuel-based resource consumption. This can hardly continue. Extensive resource consumption combined with modern technology and globalization accumulates huge environmental and social costs and, unlike at the time of the West's industrialization, humanity today far exceeds this planet's capacity to absorb these costs. Furthermore, emerging Asia is vulnerable to closely related issues, such as climate change, due to its geographic location, demographics, and status of pollution.

### Deforestation, pollution and climate change limit growth opportunities

Concerning environmental issues, perhaps most important for investors are the risks imposed by deforestation (pollution, floods), pollution (air and water) and climate change (droughts, floods, storms).

*Significant deforestation and forest degradation*

The rate of deforestation is high in emerging Asia, as vast areas of forest are legally or illegally logged, or burned down for palm plantations or farming. Global deforestation accounts for 15–20 per cent of greenhouse gas (GHG) emissions. In Indonesia, deforestation, peat bog degradation, and forest fires have led to the country's position among the world's three largest greenhouse gas emitters.[2] Indonesia's tropical rainforests will disappear by 2020 if the current rate of deforestation continues. Luckily, perhaps, Indonesia announced in 2010 that it signed a two-year moratorium on new concessions to clear natural forests and peatlands.[3] Losing the positive effects of forests often leads to impaired water quality and droughts, as well as the loss of biodiversity and entire livelihoods. Further effects are severe soil erosion and reduced flood protection.

*High incidence of air pollution*

Air and water are the most basic sources of life, and polluting them has severe effects. The World Health Organization (WHO) estimates that two-thirds of diseases attributable to air pollution worldwide occur in emerging Asia, causing 0.5–1 million premature deaths per year. Air pollution harms workers and animals, damages crops and buildings, and hinders industries that rely on clean production environments (e.g. companies producing semiconductors). Thus, pollution not only severely affects people's health, but also poses a significant risk to businesses and investors. Burning forests, transportation, and industrial activity are key polluting factors. The WHO measures air pollution according to the level of particulate matter (PM10) in the air. The world's highest annual average PM10 concentration is measured in Asia (35–220 PM10, vs. 20–70 in Europe and 20–60 in Canada and the US). Severe particle emissions cause a giant layer of air pollution covering much of South Asia and the Indian Ocean, called 'Asia's Brown Cloud' due to the brown colour stemming from 'an unhealthy mix of ozone, smoke, and other particles from human activities.'[4] The cloud not only significantly alters the Asian monsoon pattern, but also affects the entire world as it travels the globe.

---

*Polluters must fear regulatory action*

In the Chinese province of Hunan, the local environmental protection bureau threatened to suspend production at 832 paper factories if they did not improve their environmental standards. A total of 234 paper plants around Dongting Lake were closed immediately.[5] Already in 2006, the environmental protection bureau of Anhui Province had fined or closed 2,362 firms based on environmental grounds.[6]

*Increasing effects of climate change*

Emerging Asia is particularly vulnerable to rising temperatures and sea levels. This is due to a combination of the geographic location, long coastlines, and low-lying land areas, as well as high population densities and a high incidence of poverty. The Intergovernmental Panel on Climate Change (IPCC) states with 'high confidence'[7] that the following effects on Asia are gradually increasing and compound each other: more frequent and severe weather events in the form of storms, droughts and floods resulting in lower crop yields and a higher incidence of disease, and thus migration and increased pressure on urban areas; rising sea levels and declining river runoff, which increase the risk of flooding and diseases such as cholera, while affecting infrastructure and the aquaculture industry.[8]

## Society – low work standards, child labour, product safety and food security issues impose risks

A significant share of emerging Asia's economic growth is still based on low-value added manufacturing. In combination with global competition, constant pressure on margins and limited regulation, this leads to a variety of problems that are not acceptable in most of today's societies and which can have severe implications for investments.

*Low work, health and safety standards*

Problematic work, health and safety standards have become unacceptable and much publicized in the developed world and emerging Asia. Consider the scandals faced by Nike through the 1990s, with Phil Knight, one of Nike's founders, stating in 1998 that 'the Nike product has become synonymous with slave wages, forced overtime, and arbitrary abuse.'[9] The related scandals mostly affected sales in Europe and the US at the time. However, consumers in emerging Asia are becoming an important target group and are increasingly sensitive to those issues, which often relate to their direct living environments. The theme is therefore relevant for Asia-based and Asia-focused firms. Throughout the decade of 2000, however, the International Labour Organization (ILO) had to confirm a variety of allegations in Asia, almost a third of which concerned anti-union discrimination. About 50 per cent of Asian governments reacted by ratifying the two main tools of the ILO.[10] Most Asian countries have regulatory frameworks to ensure workers' right of free association with labour unions, as well as sufficient work, health and safety standards. Yet the challenge still lies in the often limited enforcement.

*High occurrence of child labour*

Per 2009, UNICEF estimated 150 million children 5–14 years old world-wide were engaged in child labour. In emerging Asia, at least 13% of children 5–14 years old engaged in labour, and even over 30% in Cambodia and 20–29% in Laos.[11] Apart from the ethical problem of child labour, those children usually go without any education and have low life expectancies – their lost productivity is a critical loss to Asian economies striving for higher value-creating industries. While child labour is somewhat more tolerated in emerging Asia – as it was in the West during industrialization – it is a troublesome issue for interna-tional firms. A prominent example is the public outcry that followed a BBC documentary in the year 2000, where a journalist interviewed 12-year-old girls working under poor conditions at a Gap Inc. plant in Cambodia. Especially the most exposed firms reacted with the develop-ment of comprehensive sets of requirements for suppliers and control-ling mechanisms, yet high rates of child labour prevail.

*Problematic product safety*

Asia is the key production hub for the world's consumer goods and has long been praised for making those products readily available at reasonable prices. However, there are product quality and safety issues involved, which often severely impact consumers, businesses and inves-tors. Examples abound, from the US firm Mattel having to recall 14 million China-made toys containing excessive amounts of lead during 2007/2008, to the 2008 scandal around melamine-tainted dairy-based products, mainly milk and infant formula, made in China. The mela-mine scandal caused a number of deaths and thousands more were taken ill, and it is named by the WHO as one of the largest food safety events it ever had to deal with.[12] The industry-wide occurrence on this large scale, systematic disregard of legal structures and consumers' interests, as well as the ineffective handling of the issue by the Chinese govern-ment, are bound to leave investors concerned that similar product-related scandals could happen at any time.

*Endangered food security and effects on poverty*

Increasing food prices not only increase social problems such as poverty and hunger, but also affect the attractiveness of markets, as they limit purchasing power and economic development opportunities. Food prices are a crucial social issue in Asia, as individuals spend a relatively large pro-portion of their income on food and beverages. For example, the income share spent on foods is about 20 per cent in Indonesia, 35 per cent in

Vietnam and 45 per cent in the Philippines. Asia's poor (income below USD1 per day) suffered the most from rising food prices as they spend 60–80 per cent of their income on foods. Increased food prices eliminated some advances in poverty reduction, and amplified social pressures. The factors that increase food prices are expected to intensify. Asia's population, along with demand for feedstock-intensive products such as meat and dairies, continues to grow, while the IPCC expects Asian crop yields to decrease due to rising temperatures and more extreme weather events.[13]

### 'Global food crisis', 2008

From late 2007 to mid-2008, prices of basic foods such as rice and wheat increased due to speculation, adverse weather events, and greater demand for biofuels, meat and dairy products (especially in Asia), as well as ineffective agricultural policies and market mechanisms. While prices have come down from the peaks of 2008, some products that are specifically important to Asians and Asia's poor are still far more expensive than they used to be. The UN's Food and Agriculture Organization reports that rice, for example, trades at about a 75 per cent higher price than it did in early 2007.[14] It is a critical fact that local prices at Asian markets often did not revert to pre-crisis levels. For local markets in Asia, adverse environmental events such as abnormal monsoon patterns – droughts, floods – and increasing demand for meats often offset governmental support programmes. That led to stronger price increases compared to global markets. Global prices for maize and wheat, for example, were down to about early 2007 prices by early 2009. Critically, however, prices in Asia are still at a higher level, with more than 50 per cent of local Asian markets reporting prices more than 25 per cent above the level of early 2007.

### Governance – suboptimal shareholder and legal structures compromise investment environment

The transparency and accountability that come with good governance are the foundation of an attractive investment environment. Yet investors face some critical governance challenges in emerging Asia.

### Risks arise from concentrated shareholder structures

Family-business ownership, single-shareholder control, and a convergence of major shareholding and management are common in Asian firms, affecting transparency, board effectiveness, and the consideration of external stakeholders' interest. Transparency is sometimes limited for investors, especially regarding family-controlled firms with often interlocking networks of subsidiaries, sister companies, and publicly listed firms.

---

*Chaoda modern agriculture, China*

Chaoda Modern Agriculture claims to own 5,000 hectares of land in Jilin Province. Yet research indicates that 2,500 hectares is closer to the truth. The firm was shunned by all major analysts due to fears of scandals and fraud detection.[15]

---

Board independence and effectiveness are often the aim of regulation but are limited by concentrated shareholder structures. The OECD best-practice model suggests independent, two-tier board structures with active and critical directors, and the CEO and Chair positions held by different people. Yet a high incidence of rather dependent, single-tier boards is observed in emerging Asia, where directors have little engagement in strategy-setting and critical analysis, and CEO/Chair positions are held by the same individual.

Furthermore, concentrated shareholder structures lay the ground for a low degree of management consideration of the interests of internal and external stakeholders. Such disregard means missing valuable input, and can lead to firms missing out on operational or market opportunities, as well as risking stepping into widely publicized and costly PR pitfalls. Such behaviour hurt several Asian firms unwilling to support earthquake victims in China, for example.

---

*Chaoda modern agriculture, China*

The board of Chaoda Modern Agriculture was prominently criticized for its weakness when it let Mr Ho Kwok, founder and major shareholder, decide over the directors' heads to purchase a Thai mining company. The deal was seen as disadvantageous to shareholders as it had no apparent strategic fit to Chaoda.[16]

---

### Risks arise from a high legal diversity and limited investor protection

Another relevant feature of the Asian business landscape is its high legal diversity. The legal frameworks of Thailand and the Philippines, for example, are based on French civil law, while German civil law provides the legal base in China, Taiwan and South Korea. UK common law inspired the legal structures of Hong Kong, Singapore and Pakistan. Additionally, religious or traditional social norms often overlie legal and regulatory structures. Such an environment of diverse and culturally differently interpreted legal frameworks provides ample pitfalls for both firms and investors, which makes the highest forms of governance, transparency and accountability ever more important.

On a more detailed level, the limited existence of regulation to protect the interests of minority shareholders poses additional risks to investors. Various cases of the exploitation of non-controlling shareholders have been reported.

---

*Resorts world, Malaysia*

In December 2008, Malaysian casino operator Resorts World (now Genting Malaysia) purchased a 10 per cent stake in US-based Walker Digital Gaming for USD69 million. Resorts chairman Lim Kok Thay is also director of the seller, and the deal was considered to be engineered by a group around him. The deal led to a slew of rating downgrades, as Resorts paid a hefty premium for an acquisition whose current benefits are not immediately value-accretive to the group. It incurred a 14 per cent share price decline, reducing the firms' market value by USD610 million,[17] with no opportunity for minority shareholders to investigate or otherwise explore options to recoup their losses.

---

## Key socio-economic and cultural sustainability drivers

Sustainable investing approaches that were developed in the US and in Europe (please see additional details in the Appendix) must be adapted to the significantly different contextual drivers of the sustainability theme in emerging Asia.

### Western bottom-up vs. emerging Asia's top-down approach to sustainability

In the West, civil society has pressured companies and regulators towards sustainability initiatives in what could be called a 'bottom-up' approach. Investors looking at the Asian sustainability theme from this perspective, however, could be misled. There is a fundamental difference in that civil society activity is limited (if growing) in Asia, and sustainability themes are mostly pushed ahead by governments in what can be called a 'top-down' approach. We see the following three drivers as decisive for the two different developments:

1. Economic development – continuous vs. rapid
2. Power concentration – diversified vs. concentrated

3. Cultural focus – truth-seeking and individualistic vs. harmony-seeking and communal

*Driver 1 – rapid speed of economic development occupies*
*individuals' attention*

Emerging Asia lacks a strong civil society due to late, but now rapid, economic development...

The initiators of modern industrialization, Western economies developed 150 years earlier and less erratically than their counterparts in emerging Asia, as did ESG problems. Along with democratization, 'civil society' emerged to counter those issues. In a way, Western societies had the 'luxury' of developing civil society structures to counter ESG problems from the comfort of continuous economic development and accompanying relative wealth – a luxury that emerging Asia did not have. Leveraging modern technology and globalized markets, economies like China are currently undergoing a major economic and social shift. Since the launch of market-based economic reforms in 1978, China's GDP has grown by almost 10 per cent each year,[18] and the GDP of developing Asia has grown by 5–11 per cent, more than double the GDP growth rate of the world (–1 to 5 per cent) or the EU (–4 to 4 per cent) over the same period.[19] China's GDP per capita (constant prices, national currency) increased more than 10-fold, from RMB 807 in 1980 to RMB 8,539 in 2008.[20] This major shift understandably focuses minds on staying on the economic winners' side, coined in China as the 'get-rich-quick' mentality, rather than on sustainability issues. Going forward, however, investors can expect civil society activity in emerging Asia to increase, as Asia's citizens gain access to the means for enabling this – free time, financial independence, the Internet, literature, telephones, travel, legal support, and so on. In this context, it is pertinent to realize that many Asian individuals are confronted with ESG problems to an incredibly higher degree than most Westerners are today, implying great potential for activity to come.

*Driver 2 – concentrated power structures limit individuals'*
*ability to engage*

... as well as the limiting effect of concentrated power structures in governments and businesses...

Politically, most Asian countries are governed by relatively autocratic structures. The People's Republic of China, for example, has been governed by the authoritarian Chinese Communist Party (CCP) since 1949. As another example, the wealthy Republic of Singapore is largely governed by the family of Lee Kuan Yew.[21]

On a broader level, it can be interesting to look at the theme of 'freedom', as classified by the organization Freedom House, which rates a country's level of political rights and civil liberties, and classifies countries as 'free', 'partly free' and 'not free'.[22] Compared with Western Europe or the Americas, a significant share of countries in the Asia-Pacific region are still classified as 'not free'.

In addition, the CFA Institute, with the Chartered Financial Analyst (CFA) designation awarding the arguably most prestigious certification for finance professionals, confirms the notion that a high occurrence of power concentration at company level is observed. Many Asian firms are controlled by a family or a single-shareholder group. Government ownership is common, and investors should be aware of a tendency that cash cows from quasi-monopolistic businesses sometimes further limit the need for transparency and accountability.[23]

Furthermore, freedom of speech, of the press and of unions is often reported as rather limited in countries with high power concentration. This does not provide an environment supportive of bottom-up movements as seen in the West, which were supported by more diversified power structures. The activity of new media such as the internet and mobile telephony helps to accelerate civil society and 'freedom' today, despite some Asian governments reportedly limiting content and access. These media provide an almost uncontrollable platform to exchange ideas and organize groups, and offer huge potential. The first ever Asian blogging conference in Hong Kong in 2009 put the spotlight on prominent activists circumventing governments' and businesses' powers. The development is attracting substantial attention from the media, and should equally interest investors as it indicates the rise of a vocal civil society.

### Driver 3 – harmony-oriented culture limits individuals' interest in engaging

...and a cultural background that focuses more on harmony and the community, rather than the truth-seeking and individualism-oriented belief systems of the West.

The impact of culture is also important. Consider the fundamental differences between Taoism and Confucianism – which strongly influenced Asian belief systems – and the Greek philosophy on which Western culture is based.

Greek philosophy laid the ground for the Western belief system of individualistic, 'truth-seeking' and democratic societies, wherein 'every vote has equal weight'. Thus, Europeans/'Westerners' developed a culture of putting great emphasis on the concept of truth-seeking and individuals' freedom and 'rights'. Westerners tended to create rather small and homogeneous states, with an inherent role and room for criticism and civil society.

This starkly contrasts with Chinese culture, which continues to have a major influence on emerging Asia. The Chinese counterpart to Greek 'agency' is 'harmony'.[24] Based on the philosophy of Confucianism and Taoism, it is a framework of rules and guidelines. The aim is to achieve a harmonious society. The Tao, 'The Way', emphasizes achieving peace with oneself and one's surroundings through empathy, moderation, humility, naturalness, 'non-action' (wu wei), 'absolute simplicity of living' and 'refusal to assert active authority'.[25] Thus, Taoism to a certain degree rather inspires individuals to accept and deal with situations they are confronted with, as opposed to questioning and challenging their background and whereabouts. Furthermore, in Confucianism, every individual has his or her place in society and must obey, respect and listen to higher-ups and authorities, with the goal of a state governed by moral virtue rather than by the use of coercive laws. Confucianism was promoted as a sort of 'state religion' by some Asian governments.

As with the above drivers of economic development and power concentration, the cultural theme is undergoing massive change in Asia as well. With increased economic and cultural interchange with the West, emerging Asia is experiencing a certain 'Westernization' in culture – including individualistic and truth-seeking tendencies. The divergence of Asian and Western culture fosters Asian civil society, similar to the effect of increased standards of living and access to media.

*Outcome – regulators drive sustainability theme*
*(not NGOs as in the West)*

Based on the described characteristics of (1) economic development, (2) power concentration and (3) cultural focus, sustainability in the West developed through a continuous bottom-up approach. From the comfort of early industrialization and wealth creation and diversified power structures, based on individualistic and truth-seeking belief systems, Western citizens addressed industrialization's ever more apparent ESG problems through civil society movements. Through continuous development, efforts were institutionalized and professionalized by the means of non-governmental organizations (NGOs) such as WWF (1961, Switzerland) or Greenpeace (1971, Canada). Such NGOs developed into powerful and professional organizations, with Greenpeace, for example, reporting EUR212 million revenues for 2007.

Their achievements are manifold, including manufacturers' attention to child labour in their production processes (Nike, Gap), or regulatory actions, such as the 1987 'Montreal Protocol on Substances That Deplete the Ozone Layer'.

To evaluate the sustainability theme correctly, investors must be aware of a fundamental difference when it comes to Asia. As civil society activity is low in emerging Asia, searching for a civil society-driven bottom-up approach will vastly underestimate the level of Asian societies' activity on the sustainability theme. Yet, as opposed to the West, Asian governments are the main drivers of sustainability activity. Governments from China to Indonesia have severe ESG issues at their doorstep and realize the case for sustainable development, both as a reaction to possible threats as well as in aspiring to achievements such as more resource-efficient and competitive economies. In the manner of often autocratic and powerful governments, various ESG-related laws and initiatives are promptly pushed ahead. Consider China's various laws such as 'Measures on Open Environmental Information' where excessively polluting factories were blacklisted and eventually shut down, as well as a 'Green Credit Policy'[26] that mandates environmental assessments of problematic projects. Other initiatives range from a sudden ban on plastic bags to mandatory sustainability reporting for state-controlled firms,[27] or the recent introduction of automotive fleet $CO_2$ emission reduction targets that are as stringent as those mandated within the European Union.[28]

### Emerging Asia's focus on social themes

Another major theme important in evaluating firms' ESG performances accurately across markets is Asian societies' focus on social issues.

*Driver 1: Social initiatives show higher direct relevance;*
*early stage of the theme*

Some governmental services that many Europeans take for granted – education, childcare, health care, and so on – are still not fully established in some regions in emerging Asia, and firms' social initiatives can have a significant and direct impact on individuals' lives. Furthermore, they are important in developing potential markets and employees. For example, while the CEO of CIMB Group, one of emerging Asia's largest banks, comments on sponsoring 500 University of Malaya graduates with the words 'We welcome this opportunity to give back to society', the University's Vice-Chancellor notes that 'The graduates will provide a pool of potential human resource for CIMB Group.'[29] The focus on such 'quick wins' and social topics is also typical of an early stage of ESG awareness, where emphasis is often placed on the most direct and clear impact of the ESG theme – frequently social and philanthropic initiatives. Furthermore, such initiatives are often less complex to implement than comprehensive environmental management systems or governance frameworks, for example.

*Driver 2: Harmony-oriented culture demands social activities*

As mentioned earlier, Asia is influenced by Taoism and Confucianism. The focus on harmony and a functioning society based on individuals behaving 'correctly' towards their peers also means that the powerful must do their best to support the weak. This applies to CEOs and their firms as well, which explains Asians' attention to philanthropic and other social initiatives. The International Finance Corporation comes to a similar conclusion, stating that Asian firms understand sustainability largely as '... referring to the firm's philanthropic activities in the community [...] guided by a collectivist and community oriented culture'.

# Sustainable investing in emerging Asia – status and outlook

Specifically in emerging Asia, sustainable investing is becoming a much discussed subject. As a Chinese investment manager put it: 'It is just something you can't ignore nowadays ... part of the pressure is from our government, which is looking for sustainable growth now. You can see how it is taking gradual steps towards controlling pollution, working against various social problems, and advocating business ethics and transparent financial disclosure and reporting. Managers who ignore those changes would inevitably face more risks and lose investment opportunities.'[30]

## Exchanges actively play a critical role

> Regulated exchanges are among society's key institutions for valuing sustainable development, rewarding best governance practices, and channelling fresh investment toward innovative enterprise.[31]
>
> Tom Krantz, Secretary General of the World
> Federation of Exchanges

The rising interest in sustainable investments offers attractive business opportunities for exchanges as investors look for ESG data, related products and marketplaces. Exchanges want to secure their share of related fees and commissions and work to:

1. raise listed companies' ESG awareness and performance, and thus ESG data quality and quantity;
2. use such firms' ESG data to offer and support relevant products and services;
3. provide marketplaces for specific sustainable investment niches.

A directly related outcome is the rise of sustainability indices offered by the 53 regulated member exchanges of the World Federation of Exchanges (WFE). The number of such indices rose from just one in 1999 to 48 worldwide in 2009.[32] Various indices relate to emerging markets, and one is run by each of the exchanges in China, Indonesia, Taiwan and South Korea. The organization stated in a 2009 special report on sustainable investing that 'The spotlight of this global shift towards "sustainable investment" is now turning to the emerging markets.'[33]

Exchanges and governments in emerging Asia work towards better ESG disclosure and performance of listed firms to increase investment inflows and trading volumes. It is understood that key drivers for such improved ESG reporting include the development of national sustainability indices, as well as ESG reporting and listing requirements, with Asian exchanges pushing the right buttons. Further information on Asian exchanges' sustainability activity is provided in the Appendix.

### Companies' ESG reporting and data availability increases

ESG disclosure on corporate websites, annual reports or separate sustainability reports is becoming routine practice in some developed markets, but is still in the developing stage in emerging Asia. The double downside of this is that it limits investors' as well as firms' abilities to leverage data on ESG risks and opportunities. As outlined by the International Finance Corporation, about 60 per cent of asset managers surveyed for a report mentioned limited transparency and a lack of information/expertise as the main obstacles to implementing ESG principles in their investment processes.[34]

Interestingly, about 22 per cent of the respondents answered that it is 'unrealistic to expect emerging market companies to meet the same ESG standards applied by investors to developed market companies'. Yet, while the overall level of firms' ESG reporting and performance is lower than in some developed markets, substantial ESG data are available and both reporting quality and quantity are increasing. In

China, for example, many large, particularly listed companies (290 in Shanghai and 88 in Shenzhen as of 20 May 2009) have begun to release public sustainability reports,[35] while government-controlled firms have been mandated to do so as well. The International Finance Corporation assessed ESG reporting by large listed firms in selected Asian countries. Its results verify the increasing ESG data availability and the impact of national characteristics such as regulatory and voluntary structures on ESG reporting levels, with Vietnam showing a very low level of reporting compared with Malaysia and Indonesia, where governments have been conscious of the issue for longer.[36]

Due to increased data availability, emerging Asia's ESG leaders can be clearly identified. Importantly for investors, the distribution of ESG leaders and laggards is much greater than in developed markets, as are the associated risks and opportunities.

Leaders are often subsidiaries of international companies, or local firms that are highly exposed to ESG issues due to their business model. Unilever Indonesia, for example, publishes comprehensive efficiency-improving initiatives as well as data on environmental themes such as water consumption, waste, emissions or energy use. ESG leaders often successfully leverage sustainability themes to drive their competitiveness.

Investors should also consider the increasing ESG focus of international firms with regard to their Asian suppliers. Staples, the world's largest office supplies retailer, for example, cancelled its contract with Asia Pulp & Paper (APP) after it failed to improve on highly controversial environmental practices (rainforest clearcutting, etc.). This issue is being reported in the media and draws the attention of investors and other APP customers.

## Sustainable AuM have increased sharply, and are set tocontinue doing so Status of and outlook on global and emerging Asia sustainable AuM

In a 2009 survey by research organization EIRIS, about 70 per cent of US and EU investment managers and asset owners named limited ESG disclosure as generally restricting their willingness to invest in emerging markets such as emerging Asia. According to the survey, 86 per cent believe that climate change, for example, will have a significant effect on their emerging market (EM) portfolios, yet two-thirds had difficulties finding enough fund managers and consultants versed in related sustainable investment methodology.[37] As a result, significant assets are held back due to ESG concerns. To answer that unmet demand, sustainable investing products were developed, which have experienced substantial growth over the past years. On a global level, AuM considering sustainability themes almost doubled from USD2.7 trillion in 2002 to USD5 trillion in 2009, representing about 7 per cent of absolute global AuM (investment funds and discretionary mandates).[38] Net asset inflows are set to increase as the 'mainstreaming', the broad implementation of the sustainability theme in investment processes, moves ahead. A key enabler herein is the fact that ESG data availability will significantly increase as ESG reporting becomes the mode d'être for firms around the world and key data providers like Bloomberg and Reuters market their currently implemented ESG data platforms. A key driver to implementing such ESG data in investment processes is investors' increasing understanding of the business case for doing so, supported by related regulation and customer interest. Growth is expected to accelerate as large players such as pension funds come on board, as is currently observed especially in the US, Scandinavia and the UK. Thus, the consensus on sustainable AuM predicts considerable future growth.

If one takes past global sustainable AuM growth rates as a proxy, global sustainable AuM could reach about USD9 trillion in 2015.[39] Based on past growth rates observed in Europe, global sustainable AuM could reach about USD13 trillion in 2015.[40] The consultancy Booz & Co., for example, arrives at a more aggressive estimate, with global sustainable AuM growing by 25–30 per cent per year to reach USD26.5 trillion, or 15–20 per cent of total global AuM in 2015.[41] That may sound quite optimistic to some investors, yet could be plausible if mainstreaming including large players occurs. After all, more than 650 signatories with combined AuM of over USD18 trillion, including some of the largest pension funds, have already declared their intent to do so by signing the United Nations Principles for Responsible Investment (UN PRI).

In emerging Asia, the 2009 level of USD20 billion sustainable AuM represents an increase by factor 400 from USD50 million in 2002. With a relative share of only 0.4 per cent of global sustainable AuM, ample room for further growth exists.[42] Sustainable AuM in emerging Asia in 2015 could amount to about USD1.5 trillion if the region were to reach the global market share of sustainable AuM in 2009.[43] Booz & Co. estimates sustainable AuM to grow to USD2.8 trillion in Asia by 2015, 10 per cent of total AuM in that region. With the penetration estimated on a global level, emerging Asia sustainable AuM could reach USD3–4 trillion in 2015.[44]

## Overview of emerging Asia 'sustainable' labelled equity funds and key characteristics

The International Finance Corporation estimated that, out of the USD20 billion emerging Asia AuM considering sustainability themes, about USD1 billion was invested in products explicitly labelled 'sustainable'. Looking at September 2009, Morningstar data arrives at a similar estimate of USD1 billion invested in 14 emerging Asia equity funds labelled 'sustainable'. The 14 identified funds represent about 2 per cent of the total number of funds, and about 1 per cent of total AuM in the region.[45]

Sustainable investing is clearly a new theme in emerging Asia. Half of the assessed funds were launched between 2007 and 2009. The quality of funds' sustainable investment approaches appears to vary and transparency is limited. As illustrated in the pie chart below, six of the 14 funds do not publish any information on the implementation of sustainability themes. Four funds do report selected information and appear to exclude some industries such as tobacco, alcohol or armaments. Only four funds emerge as looking for Asian sustainability leaders by not only excluding problematic and high-risk business activities, but additionally considering firms' ESG performance. It is thus critical for investors to assess funds thoroughly and demand transparency if they wish to invest in products that effectively utilize ESG data.

Thus, while the underlying case for sustainable investments in emerging Asia is strong, investors still need to pay close attention to the quality and transparency of the products offered. Key success factors investors might want to consider include the following:

No information disclosed: 42 per cent
Only exclusion criteria disclosed: 29 per cent
Exclusion criteria and best-in-class approach disclosed: 29 per cent
(Disclosure of applied sustainable investing approach by emerging Asia
   sustainable equity funds)

The general sustainability approach should be well defined and suitable for the sustainability theme in emerging Asia, including regional and cultural specifics. It should clearly separate ESG leaders from laggards along a defined set of meaningful criteria.

The research and investment process executing that approach should include locally experienced and emerging Asia-based resources for sustainability and financial research to consider the local context and gather relevant data. State-of-the-art market and stock analysis, as well as portfolio management capabilities, are just as important as for any other financial product. Strong risk management capabilities help to manage industry and country tilts related to the sustainability theme. A close exchange between sustainability research and financial research adds critical value, but resource separation is crucial to avoid conflicts of interest and allow staff to focus on both processes.

All processes must be repeatable and credibly documented, including insightful and relevant monthly, quarterly and general reporting, and sustainability reports at portfolio and company level. Furthermore, investors should have the opportunity to contact the involved professionals, including sustainability researchers, to gain meaningful additional information if required.

## Conclusion

Considering the sustainability theme when investing in emerging Asia today is imperative – in terms of both risks and opportunities. In terms of risks, emerging Asia faces some of the world's most severe ESG problems. On the environmental side, air and water pollution have reached levels where citizens are severely harmed and economic growth is hindered. The world has now reached its absorption capacity. A prominent example of this is climate change, the effects of which threaten especially the geographically and demographically exposed region of emerging Asia. With regard to social issues, low work standards, child labour and problematic product safety receive major attention, and societies around the world increasingly resent culpable firms and their products. Another important risk factor for investors is the notion that good governance, the foundation of an attractive investment environment, is limited. This is due to concentrated shareholder structures, limited regulation and minority-shareholder protection, and complex legal structures. Such sustainability issues can limit emerging Asia's further development, and put otherwise promising investments at risk.

Yet where there is risk there is also opportunity. This principle applies especially to the sustainability theme in emerging Asia. This can be very performance-relevant, as emerging Asia's often strong-handed governments and regulators swiftly counter their economies' substantial sustainability challenges and increase legislative pressures. Additional pressure can be expected from investors and consumers in emerging Asia and elsewhere, and from an increasingly vocal civil society. This can put firms that consider sustainability issues at a significant advantage over their often vastly lagging competitors. Studies show that a large share of asset owners and investors understand the sustainability-related risk associated with emerging Asia investments, and hold significant assets back from that otherwise highly attractive market.

What appears vastly underestimated, however, is the fact that data to limit portfolios' sustainability risk and to identify respective leaders do indeed exist. The availability of such data effectively opens up new investment opportunities via 'sustainable investing' products. However, such sustainable investing approaches must consider very specific drivers and characteristics of the sustainability theme in emerging Asia. Two aspects may lead observers to underrate the status and speed of sustainability-related activity in emerging Asia. Firstly, sustainability is not driven in the West's bottom-up manner based on non-governmental organizations or political parties, but in a top-down approach led by strong governments, sometimes together with stock exchanges. Furthermore, emerging Asia's society focuses on social issues first, as opposed to the more evenly distributed view across ESG issues observed elsewhere. Considering such issues is critical to a correct assessment of firms' sustainability positioning.

Significant opportunities arise, therefore, from the notion that markets probably underrate emerging Asia's significant sustainability challenges and powerful counteractions, and the availability of investment process-relevant data. Potentially highly performancerelevant sustainability issues are probably not fully integrated into mainstream investment valuation and portfolio construction. The profit potential of doing so ahead of mainstream investors is amplified by emerging Asia's already fundamentally attractive investment opportunities. The logical assumption that follows is that emerging Asia's sustainable Assets under Management (AuM) will continue the explosive growth observed in the past, from USD1 billion AuM in 2009 to USD1.5–4 trillion AuM by 2015.

Until then, however, the current, naturally temporary information asymmetry can provide an outstanding investment opportunity. Via selected available investment products, investors can lend critical support to the drive towards sustainability, while reducing significant sustainability risk exposure and profiting from the promising positioning of emerging Asia's sustainability leaders. Thus, the right time to look at sustainable investments focusing on emerging Asia has arrived.

# Notes

The Vontobel Group offers the unique combination of an independent Swiss private bank with the innovative strength of an active international asset manager. Our integrated business model with the three business units Private Banking, Investment Banking and Asset Management ensures close cooperation and allows us to successfully pool our expertise and resources – for the benefit of our clients and business partners. Each day, around 1,300 Vontobel employees around the world create sustained added value for our clients: they diligently manage and monitor the client assets entrusted to us, while carefully tracking developments in the financial markets and observing global events. Whether they are in the heart of Zurich, in New York or Dubai – employees in 19 international locations identify trends and devise appropriate innovative investment strategies and products everywhere that our clients are based.

Vontobel has been committed to a values-based, long-term approach for generations, and is therefore a competent, credible partner when it comes to sustainable investment. We offer clients various first-class investment solutions such as portfolio management mandates, investment funds and structured products which promote sustainable investment. When selecting sustainable companies, we cooperate exclusively with qualified partners. The investment criteria employed extend beyond purely financial aspects, and therefore create additional value as well as capture potential long-term returns. The principles of our sustainable actions are firmly rooted in our Mission Statement and in our Sustainability Guidelines.

1. To assess the specific cultural and socio-economic characteristics of 'emerging Asia' to the fullest, this paper does not include India but focuses on the culturally more homogeneous group of China, Hong Kong, Indonesia, Malaysia, the Philippines, Taiwan, Thailand and Vietnam.
2. World Bank, Indonesia and Climate Change: Current Status and Policies (World Bank, 2007).
3. Sunanda Creagh, 'Indonesia puts moratorium on new forest clearing', Reuters (27 May 2010).
4. NASA, *NASA Eyes Effects of a Giant 'Brown Cloud' Worldwide* (NASA, 15 December 2004).
5. Rob Gutro 'Hunan paper factories ordered to clean up', *China Daily* (18 January 2008).
6. 'Anhui Province Shut down 379 Polluting Enterprises', *Xinhua News Agency* (7 February 2006).
7. International Panel on Climate Change, *Climate Change 2007: Impacts, Adaptation and Vulnerability*, IPCC Fourth Assessment Report (AR4) (2007).
8. *Emerging Risk: Impacts of Key Environmental Trends in Emerging Asia* (International Finance Corporation, April 2009).
9. R Locke, *The Promise and Perils of Globalization: The Case of Nike*, MIT Working Papers (July 2002).
10. These are: The Freedom of Association and Protection of the Right to Organize Convention, 1948 (No. 87), as well as the Right to Organize and Collective Bargaining Convention, 1949 (No. 98).
11. UNICEF, Progress for Children (September 2009).

12. Lisa Schlein, China's Melamine Milk Crisis Creates Crisis of Confidence, US Fed News Service (26 September 2008).
13. IPCC, *Climate Change 2007: Impacts, Adaptation and Vulnerability. Contribution of Working Group II to the Fourth Assessment Report of the Intergovernmental Panel on Climate Change* (IPCC, 2007).
14. Food and Agriculture Organization (FAO) of the United Nations, 'Crop Prospects and Food Situation preview No. 3' (FAO, July 2009), at http://www.fao.org/docrep/012/ai484e/ai484e01.htm accessed on 5 January, 2010
15. Vontobel Financial Research.
16. Ibid.
17. Ibid.
18. World Bank, *Fighting Poverty: Findings and Lessons from China's Success* (World Bank, 2006).
19. International Monetary Fund (IMF), World Economic Outlook Database.
20. IMF, World Bank.
21. Lee Kuan Yew served as Prime Minister from 1959 to 1990. Yew's eldest son, Lee Hsien Loong, has been Singapore's prime minister since 2004, with his father holding the position of 'Minister Mentor'.
22. Freedom House is a Washington-based, privately and governmentally (National Endowment for Democracy, USAID, US State Department, Dutch government) funded non-profit think tank.
23. *Shareowner Rights across the Markets: A Manual for Investors* (CFA Institute for Financial Integrity, April 2008).
24. Nisbett, 'The Syllogism and the Tao', *The Geography of Thought* (The Free Press, 2003), pp. 1–19.
25. A Waley, *The Way and Its Power* (1958).
26. Syntao, *Guidance on Implementing Environmental Protection Policies and Rules and Preventing Credit Risks. Described in Green Credit Policy Starts in Beijing* (Syntao, 8 September 2009) at http://www.syntao.com/E_Page_show.asp?Page_ID=11922
27. *Notification on Issuance of The Guidelines on Fulfilling Social Responsibility by Central Enterprises*, Sino-German Corporate Social Responsibility (CSR) Project, at www.chinacsrproject.org; *Notification on Issuance of The Guidelines on Fulfilling Social Responsibility by Central Enterprises*, State-owned Assets Supervision and Administration Commission of the State Council (29 December 2007).
28. More information on regulatory initiatives is provided in the Appendix.
29. 'CIMB Group and University of Malaya launch training programme for students', CIMB Group Press Release (23 April 2008).
30. *Gaining Ground: Integrating ESG factors into investment processes in emerging markets* (International Finance Corp. and Mercer Investment Consulting, March 2009).
31. D Siddy, 'Exchanges Push the Sustainability Agenda', *Responsible Investor* (17 September 2009).
32. Ibid.
33. 'Green shoe for green markets', World Federation of Exchanges (August 2009).
34. International Finance Corp., *Undisclosed risk: Corporate environmental and social reporting in emerging Asia* (IFC, April 2009).

35. International Finance Corp., *Sustainable Investment in China 2009* (IFC, September 2009).
36. International Finance Corp., *Undisclosed Risk: Corporate Environmental and Social Reporting in Emerging Asia* (IFC, April 2009).
37. Emerging Markets Investor Survey Report: *An analysis of responsible investment in emerging markets* (EIRIS, June 2009). The study covered 67 respondents with over USD130 billion of emerging market assets under management; International Finance Corp., *Sustainable investing in emerging markets: Unscathed by the financial crisis* (IFC, July 2009).
38. Eurosif, *European SRI Study* (2008) and Robeco, *Responsible Investing: a Paradigm Shift* (2008). Sustainable AuM are estimated to be on the same level as in 2007/2008 due to the combined effects of the financial crisis and inflows in sustainable AuM and the high 'stickiness' of those assets.
39. 10.8 per cent compound annual growth rate CAGR 2003–2009 Calculated based on: *Towards sustainable and responsible investment in emerging markets* (International Finance Corporation, October 2003) and *European SRI Study* (Eurosif, 2008).
40. Seventeen per cent compound annual growth rate CAGR, 1999–2009. From: Vigeo, *Green, social and ethical funds in Europe. 2009 Review* (Vigeo, October 2009).
41. *Responsible Investing: A Paradigm Shift* (Robeco: Booz & Co., 2008).
42. International Finance Corporation, *Towards sustainable and responsible investment in emerging markets* (IFC, October 2003).
43. Seven per cent (global market share as reported by Eurosif 2008) of Asia Pacific ex Jp. 2015 AuM USD21.7 trillion (based on: *Delivering on the Client Promise* (The Boston Consulting Group, September 2009)).
44. Fifteen to twenty per cent (global market share estimated in Booz & Co. and Robeco, *Responsible Investing: a Paradigm Shift* (2008) of 2015 AuM USD21.7 trillion (based on: *Delivering on the Client Promise* (The Boston Consulting Group, September 2009)).
45. Based on September 2009 Morningstar Data. Morningstar Global Categories: Asia ex Japan Equity (five funds), China & HK Equity (four funds), Other Asia Equity (Malaysia two funds and Indonesia two funds), Taiwan Equity (one fund). Total number of funds in the set: 821. Total AuM in the set: USD141.5 billion.

# 16
# Sustainability Reporting: Measurements and Goals for a Sustainable Future

*Nelmara Arbex*

## Introduction

Capitalism is at a tipping point, and consequently there is everywhere an urgent need for change and for sustainable economic solutions. There is no sustainable solution for the planet without Asia. It is hard to discuss 'Asia' as a homogeneous unit, since it covers 30 per cent of the Earth's land surface and is home to almost 4 billion people – 60 per cent of the world's current population. The region contributes a total GDP of around US$18.5 trillion per year,[1] which is 30 per cent of the world's total.[2]

Of the 47 countries that make up the continent, the 10 largest economies, according to nominal GDP, are Japan, China, Russia, India, South Korea, Turkey, Indonesia, Saudi Arabia, Taiwan and Iran; these are followed by Thailand, the United Arab Emirates, Malaysia, Israel, Hong Kong, Singapore, Philippines, Pakistan, Kazakhstan and Kuwait. Think for a moment about this variety! Not only is the region immense in size, it also encompasses huge cultural and economic variety. This unquestionably adds to the challenge of finding and implementing large-scale sustainable solutions. The current economic development model has brought Asian countries to a critical point. As with everywhere else in the world, business leaders, political leaders, experts and activists are all struggling with the question: 'How can we keep business growing, maintain profitability, protect the planet's resources and create wealthy citizens - all at the same time?' And there is no answer to this question – yet.

While the profitability of Asian companies and the GDP of most Asian countries continue to grow, the current situation regarding water resources, biodiversity, climate stability, fishery and agricultural areas, as well as poverty, public health and human rights, is not the one we would wish for our children and grandchildren.[3]

The few world indicators we know about this crisis signal a very critical scenario:[4]

- Globally, the world's richest 1 per cent own 40 per cent of global wealth. In comparison, the poorer countries of the Asia-Pacific region, China and India own in total just 7 per cent of global wealth.[5]
- Extreme poverty affects at least 10 per cent of the population in parts of the Asia-Pacific region. In Bangladesh and India, two of the most heavily populated countries in the region, more than 40 per cent of the population live on less than US$1.25 a day.[6]
- Temperatures on earth are rising due to climate change. Carbon emissions play a large part in this, and as a consequence the sea level will rise, there will be a degradation of biodiversity and both food and water supplies will be endangered.[7]
- While Asian $CO_2$ emissions per capita are quite low in comparison to large developed countries such as Canada or the USA, the sheer size of the population means that, if each person in Asia were to emit $CO_2$ at the same level as the developed countries, the consequences for climate change would be catastrophic.[8]
- Water withdrawal has increased sixfold since the beginning of the twentieth century, and water resources are increasingly being depleted. Lack of basic sanitation for approximately 1 billion people is the source of water-borne diseases.
- Eighty-four per cent of total water withdrawal in Asia is for agricultural purposes.[9] Where large amounts of water are diverted or withdrawn from groundwater for agricultural use, local environmental problems occur, such as saltwater in deltas, land subsidence, salinity and alkalinity.[10]
- Average abundance of species declined by 40 per cent between 1970 and 2000.[11] Human exploitation and habitat destruction are fragmenting ecosystems and affecting their capacity to maintain biodiversity.[12] Also monoculture, that is, the culture of a small group of selected species for market purposes, greatly reduces biodiversity.
- In 2008, Asia and the Pacific had the world's highest number of threatened species, with almost one-third of all threatened plant and all threatened animal species.[13]
- Basic political and civil rights are denied to 36 per cent of the world's population.[14] There are estimated to be around 218 million child

labourers and over 12 million people suffering some form of forced labour around the world.[15]

The expectation that companies will act to help solve these problems has increased dramatically in the last decades because of the amount of power, knowledge and resources that companies concentrate. What can companies – or Asian companies – really do to contribute to the solutions for these challenges?

From the Global Reporting Initiative (GRI) and its network's perspective there is an answer – Sustainability Reporting – which is related to the ability to transform sustainability challenges into practical tasks to be planned and managed and also reported so that these efforts and challenges are made public. A short description of GRI, its history and development in Asia and other issues related to sustainability reporting will be presented in the next sections.

## Transparency as a tool to face the future

For business' and society's development – as well as to protect the quality of life of people on the planet – equitable access to natural resources, stable climate conditions and social peace are critical. Consequently, it is in the interest of both business and society to monitor and set goals which can help to find solutions to the problems described.

In recent decades, an impressive number of frameworks and tools have been developed by many organizations to help measure and monitor environmental and social impacts. International organizations have proposed standards such as the UN Global Compact Principles, the UN Principles for Responsible Investment (PRI) and the European OECD MNE Guidelines. Other international frameworks include the US-based CERES Principles, the SA8000 workplace standards, the AA1000APS standards, GHG-WRI measures from the World Resources Institute, the Carbon Disclosure Project and the forthcoming ISO26000.[16] Few of them are as inclusive and interactive as the GRI Guidelines for Sustainability Reporting.

The ability to benefit from dialogue with different stakeholders and to communicate about sustainability-related issues is extremely important for business in the twenty-first century. Universal access to the internet and other technologies, as well as the new generation of civil society organizations (CSOs) using these technological platforms, have contributed changes to the landscape in which business operates. It has become much more difficult for any organization to hide its problems or to avoid answering uncomfortable questions.

To illustrate this situation, in April 2010, *Harvard Business Review* published a cover story called 'Leadership in the Age of Transparency.'[17] The explanation of the title was a provocation to business leaders and executive managers: 'Consumers know everything about your company, not just its carbon emissions but its countless other "invisible" effects on the globe. That has changed the rules of business forever.'

There is increasing pressure on organizations to be transparent about how they go about their business and how their decisions are made. It may be that investors want to know – or the authorities, the neighbouring communities, the staff or their families. In fact, everybody wants to know for one reason or another.

So, what is the best way for organizations to communicate, in a transparent way, about their economic, environmental and social impacts? One answer can be that organizations (for profit or not) might consider preparing a *Sustainability Report*.

The GRI sustainability reporting process helps organizations to:

- understand the connection between their goals and the economic, social and environmental impacts that are created by their everyday activities;
- measure these impacts;
- dialogue with stakeholders, to define focus and to manage and identify opportunities;
- communicate achievements and challenges;
- change internal processes and create plans based on the information acquired.

As one will gather from the above, the reporting process is also a strategic management exercise to position organizations to face a much more transparent future. The importance of measuring, managing and reporting on Asian organizations' plans and efforts towards sustainability cannot be overemphasized because of the importance of Asia in the present and future of the planet.

## About GRI and the GRI guidelines development

The GRI was established in 1997 as a program under Ceres, a US-based organization.[18] In 2000, the GRI became an independent, international, non-governmental organization and moved its headquarters to Amsterdam, The Netherlands.

**Box 1.1**

When discussing current practices for managing and reporting on sustainability issues in Asia, it is important to note that the context in which business and governments operate has greatly changed over the last 10 years. This is not only because of the financial crisis or symptoms of the environmental crisis but also because of the ICT revolution, which has changed how we deal and interact with information.[19]

This revolution has several aspects: one of them is the increasing number of people with access to the Internet, where they can read and contribute content at any time, in any language. On the other hand, there are the organizations 'under scrutiny'. Companies and governments can be on both sides.

The website 'Internet World statistics' displays the following information about internet use in Asia.[20]

|  | % World Population | Internet users | % of Population with Internet Access | User Growth (2000–9) |
|---|---|---|---|---|
| Asia | 56.3 % | 764,435,900 | 20.1 % | 568.8 % |
| Rest of the world | 43.7 % | 1,037,894,557 | 35.1 % | 320.7 % |

The GRI Guidelines for Sustainability Reporting were created at the end of the 1990s to help business managers to take into account, in their decision-making, the wider impacts of their decisions; to help shareholders to evaluate the full performance of their investments; and to create a common language for all society to dialogue on how to monitor and communicate economic, social and environmental performance of organizations. Companies voluntarily follow the GRI Guidelines for sustainability reporting.

The first GRI Sustainability Reporting Guidelines were issued in 2000 and the second version, G2, followed in 2002. In October 2006 the current version, the G3, was launched. The GRI Guidelines are created through a multi-stakeholder consultation process involving around 3,000 people from over 50 countries. The multi-stakeholder process behind the development of the GRI Guidelines makes them unique in terms of acceptance and representation around the world.

The GRI Guidelines are a free public good and can be downloaded from the GRI website in over 20 languages (www.globalreporting.org). GRI also launched a reporting template for beginners, *Let's Report*, which is available to download for free from the GRI website.

Around 10 publications have been launched to support organizations in using the GRI G3 Guidelines, related to basic concepts and learning activities, as well as technical research in specific reporting topics and 'in depth' studies.

Aiming to create a global language to manage and communicate on sustainability performance all around the world, GRI has built an international network of Certified Training Partners, who teach the same concepts and the same process in local languages in more than 30 countries. At the time of writing this chapter, around 2,500 professionals had participated in the GRI Certified Training sessions.[21]

Introductory GRI workshops have also been implemented over the last 3 years and were offered in more than 20 developing countries.

All this helps to explain GRI's framework penetration. The uptake of the GRI Sustainability Reporting Guidelines has increased rapidly, and in 2009 over 1,300 reporters using the Guidelines were known to GRI, as shown in Figure 16.1.[22]

## GRI sustainability reporting in Asia

GRI has always counted on support and participation from Asian collaborators at different levels: in the Board of Directors, in the Stakeholder

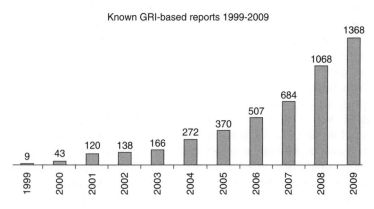

*Figure 16.1*  Numbers of known GRI Guideline-based reports
*Source*: See Chapter Appendix 1

Council, in the Technical Advisory Council and among the Secretariat's staff.

In the last year, two new very important senior representatives from the GRI Secretariat were created with focus on India and China – the GRI Asian Focal Points. They are local extensions of the GRI Secretariat and their aim is to strengthen the presence of GRI and to expand GRI's network within their regions.

The GRI G3 Guidelines have been published in four Asian languages to date (Japanese, Chinese, Korean and Turkish) and will be offered soon in Bahasa Indonesian. *Let's Report*, mentioned in the section above, is also offered in Japanese, Korean and Chinese.

The same expansion is also to be found in the GRI Certified Training Partners network. In April 2010, when this chapter was being written, GRI had three Certified Training Partners in Republic of Korea and one in the process of certification, one Certified Training Partner in Japan, three Certified Training Partners in Chinese-speaking countries (specifically Mainland China, Macau, Taiwan, Hong Kong, Singapore) and three in the process of certification, four Certified Training Partners in India and one in the process of certification. GRI has also selected Training Partners in Indonesia, Thailand and Malaysia.

Around 400 participants had attended Certified Training offered by Asian training partners by April 2010.

In 2009, introductory workshops on the basics of sustainability reporting were given by GRI staff in the following Asian countries: India, Sri Lanka, Malaysia, China, Republic of Korea, Armenia, Georgia and Azerbaijan.

These efforts are starting to show results, as Asian participation in the GRI sustainability reporting community is increasing, as shown in Figure 16.2. In 2009, 279 known GRI-based sustainability reports came out of the Asian region, representing a healthy 20 per cent of all known GRI Guideline-based reports.[23]

## What is the GRI sustainability reporting process?

The GRI Sustainability Reporting Guidelines comprise different sections: some explain how a company should describe its activities; others offer advice on how to explain the governance bodies of the organization. There are also sections containing descriptions of the reporting process itself, Reporting Principles to guarantee the quality of the process and final report, and instructions on measuring and following up economic, environmental and, social performance.

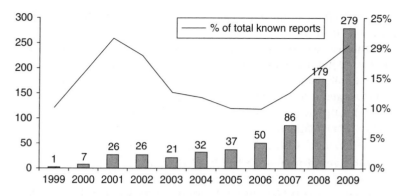

*Figure 16.2*  Numbers of known GRI-based reports from Asia
Source: See Chapter Appendix 1

Another way to look at the Guidelines is by organizing this information into steps to be followed when preparing a GRI reporting process. The GRI sustainability reporting process can be divided into five phases:[24]

- *Prepare*: During this phase reporters plan the reporting process. They should come up with an overview of what the final report might contain, the processes necessary to organize this and ways to prepare the organization to go through these processes.
- *Connect*: During this phase reporters should identify their main internal and external stakeholders and discuss with them their concerns to help decide what to report on.
- *Define*: In this phase reporters need to define the content of the report, based on input from stakeholders, assessment of the basic principles of the GRI Guidelines and analysis of the company's current commitments and capabilities. They also decide which GRI performance indicators will be included in the report.
- *Monitor*: During this phase reporters monitor and collect the information needed to report on the chosen indicators.
- *Report*: The final stage of the reporting process is to actually prepare the report. It is important to choose the correct format and make sure the approval of the Board or highest decision-making body of the company is obtained before the report is released.

Each of the above phases brings challenges to the reporting organization. Local and cultural issues will also play a role: for instance, in the

'Connect' phase when organizations should try to listen to different groups to identify critical issues to be managed, this can cause some discomfort if consultations and dialogue between different groups in society are not usual. Even if this is the case, it is important to consider the fact that in a very interconnected society there is a real reputational and managerial risk for organizations avoiding dialogue. The 'Monitor' phase can also be a challenge in contexts where data organization is not common practice.

## Main drivers for sustainability reporting

The reason why organizations decide to go through a process and publish information on their social-environmental-economic performance through a sustainability report varies, as the reader will see in the following sections.

There are regulatory and non-regulatory drivers behind this decision. There are also market and social forces that may act as drivers in this scenario.

As previously stated, universal access to the Internet generates a powerful and consistent demand for transparency and coherency, as information can be published, discussed and compared in a very short period of time. The urgency of the social, economic and environmental issues society is facing, combined with the access to information, is also generating a movement that demands accountability and responsibility from companies when producing goods and services. These social forces can also be seen as market forces, when companies have to establish codes and auditing mechanisms to manage their supply chains. Branding, competition, market access, and so on have been intensively influenced by social and non-regulatory issues.

There are two other drivers that shape the sustainability reporting field: regulators and investors. The last 5 years, in particular, have seen extensive production of information disclosure regulations in the region, mainly (but not exclusively) related to environmental aspects. This can be easily confirmed by reading the latest version (May 2010) of the publication *Carrots & Sticks – promoting transparency and sustainability*.[25] This publication provides an up-to-date and expanded overview of mandatory and voluntary approaches to sustainability reporting and assurance. Among the 30 selected countries covered by the publication, four are from Asia: China, India, Indonesia and Japan.

China appears with mandatory and non-mandatory standards and assurance standards. The mandatory standards relate to

'Environmental Information' for all companies, 'Environmental Information' for companies listed in the Shanghai stock exchange and a third one on 'Corporate Social Responsibility' for state-owned companies.

India also has mandatory and non-mandatory standards. These are very general, although the country also has an extensive set of environmental laws, specific regulatory mandates and frameworks to implement and enforce environmental policies objectives.

Indonesia appears with few mandatory standards, generally related to Corporate Social Responsibility, focusing on all companies, or on listed or state-owned companies. The mandatory standards in Japan are quite specific and mainly cover environmental protection, polluting activities, recycling or global warming, or are related to specific sectors, such as railways or civil aeronautics. South Korea has no mandatory standards in this field.

Interesting complementary information on mandatory requirements for reporting in Asia can be found in the 2009 publication *Undisclosed Risk: Corporate Environmental and Social Reporting in Emerging Asia*, a joint publication produced by the IFC (International Finance Corporation) and WRI (World Resources Institute).[26]

This publication provides an investor perspective on corporate sustainability reporting in six Asian countries – India, Indonesia, Malaysia, Philippines, Thailand and Vietnam – from the 10 largest companies in each country. The foreword notes that:

> The current global financial crisis has highlighted the need to manage risk and has given new impetus to an old debate in the investment community on how to value environmental risks. [...] Re-directing capital injected into South and Southeast Asia's growing economies toward less environmentally destructive economic activity will not only reduce investment risk, it will also help support the region's long term prosperity

The section 'Findings and Conclusions' makes the following observations:

> 'although regulations can establish a minimum standard in these emerging Asian markets, they are often not sufficiently prescriptive to result in sustainability reporting that is useful for investors,' and 'There is a real risk for companies who do not report on environmental and social factors. Not formally reporting on sustainability factors

can amplify the financial impact on a company's share price, when environmental and social information is leaked to the public.'

## Why do companies report?

The rationale for each organization's decision to publish a sustainability report may be different: the motivation may be internal or external, tangible or intangible, financial or moral – and also it may change over the course of time. But there seems to be one reason they all have in common: the organizations believe that they will benefit from it in one way or another.

When asked, GRI reporters have identified the following initial *motivations*:[27]

- *To show commitment and to be transparent*: Issuing a sustainability report is a good way for companies to react to increased demand for information on how responsible their operations are.
- *To demonstrate the ability to participate in competitive markets*: Demonstrating an understanding of the link between its everyday activities and sustainability is seen as a strength and demonstrates the quality of the company's management skills. This again strengthens the position of the company in competition with its peers.
- *To plan activities, become more sustainable and better position the company*: The reporting process can serve as a tool for companies to better understand their contributions to solving the current sustainability challenges.
- *To comply with regulations*: In most countries sustainability reporting is still voluntary; in others it is already a legal requirement. Some companies report in order to be ready to comply with future legislation in this respect.

After organizations have completed a reporting process they are better able to describe the value they found in the process.[28] The main *internal* values were identified as the following:

- *To develop vision and strategy*: It can be difficult to know where to start. The GRI reporting process can help an organization get started by focusing on the most important issues.
- *To improve management systems, improve internal processes and set goals*: Sometimes companies realize while they are gathering information for the report that there is room for improvement in their

management systems, or they may even not have any systems in place at all.

- *To identify weaknesses and strengths*: Sometimes the outcome of the company's performance on a certain indicator can be a surprise – either positive or negative.
- *To attract and retain employees*: Research has shown that staff find it very motivating if their company is working towards improving their sustainability performance. Some research even indicates that some young professionals today prefer to work for companies that have clear policies on sustainability.
- *To connect departments and encourage innovation*: During the whole reporting process the different departments of the company need to work together in different ways, for instance in connection with the collection of data. This is seen as positive, as it increases interdepartmental cooperation and people become more aware of what others are doing.
- *To raise awareness with the Board*: This can help bridge the gap between the Board and the everyday activities of the organization, as these will have to be discussed by the Board during the reporting process.
- *To achieve competitive advantage and leadership*: Some reporters remarked that by being the first in their sector or region to issue a sustainability report they were now being seen as pioneers and other companies were following in their footsteps. Others remarked that the fact that they can provide their clients with a sustainability report gives them a direct competitive advantage.
- *To attract investors*: Investors today are much more demanding of companies than previously. The creation of special sustainability stock markets supports this and it seems that many investors prefer to invest in companies that can demonstrate their sustainability awareness and that they operate accordingly.

The main *external* values were seen as follows:

- *To enhance reputation, achieve trust and respect*: A well-balanced sustainability report, where both positive and negative aspects are reflected upon, can create trust and respect. Third parties, such as investors, are more likely to give a company the benefit of the doubt if they are convinced that it is being honest and open about its performance and not excluding the less favourable aspects.

- *To show transparency and dialogue with stakeholders*: The reporting process is an opportunity for the company to engage with its main stakeholders and to both listen to and dialogue with them to get their feedback on the company's performance.
- *To demonstrate commitment to sustainability*: The reporting process enables the company to show that it is serious about making a contribution to solving the current sustainability challenges and also how it is planning to do this.
- *To enable comparability and benchmarking*: This is one of the core elements of the GRI Guidelines – to create a common language and common metrics so that sustainability practices, knowledge and experience may be compared and shared among companies worldwide.

## Future sustainability reporting trends

In 2010, GRI started a new programme called 'Future Trends in Sustainability Reporting.'[29] It is briefly introduced here as the sustainability agenda, as well as the reporting format, will move quickly in the next years, particularly in Asia.

In May 2010, GRI and Volans launched a publication entitled *The Transparent Economy*. This report is particularly aimed at business and government leaders and offers some pointers to future trends in sustainability reporting. The goal was also to explore how reporting and transparency will contribute to building a new economy.

Following desk research and interviews, several trends emerged in the sustainability reporting agenda: (1) traceability; (2) integrated reporting; (3) the role of governments in leading change towards the transparent economy; (4) the need to aggregate information on social impact issues across nations, cities, industries, companies and supply chains; (5) the need to aggregate information on environmental impact issues across nations, cities, industries, companies and supply chains; (6) the growing importance of environmental boundaries; (7) the role of ranking and rating schemes in driving competition; (8) social rights agenda and (9) the continuing – and in some areas growing – presence of shadow economies involved in drugs or sex trafficking, the weapons trade, illegal waste dumping and corruption.

These topics were presented in a survey to the GRI reporting community and six main trends were identified (leading to the acronym TIGERS):

---

**Box 2**

**TRACEABILITY**: BUILDING SEE-THROUGH SUPPLY CHAINS
Consumers and retailers want transparent global supply chains.
**INTEGRATED REPORTING**: FEEL THE FORCE
Integrated reporting means embedding sustainability system-wide.
**GOVERNMENT LEADERSHIP**: NEW RULES AND INCENTIVES
They lagged for years – but governments must now lead.
**ENVIRONMENTAL BOUNDARIES**: OUT OF OUR BOX
Climate change isn't the only great environmental change we face.
**RATING & RANKING**: ON YOUR MARKS
We need to do more to spur competition around sustainability reporting.
**SHADOW ECONOMIES**: TACKLING THE DARK SIDE
We forget the illegal side of the economy at our peril.

---

GRI believes that this agenda will be extremely important for Asia, as many of the world efforts and eyes will be on this region. In his conclusion, the author John Elkington provokes the following discussion:

> ... a shift toward sustainability is expected to trigger trillions of dollars in new investments in infrastructure, technology and human services, creating new opportunities for business to thrive and grow. A study commissioned by WBCSD indicates that this investment could reach US\$ 3–10 trillion per annum in 2050. So how will business innovators report their progress in related areas –and to whom?
>
> Whether we are focusing on the upside or downside of all this, we must develop the confidence, the resources and the tools to rate and rank the progress made at all levels: nation states, cities, businesses and financial markets.
>
> Ultimately, as we have seen, markets are conversations. The business of business these days includes developing, maintaining and extending market conversations – even if it means diving into areas like open data and apps. Whatever the technology, however, honesty, transparency and candor will be critical.
>
> To drive the levels of transformative change now needed, we need not just a shift to integrated accounting and reporting, though they are important but an integrated, multi-sectoral and long-sighted social movement to push for a new Age of Transparency – what Jeremy Rifkin is heralding as the "Empathic Civilization".'

Appendix 1: *Known GRI reporters in Asia, by country*[30]

| | 1999 | 2000 | 2001 | 2002 | 2003 | 2004 | 2005 | 2006 | 2007 | 2008 | 2009 | Total |
|---|---|---|---|---|---|---|---|---|---|---|---|---|
| Bangladesh | – | – | – | – | 1 | – | – | 1 | – | – | – | 2 |
| Cambodia | – | – | – | – | – | – | – | 1 | – | – | – | 1 |
| China | – | – | 1 | 3 | 1 | 3 | 3 | 6 | 8 | 16 | 47 | 88 |
| India | – | – | 1 | 3 | 1 | 5 | 4 | 5 | 6 | 20 | 20 | 65 |
| Indonesia | – | – | – | – | – | – | – | 1 | 3 | 6 | 1 | 11 |
| Israel | – | – | – | – | – | – | 2 | – | 3 | 6 | 13 | 24 |
| Japan | 1 | 7 | 23 | 17 | 14 | 19 | 18 | 18 | 26 | 64 | 86 | 293 |
| Jordan | – | – | – | – | – | – | – | – | 1 | 1 | 2 | 4 |
| Malaysia | – | – | – | 2 | 1 | 1 | – | 1 | 1 | 4 | 6 | 16 |
| Mongolia | – | – | – | – | – | – | – | – | 1 | 1 | 1 | 3 |
| Pakistan | – | – | – | – | – | – | – | – | 1 | 1 | 1 | 3 |
| Palestinian Administered Areas | – | – | – | – | – | – | – | – | 1 | – | – | 1 |
| Philippines | – | – | – | – | – | – | 1 | 1 | 2 | 5 | 9 | 18 |
| Republic of Korea | – | – | – | – | 3 | 4 | 8 | 14 | 27 | 37 | 55 | 148 |
| Saudi Arabia | – | – | – | – | – | – | – | – | – | 1 | 2 | 3 |
| Singapore | – | – | – | – | – | – | – | – | – | 4 | 8 | 12 |
| Sri Lanka | – | – | 1 | – | – | – | – | 1 | – | – | 2 | 4 |
| Taiwan | – | – | – | 1 | – | – | – | – | 2 | 7 | 13 | 23 |
| Thailand | – | – | – | – | – | – | – | – | 1 | 1 | 3 | 5 |
| Turkey | – | – | – | – | – | – | 1 | 1 | 1 | 2 | 2 | 7 |
| United Arab Emirates | – | – | – | – | – | – | – | – | 2 | 2 | 6 | 10 |

At the end of the publication, suggested recommendations are set out for business leaders, governments, financial market, GRI community and consumers. The evolving pattern of sustainability reporting is part of the nature of the sustainability challenges themselves, one of them being managers' continuous efforts to measure and manage sustainability impacts from their organizations' everyday performance. Sustainability reporting is a key tool to pave the road to a sustainable future, but it is not as well defined and stable as most of us would like.

## Notes

1. Wikipedia (2010) List of Asian countries by GDP, http://en.wikipedia.org/wiki/List_of_Asian_countries_by_GDP (accessed 29 April 2010).
2. Wikipedia (2010) List of countries by GDP (nominal), http://en.wikipedia.org/wiki/List_of_countries_by_GDP_%28nominal%29 (accessed 29 April 2010).
3. Various publications have appeared from the 1970s onwards, alerting us to the dangers of this model of development. One of the most remarkable of these was DH Meadows, *The Limits to Growth; A Report for the Club of Rome's Project on the Predicament of Mankind*, 2nd edn (Universe Books, 1972). This put forward some core aspects that should be monitored, and the authors indirectly suggested that all governments should be involved in such monitoring. These core aspects included: world population, industrialization, pollution, food production and resource depletion.
4. NJ Themelis, 'An overview of the global waste-to-energy industry', *2003-2004 Review, Waste Management World* (2003), pp. 40–7.

    UNESCAP, *Statistical Yearbook for Asia and the Pacific 2009* (UNESCAP, 2009), at http://www.unescap.org/stat/data/syb2009/11-Access-to-water-sanitation.asp, accessed date 29 April 2010.

    Food and Agriculture Organization of the United Nations (FAO) and International Fund for Agricultural Development (IFAD), 'Chapter 7: Water for Food, Agriculture and Rural Livelihoods', *Water, a shared responsibility; The United Nations World Water Development Report 2* (Barcelona, Spain: UNESCO Publishing and New York, NY, USA: Berghahn Books, 2006), p. 245.

    World Water Council, 'Water Crisis: Facts and Figures', World Water Council, 10 January 2008, at http://www.worldwatercouncil.org/index. php?id=25, accessed date 13 March 2008

    World Health Organization (WHO) and United Nations Children's Fund (UNICEF), 'Chapter 5: Basic Needs and the right to Health', *The United Nations World Water Development Report: Water for People, Water for Life* (Barcelona, Spain: UNESCO Publishing and New York, NY, USA: Berghahn Books, 2003), p. 123.

    World Water Council, 'Water Crisis: Facts and Figures', World Water Council, 10 January 2008, at http://www.worldwatercouncil.org/index. php?id=25, accessed date 13 March 2008
5. JB Davies, S Sandström, A Shorrocks and EN Wolff, 'The World Distribution of Household Wealth', Discussion Paper No. 2008/03 (UNWIDER, 2008), at http://

www.wider.unu.edu/publications/working-papers/discussion-papers/2008/
en_GB/dp2008-03/_files/78918010772127840/default/dp2008-03.pdf, accessed
date 28 April 2010.

6. Asian Development Bank, 'Key Indicators for Asia and the Pacific 2009'
(Asian Development Bank, 2009), at http://www.adb.org/Documents/
Books/Key_Indicators/2009/pdf/Key-Indicators-2009.pdf, accessed date
29 April 2010.

7. KL Denman, G Brasseur, A Chidthaisong, P Ciais, PM Cox, RE Dickinson, D
Hauglustaine, C Heinze, E Holland, D Jacob, U Lohmann, S Ramachandran,
PL da Silva Dias, SC Wofsy and X Zhang, 'Couplings Between Changes in
the Climate System and Biogeochemistry', *Climate Change 2007: The Physical
Science Basis. Contribution of Working Group I to the Fourth Assessment Report of
the Intergovernmental Panel on Climate Change*, S Solomon, D Qin, M Manning,
Z Chen, M Marquis, KB Avery, M Tignor and HL Miller (eds), (Cambridge,
United Kingdom and New York, NY, USA: Cambridge University Press,
2007), p. 514, at http://ipcc-wg1.ucar.edu/wg1/Report/AR4WG1_Print_Ch07.
pdf, accessed date 15 April 2008.

8. UNESCAP, *Statistical Yearbook for Asia and the Pacific 2009* (UNESCAP, 2009),
at http://www.unescap.org/stat/data/syb2009/11-Access-to-water-sanitation.
asp, accessed date 29 April 2010.

9. Food and Agricultural Organization (FAO), *Aquastat: General Summary Asia*,
at http://www.fao.org/nr/water/aquastat/regions/asia/index4.stm, accessed
date 29 April 2010.

10. Ibid.

11. Secretariat of the Convention on Biological Diversity, *Global Biodiversity
Outlook 2* (Montreal, Canada: Secretariat of the Convention on Biological
Diversity, 2006), p. 25. http://www.cbd.int/doc/gbo2/cbd-gbo2-en.pdf,
accessed date 15 April 2008.

12. Ibid., p. 30.

13. UNESCAP, *Statistical Yearbook for Asia and the Pacific 2009* (UNESCAP, 200),
at     http://www.unescap.org/stat/data/syb2009/26-Biodiversity-protected-
areas-forests.asp, accessed date 29 April 2010.

14. Freedom House, *Freedom in the World 2008: Selected Data From Freedom House's
Annual Global Survey Of Political Rights And Civil Liberties* (Washington, DC /
New York, NY, USA: Freedom House, 2008).

15. United Nations, *Report of the independent expert for the United Nations study
on violence against children*, Item A/61/299 (General Assembly, 2006), p. 10,
at http://www.un.org/ga/search/view_doc.asp?symbol=A/61/299&Lang=E,
accessed date 13 March 2008.
   International Labour Organization (ILO), *A Global Alliance Against Forced
Labour: Global Report under the Follow-up to the ILO Declaration on Fundamental
Principles and Rights at Work 2005* (Geneva, Switzerland: International
Labour Office, 2005), p. 10.

16. The acronyms listed above: UN PRI – United Nations Principles for
Responsible Investment; OECD MNE Guidelines – Organization for
Economic Development Guidelines for Multinational Enterprises; SA8000 –
Social Accountability International's Social standard; AA1000APS –
AccountAbility Principles Standard; ISO 26000 - International Organization
for Standardization Social Responsibility Standard.

17. C Meyer and J Kirby, 'Leadership in the Age of Transparency', *Harvard Business Review*, April 2010.
18. Internet World Stats, Internet users and Population Statistics for Asia, 2010, http://www.internetworldstats.com/stats3.htm, accessed date 29 April 2010.
19. Ceres is an active network of investors, environmental organizations and other public interest groups working with companies and investors to address sustainability challenges.
20. ICT is an acronym for 'information and communication technologies', which broadly refers to forms of technology employed for information and communication exchange. This includes the Internet, or World Wide Web, and the mobile phone, but also applications that utilize these media, such as text messaging, web chat programs and online data exchanges.
21. For more information, see the GRI website under 'Learning and Support'.
21. Actual figures may be much higher. As the Guidelines are a free and public good, GRI relies on organizations informing it of their usage in order to tabulate these results.
23. See Appendix 1 for country-specific details.
24. GRI, *The GRI Sustainability Reporting Cycle: a step-by-step guide for small and not so small organizations* (GRI, 2007).
25. GRI, UNEP (United Nation Environmental Program), KPMG and Stellenbosch University (2010), *Carrots and Sticks*, available from May 2010 (in print).
26. IFC & WRI, *UNDISCLOSED RISK: Corporate Environmental and Social Reporting in Emerging Asia* (2009), at http://www.wri.org/publication/undisclosed-risk-asia, accessed date 29 April 2010.
27. GRI, *GRI Sustainability Reporting: How valuable is the journey?* (Amsterdam, The Netherlands: GRI, 2008).
28. Ibid.
29. See www.globalreporting.org/FutureTrends/ for a link to the pdf copy of *The Transparent Economy*.
30. GRI, GRI Reports List, at http://www.globalreporting.org/ReportServices/GRI ReportsList, Accessed 24 April 2010. The GRI Reports List is updated on a Weekly basis.

# Conclusion

## Corporate Social Responsibility: Perspectives from Asia – The Future and Its Challenges

*Geoffrey Williams*

CSR in Asia is not the same as it is in the West. The studies in this volume illustrate this premise with a varied and comprehensive overview of issues affecting the development and implementation of CSR in a range of countries across the region. A key focus has been the need to take into account the CSR expectations and the perspectives of various stakeholders in Asia, which often differ in important ways from those in the West. Increasingly, Asian stakeholders are asserting these differences and demanding new approaches appropriate to this part of the world. In this concluding chapter we will look at some of these differences and some of the challenges and opportunities for CSR in Asia in the future.

### Understanding and engaging with Asian stakeholders

Asia is a multicultural and multi-faith region with numerous religions and denominations including Islam, Hinduism, Buddhism, Christianity, Taoism, Judaism, Sikhism, Jainism, Shinto and Confucianism, to name a few. The role of religion and culture in Asia and their impact on CSR has been discussed widely in studies that build on existing sociocultural frameworks of analysis.[1] The themes of religion and culture and their impact on stakeholder attitudes also feature strongly across the studies in this volume. These differences pose challenges to companies in Asia, especially those from overseas, but these challenges are not insurmountable.

In all parts of the world, responsible companies are successful when they identify their most important and relevant stakeholders, engage with them to uncover their concerns and, to the best of their ability,

UNIVERSITY OF WINCHESTER LIBRARY

address these needs through the management and operation of their business and through the products they sell. This basic CSR proposition is no different in Asia from anywhere else in the world, and in general the stakeholder groups identified by the contributors to this volume are similar to those identified elsewhere. They include consumers, employees, supply chain partners, civil society groups, non-governmental organizations (NGOs) and institutional and private shareholders. The differences arise in the extent and nature of their roles in the CSR matrix and in the issues they prioritize. Understanding these issues and how to address them is the key to successful CSR policies in Asia.

The evidence suggests that multiple stakeholder groups also play an important part in the implementation of CSR programmes in Asia. That is, stakeholders are not just recipients but are actively engaged in the delivery of CSR programmes themselves. This phenomenon is illustrated clearly through the discussion by the authors of various examples and live cases. These examples also show a clear message that, in order to be effective in an Asian context, CSR programmes and strategies should address issues that are important to Asian stakeholders and be implemented in ways that meet the challenges of Asian development. They also suggest that CSR practices that are common and successful in Asia may seem unusual, superfluous or irrelevant to Western observers, and in turn CSR practices that are successful in the West may not be successful in Asia.

## The hierarchy of stakeholders in Asia

A particular feature of CSR in Asia is that various stakeholder groups that have been important drivers of CSR in the West appear to play a less important, but growing, role in Asia. For example, the influence of consumers, organized labour and investors is seen to be weaker in Asia. Whereas many CSR initiatives in the West are driven from the 'bottom up', in Asia they are more often 'top-down'. Leadership comes either from the Chief Executive Officer and the Board or Directors or, higher still, from the Government and Regulatory Authorities. Asian governments and regulators appear to play a more important role in CSR issues than in the West, and often this is as much in the form of official sanction for CSR programmes as for obligation or compulsion. There is a clear trend from voluntary guidelines, which have largely been ignored, to more comprehensive regulations for the management of environmental, social and governance issues by Asian companies, international companies based in the region and those trading with or within Asia as a whole.

## The hierarchy of issues in Asia: social versus environmental CSR

Another theme that emerges from the various authors is the primacy of social development and economic sustainability over environmental concerns such as climate change, carbon emissions and energy conservation. Environmental issues are important in Asia, but there appears to be a powerful consensus that socio-economic development cannot be sacrificed to achieve environmental aims.[2] Indeed, the failure of the Copenhagen Summit to agree binding international targets on carbon emissions and greenhouse gas reductions is seen by many to be due to the insistence on the importance of social and economic priorities by Asian and other developing countries.[3] The positions taken by the Asian economic powerhouses of China and India in many respects turned the Western environmental hegemony on its head.[4] Ironically, Asia has gained a leadership position on environmental issues by insisting on social priorities.

## Non-governmental organizations and Asian CSR

Almost all authors in this volume have noted that local and international NGOs are playing an important role in CSR in Asia, but again the emphasis is rather different. In particular, local NGOs are more likely to take a bigger role in implementation of CSR programmes in collaboration with companies. International non-governmental organizations (INGOs) play a bigger role in lobbying, but their Western audience is sometimes more receptive to their campaigns than Asian stakeholders.

High-profile INGOs often draw on their experiences with companies in Europe and America to create vocal campaigns in Asia on various demands for greater social or environmental responsibility from Asian companies and international companies active in the region. Some INGOs take a proactive advocacy and engagement approach. The Worldwide Fund for Nature (WWF) advocates voluntary initiatives to provide incentives for CSR programmes to focus on long-term sustainability rather than short-term financial returns. WWF acknowledges that binding rules are often necessary to encourage and support voluntary initiatives that make effective progress toward sustainable development in Asia.[5]

Other INGOs are more critical or even confrontational. For example, Friends of the Earth (FoE) have been very much more aggressive than many other INGOs. A particular focus of their ire has been the behaviour of companies in the oil palm industry. Their 2007 report on Wilmar International, a Singapore company with operations in the Sambas District, West Kalimantan, Indonesia exposed legal, environmental and social breaches of the oil palm plantation companies of the Wilmar Group.[6] They have also exploited the global reach of regulations to carry out their campaigns. In 2009 FoE used legislation in the United Kingdom to obtain a ban on the broadcast of a promotional campaign by the Malaysian Palm Oil Council (MPOC), which they claimed made false statements about the environmental benefits of palm oil.[7]

By adopting confrontational methods in Asian societies where consensus is preferred, INGOs often achieve little more than publicity impacts. They are often criticized for their 'hit-and-run' approach, and, while their campaigns may expose bad practice and sometimes even end it, they often fail to follow-up with remediation afterwards. INGOs are also accused of not understanding the materiality of issues in the Asian context. The issues of concern to INGOs are not always of similar concern to local stakeholders in Asia. Oil palm cultivation, for example, is seen as a key strategic industry for Asian economic development and provides jobs and investment on a huge scale. It is also seen as a potentially viable response to issues of food shortages and carbon control through its use in biofuels. Palm oil companies themselves, sometimes through organizations such as the Roundtable for Sustainable Palm Oil (RSPO), argue that their environmental management and selective protection of biodiversity is seen by many objective observers as global best practice.[8] Aggressive campaigns by INGOs do not always achieve the CSR response that is hoped, and sometimes cause defensive responses by Asian companies and a refusal to cooperate on international programmes. In the palm oil sector, planters in Indonesia and Malaysia have responded with their own standards and industry advocacy group.[9]

## The changing CSR landscape

In the past, low incomes and sociopolitical exclusion have disempowered many stakeholders so that their influence on CSR issues has been restricted by their economic dependency. Although this situation persists on a widespread basis, the rapid growth of per capita GDP, personal incomes and emerging consumer classes in Asia are creating a change in the CSR landscape, which presents both opportunities and risks for enterprises of all types.

These changes are stronger in higher-income countries, where consumption patterns can influence company CSR programmes in a positive way by demonstrating new models for business success based on sustainable living and socially responsible lifestyle choices. In turn these encourage corporate innovation in CSR delivery that improves people's lives and adds value to society. So, to some extent, higher disposable incomes coupled with the changing preferences and consumption choices of Asian consumers are making a contribution in shaping the CSR agenda in Asia in a way that they have not done in the past. They are also offering an alternative perspective on how corporations in Asia can work towards building partnerships with consumers through different channels of social and cause-related marketing. Just as in the West, this discussion centres to a large part on the management of brands in Asia and issues such as reputation, brand positioning and brand protection.

Employees are also developing a more influential role, albeit slowly and to different extents in different countries. Employees are, of course, a critical resource in Asia, especially when capital is less abundant. There are, therefore, manifold dimensions of employee CSR embedded within Asian human resources approaches, including decent work policies and practices, employee training, health and safety standards, human rights, work ethics, and diversity and tolerance in the workplace. As incomes rise, issues and concerns of employees become more sophisticated and include work-life balance, career development, voluntarism and management-based ethics.

These issues are becoming more acute as economic development progresses and workers become less disempowered. Even if incomes are low and conditions are bad, employers in Asia are beginning to recognize that they become targets for NGO campaigns or risk industrial disputes which cause downtime and low productivity. Where incomes are higher, employees are more mobile, and there is growing evidence that they are demanding more from employers. A recent survey for the Hudson Highland Group employment consultancy in China, Hong Kong and Singapore, for example, showed that work-related stress was rising, mainly due to heavy workloads, and employees were leaving more frequently, demanding higher pay or simply refusing job offers more often when making employment choices.[10]

These changes encourage enterprises themselves to take on the role of change agents in CSR. This is a growing feature emerging among companies in Asia of all forms, including small-scale enterprises, medium-sized companies (SMEs) and multinationals (MNCs) alike. It is also a feature across various important sectors, including Banking and Finance, Infrastructure, Power and Fast-Moving-Consumer-Goods (FMCGs). The various case studies in this volume offer insights into the role of companies in the development of modern CSR in Asia in the context of these challenges.

## Media, new media and CSR in Asia

Media outlets of various forms play a critical role in shaping the changing of the CSR landscape and spreading CSR awareness across Asia. Media houses are central institutions in the public sphere, but in Asia traditional media such as print and television have historically been relatively conservative when compared with Western counterparts. This, of course, has various causes, from direct censorship and government control through to self-censorship and commercial imperatives. Concentrated ownership in the media sector is also a constraint on freedom of publication. Nonetheless, traditional media can still play a role in spreading awareness and empowering people while monitoring governments and corporations and holding them accountable.

In recent years, the advent of the Internet, digital information sources, social networking media and blogging have brought about a transformation in the way people communicate and share knowledge and information. These forms of new media have been particularly significant in Asia. The hugely dynamic Asian information technology and communication (ITC) industry provides access to new media in both English and regional languages in a way that is more open and accessible than has been experienced before.[11] They have played the roles of facilitators, assessors and campaigners by unearthing and communicating to a mass audience some of the biggest CSR stories in the world, such as the China Baby Milk scandal and many more.[12] This in turn has played an important role in shaping the relationship between corporations and their stakeholders in Asia. According to one study, China has 81 million bloggers engaged in online discussion about contemporary issues out of a community of 340 million Internet users.[13] So even in countries where censorship and restrictions on freedom of speech is common, companies cannot hide their CSR derelictions, nor can they rely on the self-regulatory reticence of traditional media as a way of keeping stories out of the public domain.

There are three lessons from these changes that can be usefully learned by Asian companies and Western companies operating in Asia alike. First, a clear vision of responsible business behaviour is emerging from the increasingly well-informed discussions amongst Asian stakeholders. This vision is likely to differ from Western perceptions, and 'one-size-fits-all' CSR strategies based on Western premises are unlikely to fit this frame comfortably. Second, new media options and widespread access to the Internet provide an easier and relatively open forum for Asian stakeholders to air their views. This helps them to build a momentum of agreement amongst like-minded people which can quickly outpace corporate communications responses and crisis plans. Third, it is neither necessary nor sufficient for companies to guess at stakeholder concerns or adopt 'off-the-shelf' Western issues and models. Companies can and should engage with new media forms to uncover the views of the increasingly sophisticated Asian stakeholder discussion. Very few companies have developed strategies to do this, and rely on crisis reaction rather than strategic programmes that anticipate Asian concerns.

## Creating CSR professionals and supply chain capacity

The CSR function in most Asian companies invariably sits in the Corporate Communications or Corporate Affairs Department and is often seen as little more than an extension of the public relations function. As a consequence, the professional role of CSR managers is often under-recognized. Whereas many corporate communications managers will have professional training or even university degrees in marketing, communications and public relations, CSR managers very rarely have similar professional training in CSR or sustainability issues. Often they learn on the job through ad hoc workshops or conferences, or they simply apply corporate communications concepts to CSR programmes that are focused on one-off projects and publicity events.

A strategic role for CSR managers, in, for example, Corporate Strategy Departments, is less common, but is becoming more of a feature in particular industries such as oil and gas or plantations, where CSR issues are more acute. There is also an increase in the number of professional institutions and better-quality education on CSR.[14] This is helping to increase understanding of the strategic role of CSR and its value as a separate specialist management function. These are supporting new certification and qualification programmes for CSR managers, which are helping to improve CSR performance through the professionalism and the credibility of CSR managers.[15]

In order to be fully effective, these programmes need to extend into the supply chain in Asia, since supplier codes of conduct and voluntary standards may be insufficient. Proper training and capability-building can help to ensure that supply chains are free from labour abuses and human rights violations. Such programmes can also help companies protect their brands by creating a professional monitoring and measuring capability to help ensure that their supply chains achieve full compliance with their environmental and social objectives.

Supply chain capacity-building is needed at a number of levels, beginning with the development of modern management training for factory and plant managers, which is often rare. There is also a need to create employee awareness programmes. Many workers are often unaware of the labour laws that protect their entitlement to minimum wages, decent working hours, overtime compensation and health and safety protection. Some international companies working in Asia protect their brands by providing workers with such training directly and with mechanisms to air grievances in the absence of collective bargaining and freedom of association. These issues, of course, are needed in addition to providing workers with good-quality skills training and vocational development.

## Developing a clear CSR strategy

Although there is evidence of significant progress in CSR across companies in Asia, it is also clear that management of CSR tends to be unstructured or, at worst, piecemeal. Clear CSR strategies are the exception rather than the norm, and the centrality of strategic CSR, which is considered as more common in Europe and the US, has yet to be established as a key component of business management across Asia. Successful CSR programmes create a vision for CSR within a company that reflects a clear understanding of the context of CSR in Asia. Structured programmes can benefit from the following features:

- Assessment – conduct a CSR assessment to provide a comprehensive analysis of the current CSR position based on international standards and best practice.
- Stakeholder Mapping – to identify the most relevant stakeholders and the issues of concern to them.
- Gap Analysis – produce a gap analysis to provide a detailed report on current gaps in CSR strategy.
- Stakeholder Engagement Analysis – to deliver a stakeholder engagement proposal based on the needs of relevant stakeholder groups, and design and undertake effective engagement exercises.
- Assessing Materiality – using the assessment of capability and the issues of concern to stakeholders to craft the CSR strategy to create meaningful policy statements and strategy.

- Implementing CSR Policy – and evaluate future development and ongoing work.
- Measure and Monitor CSR – evaluate outcomes and impacts using metrics such as Social Return on Investment (SROI).
- Transparency, Reporting and Accountability – develop a framework for effective CSR reporting relevant to corporate sustainability context.

OWW Consulting Sdn Bhd 2010

Structured programmes of this type are rare across Asia, but, in line with the development of professional CSR functions and training courses, are beginning to be seen more often than in the past. The trajectory of their future development will very much depend on the overall drivers of CSR in the region and the demands of various stakeholders for more structured and better-managed CSR programmes.

## Challenges and opportunities for CSR in Asia

### Corporate governance

Corporate Governance in Asia has been and continues to be a thorny issue for investors, companies and regulators alike. A comparison of Asian Corporate Governance frameworks shows a huge variety of approaches in Asia, due in large part to their history and development. This has led to British-type systems in Singapore, Hong Kong and Malaysia, a Dutch-influenced system in Indonesia and elements of Japanese approaches in Korea.[16] There are also multiple local variants, and family-run businesses or dominant shareholder structures are common. The insistence of international and local stakeholders has led to changes in the Corporate Governance regimes of many Asian countries, and to some extent these have reduced the divergence from international norms.[17]

Good systems do not guarantee good practice, and criticisms of Asian Corporate Governance from Western observers have been manifold. Corporate Governance in many companies in Asia has been characterized as lacking in transparency and having governing bodies and boards of directors that are dominated by non-independent directors influenced by personal incentives. There are also claims of an absence of clear board committees and systems for audit and control, as well as a legal mapping of responsibilities and accountability remedies. These limitations frustrate the control of managers by shareholders and investors alike. The role of shareholders in the control of companies often highlights the effectiveness of voting systems at general meetings, proxy voting and minority shareholder protection as key areas of concern.

Since the global financial crisis of 2008 these criticisms are losing traction in the light of egregious Corporate Governance failures in the West and the clamour for reform there.[18] This has taken the spotlight off Corporate Governance in Asia, first because by and large Asian companies did not suffer the same failures, and second because the reforms in Asia are now more properly understood as part of a global rather than a regional or country-specific problem. This new swell of global concern offers Asia an opportunity to consider Corporate Governance reform in a more balanced and less reactive way in the context of wider global efforts to improve company management at the Board of Directors level. The journey remains difficult, but it is no longer one that Asia must tread alone.

### Shareholder rights

Milton Friedman's 1970 article in the *New York Times*, 'The Social Responsibility of Business is to Increase its Profits,' is often quoted and misquoted as an assertion that the sole aim of business is to maximize profits irrespective of other considerations.[19] Unfortunately very few people have actually read this article, and most go no further than to read the title and draw their own conclusions. In fact, Friedman merely states the widely held view that issues surrounding the social responsibility of business raise a 'Principal-Agent' problem of how well managers, the Agents, are controlled by owners, the Principals. In particular, from the perspective of the 1970s Friedman argued that managers were often overstepping their duties to the company by implementing CSR programmes that had not been approved by shareholders. He said that a manager:

> ...has direct responsibility to his employers. That responsibility is to conduct the business in accordance with their desires, which generally will be to make as much money as possible while conforming to the basic rules of the society, both those embodied in law and those embodied in ethical custom.

Laws and ethical customs have changed since 1970 and today demand that companies and their managers have a greater awareness of the environmental, social and governance issues that impose costs and risks on their businesses and which offer profitable opportunities if managed proactively. Indeed, in some instances they risk being sued if they don't take this into account.[20] This is as true in Asia as it is anywhere else, and as a consequence the balance between profit and social and environmental issues is much the same, but the Principal-Agent problem may not be the same. Shareholders in Asia do not necessarily have problems in preventing managers from respecting CSR issues; instead, they have problems ensuring that managers respect those principles.

As Asian firms have grown, they have opened up to capital markets to gain access to investment funds, and this has accentuated the agency problem more clearly in the Asian context. The role of shareholders as one of the guardians of CSR principles has risen in Asia, but the agency problem means that shareholders often do not have sufficient control over managers to regulate them on key CSR issues. Added to that, lack of transparency means that information on CSR management and performance is often not available even to the Board of Directors. It is also difficult for shareholders to coordinate efforts or gain sufficient mass to change management policies and practices. Finally, a lack of legal sanctions and poor enforcement means that minority shareholder rights are often weakly protected. As a consequence many managers simply ignore CSR issues, environmental protection and decent work practices. This causes risks for shareholders that they often cannot control through existing systems, and so CSR violations persist beyond their influence.

In Asia there remain a large number of family-owned and run companies, and the number of single-owner or dominant-owner firms is also large compared with the West.[21] To some extent this has reduced the agency problem in the past, since managers and owners have been the same people. Also, to the extent that the tradition of benevolent ownership has influenced corporate behaviour, it has substituted for formal CSR or even taken on a more strategic CSR role.[22] Nonetheless, these Asia-specific traits cannot compensate for the weakness of control of managers, which poses significant risks for stakeholders across all CSR domains.

## Corruption in Asia

Corruption is a global problem, which causes many problems beyond the legal issues. From an economic perspective, it inhibits investment, limits trade and reduces growth. In addition, it can cause failure in CSR implementation and is associated with serious CSR issues such as trafficking, child labour, human rights and errant legal enforcement of all forms of laws, regulations and standards, including in the environmental, social and governance domains. In Asia, corruption is a particular issue because of the widespread perception that it is endemic. These perceptions are fuelled by media reports about various derelictions in Asia, including, inter alia, corruption, bribery, money laundering, falsification of accounts and insider-trading.

In Transparency International's *2009 Corruption Barometer* more than half of the respondents in Asia said that they believed that bribery is commonly used in the public sector to shape policy and regulation in favour of the interests of companies. There is also a growing perception of corruption within the private sector in Asia and by private companies themselves. Half of the survey respondents in Asia said that they perceived the private sector to be corrupt.[23] The Kroll *Global Fraud Report 2009/2010* showed a rise over the year earlier from 10 per cent to 15 per cent in the number of companies reporting actual cases of bribery, and the proportion of companies in Asia that consider themselves highly vulnerable to corruption and bribery also rose. Major areas open to corruption in Asia are vendor and procurement fraud and bribery of officers to avoid enforcement of regulatory breaches.[24]

Contrary to many widely held perceptions, stakeholders in Asia are not tolerant of corruption, and many are vocal in its condemnation.[25] Anti-corruption authorities in Malaysia and Indonesia have been established and given special powers to tackle corruption directly.[26] While anti-corruption frameworks exist in comprehensive forms, many observers note that they lack credibility and impact; failure of enforcement is most often cited as the major issue.[27] Many people have pointed to the fact that corruption exists in all parts of the world and note, for example, that the world's biggest fraudster, Bernard Madoff, is not from Asia. Nonetheless, while Madoff's crimes are huge in financial terms and devastating to the people he defrauded, the justice system in America has eventually prevailed in identifying, investigating and prosecuting his crimes.[28] As things stand, Asia can only look forward in wistful hope to a similarly effective system.

## The environment and climate change

There is widespread equivocation about environmental issues and climate change in Asia, which arises from two main sources. First, climate change is often viewed as a consequence of Western economic development and high consumption, as the views of Indian Prime Minister Manmohan Singh so clearly reveal. Further, Asia is seen by many to have relatively good indicators on environment in some areas. According to World Bank statistics for 2010, energy use per capita in Asia is one third of that in the Euro Area, energy generated by biomass is more than twice the proportion of the total and energy from hydroelectric sources is 60 per cent greater. Compared with high-income countries, the figures are one-quarter, three and a half times greater and one-third greater respectively. Of course, these relative figures disguise the trend due to rapid economic growth; for example, $CO_2$ emissions in Asia grew by 132 per cent from 1999 to 2006 compared with 3.8% in the Euro Area, and the future trajectory is likely to narrow these gaps further.[29]

They also disguise pressing environmental concerns such as access to clean water and sanitation. Problems such as these are often taken as economic rather than environmental issues. Indeed, access to clean water is also taken as a human rights issue. This raises a second source of resistance to environmental programmes, which comes from a widespread determination not to sacrifice socio-economic development for environmental protection. These arguments are compelling to some, but for others they fail to account for the damage to socio-economic development and quality of life due to poor environmental management and man-made environmental disasters. $CO_2$ damage as a percentage of Gross National Income (GNI) is five and a half times greater in Asia than in the Euro Area, and particulate emissions damage as a percentage of GNI is seven times greater.[30]

Whatever the sources of resistance, various forms of pleading, persuasion or threats from the West have not changed attitudes or practices in Asia much. Even statutory environmental regulation has not been effective. For example, the government of China has introduced a range of environmental laws, but the environmental NGO Greenpeace has been vocal in its criticism of companies that systematically disregard these regulations, and has identified weak enforcement by the Chinese government as a key cause. Their report of 2009 highlighted 28 major multinational and Chinese corporations that violated Chinese environmental regulations with apparent impunity.[31]

## Climate change opportunities

The various business risks associated with climate change, including the socio-economic impact of environmental degradation, regulatory sanctions or NGO pressures, have not gained much momentum across Asia. Indeed, there is a widespread scepticism about environmental issues, which is part of the public policy consensus as well as the business conversation. Nonetheless, signs of change are emerging from a much more pragmatic source. This is the growing view that Asia has a potential advantage in environmental resources which offer realizable business opportunities from climate change responses. This means that for some businesses environmental issues have become a positive strategic business option rather than simply a source of risk.

The economic benefits of environmental protection are beginning to make sense to some Asian companies. From a basic level, energy conservation reduces costs directly and is passed almost seamlessly into higher profit margins, while at the same time reducing energy-related greenhouse gas emissions. Waste reduction and recycling are also clear sources of cost saving, which for many Asian companies are becoming real sources of financial advantage. Even in areas such as protection of biodiversity, where economic advantages have been quite obscure, companies are beginning to see that preservation can create greater value-added than destruction. International research such as The Economics of Ecosystems and Biodiversity (TEEB) study is helping to uncover the economic value drivers in material ways.[32]

Many Asian companies are also able to exploit cost advantages to create low-carbon technologies and green products on a viable economic scale to meet international demand. Following the standard industrialization model of 'Import, Imitate and Innovate', Asian companies are rapidly developing capability in manufacturing of environmental products in the same way as they have with cars, computers and consumer goods. To this extent the low-cost advantages of Asia offer the prospect of producing and supplying low-carbon goods on an industrial scale which will far outstrip the output levels possible in the West.

Even in the debate between environment and economic development, low-carbon and alternative renewable energy sources such as geothermal or hydroelectric power are seen as a cheaper and almost inexhaustible way of meeting energy demand to fuel long-term economic growth. The environmental benefits and low-carbon footprint are seen almost as a by-product. The International Labour Organization (ILO) has a Green Jobs Agenda programme that highlights environmentally friendly employment as a key source of economic and social value added over the long term.[33]

Investment opportunities for cleaner technologies in Asia are growing as a consequence, and new initiatives to underpin this investment are beginning to emerge. The Asia Carbon Group, which plans to establish a trading platform, the Asia Carbon Exchange and the Asia Carbon Fund for investment in sustainable development projects are examples.[34] The Asia-Pacific Partnership on Clean Development and Climate, a collaboration between business and the governments of Australia, China, India, Japan, Republic of Korea and the United States, aims to support investment and trade in clean energy technologies, green products and services that support them in strategic market sectors.[35]

## Supply chain issues in Asia

Supply chain management has become a critical area of focus in the context of CSR in Asia. Traditional models of supply chains view the management issue as the effective integration of supply and demand coordination within and across companies and production partners. These models have developed into modern supply chain systems which incorporate issues of ethical sourcing and environmentally friendly production and logistical solutions.[36] In many regards they have become essential for some companies to maintain their licence to operate.

Asia is the source of an increasingly large share of global GDP as a supplier of raw materials, components and finished goods. Asian companies are therefore an important part of the supply chain for major international companies and underpin many companies with significant global brand value. Historically, supply chain pressures in Asia focused on anti-sweatshop issues, but today they have become more complicated and include concerns about labour and human rights abuses, environment protection and product responsibility.

High-profile issues originating in Asian supply chains have hit major global brands hard. Recent examples include the exposure of child labour issues in the supply chain for the US clothing retailer Gap in 2007[37] and another clothing firm, Primark, in the UK the following year.[38] Issues in the clothing and fashion industry attract a lot of attention, perhaps because of their universal appeal to everyone's basic need for clothing. Oxfam in Hong Kong, for example, has focused its recent campaigns on responsibility and transparency in the clothing supply chain in Asia. It argues that well-managed supply chains can empower the poor and companies can address poverty directly through their supply chain operations if the focus is on social mobility capability development.[39]

## Supply chain certification in Asia

Supplier codes of conduct and the use of social and environmental accountability standards have become a common approach for businesses involved in outsourcing, purchasing and trade in the West, but remain relatively underdeveloped in Asia.[40] For example, the Forest Stewardship Council (FSC) certification for sustainable wood products had 90 forest areas of 3.9 million hectares certified in Asia by mid-2010 out of 1,024 global certificates covering 135 million hectares.[41] Even for issues that affect Asia most acutely, certification is still underdeveloped. In the oil palm industry, for example, palm oil production certified by the Roundtable for Sustainable Palm Oil (RSPO) amounted to about 5 per cent of global palm oil production by mid-2010.[42]

Even where supplier certification exists, there are risks for international manufacturers and retailers sourcing from Asian supply chains. First, verification is a major problem. It is often impossible for companies to know with certainty whether labour and environmental standards required under contract or certificates are actually being maintained. This is especially true when there are 'chain-of-custody' issues where products change hands between various suppliers, traders or transportation companies during the supply process.[43] Many suppliers are accused of 'box-ticking' to achieve initial certification and falsification of data to maintain accreditation year-on-year. Fraud and corruption are considered to be common, and sophisticated and monitoring infrastructure in vulnerable markets is often underdeveloped. Independent international organizations such as the Fair Labor Association offer a partial and well-respected inspection process which covers many Asian markets, but, with the best will in the world, their coverage is by no means universal.[44]

A second problem with certification arises from the costs both for the suppliers themselves and for the companies they supply to. Global supply of manufactured goods and commodities has been under significant downward pressure for many decades, and cost efficiencies and scale economies in Asia have been a major cause of this trend. Costs of certification to suppliers cannot always be passed up the supply chain to final retail customers, and unless final buyers there are prepared to pay a premium for certified goods then margins at all stages in the supply chain are squeezed. This may simply be unsustainable from a financial perspective. Sometimes this problem is acknowledged and accommodated by cooperation agreements between buyers and suppliers. Or, as in the case of palm oil in Malaysia, government support is provided.[45]

A third major issue is the question of how companies should respond when violations of environmental and social problems are identified in their supply chain. One obvious response is to end contracts with noncompliant suppliers. This may not remove the problem, and may itself be taken as a dereliction of responsibility if large multinationals are seen to simply walk away, leaving child labour issues or other violations to continue unchecked. Active engagement with suppliers may be more effective. Gap, for example, responded to its child labour issues by providing help and support for the children involved, although for some, including the international children's charity Save the Children, their efforts may not have gone far enough.[46]

## Product responsibility

The concept of product responsibility varies by industrial sector according to the production and use of the products concerned. At a basic level it includes the provision of clear and accurate product information, including instructions and cautions on use. It also requires that marketing is not misleading or aimed at inappropriate audiences, such as high-sugar food advertising during children's television programmes. Beyond this, it also covers fair contractual arrangements and consumer protection.

Product responsibility can go beyond regulatory compliance to be a key feature in the promotion of sustainable consumption. It can help to minimize the environmental and social risks from the use of products and services. Promoting sustainable consumption can involve design, manufacture, distribution, marketing and post-sale support. It can also promote 'cradle-to-cradle' features that accommodate environmental issues into design, production and use and then extend to the collection and recycling of products at the end of their useful life. Companies that reclaim fast-moving-consumer-goods (FMCG) and mobile telephones for recycling are common examples.

Consumer products scandals and recalls in Asia raise a perception of poor, even deadly, quality standards amongst Asian manufacturers. From the Sunlu Baby Milk Scandal[47] to the Toyota brake failure recalls,[48] product quality standards are of concern across a wide range of sectors and appear to be a recurring theme for some companies, sectors or countries. The consumer attention that is drawn by these incidents damages a company's reputation and calls into question the responsibility of the senior management for quality and safety issues. This can have an impact on brand, reputation and sales, and ultimately damage financial performance and the attraction of the shares on the stock market. In the words of the international financier Warren Buffett:

> It takes 20 years to build a reputation and five minutes to ruin it. If you think about that, you'll do things differently.
>
> Warren Buffett

Indeed, in some cases the penalties are even more severe; in the Sanlu case two senior managers faced capital punishment.

The increased attention paid to corporate responsibility for product failures has led to calls for greater regulation and statutory consumer protection. Thailand, for example, adopted a new legal framework for product responsibility in 2008. This covers sale of local or imported goods that may be potentially dangerous due to defective manufacturing or because directions of use have not been properly labelled, are incorrect or unclear. Manufacturers, importers and vendors are jointly liable to the injured party whether or not the injury is deliberate, or due to negligence. The injured party needs only to prove that injury occurred during normal use or storage of a product and proof of negligence is not necessary.[49] Again, of course, legislation is only as effective as its enforcement, and judicial remedies may be slow to protect consumers from dangerous goods.

## Decent work and labour practices

The issues at Gap and Primark are just two examples that expose poor workplace practices and associated labour and human rights issues in Asia. These continue to be a challenge for local and multinational companies operating in Asia, who often find it difficult to manage or even to be aware of issues in the plants and factories of their primary and subsidiary suppliers. Common concerns include dangerous working conditions, exploitative hours, irregular payment of wages and overtime compensation, or even the unlawful withholding of pay altogether. While most countries in Asia have employment laws covering minimum wages, working hours and fair remuneration, enforcement is a recurring problem. Similarly, comprehensive health and safety standards exist in most countries, but corruption of officials leads to widespread abuse.

## Human rights

International conventions, such as those advocated by the International Labour Organization (ILO), have been widely, although not universally, adopted to prevent the worst forms of human rights abuses in the workplace, such as child labour, trafficking and forced or slave labour. Unfortunately, because many workers are migrants, either from rural to urban areas or from one country to another, their rights are regularly abused. Migrant workers are often not aware of their rights, and, even if they are, access to the judicial system is often denied to them or is prohibitively expensive. This is not an issue unique to Asia, but in the context of poor legal enforcement the consequences are often more severe. The legal maxim that 'Justice delayed is Justice denied' is an all too common feature in the administration of labour law in Asia, and is especially acute in China, Malaysia, Thailand and India. Indeed, in some countries, including China, Japan and Korea, migrants do not enjoy the same protection under the law as local workers.

## Poverty

Although some countries have successfully dealt with income growth and distribution, poverty remains the most pressing issue across Asia as a whole, and the region is home to two-thirds of the world's poor. Poverty can undermine governance, political stability, social cohesion and the overall well-being of the economy. Companies can play an important role in the process of poverty alleviation, and in the absence of government programmes businesses may have no option but to address social issues due to poverty. Most obviously, they can create employment opportunities, directly and indirectly, that have positive impacts on the communities in which they operate. They can also be catalysts for wider economic development at a community level by developing pro-poor community investment projects that specifically aim to provide jobs and contracts for local suppliers. Microfinance or micro-franchise programmes can encourage social entrepreneurship, especially among marginalized groups. They can also focus on environmental community investment strategies to address climate change issues, which affect the poor disproportionately.[50]

### Pro-poor business models

More widely, businesses can help to develop resilience in local communities to economic or environmental challenges by creating a holistic form of sustainable development. For example, companies can work on industry or sector-level initiatives to create easily adoptable standards to spread technology and good practices. They can also promote public policy through advocacy and dialogue to strengthen public governance and institutions that assist adaptation. By working with communities they can use core corporate competence and individual efforts to increase climate resilience in developing countries, enterprises and communities as a whole. They can create strategic partnerships and alliances with civil society, other businesses, NGOs, research institutes and community organizations and increase public-private investment and hybrid financing vehicles.[51]

### Business at the bottom of the pyramid

Even in countries with low per capita income there is a huge potential market at the 'Bottom of the Pyramid'.[52] It is estimated that around 2.7

billion people live on less than US$2 per day, but their collective purchasing power may be as much as US$5 trillion.[53] This offers scope for new markets and extra sales for companies that currently focus on middle and high-income groups. It can also offer greater mutual benefits and opportunities if firms recognize low-income stakeholders as partners. Companies can help to build sustainable livelihoods by engaging with low-income customers, for example, through direct employment from low-income groups, micro-franchising and outsourcing of sales to community cooperatives or the targeted development of supply chains in poor rural areas. In particular, companies can benefit from supporting and engaging with Social Enterprises in their business operations through profitable commercial activities or inclusive businesses. Social Enterprise Partnerships can help them in achieving their CSR goals while at the same time creating economically sustainable business environments.[54]

### Social enterprise and social entrepreneurs

Social Enterprise models are different from CSR.[55] Social Enterprises are organizations that start with a social or environmental aim and use commercial business processes in order to meet those aims.[56] By contrast, CSR is a way in which organizations with a primarily commercial aim can address their social and environmental responsibilities.

Nonetheless, large companies can gain a great deal from partnerships with Social Enterprises through joint ventures, direct investments or sourcing inputs from Social Enterprises. These partnerships can and should be viewed as part of a CSR programme for a commercial firm and part of the commercial programme of a Social Enterprise. In this way they can be symbiotic relationships, which become sustainable simply because of mutually aligned organizational incentives. Working with Social Enterprises can also be useful to create a training ground for leadership programmes and can have benefits for staff motivation, company loyalty and human resource management. In turn, Social Enterprises can benefit from management experience and knowledge transfer from larger commercial companies.

An example is the collaboration between the international food giant Danone and the Grameen organization in Bangladesh through the establishment of Grameen Danone Foods Ltd in 2006. The social aim is to provide a fortified yogurt drink called *Shakti Doi* at affordable prices, to help reduce malnutrition among Bangladeshi children.[57] The business model is built on local supply chains and local employment, and so adds economic value directly and indirectly into the communities in which the factory operates. Grameen offers micro-loans to buy cows and feed to provide the raw milk, and helps vendors to create infrastructure to sell its milk and yogurts in small-proximity stores. Grameen micro-entrepreneurs also sell the yogurt door to door through micro-franchise agreements. The production and sales process is also environmentally aware. Natural resource use is minimized using solar panels and rain-water harvesting, and biodegradable cups made from cornstarch also contribute to minimizing the environmental footprint.[58]

From Danone's perspective, the company has achieved sales in a market that would otherwise be outside its economically viable sphere. Danone products would normally be too expensive unless this business model was adopted. From an investment perspective it also recovers its costs over a reasonable period. In addition, the collaboration supports Danone's CSR programmes and emphasizes its social responsibility through its products rather than through donations. This builds brand value and enhances Danone's reputation internationally as a producer of responsible, healthy food products.

### Measuring CSR impact

One persistent feature of CSR in Asia is the absence of impact measures, that is, metrics or other indicators to evaluate whether or not a CSR pro-gramme is effective. In the absence of proper impact measurement CSR programmes become at best input-focused, that is, measured by the size of the donation, or at worst unstructured and wasteful. Community Investments in particular must be conducted within the context of a return on investment matrix, otherwise there is no way of knowing whether they are worthwhile or not. Creating CSR programmes in the context of clear CSR impact metrics provides a structure for the design, management and implementation of projects and adds to the long-term sustainability. It also helps to evaluate and create partnership and col-laboration models for delivering CSR with Asian Community Based Organizations (CBOs). Without a focused measure of return resources often do not even get to the intended recipients due to poor tracking, leakage and corruption.

CSR impact measures do exist, however, and are relatively easy to apply. In the United Kingdom, for example, the concept of 'Social Return on Investment' has been developed with funding from the UK Government to help organizations understand the non-financial impact of their activities on communities and evaluate them through moneti-zation and proxy values.[59] In Malaysia, the 'Silver Book' guidelines for management of community projects by Government Linked Companies

(GLCs) provide clear metrics to evaluate potential CSR impact as part of the selection process for programmes in GLC CSR portfolios.[60] These are linked to the extent to which the programmes help meet Malaysia's National Development Targets, which overlap in many respects with the Millennium Development Goals (MDGs). Other examples include the TATA Power CSR Impact measures, which aim to create a version of the UN Human Development Index at the community level, as a way of mapping the impact of TATA's CSR initiatives.[61]

## And so to the future

CSR in Asia is not the same as it is in the West, and its future will not be the same. The issues highlighted in the studies in this volume point to the need to take into account the CSR expectations and the perspectives of various stakeholders in Asia. These differ in important ways from those in the West, and increasingly assertive Asian stakeholders demand new approaches that reflect these differences. Whatever the issues and whatever the approaches to the challenges and opportunities for CSR in Asia in the future, the responses will be uniquely Asian.

## Notes

1. Issues of culture, choice and ethics in CSR in Asia are covered, for example, in G Williams and J Zinkin, 'The Effect of Culture on Consumers' Willingness to Punish Irresponsible Corporate Behaviour: Applying Hofstede's Typology to the Punishment Aspect of Corporate Social Responsibility', *Business Ethics: A European Review*, vol. 17, issue 2 (April 2008), pp. 210–26. Issues of religion and CSR are covered in, for example, G Williams and John Zinkin, 'Islam and CSR: A Study of the Compatibility Between the Tenets of Islam and the UN Global Compact', *Journal of Business Ethics*, vol. 91(4) (February 2010), pages 519–33, and S Brammer, G Williams and J Zinkin, 'Religion and Attitudes to Corporate Social Responsibility in a Large Cross-Country Sample', *Journal of Business Ethics*, vol. 71(3) (March 2007), pp. 229–43.

   The general issues of culture, choice and ethics, especially in Asia, are covered, for example, in R Nisbett, *The Geography of Thought: How Asians and Westerners Think Differently...and Why* (New York, NY: The Free Press, 2003), G Chan and GTL Shenoy, *Ethics and Social Responsibility: Asian and Western Perspectives* (Singapore: McGraw-Hill Education (Asia), 2009), or in journal articles such as S-H Chuah, R Hoffmann, M Jones and G Williams, 'An economic anatomy of culture: Attitudes and behaviour in inter- and intra-national ultimatum game experiments', *Journal of Economic Psychology*, vol. 30(5) (October 2009), pp. 732–44, or S-H Chuah, R Hoffmann, M Jones and G Williams, 'Do cultures clash? Evidence from cross-national ultimatum game experiments', *Journal of Economic Behavior & Organization*, vol. 64(1) (September 2007), pp. 35–48.

2. See, for example, the comments of Indian Prime Minister Manmohan Singh in July 2009 before the Copenhagen Summit: http://www.bloomberg.com/apps/news?pid=newsarchive&sid=aqr.54wsxvmI
3. There are a number of opinion pieces and editorials on this issue; see, for example, Roger Harriban at the BBC, http://news.bbc.co.uk/2/hi/science/nature/8423822.stm, or the editorial in the leading science journal *Nature* at http://www.nature.com/nature/journal/v462/n7276/full/462957b.html
4. See, for example, the views expressed by Mark Lynas on CNN at http://edition.cnn.com/2010/TECH/science/01/04/climate.mark.lynas/index.html
5. See D Pamlin ed. *WWF Discussion paper: Corporate Social Responsibility, An Overview* (Stockholm, Sweden: WWF, 2009).
6. Friends of the Earth, *Policy, practice, pride and prejudice: Review of legal, environmental and social practices of oil palm plantation companies of the Wilmar Group in Sambas District, West Kalimantan (Indonesia)* (Amsterdam: Milieudefensie (Friends of the Earth, the Netherlands), 2007) can be downloaded at http://www.foeeurope.org/publications/2007/Wilmar_Palm_Oil_Environmental_Social_Impact.pdf: the press release for the report is at http://www.foeeurope.org/press/2007/July3_PDC_Wilmar_PalmOil.htm
7. The Advertising Standards Authority adjudication is at http://www.asa.org.uk/Complaints-and-ASA-action/Adjudications/2009/9/Malaysia-Palm-Oil-Council/TF_ADJ_46897.aspx
8. You can find advocacy material of palm oil at the Malaysian Palm Oil Council (MPOC) website http://www.mpoc.org.my/. International best practices are advocated by the Roundtable for Sustainable Palm Oil (RSPO); their website is at http://www.rspo.org/
9. See articles by A Ekawati, 'Indonesia's Palm Oil Industry Seeks New Standards', *Jakarta Globe*, 2 February 2010, http://www.thejakartaglobe.com/nvironment/indonesias-palm-oil-industry-seeks-new-standards/356250 or J Wong, 'Palm oil players in M'sia, Indonesia form group', *The Star*, 4 May 2010, http://biz.thestar.com.my/news/story.asp?file=/2010/5/4/business/6182619&sec=business
10. See the Hudson Highland press release at http://china.hudson.com/documents/Hudson-Report-Q3-2010-Asia-Press-Release.pdf for further information on this topic.
11. An Edelman study entitled *Public Engagement: The Evolution of Public Relations* presented by Richard Edelman at a Grunig Lecture at the University of Maryland on 30 October 2008 suggested that the growth of Internet users in China is around 40 per cent per year. In Korea 45 per cent of the population use blogging and 47.8 per cent subscribe to a popular online social network called CyWorld.
12. See the China Daily article at http://bbs.chinadaily.com.cn/viewthread.php?gid=2&tid=615705
13. Edelman, *The Dragon & The Mouse. Public Affairs and Social Media in China* (Hong Kong: Edelman and Public Affairs Asia, 2009).
14. See, for example, the Academy of Responsible Management (ARM) at www.responsibleacademy.com
15. Examples include the Professional CSR Manager Programme at the Malaysian Institute of Management, the Professional Diploma in CSR at Universiti Sains

Malaysia (USM) and the GRI Certified Trainer programmes run across Korea, India, Malaysia, Indonesia, Thailand and Chinese-speaking countries.

16. For an overview see the Asian Corporate Governance Association at http://www.acga-asia.org/.
17. See, for example, J Roche, *Corporate Governance in Asia* (London: Routledge, 2005) for an overview of such issues.
18. See an overview of Wall Street reform bills at http://en.wikipedia.org/wiki/Wall_Street_reform
19. See M Friedman, 'The Social Responsibility of Business is to Increase Its Profits', *The New York Times Magazine*, 13 September 1970. A full copy of the text can be found at http://www.stthomas.edu/cathstudies/cst/facdevelop/CITII/CITII%20links/Friedman_1st_page.pdf
20. See the UNEP FI report covered in http://www.responsible-investor.com/home/article/fiduciary_2/
21. Companies with a single controlling shareholder account for more than half of all listed companies in Hong Kong, China and Indonesia, according to the CFA *Shareholder Rights Across Markets. A Manual for Investors* (New York, NY: CFA Institute for Financial Integrity, 2008).
22. Examples include the TATA Group in India or the YTL Group in Malaysia, but there are many across the region.
23. D. Zinnbauer, R. Dobson and K. Despota, (editors). Transparency International *Global Corruption Report 2009*, (Cambridge UK: Cambridge University Press, 2009). Available at http://www.transparency.org/publications/gcr/gcr_2009#dnld.
24. See *Global Fraud Report: Annual Edition 2009/2010* (New York: Kroll, 2009).
25. TA Aziz, *Fighting Corruption: My Mission* (Kuala Lumpur: Konrad Adenauer Foundation, 2005) provides an overview in a compilation of speeches by one of the leading anti-corruption campaigners in Asia.
26. Lim Kit Siong, the Parliamentary Leader of DAP, one of Malaysia's main opposition parties, discusses this point succinctly in his blog site at http://blog.limkitsiang.com/2009/11/16/indonesia-100-corruption-conviction-rate-against-ikan-yu-%E2%80%93-malaysia-0/. His section devoted to corruption provides a comprehensive account: http://blog.limkitsiang.com/category/corruption/
27. The Malaysian Anti-Corruption Commission (MACC) or SPRM (Suruhanjaya Pencegahan Rasuah Malaysia) website is at http://www.sprm.gov.my and the Indonesian Corruption Eradication Commission or KPK (Komisi Pemberantasan Korupsi) website is at http://www.kpk.go.id/
28. The Madoff case is, of course, well known; see, for example, the *Wall Street Journal*: http://online.wsj.com/article/NA_WSJ_PUB:SB123685693449906551.html
29. Source: World Bank, *The Little Green Data Book 2010* (Washington DC: World Bank, 2010).
30. Ibid.
31. The main breaches were those that require publication of pollution information within 30 days of notification by the local environmental bureaux that the company had breached pollution standards. See Greenpeace, *Silent Giants: An Investigation into Corporate Environmental Information Disclosure in China* (Hong Kong: Greenpeace China, 2009).
32. The TEEB website is at http://www.teebweb.org

33. See the ILO Green Jobs WebPages at http://www.ilo.org/integration/themes/ greenjobs/lang--en/index.htm

34. See Asia Carbon Global Website at http://www.asiacarbon.com/

35. See the website of the Asia-Pacific Partnership on Clean Development and Climate at http://www.asiapacificpartnership.org/

36. See, for example, PH Rao, *Greening the Supply Chain: A Guide for Asian Managers* (New Delhi: Response Books, 2008).

37. The issues at GAP and the remedies the company proposed are discussed by Amelia Gentleman in her *New York Times* article *Gap Campaigns Against Child Labor*, published on 16 November 2007, which can be read at http:// www.nytimes.com/2007/11/16/business/worldbusiness/16gap.html?ex=1 352869200&en=cb61f65092b69228&ei=5088&partner=rssnyt&emc=rss

38. Primark faced an expose on a BBC documentary Panorama in June 2008, referenced at http://news.bbc.co.uk/2/hi/business/7456897.stm. Primark's response is discussed at Ethical Consumer at http://www.ethicalconsumer. org/CommentAnalysis/CorporateWatch/primark.aspx

39. The campaign focuses on supply chain issues in the clothing and textile industry: see *Good Fashion: A Guide to Being an Ethical Clothing Company* (Hong Kong: Oxfam Hong Kong, 2009).

40. International certification schemes such the Forest Stewardship Council (FSC), the Marine Stewardship Council (MSC) and the workplace practice standard SA8000 are examples but are relatively underused in Asia.

41. There were also 3,511 Chain-of-Custody Certificates in Asia out of a global 18,073; see *Global FSC certificates: type and distribution August 2010* (Bonn: Forest Stewardship Council, 2010), available at http://www.fsc.org/fileadmin/web-data/public/document_center/powerpoints_graphs/facts_figures/ Global-FSC-Certificates-2010-07-15-EN.pdf

42. RSPO Certified output of 2.5 million tonnes by mid-2010 is taken from the RSPO website at http://www.rspo.org/?q=page/520. Global output is estimated at around 50 million tonnes at the same time.

43. See, for example, the Chain-of -Custody issues at Programme for the Endorsement of Forest Certification (PEFC), an international forestry certification scheme, at http://www.pefc.org/standards/chain-of-custody

44. Information on the Fair Labor Association (FLA) can be found at http:// www.fairlabor.org/

45. The Malaysian government was reported to be considering support of RM20 million in August 2010 in addition to the RM50 million it has already provided for smallholders to help them in RSPO compliance. See the Malaysian National Press Agency Bernama article *Government Considering RM20 Million Allocation For Oil Palm Smallholders* at http://bernama.com.my/bernama/v5/ newsbusiness.php?id=518425

46. See Amelia Gentleman's *New York Times* article ibid.

47. See the *New Scientist* article on general problems in milk powder in China at http://www.newscientist.com/article/dn14791-melamine-widespread-in-chinas-food-chain.html

48. See Toyota's view at http://www.toyota.com/recall/ and an general overview at http://en.wikipedia.org/wiki/2009%E2%80%932010_Toyota_vehicle_recalls

49. M Clark, R Chomsri and J Sok, *Focus: Thailand - Product Liability New product liability legislation in Thailand* (Sydney: Allens Arthur Robinson, 2008).

50. See, for example, J Nelson, 'Corporate Action on Climate Adaptation and Development: Mobilizing new business partnerships to build climate change resilience in developing countries and communities', in *Development in the Balance: How Will the World's Poor Cope with Climate Change?* (Washington DC: Brookings Institution Press, 2008).
51. See, for example, *Development in the Balance: How Will the World's Poor Cope with Climate Change?* (Washington DC: Brookings Institution Press, 2008).
52. See, for example, CK Prahalad, *The fortune at the bottom of the pyramid: eradicating poverty through profits* (Upper Saddle River, NJ: Wharton School, 2010).
53. World Business Council for Sustainable Development, *Doing Business with the World* (Geneva: WBCSD, 2007).
54. A number of case studies of this type can be found in M. Yunis, *Building Social Business* (New York, NY: Free Press, 2010).
55. This point is emphasized clearly by M. Yunis in *Creating a World Without Poverty: Social Business and the Future of Capitalism* (New York, NY: Public Affairs, 2007), pp. 15–17.
56. For a full explanation and discussion of social businesses see M. Yunis, *Building Social Business: The New Kind of Capitalism That Serves Humanity's Most Pressing Needs* (New York, NY: Public Affairs, 2010).
57. An overview of this project can be found at http://en.wikipedia.org/wiki/Grameen_Danone
58. See also S Prasso, 'Saving the World with a Cup of Yogurt', *Fortune Magazine*, 15 March 2007, at http://money.cnn.com/magazines/fortune/fortune_archive/2007/02/05/8399198/index.htm
59. See the SROI Network at http://www.sroi-uk.org/
60. The Silver Book can be found at the GLC Transformation Programme Website: http://www.pcg.gov.my/trans_manual.asp
61. As described in *Successful Companies Of The Future Will Be Those That Differentiate Business Through Strategic CSR* by Prakash Tewari, Head, Community Relations & Rehabilitation and Resettlement, The Tata Power Company Limited, India at the Global CSR Summit, 29–30 June 2010, Raffles Town Club, Singapore.

# Index